# Joseph Beuys and History

# Joseph Beuys and History

**Daniel Spaulding**

**PRINCETON UNIVERSITY PRESS**
**PRINCETON AND OXFORD**

Published by Princeton University Press,
41 William Street, Princeton, New Jersey 08540

In the United Kingdom: Princeton University Press,
99 Banbury Road, Oxford OX2 6JX

GPSR Authorized Representative: Easy Access System Europe - Mustamäe tee 50, 10621 Tallinn, Estonia, gpsr.requests@easproject.com

press.princeton.edu

Jacket image: Joseph Beuys, *La Rivoluzione siamo Noi* (We Are the Revolution), 1972. Phototype on polyester sheet with handwritten text; stamped. 75 1/4 × 39 3/8 in. (191.14 × 100.01 cm). The Broad Art Foundation. © 2025 Artists Rights Society (ARS), New York / VG Bild-Kunst, Bonn.

ISBN 978-0-691-27954-1
ISBN (ebook) 978-0-691-27955-8

Library of Congress Control Number: 2025946194

British Library Cataloging-in-Publication Data is available

Editorial: Michelle Komie and Annie Miller
Production Editorial: Terri O'Prey
Text Design: Heather Hansen
Jacket/Cover Design: Heather Hansen
Production: Steven Sears
Publicity: William Pagdatoon
Copyeditor: Cindy Milstein

This book has been composed in Adobe Text Pro with Edu Whyte Inktrap

Printed in the United States of America

1 3 5 7 9 10 8 6 4 2

# Contents

**Joseph Beuys and History**

# Introduction. Economimesis

## 1.

According to Joseph Beuys, capitalism was scheduled to end in 1987, about a year and a half after what turned out to be the day of his death. Or perhaps, by another of his reckonings, it was to end on May 1, 1984. In a photograph taken in Düsseldorf on March 27, 1981, Beuys sits on the edge of a table, his back to us, with a white phone receiver at his ear (fig. 1). Nothing of his face can be seen. Behind him stands a blackboard on which the number 2277 has been scrubbed out and replaced with the number 1133. With this modification, the sentence on the board now reads *Nur noch 1133 Tage bis zum Ende des Kapitalismus*—"Only 1133 days left until the end of capitalism." 2277 days from March 27, 1981, would have been June 21, 1987: summer solstice. Beuys died of heart failure on January 23, 1986. By moving the date up a little over three years, he gave himself the pleasure of witnessing capitalism's downfall in the flesh on International Workers' Day three years hence.

The countdown began earlier. There is a multiple—that is, an editioned artwork—of his from 1980 titled *Nur noch 2425 Tage . . .* (Only 2425 more days . . .) (fig. 2). The work consists of a picture frame in which are mounted two prints from a contact sheet. On the left, Beuys appears again in trademark hat and vest. He is gesturing toward a small piece of machinery. On the right is the blackboard we have encountered already, here in an earlier state with a pair of illegible flyers attached. These are probably from the artist's Free International University (FIU), founded in 1973—one of several pedagogical initiatives that he led in the 1970s. There is no way to be sure of when exactly this photograph was taken. Assuming that it is from 1980, like the multiple of which it is a part (which is by no means certain, since

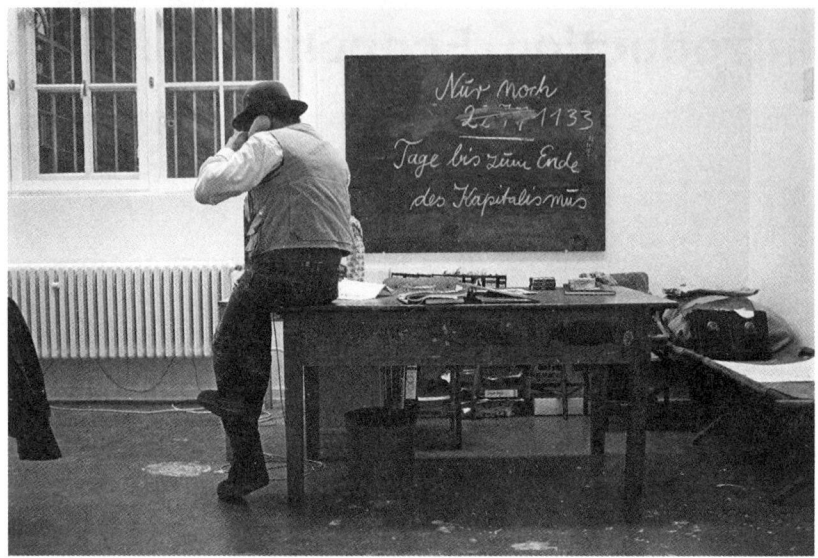

**Fig. 1.** Joseph Beuys in Düsseldorf, March 27, 1981.

an earlier photograph might easily find its way into a later work; Beuys often did such things), the window for capitalism's demise would thus fall between August 22, 1986, and August 22, 1987. This leaves an overlap of two months ( June 21 to August 22) with the erased nonaccelerated calculation in the photo from March 27, 1981.

The revised schedule—one doubts the choice of May Day in George Orwell's year was inadvertent—did not wholly supersede the longer time frame. Perhaps the most interesting single manifestation of this series is a work called *Nur noch 2190 Tage bis zum Ende des Kapitalismus (Denkmaschine)*, or "Only 2190 more days until the end of capitalism (thinking machine)," also from 1981 (fig. 3). These 2190 days equal exactly six years, minus the leap day or two that necessarily would intervene over that period (namely February 29, 1984, if we take 1981 as a starting point). This object is exceptional in Beuys's oeuvre: he used a computer to generate art. The piece consists of a large stack of folded continuous form paper, recognizable by its distinctive perforated margins, on which are printed programming commands that generate a countdown from 2190 to 0.[1] As displayed, only the first sheet is visible, meaning that viewers must take the rest on faith. The work thus exists in a state of latency that, as we will

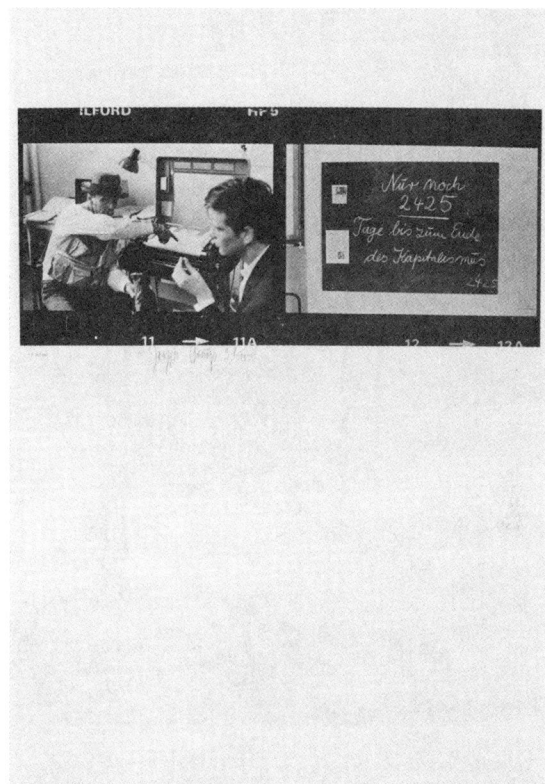

**Fig. 2.**
Joseph Beuys, *Nur noch
2425 Tage* ... (Only 2425
days left ...), 1980. Offset
on cardstock. 27⁷⁄₁₆ × 19⅛ in.
(69.7 × 48.6 cm). Walker
Art Center, Minneapolis,
1992.438.

see, is characteristic of much of the artist's materialized thinking about economics, politics, and history. Since we do not know the exact date in 1981 on which the program was run, we again have no choice but to admit the widest potential range. Shifting the window accordingly, we arrive at a possible terminus for capitalism between December 31, 1986, and December 30, 1987. The Berlin Wall was breached on November 9, 1989, a bit over three years and nine months after the artist left this earth.

Beuys living, Beuys dead. Capitalism living, capitalism defunct; socialism in bloom—in the East German media, at least—and socialism gone. At the turn of the 1980s, Beuys had an approximately five-year plan. History turned out differently. The wobbliness of the exact chronology notwithstanding, Beuys's implication, in this series of objects and actions, seems to have been that humanity might not only survive capitalism but also bring it to a punctual conclusion within a living future, though not within his

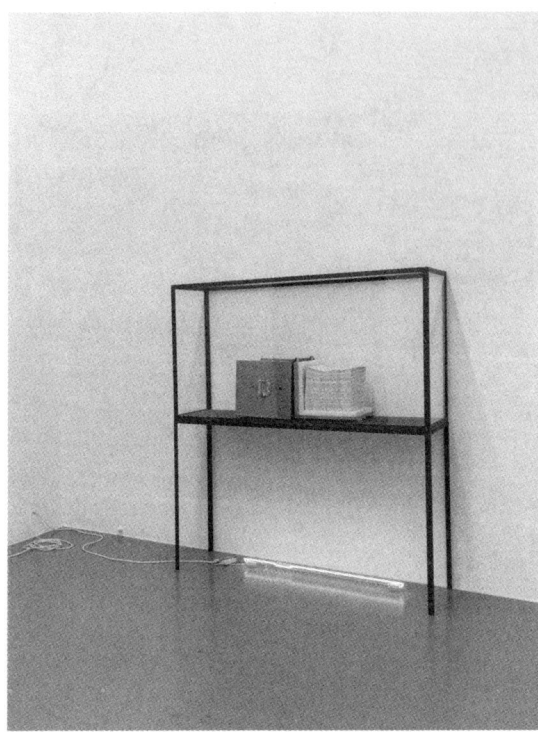

**Fig. 3.**
Joseph Beuys, *Nur noch 2190 Tage bis zum Ende des Kapitalismus (Denk-maschine)* (Only 2190 days until the end of capitalism [thinking machine]), 1981. Metal, glass, wood, and paper. Dimensions variable. Galerie Crone, Berlin and Vienna.

own, as things transpired. That is, unless we except the May Day prophecy, which was no more fulfilled than the rest.

It would be cruel to adduce this welter of dates to mock Beuys's naivete or even wring pathos from his optimistic anticapitalism, so foreign as it is to our more recent "capitalist realism" (a term that originated in Beuys's circle: his students Konrad Lueg and Gerhard Richter coined it for a performance at a furniture store in Düsseldorf in 1963).[2] Cruel and unwarranted. Beuys lived through at least one of his failed predictions; given that he died early, at the age of sixty-four, he must have hoped to live through the others. To say that the *Nur noch* series cannot have been meant to be taken literally is not to say that it was unserious. What I mean to suggest by starting with this little-known body of work is that Beuys's art and thinking had a direct, practical relation to an imagining of capitalism's end along with its expected replacement by something that he called "free democratic socialism." This is no coinage of mine; the phrase was one the artist's slogans. It remains to be seen what exactly "free democratic socialism" meant and what relation it had to the staggering multifariousness of his artistic practice, which is often called the most important to have emerged in post–World War II Germany: from the early "actions" that he staged in the orbit of the international Fluxus movement during the 1960s; to his sculptures and installations that incorporate unusual materials such as felt and fat; to his discursive activity as a tirelessly self-theorizing writer and interviewee, by means of which he propagandized his notion of "social sculpture" (an art that takes social relations as its material, or to put it differently, takes social relations as art). The task of this book is to relate the various things that Beuys did and made to a sense of history for which socialism is thinkable. To relate is not to identify. The possibility that what Beuys did sometimes bore little connection with what he claimed to be doing is real.

His premature death from heart failure was a fluke, but it is not by chance that I have introduced Beuys in a way that makes mortality unavoidable. There are few artists of the twentieth century whose work is so saturated with the negative as his. Death is everywhere, as is historical trauma: his drawings and sculptures are littered with decomposing organic matter and fecal-looking stains, and his "actions" pervasively thematize wounding. This is true most notoriously in his many, though mostly indirect, evocations of the National Socialist period, through which he passed as a member of the Hitler Youth and soldier in the Luftwaffe. (He served in the air on the Eastern Front and then in the final months of the war on the ground in the West.) There is no getting around the issue of the "German past," to employ a euphemism.

Yet my approach to the deathliness of Beuys's art takes a different tack. The *Nur noch* series is oriented to the future. Beuys, however, imagines this future as an ending, a literal perishing, not of any biological individual—such as the artist himself—but rather of a mode of production. He could only have looked forward to the prospect. Though his terminology was different, Beuys was as relentless in his critique of capitalist modernity as any Marxist revolutionary. The way to free democratic socialism was for him a passage through the valley of death. His utopia is a companion of the negative. The problem is figuring out how. To note that each of his countdowns, whatever their internal inconsistency, all proved equally false, for reasons that go beyond the contingent fact of one man's lifespan, is to skirt the issue of falsifiability as such. Beuys *did* choose a date, or rather several, for his improbable millenarian event. He thus made the event a material test of his capacity for prognostication. There had to have been some irony involved. Though sometimes taken for one, Beuys was not a fool, and his statements from the 1980s betray little sense that the overthrow of capitalism might really be imminent.

## 2.

Matters are weirder. What I want to get across in the chapters that follow is that Beuys's anticapitalism is persistently mediated through an aesthetic figuring of capitalism, or more properly, a mimetic relation to what Karl Marx and his followers call the value form of the commodity—that is, the form in which a thing's material specificity gives way to an abstract representation of itself in the mirror of other commodities, and above all, money, the general equivalent of all commodities. This kind of mimesis is not the same as mimetic representation in its traditional sense—which would be impossible in the case of something so abstract and totalizing; one cannot paint a portrait of capital—nor does it constitute a strategy of subversive "mimetic critique" that simultaneously apes and undermines its target.[3] Beuys occasionally seems to instantiate the latter model, as in the signed banknotes of his *Kunst = Kapital* (Art = capital) series, which will appear in this book's second chapter. Yet satire is not the main thrust of his aesthetic politics. The object of mimetic approximation in Beuys's work is not a thing but rather a relation, meaning that the mimesis at stake here is an emergent property of a nonrepresentational alignment between an aesthetic logic and a social form. That is, Beuys's art starts to *behave* like capital instead of looking like it. And since capital totalizes—it tries, at least, to mediate everything in the world—so, too, does Beuys's art. This vast structural mimesis does, however, get concretized in his art's taking on of traits associated with particular moments in capital's process—most important, that of the value form. The value form is the mode of a commodity's being in which it is exchangeable for anything else. I will argue that an analogous universal fungibility is the horizon of Beuys's *erweiterter Kunstbegriff*, or "expanded concept of art."

This would at first seem to throw us back onto familiar terrain. What could be more familiar than the convergence of commodity and artwork in Marcel Duchamp's readymades, or in Andy Warhol, or any number of other canonical practices? The value form of the commodity is not the same as the commodity as a physical thing, though. Commodities can be mimicked easily; the value form less so, since it is wholly relational, meaning it has no existence except in the act of exchange and thus is a moment in a process rather than a material thing. Beuys's weirdness has to do with his figuring of value accumulation as process instead of object. What this process does, above all, is to separate things from themselves, to produce nonidentity: the non-identity of a commodity with money, its form of representation; of labor power with its alienated objectification; and of substance with concept or number. In disidentifying things from themselves, commodity exchange at the same time generates the abstract identity of value. We will want to see how this sort of nonidentity is or is not like the nonidentity of a stack of printer paper with the mythos of revolution.

This is to frame the question in a manner that is open to dispute. For one thing, we may seem immediately to contradict ourselves in saying, first, that Beuys aimed to achieve free democratic socialism, and second, that the capital relation was his art's structuring object of mimesis. For how can a body of work be at once anticapitalist and formed in capitalism's image? Indeed, his socialism has often seemed muddled, if not embarrass-ing. (His interlocutors do not always appear to have known what to make of it. In an interview from 1973, for example, critic and art historian Achille Bonito Oliva abruptly changes the subject—to Duchamp, as it happens— after the artist declares that "socialism means love.")[4] Or if not embarrass-ing, then epiphenomenal. From the present perspective, his anticapitalism may seem less fruitful than his expansion of the concept of art to include abject materiality, bodiliness, performance, and social relations, or his reckoning with the Nazi past, or his invention of an ecological aesthetics.

I think this is not the case, but it will take time to show how. Both the oddness and historically specific conditions of possibility of such a type of socialism are this book's object of study. Hence although the topics just named receive their due in the account that follows, it is the link between the moment of abstract universality in the value form, on the one hand, and on the other hand, the universality of an "expanded" aesthetics that is my keynote, even in the discussion of works that do not appear to fore-ground economic concerns. To start with, for all that the *Nur noch* series obviously thematizes capitalism, the relevance of value form analysis to it is not immediately evident, at least not as I have presented my examples so far. The same will be true of any number of isolated works. One of the distinctive and arguably problematic aspects of the artist's oeuvre is that its particularities often feel inassimilable to its overweening conceptual armature; "formal analysis" as art historians like to teach it founders on the mediating step from the individual object to its metaphoric schema. Yet there are some projects—generally larger, culminating statements, as it were, in major public exhibitions—that approach a holistic summary of the work's structuring logic by, in effect, allegorizing themselves.

So I will have to move on to what, for lack of a better term, must be called the "major" works of the period in which Beuys turned decisively toward political, environmental, and economic themes: the later 1960s through the 1970s. It is arguable that Beuys was "the first artist to address the history of fascism."[5] He was, though, much more certainly the first artist not only to make environmentalist concerns an integral part of his practice but also to make his environmentalism inseparable from a total critique of capitalism.[6] This makes him tremendously important for the present and future. It doesn't, however, get his interpreters clear of the messier, more disturbing facets of his work and character, even or especially for anyone who shares his fundamental sense of the tasks that face humanity in the present. By the end of this book, it should be evident why I think it is just these contradictions that tell us most about his ecology and politics, and thus something, too, about the possibility of an opposition to capitalism after the breakdown of its classical (that is, socialist) forms. Beuys was a socialist but not a Marxist, for understandable reasons, since Marxism turned out to be so deathly in most of its twentieth-century manifestations. One reading of the *Nur noch* pieces is as a simple parody of Marxism's romance with the inevitable.

## 3.

It will take some time to arrive at the coordination of capitalism, utopia, and death that is of concern here. What follows will therefore remain displeasingly abstract until I have developed these claims more concretely through the analysis of particular works of art. So what does this look like in practice? For one thing, it looks like the *Honigpumpe*, or honey pump, that Beuys installed in Kassel, Germany, for the exhibition *documenta 6*, which took place during summer and autumn 1977 (plate 1). *Honigpumpe* is my most important case study—to such an extent that the present book might almost have been a monograph on this installation alone. It is a complex thing, but not so much so that it can't be summarized in a few sentences.

(I will have more to say about it in chapters 2 and 3 after dealing with different artworks in chapter 1.) Viewers entering the Fridericianum—the museum in which *documenta* was held—first would have seen, or more likely heard, a motor running in the lowest level of the building. This motor pumped honey into the Fridericianum's exhibition spaces above, where the substance flowed in swags of plastic tubing strung along the curving walls of the museum's central atrium. Photographs and video of the installation, which no longer exists in its original form, are visually striking, but in a way that does not much resemble art as we usually know it. The machine is loud, messy, not self-contained, industrial looking, and hard to totalize as a gestalt. It probably confused many of its viewers. Over the exhibition's hundred days, Beuys also organized a series of workshops and panel discussions in these spaces on topics of politics, economics, and aesthetics. It was in a similar pedagogical context that Beuys must have erased the number 2277 a few years later. His intervention in Kassel thus had two components: first, the pump itself, which was a kind of sculpture or installation at the edge of what, even in the wake of postminimalist process art, would not have been recognizable as art at all, and second, an educational program (a textbook example of social sculpture). The work is an economy that integrates or at least juxtaposes thermodynamics with an exchange of signs.

I will say more about *Honigpumpe* later, so here I will just ask a question and respond with a tentative answer. What does honey stand for in this work? To begin with, it stands for blood. The pump is a "heart" that sends liquid coursing through the "body" of the art institution. Beuys made this connection in interviews he gave at the time. The analogy also becomes explicit in a later screen print that diagrams the apparatus (fig. 4). In this print, the motor is labeled *Herz*, or "heart." Blood, though, is also money. In other statements and writings from the 1970s, Beuys more than once asserted that money is to the economy what blood is to the body: a substance that must circulate if the system is to maintain its existence. (Chapter 2 considers the nuances of this analogy.) Finally, Beuys compared the circulation and accumulation of honey, and by extension blood, to the circulation and accumulation of knowledge in collective learning processes of the sort that he aimed to stage by means of his pedagogical activities in the Fridericianum's halls. Metaphorically, that is, knowledge moves through society as money moves through the economy and blood moves through the veins. But money *accumulates* in a way that blood and probably knowledge do not. It becomes capital, and by the same measure, profit in the hands of the capitalist class.

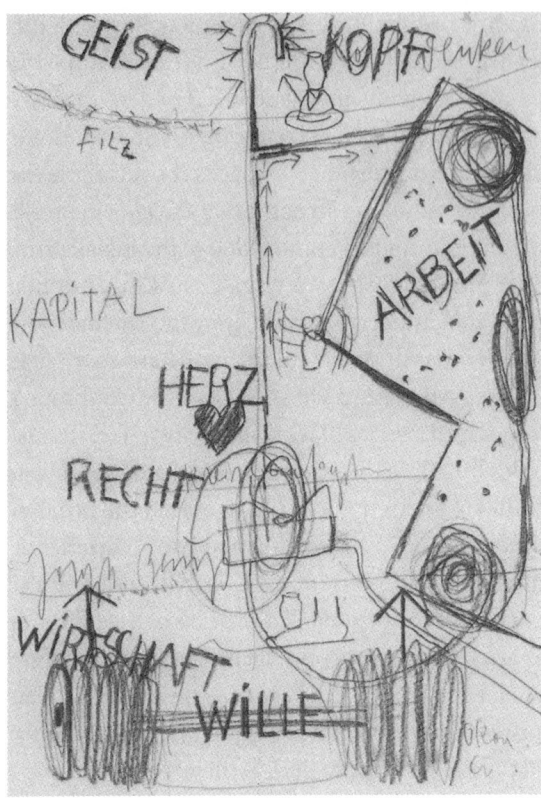

**Fig. 4.**
Joseph Beuys, *Honigpumpe* (Honey pump), 1985. Screen print. 11¾ × 8⁵⁄₁₆ in. (29.8 × 21.1 cm). Publisher: Spuren - Zeitschrift für Kunst und Gesellschaft, Hamburg. Harvard Art Museums, Cambridge, MA, 1995.560.2.

To whom does the pedagogical profit of knowledge circulation fall? To Beuys, as pedagogue in chief? And what might be the figurative equivalent of profit in the circulatory system, the realm of blood, which after all seeks homeostasis rather than ever-expanding accumulation?

Beuys overlays his metaphors, and from this blurring emerges disquieting problems around analogy as such. As will be evident even in the above compressed mode of presentation, these problems have to do with economy's relation to nature, pedagogy, politics, and the aesthetic. More pointedly, the question is whether economy, in its capitalist mode, is antagonistic to these other things, to other ways of life or being, or whether some accommodation, if not identity, might be found between them. Everything in this book—I would suggest, of course without being able to prove it, nearly everything in Beuys's oeuvre—has to do with this nexus. I spend more time on *Honigpumpe* than any other artwork because it displays these problems in arguably their most paradigmatic form.

I will not attempt a complete survey of Beuys's production, then. For one thing, he was dauntingly prolific. Most of my core objects of analysis belong to a restricted subset of his work—namely, large sculptural installations dating from the late 1960s to the late 1970s. The materiality and objective persistence of monumental sculpture brings to its highest pitch a contradiction between metaphors of flow and stasis in Beuys's work—and it is this relation that hooks the work onto capital as a social form that at once revolutionizes everything and somehow keeps everything the same.[7] I use the word "materiality" with some caution because in art discourse, at least, it often seems to describe a certain salience or vehemence of material properties to the disadvantage of social and historical concerns, which is not a precise terminology. A painting with a licked-smooth surface is just as "material" as one with high impasto; it's just material differently. When the notion of "materiality" shows up in this book, it ought to be understood as the counterpart of a tendency in Beuys to subordinate the material to concepts. Materiality, then, is part of an economy of signs and things rather than a property in its own right. By the same measure, "concept" or "meaning" ought to be understood here as an inflection of an economy that needs a material substrate.

This economy is present in works both big and small. Large sculptures, though, do bring to a special pitch the interaction between these poles precisely by stretching them to their limits—by juxtaposing sheer stuff to its metaphoric significance—and will accordingly make for a privileged focus of attention. I will by contrast have relatively less to say about Beuys's early "actions" in the orbit of Fluxus along with his late ecological projects, drawings, or production of multiples (with the exception of the *Kunst = Kapital* series of modified banknotes), and only a little a bit more about his many vitrine sculptures, although I think that my propositions apply to these other bodies of work as well. The reason for zeroing in on this strain of Beuys's oeuvre is that it delivers a particularly concentrated manifestation of the curious superimposition of metaphors with which we are concerned: metaphors of death and life, injury and healing, biology and economics, art and society.

These are abstract words that will make more sense after I have gotten under the skin of the art. Doing so requires clarifying some basic terms that circle around a striking and yet little-understood dynamic in Beuys's work and discourse: the way in which his identification of incommensurables both transgresses the modern boundaries of the aesthetic and proposes a specifically aesthetic parallel to capitalism's real abstraction. These are not the terms in which twentieth-century art has usually been theorized. Art historians are comfortable with the idea that art might resist, reflect, or acquiesce to capitalism; indeed, the very category of art in modernity perhaps owes its coherence to its exceptionality with respect to capitalist commodity production.[8] But conversely, there is no adequate existing framework with which to describe how art, in becoming like capital, might try to subsume it—which is what happens with Beuys.

## 4.

What *is* widely understood, by contrast, is that Beuys was tremendously ambitious, perhaps to the point of megalomania—as the reader may have intuited already. He aimed to totalize the concept of art. He wanted to make it the basis for a total remaking of society, economics, and politics, indeed for a coming form of life, in a mode of aesthetic politics to which we can usefully attach the rich German word *Gestaltung* (design, shaping, or form making). Art can set a date for capitalism's end; a more powerful idea of art's agency is hard to imagine. The reason this might have seemed at least plausible is that for Beuys there was or anyway should be no distinction between collective practice (political practice, for example, but also the tasks of everyday existence) and art making. The doctrine of social sculpture was not so much a technique for making art out of life as for making life into art, everywhere and always. *Honigpumpe* subsumes collective discussion to the artwork of which it was an element. Art is or wants to be the master term here—the term that synthesizes and relates everything else. Art is the Gestaltung of everything, potentially.

Yet just such a totalizing relation already existed in Beuys's world. That relation was capital. It was accordingly to the capital relation that Beuys oriented his practice. In a real sense, capital occupied the terrain that he hoped art would conquer; capital did what he hoped art could do, only badly. It was and is what mediates the reproduction of most human life on earth. Of course, no life is possible without nature too—whatever that happens to be. There is no need here to adjudicate the ontological status of "nature," or for that matter of "art" or any other concept; it's sufficient that the concepts are operative as part of the material and discursive complex that is Beuys's oeuvre, in which paired terms often function as quasistructural oppositions. One such opposition—the crucial one in this book, as I think it was for Beuys—is that between nature and intentional human practice, with nature understood in this context as autonomous, extrahuman reality, and intentional human practice understood to be, in its highest form, art.

The thrust of a work such as *Honigpumpe* is to overcome this opposition, even as it presupposes it. It does so, remarkably, not by naturalizing art (by restricting art's claim to be distinct from everything else) but instead by totalizing it, such that at its vanishing point or realized utopia, there would be nothing left that art does not touch. A totalized art simply would *be* nature, or rather a second nature; it would lie at the root of everything, as indispensable as the air we breathe or the blood that flows in our veins. But it would also still be what Germans call *Geist*: spirit, mind, or cognition. This insistence on art as art (as human practice) distinguishes Beuys's honey pump from more recent and in some respects rather Beuysian kinds of art that model or (re)produce hybrid biological/semiotic ecosystems. I have in mind contemporary artists such as Pierre Huyghe, Anicka Yi, or Candice Lin, all of whom incorporate volatile organic matter into technical metabolisms that operate in at least partial autonomy from their creators' volition.[9] There is a clear resonance between such practices and Beuys's conflation of machinery with the circulation of blood in *Honigpumpe*— with the key difference that Beuys insists on human plastic or "shaping" (*gestaltend*) agency in a way that is at odds with the renunciation of anthropocentrism in much current ecological art. From the Beuysian perspective, good ecology does not so much void Geist as extend it to the point that it becomes inextricable from the cosmos.

This involved Beuys in intervening at least imaginatively in the basic structures of human life. To repeat, societies have a double root in nature and a mode of production. In capitalism, however, the latter introduces an "irreparable rift in the interdependent processes of social metabolism"—a metabolic rift in the exchange of energy between humans and the earth.[10] Capital modifies that exchange and subsumes it to the needs of its own accumulation, even to the point of making the metabolism break down. Capital indeed comes to look like a kind of incontrovertible nature of its own: money becomes as indispensable as blood. Ongoing debates in the fields of ecosocialism and Marxist ecology, often in dialogue with feminist and decolonial ecological thought, address the problem of capital's immanence to nature and vice versa. A critique of the "Cartesian" division between nature and society, and indeed of certain interpretations of Marx's own concept of the "metabolic rift," has been a frequent refrain in this discourse.[11] If Beuys's work helps us to think about these urgent questions, it does so because his ecology was at the same time a political economy and semiotics. Beuys demonstrates both the oneness of a modern natural/social world system and the grotesqueries that result from nature's subsumption to capital accumulation. Along with capital, nature, too, was an object of Beuysian mimesis. *Honigpumpe* is an image of both the body and, more tenuously, larger natural thermodynamic systems. It likewise figures economy. But the means that Beuys used to construct his metaphor are literally mechanical; it seems that there was a propane motor (fossil fuel) involved in the installation.

This is not an isolated case. Metaphors of circulation and (life) cycles, of natural communities, such as those of the bees that make honey in the first place, recur in work after work, but they are rarely pure, rarely inseparable from something more disturbingly dead. For Beuys, nature was a compelling image of totality. The problem is that in wanting to become at once more like nature and more like capital—more totalized and totalizing, more inextricably woven into the numberless patterns of everyday life—Beuys's art became more and more riven by capital's violence, and thus more and more contradictory with respect to its own ecological telos. The increasingly vast chasms that Beuysian metaphors had to bridge are the index of the concrete problem of holding together a sense of reality in the face of capitalism's contradictoriness. As philosopher Hans Blumenberg argues, metaphor perhaps most essentially emerges in response to the disturbance of a prior homeostasis: "The element that is initially destructive only *becomes* metaphor under the duress of having to repair the imperiled consistency."[12] What is more, to model art on the automatism of either nature or capital was to risk corrupting the central idea of Gestaltung given that the latter would seem essentially to involve conscious human control. At Kassel, Beuys and his acolytes produced knowledge by means of intentional collective practice, even as honey/blood/money circulated automatically, mechanistically, to its own inhuman rhythm.[13] Any interpretation of the piece comes down to figuring out what, if anything, these two processes have to do with each other. What was the point of the work's split presentation (which was, among other things, a literal spatialization of the Marxist base/superstructure metaphor)? Why pair, much less try to reconcile, human self-determination with mechanism at all?

# 5.

I can put the argument more directly, though still in more abstract terms than I would like. In this book, I intend to prove that the negativity manifest in the art of Beuys resulted from his attempt to reconcile the automatism of capital accumulation with a principle of universalized Gestaltung (the free shaping of all social and material relations rather than only those that are usually called aesthetic). This attempt to reconcile irreconcilables depended on a third term: nature. *Honigpumpe*'s contradiction is found in the elided nonidentity between capital—a social form that accumulates—and blood, a natural substance that maintains homeostasis. If honey is blood and blood is money, and if money is also capital, then we are left with the problem of what it could mean to *extract* something from these other systems in the way that capitalists extract profit from labor. The answer may turn out to be dark.

To develop the contradiction, we need to take such inferences seriously, which is to say, literally. Paradoxical as it may sound—although I doubt that he is unique in this regard—making sense of Beuys's art requires us to take metaphors literally. (Blumenberg is useful here too: "It is no rarity to observe that metaphorics are 'taken at their word.' In the process, the metaphor is seized from the limited intention of its author, made independent, and extended in a direction that often changes the clarification into an explanation.")[14] More specifically, it requires us to treat a metaphoric economy *as if* it were a real economy. In the case I have been discussing, there are at least two economies involved: that of pedagogy or knowledge production (symbolic exchange), and that of a fossil-powered hydraulic circuit, which Beuys in turn metaphorized as akin to both the circulation of blood and circulation of money. *Honigpumpe* is an artwork, a product of conscious human intentionality. So is knowledge that comes out of a seminar. But the models, both natural and economic, to which *Honigpumpe* mimetically assimilates itself are under nobody's conscious control. Blood pumps without us willing it; money circulates whether we like it or not, and not even the most powerful capitalist in the world controls the whole of the process. Capital, even though a human social form, behaves as if it were an impersonal, natural necessity. Gestaltung, or artistic formation, involves contingent human agency even when, as in Beuys's case, it has for its paradigm natural or necessary form.

Beuys tried to make peace between these terms. In a series of case studies—*Honigpumpe* is only the first I have introduced—I will try to show that his most characteristic strategy was a mimesis of capital—not most often, however, of its most concrete instance, the commodity, but rather of the entire circuit of value accumulation, which in returning to itself passes through a series of negations (labor, money, and yes, the commodity too, all objects of Beuys's mimetic investment in their turn). This was a strange, perhaps singular way of making art. It involved Beuys in leaps across categories that it has been modernity's work to keep separate. What I call Beuys's "myth" was a self-reinforcing yet also contradictory complex of metaphors that aimed to graft a cosmology to the real totality of capital, which is a self-reproducing system. Blood's likeness to money is an instance of Beuysian myth. Mythical totalization is akin to the closure of a capitalist economy in ways that will need to be explored. Like capitalism, though, this closed loop of artistic meaning making generated waste, nonmeaning, and death.

To explain how this works, I have borrowed the term "economimesis" from the philosopher Jacques Derrida, although I use it in a different and usually more straightforward sense than his.[15] Derrida will return in my book's conclusion, at which point I will hew more closely to what he really means by his neologism. "Economimesis" is meant to sound like an oxymoron since the system of the aesthetic as it attains canonical shape in philosopher Immanuel Kant's *Critique of Judgment* would seem to oppose "free" art (mimesis) to "mercenary" art (economics). Derrida, as one might expect, deconstructs this binary opposition and demonstrates the mutual dependency of the two terms. In a methodologically similar vein, my book takes oppositions such as "nature versus culture" as discursive givens that ought to be subjected to a further turn of the screw, rather than as ontologically fixed terms to be either accepted or rejected as is.[16] Language itself already does some of this work, which is why—without ever intending to complicate ordinary language needlessly—I also do not shy away from using some exotic terminology. Neologisms can sometimes illuminate a constellation of ideas that it would otherwise be too laborious to describe sequentially; neologisms are, sometimes, concentrated dialectics.

By writing of "economimesis," for example, I mean to indicate that Beuys's practice worked as an economy, or instead, as something like an economy. His art is sticky; it adheres to other things (in the instances that matter here, to another social form); this is what mimesis signifies in the pages to follow. His art posits the uptake of form, even or especially at its

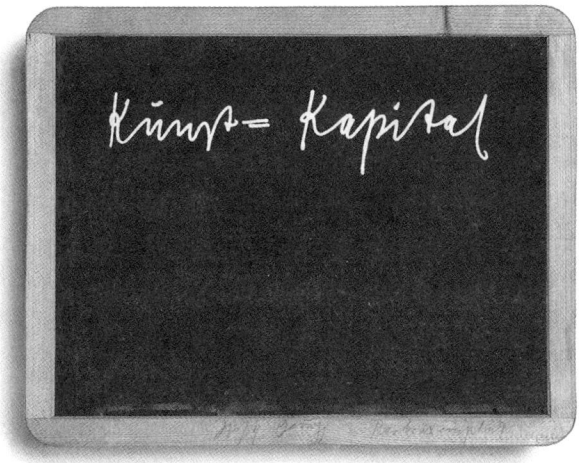

**Fig. 5.** Joseph Beuys, *Kunst = Kapital*, 1980. Silk screen on blackboard in wooden frame. 13¼ × 17³⁄₁₆ × ⅜ in. (33.7 × 43.7 × 1 cm). Walker Art Center, Minneapolis, 1992.191.

most abject, into the economy of a signifying system, somewhat as capital enlists what it can to the abstraction called value. This system facilitates a metabolism between form and meaning. Matter emerges from the process charged with spiritual (that is, human) value. At the same time, Beuys structured his practice like an organism, ecosystem, or body—that is, like nature. Growth, death, the circulation of blood, cycles of heat and cold, everything contained in what Beuys called his "theory of warmth" (*Wärmetheorie*): these are the substance of his biological aesthetics and, at the same time, phenomenalizations of his economy.

It is not as if there is a hidden kernel of economic content in these biological tropes. The economic content is quite open. More directly than by insinuation, then, Beuys aimed to identify the one representational level with the other. In the 1970s and 1980s, Kunst = Kapital (art = capital) was no less ubiquitous a slogan than his better-known pronouncement that everyone is an artist (*jeder Mensch ein Künstler*) (fig. 5). The difficult thing about these equations is that they are not literally true. Another problem is that *if* true, and if taken together, the two equations imply that everyone is a capitalist as well as an artist; or more precisely, that everyone is a capitalist to the same measure that everyone is an artist. Taking the metaphor literally makes sense of it by rendering it contradictory. A literal reading thus paradoxically puts the mediations back into the totalized metaphors that sublate them, and in the process, makes us aware of the negativity of the identical (or of what the critical theorist Theodor W. Adorno called *erpresste Versöhnung*, "reconciliation under duress").[17] It makes the metaphors uncomfortable. Derrida's economimesis in the end turns out to be a theory of disgust. So it is here too. The queasy-making aspect of Beuys's system ought to be palpable already and will return with a vengeance in my book's conclusion, when the indigestible remnants of modern history should start to stick in the reader's throat. A system that tries to reconcile everything identifies too much, perhaps violently.

My account is largely about the analogy making or semiosis that plays out as a result of this making equivalent of unlike things, which is symmetrical with and inherent to capital's making unlike of things that were once undivided as they pass through the production/accumulation process (by making labor into value and separating workers from both their means of production and what they make). Art as Beuys understands it has this in common with money: it can mediate anything. The remit of metaphor here is accordingly wider than in most art made during the twentieth century. For Beuys, art is to organism as art is to economy, which in turn implies that economy and organism are themselves homeomorphic. Then comes the crucial move, which at least notionally differentiates Beuys's totalized art from capital. If organisms and economies are both like art, then—like art—both should be susceptible to conscious human shaping, or what I have been calling Gestaltung. Art can write capitalism's obituary because what we call art is nothing but a valence of form making in general, of which politics (collective decision-making about the way we live) is another. Why shouldn't art decide that capitalism will end on May 1, 1984? Humans can do anything.

# 6.

These are tropes of what I will call "socioplasticity," a concept that I extrapolate from the artist's own term *Soziale Plastik*, or social sculpture. Socioplasticity is the semiotic field in which figures of the aesthetic mingle with figures of social and historical processes. It overlaps but is not coterminous with what the literary critic Paul de Man called "aesthetic ideology."[18] Socioplasticity is a way to talk about issues that over the past twenty years have often been discussed under rubrics such as "social practice art," "new genre public art," "socially engaged art," and so forth (the pedagogical component of *Honigpumpe* is an obvious precursor to these).[19] But it is also a way to articulate such politicized art practices with a political economy that exceeds them and to which they tend to be opposed, or at least imagine themselves opposed. To keep matters most literal and therefore closest to what Beuys meant by Soziale Plastik, socioplasticity is a way of conceiving of human collectivity as an object of Gestaltung, or more precisely as an identical subject/object since what shapes society is society itself. This is no different from a classical strain in Marxist philosophy, the paradigmatic expression of which is literary theorist and philosopher György Lukács's *History and Class Consciousness*.[20] The factor that differentiates Beuys is his tendency to privilege art as a model for general social practice in a way that perhaps both overestimates the efficacy of the aesthetic and underestimates the danger of according the artist such an exalted role.

This is the point at which Beuys's approach both converges and conflicts with my technique as a scholar. I take it as an axiom that works of art can be understood as social relations, not in the indirect sense that artworks "reflect" their context, but in the sense that every work of art produces concrete relations between discourses, materials, signs, and agents. Whether these relations are only or predominantly social, meaning human, or whether we might better understand them in terms of a more capacious relationality that encompasses nonhuman as well as human factors or agents, is a problem that we can leave in suspension. I prefer to use the term "social" because I consider my approach to belong to the methodological lineage of the social history of art. The social history of art is a history of the "concrete transactions" that constitute "the connecting links between artistic form, the available systems of visual representation, the current theories of art, other ideologies, social classes, and more general historical structures and processes," as art historian T. J. Clark once put it.[21] It does not strike me that there is any insuperable divide between this sort of materialism and newer materialisms that embed social relations in the "double internality" of "humanity-in-nature/nature-in-humanity," to quote environmental historian Jason W. Moore—even if the protagonists of various theoretical "turns" in the early twenty-first century have had an interest in maintaining otherwise.[22]

To begin with, the making of an artwork rebounds on its maker, subjectivizing them as "artist," at least in cultures in which that identity is available. In other cultures, representational activities that to us resemble art may be called "magic" or some other emic term. (Beuys often modeled what he was doing on these other-than-art practices. This is the basis for his problematic identification as a "shaman.") Every artwork, like everything else, projects a diagram of relations, including art's self-relation or autonomy; withdrawal or hermeticism is a kind of negative relationality too.[23] These patterns of relation shift over time as forms emerge and disappear in consequence of both objective factors, such as the prevailing mode of production or environmental allowances of the earth, and intentional human practice. The artwork is not an isolated object but rather a node within diagrams of relations that constantly rearrange themselves (which is how I understand the historical process)—all of which are not equal, however, because some relations and some systems are more totalizing than others, or indeed subsume others to their own reproduction (this is how I would describe capital's relation to human life and the earth).[24] A further dereifying step would be to say that there are or ought to be no "nodes," and hence no networks between them at all, only likenesses and becomings alike.[25] I argue that Beuys's art involves a becoming-like capital. But the point is that this can never exactly succeed for reasons that clarify the peculiar status of art in the modern world.

Beuys is useful for getting at these basic issues because his habit of transgressing categories obliges his interpreters to ask, "How is art like any other thing or practice (or not)? How is it autonomous from these other things and practices (or not)? What impact, if any, might art have on evidently distinct spheres of human practice, such as politics and economy? And what danger might arise when art trespasses on these other spheres?" There are more and less honest ways to answer these questions. Resistance to Beuys has mostly come from a sense that his answers were implausible or duplicitous. From such a point of view, Beuys's transgression of categories is regressive because it posits a socioplastic effectivity that his art (or perhaps art in general, or perhaps only art in modernity) cannot have. It posits, for example, a *specific* date on which capitalism will die. Art has little power to make this come true. Thus the prophecy exists—as most art does anyway—in the realms of the virtual, metaphor, fiction, nonidentity, or the "*objet ambigu*."[26] This is only a problem if the prophecy is meant to be more than a fiction. And that is the whole difficulty of interpreting Beuys. If fiction, his politics only muddles his art. If prophecy, aesthetics impinges on politics in a manner that, as it has seemed to some, can only issue in the totalitarian annexation of politics to the charismatic authority of the "genius," or on the contrary, in a mere parody of art-politics. When working as ideology, then, socioplasticity recognizes the entanglement of the aesthetic with social and historical processes while occluding asymmetries of subsumption, or domination.

Like Duchamp's readymade, the notion of social sculpture is a particularly suggestive way to think about art's entanglement with other practices and things, but it confounds orders of magnitude. Hence there is a great pathos—maybe bathos—in Beuys's attempt to subsume capitalism under art by analogy making. (I will argue that this is what *Honigpumpe* and by extension Beuys's practice as a whole aimed to do in the 1970s.) The hypertrophy of metaphor in his work, such that many take it to be overladen with mythological deadweight, is a sign of the contrariness of his way of art making to "metaphoroclasm," to coin another term that I will use elsewhere in this book. Beuys's work was an extended battle against the reduction of metaphor to real abstraction, or capitalism's practical making equivalent of all commodities as exchangeable bearers of value. At the same time, his "metaphoresis" had no other model, no other mimetic object, but this reduction of difference. The real equivalence of all things from capital's perspective has its shadow in an imagined universalization of art, under which Beuys wanted to subsume literally everything (everyone is an artist and everything is art; honey is blood is money is knowledge). To put it in terms I have already developed, the commodity form is what happens when you take metaphor literally at a general societal level. Commodity exchange is based on acting as if, not merely imagining that, ten yards of linen and a coat are the same thing, even though their use values are qualitatively distinct. Beuys's *erweiterter Kunstbegriff* (expanded concept of art) makes everything fungible too. Art is the coin of Beuys's realm; Kunst = Kapital. The purity of poet Friedrich von Schiller's "aesthetic state," then, corresponds to the mirage of a capitalism stripped of material friction.[27]

This is economimesis at work. The aesthetic, in its purity, reproduces or assimilates itself to the logic of economy, even as it remains something else—something subject to Gestaltung in a distinctive way. (In Derrida's terms, which he borrows from Kant, "free" and "mercenary" art, mimesis and *oikonomia*, turn out not to be antithetical; "their relation must be one neither of identity nor of contradiction but must be other.")[28] The above formulations are indebted to Adorno's observation that the "absolute artwork" and "absolute commodity" converge.[29] They do so, for Adorno, because the absolute artwork and absolute commodity represent two faces of the extreme point of fetishism, or the concealment of labor and production. In the commodity, social relations between people appear as relations between things. The autonomous artwork, in turn, appears to sever itself from its social determinations altogether. In both cases, the product of labor thus appears not as a product at all but rather as a self-grounding, self-moving subject. This is indeed how totalized or "expanded" art functions for Beuys. Art theorist Marina Vishmidt concisely makes this theoretical point that I intend to prove more empirically in the pages that follow:

> If we recall … that art, like capital, expels labour and declares a formal freedom from it while being just as subordinate to capital as any other form of social production (indeed, because art electively assumes capital's formal freedom as one of its own laws, we might argue that it is *more* subordinated), we can further say that this is possible because art is mimetic of capital in a very specific way: art mimetically assumes the role of the automatic subject of value.

As Vishmidt continues, "The ability of art to 'accumulate' all social phenomena as instances of itself comes to resemble what capital does, in its self-expanding movement as the automatic subject. The nominalist gesture then appears symptomatic of art as a scene of, and vehicle for, the 'mimetic subsumption' of all non-value producing sectors."[30] By "nominalist gesture," Vishmidt means to refer to the Duchampian readymade. The designation of, potentially, any arbitrary thing as a work of art mimetically subsumes nonart phenomena much as capital subsumes concrete particulars under the abstract value form.

Posed in this way, the homology between art and capital might seem straightforward and punctual. Once Duchamp decides to call a urinal *Fountain*, the operation is over; commodity and artwork have been identified. The mimetic convergence with which I am preoccupied in this book, however, is dynamic as opposed to static. The convergence is not between artwork and commodity but rather between a mode of production and a structure of metaphors. Beuys's transubstantiation of honey into blood and money, for instance, is a figure of capital's transubstantiation of labor and concrete matter into abstract value, but also a wild (utopian) counterfactual to the same. His logic was that of sympathetic magic, or the affecting of like by like: an archaism. What makes it distinctive is that he applied it to a mode of production.

## 7.

The layering of two metaphors (economy and organism) atop a notion of art defined as Gestaltung accounts for the difficulty that Beuys has met in reception, especially in the United States. For this same complex of analogies—of economy and society to art and organism—lay at the heart of the twentieth century's most ambitious and, in practice, most horrific programs of social transformation on the Right as well as Left (fascism and state communism). These programs of socioplasticity had fallen into discredit by the 1970s and 1980s, when Beuys became Germany's most famous artist. "Neoliberalism" is one name for the ideology that came after, although it is probably correct to see the discourse of neoliberalism not as a driving force but instead as a language in which to justify a more important phenomenon: the restructuring of capitalism in response to a crisis of profitability in the 1970s.[31] It was at this moment that Beuys found himself in competition with other, more violent historical actors for a vision of the future to hold against the terror of history. My example is the militant Rote Armee Fraktion, or Red Army Faction (RAF), whose last major offensive in autumn 1977 took place at almost exactly the same time that Beuys created two large-scale installations (*Honigpumpe* and *Unschlitt/Tallow*) that are keys to my reading (fig. 6).

Beuys's art is thus bound to historical catastrophe, though not necessarily in the ways his interpreters often presume. The center of gravity in my account is not the National Socialist period but rather the cresting and decline of Germany's postwar "economic miracle" in the 1960s and 1970s. This was an era that many of its own subjects, especially on the Left, experienced as a near replay of the earlier disaster. These years also saw the final triumph of the welfare state. So-called *Modell Deutschland*, with its lucrative manufacturing sector along with state-managed coordination between capital and labor, was the backdrop to the development of Beuysian socioplasticity. Free democratic socialism, of which social sculpture was meant to be a premonition, was both an image of and imagined alternative to the German social market economy. The phrase was Beuys's way

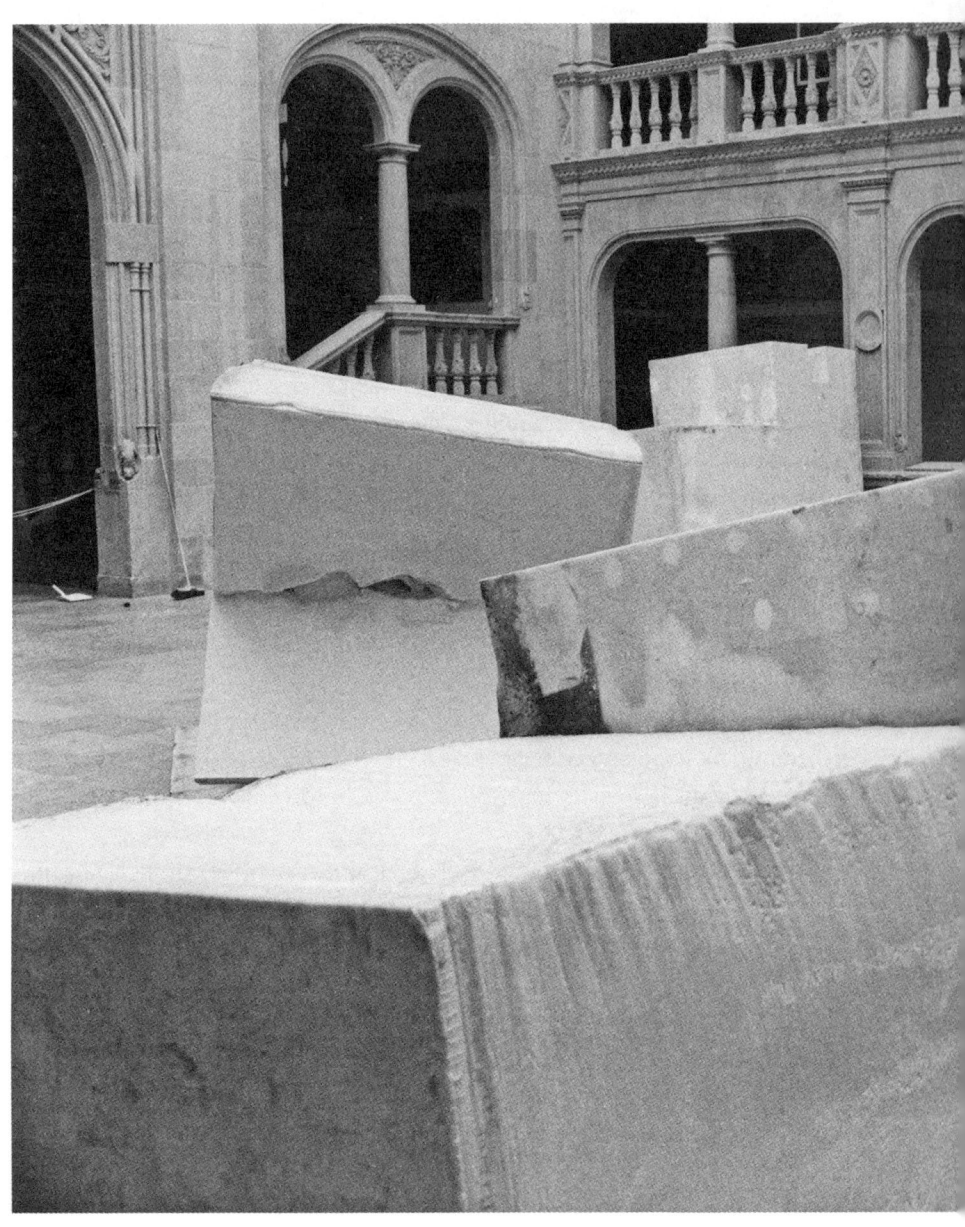

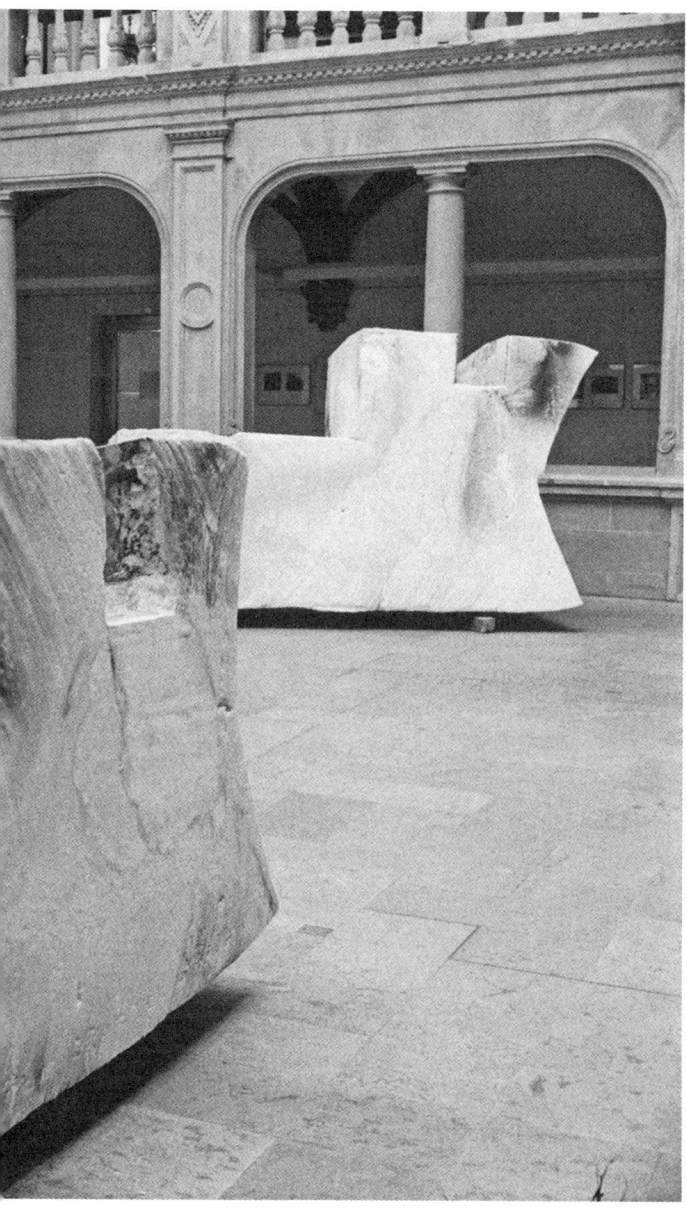

**Fig. 6.**
Joseph Beuys, *Unschlitt/ Tallow (Wärmeskulptur auf Zeit hin angelegt)* (Unschlitt/tallow [heat sculpture designed for long-term use]), 1977. Beef suet, paraffin (?), stearin, steel, and electric elements. Cut from a cast measuring 76⅘ × 376 × 120½ in. (195 × 955 × 306 cm). Dimensions variable as installed. Installation view, Westfälisches Landesmuseum, Münster, 1977. Sammlung Marx, Berlin, on long-term loan to the Staatliche Museen zu Berlin, Hamburger Bahnhof—Museum für Gegenwart.

of describing collective historical self-determination, which remains the horizon of any politics that aims to transcend the "natural history" of the capitalist mode of production.[32] His work was an attempt to answer modernity's most insistent questions: Can humans control their own destiny? And if history can be made, is disaster the inevitable result?

A politics that answers "yes" to the first of these questions and "no" to the second remains difficult to imagine as anything other than what it became in fascism and authoritarian socialism. In the Federal Republic of Germany, the persistence of Nazi personnel and command structures in positions of high governmental as well as economic power deep into the postwar era made Beuys's imagining of an alternative to liberal democracy and its economic forms difficult except in aesthetic terms. The presence of a socialist German state immediately to the east complicated matters for would-be leftists too. Worse still, Beuys's unwillingness ever to provide a full account of his participation in the Nazi war of annihilation would seem to invalidate any such attempt a priori. There are affinities with fascist rhetoric and tropes in his language that it seems impossible not to call symptomatic.[33] In the postwar decades, however, the notion that history might be made by those who undergo it had a peculiarly German variant that turned out not to be incompatible with the capital relation. None other than Konrad Adenauer and Ludwig Erhard, the architects of the Federal Republic's *Wirtschaftswunder*, or economic miracle, saw the "social market economy" as a third way between the socialism of the Eastern bloc and the unfettered capitalism that many of their contemporaries held responsible for the downfall of the Weimar Republic. So the theory and practice of economic planning—to put it more strongly, economic Gestaltung—was a contested object, with one of its more eccentric claimants being Beuys. The point of the sections of this book that veer from art history to economics is to show that even the strangest features of Beuysian theory and practice make an amount of sense within this context.

In what follows, then, I approach the disturbing echoes of the Nazi era in Beuys's work neither as an involuntary return of the repressed nor as manifestations of a right-wing political program (nor of an orthodoxly leftist one either), but rather as signs of resonance, across thirty years or so, between notions of planning and contingency in human affairs. Without contesting the singularity of the National Socialist regime, I nonetheless attempt to assess its aftermath during the postwar era—and more particularly in Beuys's socioplastic imagination—in terms of a longer duration of approaches to the "shaping" (Gestaltung) of human society and the relation of such projects to the invisible hand of the market. In Beuys's time, this constellation was rearranging itself. As I write, it may be rearranging itself again under new ecological and socioeconomic pressures (though the obvious contingency of the present world order has so far not called forth any universalizing counterproject comparable to classical socialism; neither is it clear that it can or ought to). Hence although much of my work is that of contextualization or historicization, the temporality at stake here is complex. It is not as if either the 1930s–40s or 1960s–70s alone explain what Beuys was trying to do. Only a parallax between these moments produces an adequate etiology of his economimetic procedures. Beuys projected a future—it did not come to pass, as hardly needs pointing out—that was an echo of the past as well as an image of what, at the time, was the present: that of West Germany's capitalist reconstruction.[34]

Lastly, I aim to show that Beuys's ecological politics, so easy to describe as an antimodern romanticism, turn out to have capital as their paradigm, thus adumbrating a world in which "ecology" and "nature" are by no means synonymous. In much of Beuys's work, the terms "nature" and "capital" might as well be interchangeable. Some have called this world that of the Anthropocene, or more to the point, the Capitalocene.[35] In the first half of the twenty-first century, socioplasticity's only noble aim—collective human self-determination on an international scale—has become unimaginable except as care on and for a sick planet. This is what one might by analogy call *eco*plasticity: the form in which a socialism of the twenty-first century is imaginable, though not necessarily in any comforting way.[36] The governability of the cosmos is now at stake in the possibility of ecosocialism, as it was, already and differently, in Beuys's work and thinking. Whether ecosocialism is either possible or desirable is not really at issue here, though I hope that a look back at the previous century indicates something of the direness and immensity that any planetary ecological politics would involve. Beuys makes a mockery in advance of any notion that "ecological art" could be isolated as a tidy genre alongside installation, performance, and so on. An aspiration of this book is to monstrate the joint where, in art, the desire called socialism meets the disaster called the Capitalocene. One such joint is Beuys.

# 8.

This book has three chapters. *Honigpumpe* appears mostly in the second and third, although much of what is required for the interpretation appears already in the first, which is dedicated to the function of materials in the artist's early work and the notion of myth. The second chapter is mostly about value, and the third is primarily about history. More exactly, in chapter 1, which is titled "The Matter of Myth," I try to provide an account of Beuys's meaning making and its difference from the contemporaneous practices of minimalists in the United States. To do so, I have to articulate, or rather show Beuys articulating, materials with the symbolic significance they have in the artist's spoken and written utterances—as, for example, the association of the materials of fat and felt with the idea of healing. This may seem like an archaic semiology. Whether it is or isn't, I think it is true to what I have observed in the work. The material/meaning transit turns out to be more complicated than it looks at first since it depends on something that I call "myth." Myth, in this context, is not a synonym for "made-up stories" but rather a mode of external conceptuality that grounds the transit between material form and determinate meaning. This relation turns out to be slippery in practice: a material may not really be what it ought to be according to the system; something that symbolically works as "fat" may be a compound of other waxy substances, for instance.

Myth is war on metaphoroclasm. The danger of it is that it will either regress to forms of knowledge and power that were characteristic of premodern as well as regressive modernist political regimes (fascism, most obviously) or assimilate its logic to capital's metaphoresis. Both of these things may have happened, and this is why leftist critics have often regarded Beuys with suspicion. Although I do not yet develop this argument in my opening chapter, establishing the way that Beuysian myth functions as a semiotic regime is important to the articulation of history with capital that I develop in the rest of the book since it turns out that the capital relation, too, is a way of assigning meaning to material things. The meaning at stake in the latter instance, though, turns out to be the empty, quantitative form of economic value as opposed to the "deep" spiritual values with which Beuys hoped to associate his art. So another important theme in my book is the fate of meaning as such under capitalism.

On top of socioplasticity and ecoplasticity, then, we ought to keep in mind the analogous notion of *semio*plasticity: the prospect for remaking signification in its totality in ways that were characteristic of the modernist avant-gardes, but that Beuys echoes in his project of a new myth. It ought to be evident that the metaphoric totalization involved in semioplastic myth building is dangerous. This accumulation of "-plasticities," though I derive it from Beuys's term Soziale Plastik, is also meant to resonate with current research on neuroplasticity, or the brain's ability to restructure its neural networks in response to learning processes, environmental influences, and trauma. The philosopher Catherine Malabou has developed the most robust philosophical interpretation of neuroplasticity. But of these terms, it is only "socioplasticity" that I develop consistently because in effect it subsumes the other two; the realm of collective human action retains its primacy for Beuys. Finally, it is in chapter 1 that I bring on the trope of the wound, which returns in chapter 3.

Chapter 2, "Circulatory Systems," is meant to show what happens to this structure of meaning when change and thus history enter the picture. This involves a detailed reading of *Honigpumpe* together with a reconstruction of Beuys's economic doctrines, to which the installation is intimately bound. Beuys has never enjoyed much credit as an economic thinker; his theories seem amateurish and utopian. They may be so, but they were a tool with which to think about the art-like Gestaltung of collective human life, and therefore have much to tell us about Beuysian socioplasticity and economimesis. This is so even if few would bother with Beuysian economics if the material work were not compelling on its own merits. If fat was the crucial material in chapter 1, honey takes over here. Honey is in some ways the richer (that is to say, the less "personal") of the artist's mythological substances. There is a deep vein of honey and bee lore in the European tradition, and Beuys undoubtedly meant to refer to it. The hive is an image of sociality among the ancient Greeks as much as for Rudolf Steiner, the founder of anthroposophy and a model for Beuys (Steiner lived from 1861 to 1925). Honey is the hive's product; thus honey is a figure for the results of social labor. The figurative work that Beuys does with bees in *Honigpumpe* and elsewhere is a textbook instance of "work on myth," to invoke another of Blumenberg's key ideas.[37]

By drawing out Beuys's apian metaphor, I try to make sense in turn of some of the more puzzling of his statements on economics—for example, that money is or ought to be somehow at once a collective "sculpture," a circulating substance with the character of a "bloodstream," and an institution subject to law. Beuys's economimetic operation here is a deployment of metaphor to shift money from one category to another—roughly from "economy," as we usually understand it, to the sphere of Gestaltung. If money is an artwork, the economy can be remade. But a twist emerges at this link in the chain of associations. Beuys's image of Gestaltung is the society of bees: an unconscious, inhuman kind of sociality. (Or so it would seem; Beuys in fact more subtly understood apian form making as the result of coevolution with hominids.) Autonomy and automatism again strangely overlap. This balance between control and laissez-faire was also the field of postwar German ordoliberalism, which was not so much a foretaste of neoliberalism as we have subsequently come to know it as a final version of a distinctively modern socioplastic ambition. In the last part of the chapter, I accordingly turn to contextual history to indicate how these Beuysian metaphors took shape and perhaps even came to be operative in the Federal Republic of Germany during the postwar decades, in which there was an attempt—but on a vastly larger scale than any artwork—to reconcile a stochastic, self-regulating system (free market capitalism) with collectively determined human aims.

Whether the reconciliation sticks is the question of my book's third and final chapter, "The Shape of History." The answer, inevitably, is no. We do not live in free democratic socialism. Yet the model's failure is not the final word. To start, it's worth asking whether "failure" is something we can predicate of a metaphoric/aesthetic economy at all. We can if we take it literally, as I have been saying that we should. But reversion to metaphor is fated; this is the oeuvre's way of living on. I start by introducing two more bodies of work here, the first of which is another large installation from the 1970s: *Arena—Dove sarei arrivato se fossi stato intelligente!* (Arena—Where would I have got if I had been intelligent!) (plate 2). *Arena* is a collection of photographs of Beuys's own works, including many of his performative "actions." I then go on to consider his vitrine sculptures, which likewise accumulate existing artworks, or at any rate, things that an artist has modified. In both cases, notions of sociality layer atop notions, or the real fact, of accumulation. The vitrines also highlight the ambivalence of materials in Beuys's art. They tend to be junky, if not abject, but the form suggests that of a reliquary. A vitrine contains something precious, maybe sacred. Reliquaries are, furthermore, indexes of suffering and death. Over the course of this chapter, I make a case that this distinctive ambivalence has its double root in the commodity form's exaltation and abjection of matter (commodities are bearers of an ineffable something called "value," but as such their material form is indifferent from capital's point of view) as well as in valences of wounding and trauma. This eventually leads me to interpret the doubleness of much of Beuys's art—meaning his use of actually doubled objects along with its ontological doubleness as both abject and transcendently significant—in light of capital's splitting and fusing of the world, which produces both nonidentity between things and themselves as well as the forced equivalency of unlike things.

The issue of trauma in turn leads to a consideration of the historical circumstances under which such a practice took shape, namely West Germany after World War II. I resist the impulse to reduce Beuys's art to an aftereffect of Germany's destruction. The political situation of the 1960s and 1970s, in which Beuys had to defend his "revolutionary" persona against challenges from the student Left and armed radicals, accounts for the specific modality of his aesthetic politics. The temporality of his art is hence complicated and recursive. It is an image of past, present, and future at once. Elsewhere in the chapter, I turn to the explicitly memorial role of some of Beuys's work during the period under consideration and then finally to his major retrospective at New York's Guggenheim Museum in 1979. The arrangement of the latter into distinctive "stations" allows multiple narrativizations, one of which involves what I call the darkest possible construal of the artist's work. I present the latter as a limit case rather than anything like a settled, ultimate meaning.

So that is the structure of things. My coda puts *Honigpumpe* in proximity to a contemporary, Belgian artist Marcel Broodthaers, and the RAF, fellow would-be revolutionaries, as well as a nearly contemporaneous artifact: Pier Paolo Pasolini's film *Salò, or the 120 Days of Sodom* (fig. 7). This contrast turns on the place of death in Beuys's and Pasolini's respective systems. Following critics Leo Bersani and Ulysse Dutoit, I understand death in *Salò* ultimately to be dispersive of historical violence, whereas Beuys's relatively more closed system allows no such escape precisely due to the insistence of the installation's life-affirming tropology.[38] In short, in *Salò* you eat shit, but at least you die. Beuys lacks this cold comfort. Hence the comparison with *Salò* brings to its most painful intensity the problem of the relation between Beuys's utopian rhetoric and the death-haunted materiality of so much of his art.

*Honigpumpe* is my prime example because it condenses the structure of metaphors I have outlined above at its most generative and contradictory. This work also happens to involve another crucial term in the Beuysian

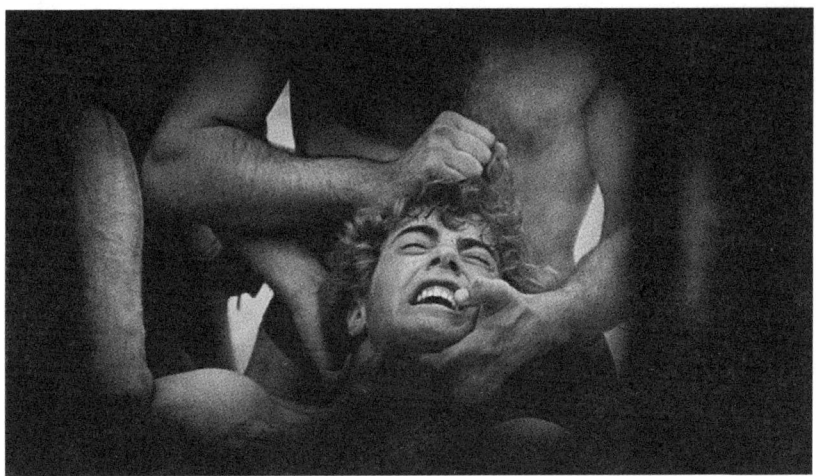

**Fig. 7.** Pier Paolo Pasolini, *Salò, or the 120 Days of Sodom*, 1975 (film still).

equation: pedagogy. Teaching is an enactment of socioplasticity because it results in cognitive changes that are usually collective. Education makes new people and new communities. Beuys proposed aesthetic education as his model for politics in general, in the tradition of an aesthetic ideology that has its German roots in Schiller, Johann Wolfgang von Goethe, and Kant—to say nothing of Steiner, who was certainly the most important single influence on the artist's thinking. There exist several studies of anthroposophical influences on Beuys's work, and I will cite these where appropriate. Nonetheless, a systematic concordance of Steinerian with Beuysian ideas seems otiose here since that would only produce a translation between the two men's conceptual systems as if the decades intervening between their periods of activity had not thoroughly changed the social and historical significance of this body of ideas. The point is rather to see how Beuys worked on and thus transformed Steinerian theory as well as Steiner's pedagogy under the conditions of postwar capitalism.

In this sense, my approach to the Steiner–Beuys relationship is again modeled on Blumenberg's notion of "work on myth" and representative of my methodology in general. Blumenberg does not aim to discover either an original or final meaning of mythical tropes but instead describes how their metamorphoses formalize changing senses of reality. In the same spirit, I have not explicitly thematized or sought to resolve the incongruity of my conceptual resources: Marxian value theory and ecological thought with

Derridean deconstruction; Blumenberg's "metaphorology" with Frankfurt School critical theory. Whether the apparatus works will become evident in the readings of the artworks, and if it does work, the reader may take this as an indication that the party lines of theory may be subject to dialectical torsion on contact with aesthetic singularity. The point of letting such dissonances stand is to work through others—that, above all, between the harmonizing bent of Beuys's aesthetic ideology and its mimesis of capital.

In *Honigpumpe*, such contradictions arose when pedagogy folded into the more totalizing social process known as the capital relation (which, perhaps contrary to appearances, is not at bottom an objective economic process but rather the production of classed subjectivities; the apparent objectivity of "economy" is a mode of class reproduction). A model of the collective production of knowledge thus collapsed into a model of capital accumulation, to disturbing effect. A question that ought to concern any writer on Beuys, then, is that of the modality in which one's own critical exposition does or does not redouble the power/knowledge effects of the artist's teaching, preeminently in the forced equations (or makings equivalent: art = capital) that are so characteristic of both Beuysian discourse and the real abstraction of the commodity's value form (the effective practical equivalence between qualitatively different commodities that emerges in the moment of exchange).[39] Throughout, I attempt to maintain an attitude of critical skepticism toward Beuys's claims about his life and art without indulging a tendency to "debunk" the same that in the literature on the artist too often marks the end as opposed to the beginning of analysis. The cognitive yield of an artwork is never exactly its truth content, if it has any. Metaphors *work*.

So while I am careful to establish facts as the evidence gives them, the truth or untruth of Beuysian myth ultimately finds its bearings not in positivist history but instead in the way it illuminates (or conceals) the predicament of art in capitalist modernity. This is not to say that our conclusions will be comforting. Beuys has always been a controversial artist. I have not structured this book as a series of arguments meant either to endorse or contest existing readings of his work, though I do engage with powerful instances of critique when it seems appropriate or unavoidable.[40] My aim, in contrast, is to offer a new account of that work's significance. I discuss metaphors so fundamental, so totalizing, and yet for those reasons so camouflaged that their role as the persistent undercurrent of Beuys's practice has so far eluded explication.

# Chapter 1. The Matter of Myth

## 1.

In this chapter, I address the question of how things relate to their meanings. The work of Beuys poses this question in especially vexing ways as it seems to involve a rift between signification and its material substrate, even as it seeks to fuse the two. The aim of what follows is accordingly to develop an account of the work's semiotics by determining the relation between its material qualities and its structure of metaphors. But we can start by bracketing the latter; we can pretend, at least, only to look.

Fond III/3 is now in the collection of the Dia Art Foundation (plate 3). It was created in 1979. As the split title indicates, this was the third iteration of the work, each of which, however, was not a modification of the same sculpture but rather a separate object. The earliest, *Fond III*, was installed as the hundredth exhibition at Alfred Schmela's Düsseldorf gallery in 1969.[1] Beuys produced works with the title *Fond* over the course of three decades. The first that is preserved is *Doppelfond* (Double fond), initially from 1954, but reworked twenty years later. In 1969, Beuys also claimed to have made a *Fond 0* in 1953. He said that this lost sculpture had been a "massive block of iron." It seems to be either the same work as or an earlier variant on a *Fond 0* dated to 1957 that is now in the *Block Beuys* installation at the Hessisches Landesmuseum in Darmstadt. (The *Block Beuys* is a permanent, seven-room installation of works by Beuys that formerly belonged to collector Karl Ströher.)[2] This work is actually made out of an unusual alloy of metals as opposed to iron alone.[3] In the same statement from 1969, Beuys describes the logic of the *Fond* series in general: "What is common to the *Fonds* is their character as a base [*Basischarakter*], a base that one stands on, from which one develops other sculptures that are more differentiated, specialized."[4] *Fond I*, despite its numbering, came after *Doppelfond*. The former is dated 1957 and consists of a preserving jar full of peach slices. *Fond II*, 1968, is made up of a pair of copper-plated tables hooked up to electric elements that pump a live charge of twenty thousand volts through the work (plate 4). It would be enough to generate a perceptible shock, if anyone were to touch it, but not enough to do serious harm.

Aside from these outliers, the rest of the *Fond* series follows a consistent formal strategy that Beuys seems to have discovered around 1968. (The titles of the earlier works may have been added at this period or later.) Like the other sculptures from the 1970s with which it shares the name, *Fond III/3* consists of a number of stacks of raw felt—in this case, they are rectangular, and there are nine of them—on top of which lie copper sheets of the same dimensions. The latter function as lids or capstones. They give the work a sense of finality. Otherwise, the piles might fall over or look as if they could. In a more abstract way, it could be said that these copper elements help the work to register as "formed" at all given that the felt sheets have imprecise boundaries. Except for the odd combination of felt with copper, the sculpture resembles something that one might expect to find in a factory or warehouse: raw material instead of finished product.

Accumulation is *Fond III/3*'s principle. No sheet of felt is superior to any other and thus the work seems nearly uncomposed. Yet the polished copper plates cut that reading short and suggest instead a relapse into the aesthetic. The metal looks precious, artisanal, although it may be just as much of an industrial product as the raw felt. Beuys sourced his materials with some care. A letter to Beuys from Heiner Friedrich, a German gallerist and cofounder of Dia, concerns the fabrication of *Fond III/3*. Friedrich details the technical specifications of the commercially available felt that could potentially be used in the work. The entry for one sample reads: "The fiber content of the felt is: virgin wool, 18 percent; reprocessed wool, 68 percent; reused wool, 19 percent; rayon, 5 percent. Rayon is a fiber synthetically derived by forcing natural plant cellulose through small holes and drying the resulting filaments. If you prefer, I am almost certain the rayon can be left out in favor of a 100 percent wool felt."[5] The stacks in *Fond III/3* are around five feet tall and therefore reach just about the eye level of an average viewer. These proportions offer visual access to the copper "seal" on top of the work, but no opportunity to look down on its surface from a position of literal or metaphoric superiority. Unlike *Brasilienfond* and *Fond IV/4*, both likewise from 1979 and both now installed near *Fond III/3* at Dia Beacon, the nine discrete elements of this work are massed together densely—in fact, the middle parallelepiped is inaccessible to touch and almost to sight, except for what little one can glimpse from the top—and hence grant no opportunity for bodily access.[6] There is no labyrinthine effect, no linear extension, and no sense of invitation either.

Felt insulates. Copper conducts. In *Fond II*, copper does so literally. The work is thus a thermoelectric system. With *Fond III/3*, the suggestion is more tenuous. Beuys metaphorized these objects as immense batteries as well as financial instruments given that the title *Fond* is similar to *Fonds*, a cognate of the English "fund." *Fond* is French for "bottom"; it can also mean the holdings of an archive, museum, or library. The word *Fond* has several meanings in the German language too. It can mean the rear compartment of a car, a background (of a painting or embroidery, for example), a basis for more advanced knowledge (in the field of pedagogy), or in the context of cooking, a stock or broth. None of the definitions fits the sculptures intuitively and hence it seems legitimate to consider the close variant, with an *s*, as a clue to the word's significance. Perhaps the culinary meaning is relevant given its implications of standing in reserve or serving as the starting point for more elaborate concoctions. These works "accumulate" energy for indeterminate artistic or spiritual purposes. To quote again from the 1969 statement, "What is primary here is the idea of the battery. These stacks of felt ... are aggregators, the copper plate is the conductor. In this way, for me, a kind of power plant, a static action, emerges from the energy and warmth storage of the felt."[7] The word "action" in the last sentence may refer specifically to Beuys's chosen term for his works of performance art. A "static action" sounds like a contradiction in terms. The idea, though, would seem to be that whereas his actions are dynamic energy economies that play out in real time, the *Fond* sculptures instead freeze and conserve potential energy, perhaps to release it in some other way, as a battery can be charged and then used for any number of purposes later on. The manifold of the artist's sculptural oeuvre then arises out of this "power plant." The *Fond* works are therefore an appropriate place to begin a consideration of his practice at large. Beuys considered them a kind of origin.

What is a *Fond*? It's a contradiction between the abstract and concrete, made concrete. Nothing could be more insistently material than a few tons of raw wool and metal. Yet the point of the work is to kick-start the circulation of a generic, indeed undetermined force or substance that the artist calls "energy." With the exception of *Fond II*, where "energy" is in fact electricity, it is hard to say that this Beuysian energy conforms to any scientific definition. To be reductive, it makes no sense to call these stacks batteries since felt is not a conductive material. Energy here might also be "economic" in the more colloquial sense of the word given the resonance between the title *Fond* and financial terminology. Lastly, Beuys's focus on movement or force is hard to reconcile with the physical characteristics of the sculptures. *Fond III/3* is unyielding, mute. The felt muffles sound as much as it impedes the transfer of heat or electricity. The work's formal strategy is as primal as can be. All of the *Fonds* except the early "preclassical" iterations result from the ur-sculptural act of stacking. They were made without joinery, without carving, without mortar or welding. Their analogs in the premodern era are dolmens, zigurrats, or burial mounds. In their own time—that is, in the second half of the twentieth century—the closest comparable art would have been that of various US minimalist and postminimalist sculptors. A good example is Richard Serra, whose 1967–68 *Verb List* (a sheet of paper with a handwritten list of activities) does not contain the infinitive "to stack," as it happens, although it does have "to store," "to collect," "to heap," "to gather," "to cover," and even, interestingly enough, "of felting" (fig. 8).[8]

Whereas Serra's list evokes an operative concept of art, though—art not as thing but rather as process or the trace of process—the *Fond* works emphasize blank accumulation. There is little in their final appearance to index the moment of making, as there is, for instance, in the pieces that Serra made by throwing molten lead against the join between the floor and wall of a room, or even the potential energy of a precarious arrangement, as in the same artist's propped and stacked metal sculptures. Beuys's stacks simply exist where they are, as they are, and it seems that they will continue to do so forever. They "accumulate" nothing but the ambiance around them. Yet they are also meant to radiate energy back to—well, to what or to whom, exactly? To the viewer? Absent the physical shock that *Fond II* might provide, it's hard to know what Beuys's "energy" is supposed to be made of. Nor is it clear how this energy is supposed to interact with the inert substance of the sculptures.

Stasis and flow are the dominant metaphors here. They're in tension. Beuys was aware of this. He often spoke of an alternation between the "cold," crystalline pole of static form and its opposite: flux, warmth, and change. Both terms could be present in a single work or they could be localized in different works that function as part of a larger schema. It might

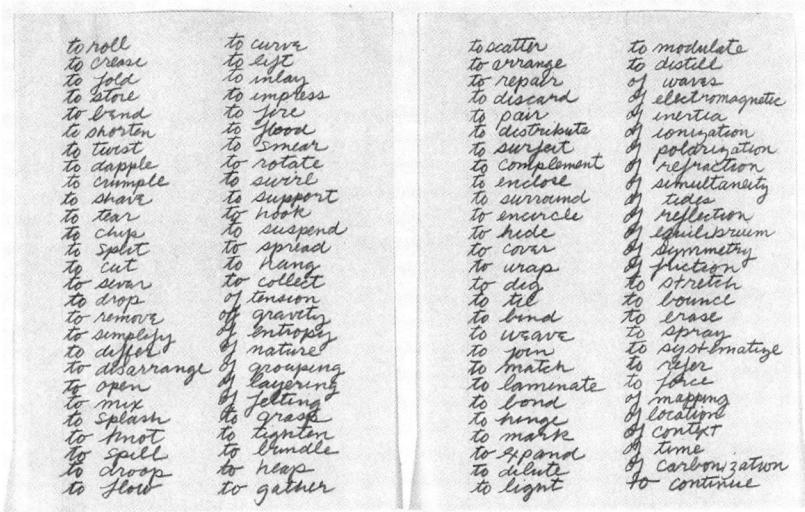

**Fig. 8.** Richard Serra, *Verb List*, 1967. Graphite on two sheets of paper, each 10 × 8½ in. (25.4 × 21.6 cm). The Museum of Modern Art, New York. Gift of the artist in honor of Wynn Kramarsky, 2011. Artwork © Estate of Richard Serra/Artists Rights Society (ARS), New York.

even be possible to reconstruct that schema in full if one were to attempt a complete survey of his oeuvre. What makes the tension between stasis and flow more obviously problematic than Serra's gravitational poetics is that these works involve different kinds of semiosis.[9] The baseline material presence of a *Fond* derives its meaning, if it has any, from its indexicality: the work indicates what it is by being a trace of its context and production. By contrast, the image of the battery or financial instrument—of circulation, accumulation, and exchange—is more definitely discursive and representational. Beuys often tied these sorts of meanings to specific materials. Felt had a meaning within what has been called his personal mythology.[10] He claimed, probably falsely, that nomadic Tatars had wrapped him in felt and fat to keep him warm after his Stuka dive-bomber crashed in Crimea in 1944. There is no direct reference to the crash narrative in any of the *Fond* pieces, except to the extent that the artist's use of felt always bears this connotation.

These sculptures are impersonal—unusually so in Beuys's oeuvre. They represent the most thoroughly objective extreme in his practice. On the other, "subjective" side are those actions (performance works) that involved the artist's body. These were frequently confounding, if not

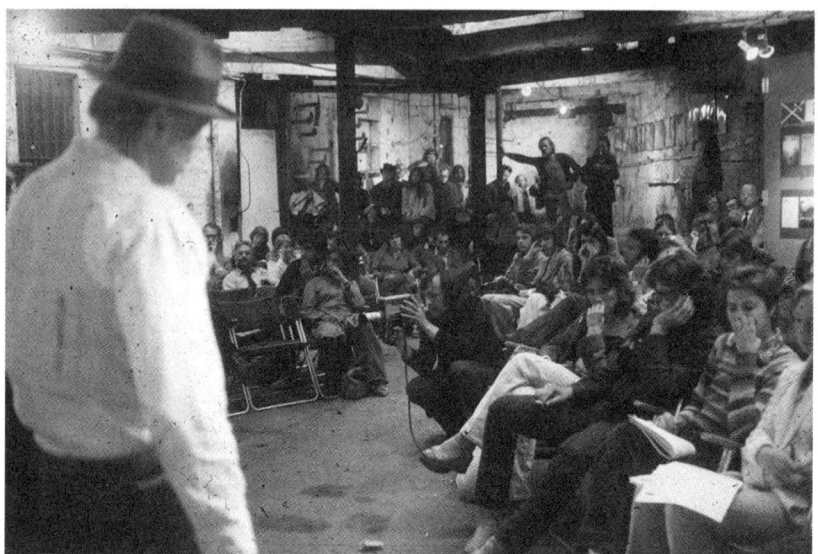

**Fig. 9.** Lecture event as part of the Black and White Oil Conference at Forrest Hill Poorhouse, Edinburgh, August 19–21, 1974. Demarco Digital Archive (University of Dundee) and Demarco Archive, Edinburgh, BEU.74.003.

impenetrable, to their audiences, but they exerted a fascination that soon attracted acolytes. From early on, interpreters made the connection between this distinctive style of performance and the practice of shamanism.[11] The latter is a problematic, generalizing word for a variety of magical operations in various cultures. Shamans typically achieve an altered state of being in the course of their rituals by means of which they contact spiritual entities. If taken seriously, Beuys's shamanism would be a powerful kind of art indeed; it might even transgress the boundaries of "art" as such. But in practice his actions could be modest too.

An apposite case study, precisely because it is so obscure, is *Three Pots Action*, which Beuys performed in 1974 at an abandoned poorhouse in Edinburgh prior to the opening of a solo exhibition at the city's Richard Demarco Gallery.[12] It involved the use of two blackboards as well as the three titular clay vessels, which Beuys carried in his arms and rolled along the walls of the room in which the action took place. After about an hour of doing so, he stacked the pots at the foot of the empty blackboards, onto one of which he then wrote the words "3 total economic Model / 2 dualistic / 1 cultural." Not much more can be said about this action. The work is underdocumented. It remains worth noting all the same because the artist's intervention prepared the building to serve as the site for a conference on North Sea oil (fig. 9). Beuys subsequently gave a talk to attendees at this conference as part of the program of the Edinburgh Arts Festival of that year. North Sea oil was Scotland's new gold mine in the 1970s. Beuys delivered its shamanistic blessing, one could say, in a building that had once undoubtedly been a place of great suffering.

To whom was he speaking? What was *Three Pots Action*? A neoliberal exorcism, perhaps.

## 2.

What does the quasiminimalist sculptor of *Fond III/3* have to do with the magician of *Three Pots Action*? Nothing except the force of his personality, it may seem. Interpreters of such works are unusually reliant on Beuys himself, their first and, from a certain point of view, most authoritative interpreter. A substantial amount of the literature on the artist neglects to mention specific artworks at all and instead merely paraphrases statements of his in interviews and other texts.[13] Many of these statements have autobiographical content, which means that much of the secondary literature is, by extension, biographical.[14] The odd thing about this fixation on the artist's biography is that it constrains even those who otherwise would be least likely to admit the authorial fallacy to do just that. Beuys dictates his interpretations. Sometimes this occurs by way of negation, as in the debunkings that constitute some of the most influential commentaries on the artist.

The least charitable interpretation of such writing is that it commits the error of taking Beuys at his word. If part of his art was his self-fashioning, then it would be unreasonable to assume that statements in the first person are any less fictional than other kinds of art. An advantage of starting with the *Fond* series is that these sculptures are relatively devoid of falsifiable trivia apart from the obviously metaphoric notion of the battery. They suggest how metaphor might be taken to function in Beuys's work if interpreters accept it *as* metaphor. It may not be much of a scoop to show that things did not happen in Crimea in 1944 exactly as he said if the story functions as a metaphor to begin with. On the other hand, perhaps it does matter immensely since Beuys implied that it did. As always, the primal scene is absent. Do we care whether it even happened? We ought to, as historians. But at the same time, if we do, we are perhaps reading the art wrongly. In effect, we would then not be reading it as art at all but rather as a kind of evidence or testimony that therefore would be falsifiable in a way that paintings, for instance, generally are not taken to be. A painting may represent an event that did not really occur, but we do not call paintings of fictional events false and paintings of real events true. An artwork that refers to a traumatic moment in the artist's personal history, however, may lose some of its power if the reality of that moment is questioned.

All of which is to say that the precise tenor of Beuys's atavism remains difficult to pin down even decades after his death. At least the catalog of options is easy to draw up: shaman, charlatan, Nazi, trickster, revolutionary, and more identities besides, few of which, when merely enumerated, tell us much about his art. Instead of seeking the artist's ultimate truth in any one of these labels, it may be more fruitful to approach them as discursive effects of his practice's structure of metaphors (and of the real historical content on which they operate). In this book, I therefore try to bracket almost entirely the guessing game that interpreters sometimes play with Beuys's life. I forsake biography for something like semiotics.[15] Beuys's self-staging is not external to the work but instead part of it. The task, then, is not to ask what Beuys was but rather *how* his production and persona worked. The present chapter aims to show that some of the distinctive qualities of Beuys's art have to do with the relation he tried to establish between material artifacts or actions and conceptual meaning—the relation between the concept "battery" and an amount of raw material, for example. I will eventually argue that this relation depends for its coherence on the more totalizing social relation called capital, or more particularly on a mimetic stance toward the value form of the commodity, though in ways that will not be specified until chapters 2 and 3. My account is unlike others in the literature. Yet to begin developing this account, I first adopt a traditional word: myth. When I write "myth" or "mythology," I refer not in the first instance to the stories that Beuys told about himself (preeminently, the one about the plane crash and Tatars in Crimea) but instead to a semiotic strategy or way of manipulating signs.

Beuys's myth operated by fixing a particular, fragile relationship between the material and conceptual aspects of his practice. It served to fix the concept of "battery" to a pile of felt and copper. If the concept fails, then felt remains felt, copper copper, and thus meaningless, it could seem; this is the danger of the operation. To say that felt has its meaning thanks to a primal, traumatic scene that may never have happened is to leave the artwork open to discrediting in a way that could stop interpretation in its tracks. Comparable practices, such as Serra's, tend not to run this danger or at least tend not to make it inescapable. Although Serra's father was a pipe fitter in a shipyard and has mentioned a childhood memory of seeing a tanker being launched as a sort of ur-sculptural experience, no serious interpreter of his work would take this as the hidden key to the meaning of his mature sculptures, at least not in the way that the Tatar legend is sometimes taken, seriously, as the key to Beuys's work.[16] It is as if Beuys simply jumps over formalization altogether. The meanings that he associated with his materials and motifs are a dangerous supplement because they raise the issue of credibility, and by extension, the possibility of failure or imposture. That Beuys is one of the last artists over whom there was a serious debate regarding charlatanism indicates that he was arguably one of the last modernists too.[17] When he calls a *Fond* a battery, it matters whether we believe him. Hence there are two pieces of evidence to consider when looking at *Fond III/3* or really most of the artist's production: what we see and what Beuys tells us that it means. His myth produces the distinction between the material and the conceptual, or at least this particular modality of it, to begin with.

I imagine that few readers will happily accept the distinction between matter, form, and (conceptual) content that is shaping up here. It seems to impose the idea that meaning comes to artworks from outside, maybe from outside materiality altogether—from a transcendent signified—when the whole thrust of modern theories of meaning has been opposed to any such possibility. Meaning, for modern semiotics and hermeneutics, is differential, contingent, and immanent to material structures. But this is not necessarily so in Beuys. To put it differently, the issue of meaning is only an issue because the present critique is immanent. I start with the danger of a breakdown between signification and its material substrate as Beuys himself seems to deliver it, and then work my way both to this semiotic mode's conditions of possibility and its wider import. It isn't necessarily a danger that the work would run in the absence of a formalized mythology, any more than would Serra's. A *Fond* is significant as it is, in some possibly elusive way, insofar as it consists of organized matter, even if the work's principle of organization is exceedingly simple: something like "to stack," to echo the *Verb List* again. Even a stack is different from its ground. Just such a barely organized gestalt was enough to sustain a few of the most influential of Beuys's contemporaries, namely the minimalists to whom I have already compared his practice.

The entrance of myth complicates things. By reason of its semiotic excess, its second order of meaning, Beuysian myth tends to suggest that organized matter on its own is inadequate to the conceptual plenitude that a metaphor such as that of the battery promises to convey. There are in fact at least three levels of metaphor in operation here. First, the *Fond* is equated to a battery. Then the battery becomes a metaphor for "basis character" or the foundational status of this work with respect to other works. This in turn implies a larger system: the existence of works that disperse or recirculate that stored, potential energy, since accumulation or stasis is only one of its poles. This progressive layering of metaphors is fundamental to the large, ambitious installations to which Beuys increasingly turned his attention in the 1970s and that are the focus of this book. But as articulated elements of a structure, such binary terms are operative in actions and more modest objects too.

Another good example of the accumulation/expenditure dyad is *Celtic* +~~~~, an action that Beuys performed in Basel on April 5, 1971. Over the course of this action, Beuys first washed the feet of some of his audience (apparently in imitation of Christ) and then collected small pieces of gelatin that had earlier been stuck on the walls of the large civil defense storage room where the event took place. After gathering the dabs of gelatin onto a platter, Beuys dramatically dumped them onto his head, after which he briefly went into what looks like an ecstatic trance and then stood motionless amid the milling audience, with a staff in his right hand, for about an hour. Accumulation ceases and becomes expenditure, in the process becoming social; then as energy pours out of the artist, he freezes into sculpture-like immobility. *Celtic* +~~~~ is obviously modeled on religious ritual. It is a baptism of sorts into socioplasticity. So another level of metaphor emerges as the oeuvre becomes a figure of social, political, and economic structures, perhaps also a means to their transformation. The exchange between stasis and flow becomes a figure for the metabolism of (human, but not necessarily only human) life with the earth, or for collective processes of social or political transformation.

Myth binds these levels of metaphor. Myth insinuates that profound content inheres in this art by magical as opposed to material semiosis. I intend to show that we can in fact reconstruct how material semiosis functions

in Beuys's art. The task requires looking at the oeuvre with an eye different from that we would turn on someone like Serra. Art history becomes
myth criticism, but only in the particular sense that we are in the process
of expositing. It is possible to pretend, temporarily, that myth simply isn't
there in *Fond III/3*; it's possible to pretend that Beuys is more like Serra
than he really is. Yet an adequate account of the work has to explain how
and why myth is one of its materials.

"Myth" means stories, but it can also name a set of strategies. Its point
of origin may ultimately have little to do with how it functions in a given
conjuncture. If it matters whether myth is exactly "believed in" is far from
certain as well. In several classic theories of myth, which are closely related
to theories of ideology, myth is a symptom. It aims to reconcile the irrec-
oncilable; it allows contradictory propositions to coexist in the mind.[18]
Symptomatic readings account for some of the strongest interpretations
of Beuys's practice, no doubt because the work lends itself to that angle of
attack; much of what he did as much as advertises its post-traumatic status.
The artist suggests that the "meaning" of a stack of felt has to be found in
a traumatic origin story. In a symptomatic reading, however, the mythic
origin explains nothing but itself. It shows how a work of art is an index of
a past event, but says little or nothing about the work *on* memory (or other
material-social conditions, for example) that the formalizing process accomplishes.[19] Whether Beuys succeeds in a work like *Fond III/3* depends
on whether a symptom can also be a strategy. (This is where traditional
"leftist," disenchanting theories of myth and ideology fall short, and where
Blumenberg turns out to be useful.) Part of the problem is just that formalization barely seems to happen at all in this sculpture, leaving bare
mythologemes to provide much of its propositional content. In practice,
this takes the form of the bluntly declarative language of the wall label.
Statements such as "felt signifies healing" avoid explanation.

Myth is pragmatics as much as ideology. It is easy enough to point out
that Beuys's mythic claims do not stand up to rational scrutiny, but then,
such claims are never meant to. Beuys's myth functioned by establishing
binaries that allowed differences to resolve into stable, repetitive, and essentially atemporal or cyclic patterns. He proposed oppositions such as
hot and cold, animal and human, and east and west that fixed meaning
to his recurrent materials (fat, felt, copper, *Braunkreuz*—his distinctive
oily reddish-brown paint—and so forth). We have seen this in the economy
of the *Fond* sculptures, where the metaphor or indeed fact of immobility

counterbalances a metaphor of flow, which by contrast is wholly notional since with the exception of *Fond II* and its electric current, the works are static systems. By means of a scheme transfer across vastly unequal scales, the economy of warmth and coolness across multiple works, or the circulation of electricity in a single work, is made analogous to natural and social processes, such as the metabolic exchange of energy between human beings and the earth. Beuys thereby conveyed the impression that each of his artworks constitutes a fragment of a vast *Gesamtkunstwerk* that would represent nothing less than a totalizing cosmology, though that system was never to be explicated in full, nor could it have been, one suspects.[20] Because it was the creation of a single man, his conceptual world lacks both the variety and resonance of real, collective myth.

His mythos may be thin, but its operations were rich. It generated a great deal of art. Consider one of his best-known actions, and moreover, the only one that took place in the United States: *I Like America and America Likes Me* from May 1974 (fig. 10).[21] Beuys, wrapped in felt, had himself driven in an ambulance directly from John F. Kennedy Airport to René Block's New York gallery, where he lived with a coyote for the eight hours the gallery was open on each of the following three days. Their tense, intimate relationship was recorded on a few minutes of 16 mm film.[22] Beuys had with him felt blankets and a walking stick—props that recur in many other of his actions and sculptures. The work was something like a confrontation between Beuys's self-presentation as a "shaman" and its real-world referent, an animal with a host of mythical associations in the traditional beliefs of various Native American peoples. Beuys had a more precise reason for his choice of companion, however:

> I would never have done it with a coyote in Europe. But there are other animals in America which could conjure up a completely different aspect of that world. The eagle, for instance, the abstract powers of the head and the intellect, in the West, powers that the Indian wore on his headdress. I believe I made contact with the psychological trauma point of the United States' energy constellation: the whole American trauma with the Indian, the Red Man. You could say that a reckoning has to be made with the coyote, and only then can this trauma be lifted.[23]

It hardly needs to be pointed out that Beuys's possible implication—that *he* can lift the trauma—is presumptuous in the extreme. It confirms

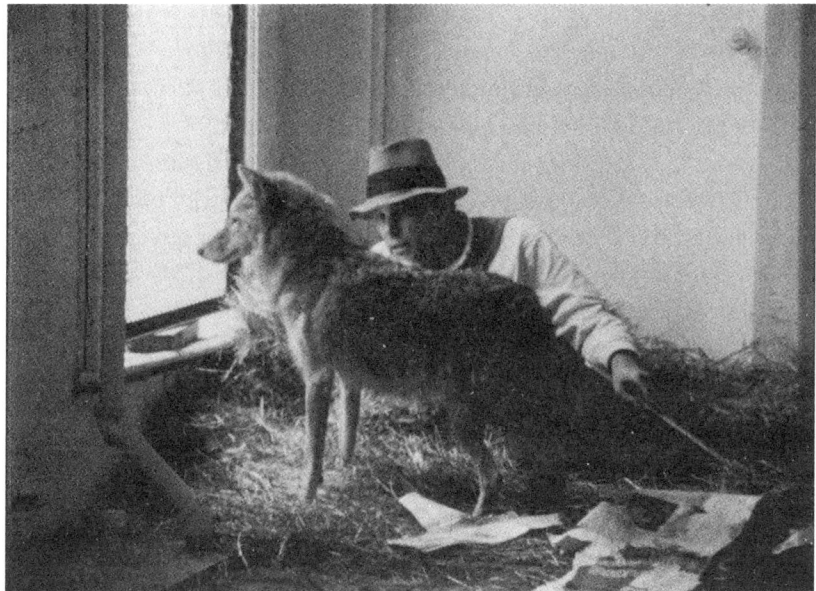

**Fig. 10.** Joseph Beuys, *I Like America and America Likes Me*, 1974 (film still).

accusations that the artist's persona as healer and shaman serves to prevent rather than facilitate a process of coming to terms with the past (above all his own: the trauma he mentions is that of the United States, not Germany).

A fissure in the work opens just here at the transition between the particularities of the performance and its verbal explication, though. So far as one can tell, what Beuys actually did bore few traces of soteriological afflatus. The work's mythic structure does not exhaust the fascination of the film, at least for this viewer. It is rather the artist's jerky and somewhat mannered movements, the document's sense of play and danger and absurdity, and of course the screen presence of the coyote that remain interesting on rewatching. It is up for debate to what extent these qualities depend on Beuys's explanation of the piece. At the same time, it's hard to claim that they wholly escape his mythopoeic drive. For Beuys, myth was a way of working. The Tatar legend had already taken hold—had already established an association between felt and healing, which then became material for the performance with the coyote, which itself became a new myth calibrated for circulation as an anecdote (the core of any myth is a memorable narrative). The coyote is a mythological readymade, the associations of which he could use as raw material for his art.[24] But if myth is excess semiosis, then the materialization of myth is also surplus to its narrative core. Anyone who has watched the video knows that life with the coyote had "meaning" beyond its threadbare association with a plane crash in Crimea thirty years earlier or Beuys's white savior complex. Perhaps myth did not exempt the artist from a reckoning with history but instead made it possible in new ways. Perhaps it allowed *I Like America and America Likes Me* to speak more eloquently about transatlantic relations than Beuys might have consciously intended.

If so, however, what real referents does Beuys's myth latch onto—or from what does it fail to escape? Is it plausible to say that it lost its grip entirely? A myth is a fiction. It need not tell the truth in order to work, but to take hold even myth does, probably, need some connection to experience, to history, to a world. As Blumenberg argues, perhaps counterintuitively, myth does not have to explain things, but it does have to correspond to a sense of how things are. A sense of how things are is not necessarily a sense of "reality" as we understand it in an everyday fashion.[25] This is why myth can be obviously fantastic. That myth need not offer explanations seems more paradoxical since myths are largely origin stories; they tell us why there are seasons, for example, or who founded a city. For Blumenberg, though, this explanatory function is less hermeneutically significant than the ways in which varying receptions of a meager narrative core allow responses to new distributions of the "absolutism of reality" (that is, limitations on human autonomy). In Goethe's eighteenth century, for instance, the ancient Prometheus myth became an urtext of modernity.[26] When this happened, Prometheus ceased to explain the origin of fire or technology in general and instead became a figure for human self-assertion. This suggests in retrospect that the function of the myth may not have been protoscientific (explanatory) to begin with.

The question to ask is whether artworks such as those I have been writing about impose meaning by fiat or produce a sense of their mediation of real, shared experiences—whether they have a public, to put it differently. This is, by the same measure, to ask whether Beuys accomplishes "work on myth" in Blumenberg's sense. Answering the question therefore requires attention to data not accounted for by the work's immanent formal relations: whether its metaphors take hold is a historical and social matter, not just an aesthetic one. Do the metaphors stand for anything? Felt equals healing by transfer of the mythic origin to all of its later symptomatic/ strategic manifestations. (The word "metaphor" is derived from the Greek *metapherō*, "to carry over," "to transfer.") Thus a *Fond* sculpture is meant to heal. But to heal what?

## 3.

The art historian Benjamin H. D. Buchloh launched the first high-profile challenge to the "Tatar legend" in his article "Beuys: The Twilight of the Idol, Preliminary Notes for a Critique," which was published shortly after the opening of the artist's major retrospective at the Guggenheim Museum in winter 1979–80.[27] I will forego summarizing the essay; the ways in which my understanding of Beuys differs from Buchloh's will be evident to anyone interested enough to compare our texts. Let's zoom in, rather, on a passage that has remarkably broad implications not only for any understanding of Beuys but also for modern and contemporary art in general:

> The historic precision and function within (as it seems) the limits of a formalist tradition and of work growing out of it (such as Serra's, [Bruce] Nauman's, or [Carl] Andre's) is altogether lacking in Beuys's works. Their opulent nebulousness and their adherence to a conventional definition of artistic signification make the visual experience of them profoundly dissatisfying. His work does not initiate cognitive changes, but reaffirms a conservative position of *metaphoricity*.[28]

The story of art after World War II is, according to Buchloh and those who share his sensibility, that of the elimination of idealistic, humanistic, and other objectionable qualities—the unity of the authorial subject, values of originality and creativity, and the spiritual vocation of culture—in favor of the literal facticity of the art object or conceptual statement, and eventually from there to a recognition of art's embeddedness in determinate social systems.[29] This is metaphoroclasm: the destruction of a model (more tendentiously, an ontotheology) of art that would ground art's meaningfulness in analogy making or scheme transfers between unlike things along the vertical axis of metaphor, as if descending from a rope hovering in the clouds of the noumenon, as opposed to drawing significance from immanent and differential semiotic relations. The only correct movement here is from enchantment to disenchantment. This is so even if the process is ambivalent in its effects and often melancholy; going back can only be regression. Beuys seems willfully to confound this trajectory.

The passage from Buchloh that I have just quoted is suggestive because it reduces his bad object to a single word: "metaphoricity." Metaphoricity is another name for nonidentity. When a thing pretends to be something it isn't, metaphor is in play. Of course, this also describes lying; hence the immemorial complaint that poets and artists are liars. If metaphor as such is the problem, though, we really are in trouble. Not even *Fond III/3* will be safe, for all of its resemblance at first glance to the "formalist tradition" and "work growing out of it," since the work's meaning depends so much on a tension between metaphors: those of stasis and flow (felt as insulator and copper as conductor). Metaphors ostensibly do not initiate "cognitive changes," curiously, given that metaphor's function is to transfer meaning from one thing to another. Metaphoroclasm's master metaphor is that of the end metaphor: an imagined breakthrough to a world in which the irrationality that stubbornly clings to art would finally give way to a new universality in which illusion ceases to be. This is a myth, too, but it's one in which Buchloh participates (if critically, self-consciously, and as a work of mourning).

In a later and slightly more forgiving treatment of the artist, it emerges that Buchloh's deepest objection to Beuys is not simply that his work is metaphoric but rather that his "artistic language" did not properly reflect on its social conditions: "What Beuys lacks most of all is the understanding that artistic languages are public entries into the symbolic order, and as such they are both historically overdetermined and socially constructed."[30] The notion of a "public entry" implies the notion of a public. A work of art that means something within the rules of a game has to play by those rules, and those rules are, essentially, those of the game that makes an artwork register as an artwork at all, or at any rate, a legitimate, nonregressive one. This is what allows for the disenchantment of a public sphere.[31]

I think Buchloh's error here, if it is one, in fact turns out to be an excess of optimism. He claims that a progressive, avant-gardist art contributes to a rational dialogue in public, somehow still, even when the advances of spectacle and the culture industry have drastically narrowed the conditions of communicative action. Buchloh does not seem to admit the more unsettling possibility that any such form of communication has become impossible. What can it mean for an artist such as Beuys to have addressed his work to a "public" that may not be there, or that may not be capable of accepting his communicative propositions as something that add up to a totality of meaning held in common, or to a totality of practice, to a world? What if his mythology *is* only private? And if the requisite structure of meaning—that is, reception—is absent, can an artistic address to such a horizon ever be anything but arbitrary, forced, or even totalitarian? Could the work ever produce its own reception, its own interpretive community, by sheer strength of socioplastic metaphor?

The question, then, is not exactly that of Beuys's success or failure as an artist in conventional terms of aesthetic quality. At issue is rather the systematicity of his oeuvre and its relation to a social world. Beuys made totalizing claims for his work. Myth, though, is antipathetic to rational argument. Its coherence instead depends on the ensemble of conditions out of which it works up its bricolage.[32] Buchloh offers one reading of these conditions: Beuys is a symptom of Germany's postwar repression of historical memory. Beuys's myth is "an attempt to come to terms" with the "blocks and scars" left by the Nazi period. Its use value is to repress the trauma of that experience. "But, of course," Buchloh writes, "the repressed returns with ever-increasing strength, and the very negation of Beuys's origin in a historic period of German fascism affirms every aspect of his work as being totally dependent on, and deriving from, that period."[33] Myth, here, is isomorphic with the Freudian symptom.

True or false, this does little to explain the specifics of his art. From this point of view, there was no necessity behind Beuys's intense way with materials. There is no reason for a work such as *I Like America* to be the strange, contradictory, and particular thing that it is; there is no reason for *Fond III/3* to be exactly five feet tall, or *Fond II* to be electrified. That his art revives a set of philosophical problems around matter and the ideal is then more or less beside the point. What counts is the regressive quality of the work, not the particularities of its regressions. This is perhaps why assessments of Beuys are often so little concerned to describe individual works of art: his practice seems to transcend its own particularity. Perhaps it even actively repulses a close reading by its repetitiveness—a quality that suggests that the meaning of the work is not to be found in its material specifics but rather in its underlying conceptual armature.[34] If Beuys makes totalizing claims, criticism can totalize in return. If his mythology is personal, then judgment on the art is judgment on the man. From being at a minimum a symptom, Beuys might shrink to nothing better than a crank.

Insofar as this book is involved in a historiographical dispute, this is where I intervene. I will try to show that the conditions of possibility for Beuys's practice are more general than some critics allow and can be explicated in a way that emphasizes the relevance of his art, in its quiddity, to problems that extend beyond the situation of the postwar Federal Republic of Germany. It may be possible to shift the etiology of Beuys's practice away from a symptomatic reading of either personal or national trauma, and instead toward the horizon of art's relation to postwar capitalism—or rather, to show how these two horizons intersect. It may be possible to tease out the fundamental metaphors that orient the Beuysian work on myth, which is undeniably work on the legacy of the Nazi period too, not for the sake of ratifying these metaphors *tel quel*, but to argue for their mediation through other social forms that regulate the metabolism of everyday life. The metaphors are not necessarily profound. In the case of Beuys, they may indeed be flimsy or even ridiculous. It is nonetheless at the level of these absolute metaphors that one can see Beuys as having formalized his art's dependency—I contend that the relation is a kind of mimesis—on a social matrix that precedes the artistic gesture or mark, and within or sometimes against which the gesture or mark will do its own mediating work.[35] To put it most directly, a *Fond* can be analogized to funds only because funds exist. Thus the very fact that Beuys is able to conflate the financial association with quasiscientific as well as spiritual valences of the "battery" idea tells us something about the structure of the society in which this condensation of metaphors became possible.

These concrete relations are not inherently resistant to historical description, and can be theorized in a more granular fashion than sweeping gestures toward "the spectacle" or "the culture industry" allow. It is at this level—at the interface between social form and aesthetic form, or between circuits of reproduction (of value and human beings) and artistic gestures—that these reflections are posed. It will not help to ask whether metaphor as such is legitimate in contemporary art. An adequate account of Beuys will necessarily reject metaphoroclasm as a categorical imperative, though perhaps not as a necessity at certain moments (there were compelling, arguably even obligatory grounds for rejecting the metaphor of society as artwork during Beuys's lifetime, for one thing). The point is rather to see the concrete mediations between metaphors and social conditions of shared experience. In this case, the question is whether any totalizing system of artistic meaning, such as Beuys proposed, could take hold in these years, and if so, what might have been the grounds for its coherence, its political horizon, its conflicts and contradictions. Could Beuys's mythology have become more than "personal"? Could it have connected to a public of some kind? Could it have made itself effective as a real principle of social transformation, social Gestaltung, socioplasticity? And could this totalization be anything more than a duplicate or negative image of an already existing social totality: that of capital and the violent social forms it needs to reproduce itself? Again, what has been injured—and what needs healing?

## 4.

*Zeige deine Wunde*: "Show your wound." This is the title of a work that bears the date 1974–75, although Beuys first installed it in a subterranean walkway in Munich in 1976 (plate 5).[36] Its initial viewers may well have been unsure what exactly was on display. Among other materials there happens to be fat, although it's almost impossible to see at first. Fat is smeared on the inside of the glass panes on the front of two sheet metal boxes, called "lamps" in catalog descriptions, that hang above the two stretchers at the rear of the room. There is more fat in the two zinc boxes beneath the stretchers; a thermometer and a test tube containing a blackbird's skull also rest in these boxes, even though these objects are barely visible in the work's present installation. The metal stretchers were built to carry corpses. There are quite noticeable depressions in both of them. Next to the boxes filled with fat are empty glass jars, to which the boxes are connected by a filter apparatus (not likely to be functional in any literal sense). On either side of the room, archaic wood and metal implements, paired too, lean against the walls. The two on the right rest against two white panels that are hung like paintings, while those on the left sit atop small blackboards of the kind once found in German primary schools; the latter rest on the floor. Mounted on the same left wall, closer to the viewer (again, as the work is currently installed), are two framed copies of the Italian newspaper *Lotta Continua*—a phrase that can be translated either as "continuous struggle" or "the fight goes on." They are still in envelopes addressed to Beuys. Each has furthermore been inscribed, in Beuys's hand, to Jörg Schellmann and Bernd Klüser, publishers and friends of the artist. This newspaper was issued by an extraparliamentary communist group of the same name. Either centered at the back of the room, in its present state, or on the right wall, in its original installation, are two large blackboards on which are written the installation's title.

"Zeige deine Wunde" is an imperative in the familiar form of address reserved for friends and family. The notion of the "wound" was a persistent element of Beuys's rhetoric. Its first public appearance was evidently in an allegorical curriculum vitae titled *Lebenslauf/Werklauf* (Life course / work course), the first version of which was distributed at the Fluxus Festival der Neuen Kunst (Festival of New Art) in the German city of Aachen in 1964.[37] Beuys here refers to his own birth in 1921 as the "exhibition of a wound." The association of birth with wounding is likewise evident in his sculpture *Badewanne* (Bathtub), which he claimed was his actual childhood tub; he applied gauze bandages, adhesive plaster, fat, and copper wire to this readymade object (fig. 11). Variants of the phraseology recur through the end of his life. In 1980, for example, he would issue a call to "show the wound we inflicted upon ourselves in the course of our development."[38] The chalk marks are faint in *zeige deine Wunde*, however. In many reproductions, they do not show up at all. The passage from the so-called lamps to the stretchers to the oleaginous mass below suggests a descent from mind to the residue of body, although the lipid film on the glass lends to this baser material the latter's metaphorics of transparency. It may be relevant that Beuys suffered a heart attack in 1975, sometime between the work's initial date and its inaugural exhibition.

There is a deathly poetics at work here, or at least there is as soon as we identify the stretchers. A standard iconography is available with which to interpret *zeige deine Wunde* as a kind of rebus, almost a linguistic proposition, the elements of which add up to a whole. Later, in my book's third chapter, we will consider this iconography and try to see whether it tells us anything useful about the work; I will also propose my own provisional alternative reading, still more or less in iconographic terms. Iconography produces a relay between discursive propositions and the facticity of an artwork. As a hermeneutic, the practice of iconography or iconology posits— or to put it more tendentiously, constructs—the conceptuality of an artwork, and by extension, the nonconceptuality or mute objecthood of all that cannot be thus conceptualized. Iconography's wager is accordingly not so much that artworks are meaningless unless they can be correlated with a text as that artworks are, under certain conditions, capable of attaining a text-like conceptuality or propositionality. This is the assumption that has always seemed to make iconology inapposite for interpreting modern

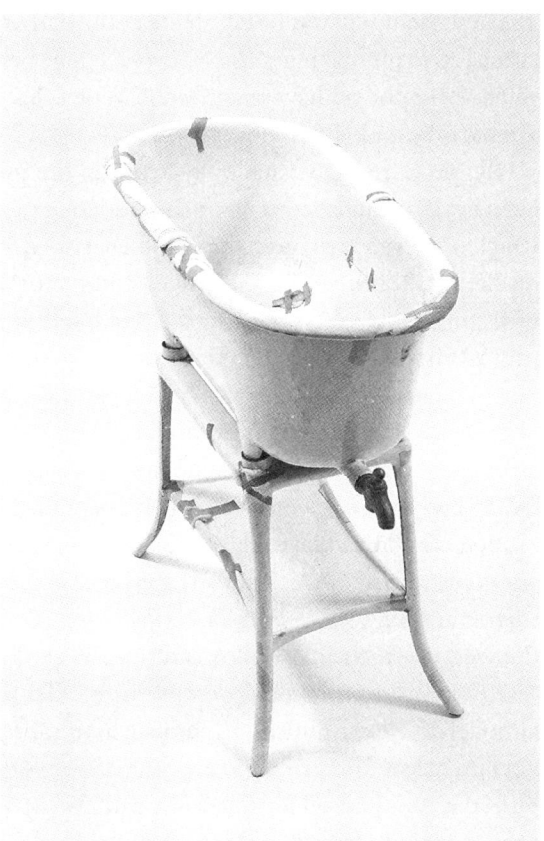

**Fig. 11.**
Joseph Beuys, *Unbetitelt (Badewanne)* (Untitled [bathtub]), 1960 (repaired 1977). Enamel bathtub with stand, adhesive bandage, and gauze. 39⅜ × 39⅜ × 17¹¹⁄₁₆ in. (100 × 100 × 45 cm). Schenkung Lothar Schirmer, Städtische Galerie im Lenbachhaus, Munich.

(or at least modernist) art. By extension, the evident openness of Beuys's work to iconographic interpretation is suspicious in itself. In an installation such as this, which consists of a number of charged objects (Are they signifiers? And of what?) in a seemingly arbitrary arrangement, Beuys secures, or perhaps doesn't, the link between matter and meaning by way of the strategy that I am calling "myth." But how?

To concretize the problem, it may be useful to discuss a material, or rather a set of materials, that is as important as felt in Beuys's oeuvre: fat and its relatives. The fat in the glass jars in *zeige deine Wunde* is associated with an arrangement that strongly suggests an operating room or morgue. Fat signals the body, but that body is wounded or dead. Something is going on here in the exchange between a material and a baseline fact of existence—to which, of course, attach vast territories of religion, superstition, and myth.

The argument will not be complete at the end of this chapter because the crucial term for making sense of this exchange between matter and myth—value—will not yet have reappeared. When that does happen, *zeige deine Wunde* may look different.

By the time Beuys made this work in the mid-1970s, fat had already been firmly established as one of his trademarks. The *Fond* sculptures with which we began turn on an opposition between felt and copper, the one an insulating substance and the other a conductor. Fat combines both properties in a single material. On the one hand, it is an inert insulator that protects bodily warmth. On the other hand, it is a source of energy. Fat is fuel. If heated, it also becomes liquid. Fat is the only organic substance in *zeige deine Wunde* apart from the blackbird's skull. If the latter is clearly an image—indeed, barely a metaphor; more like an envoy—of death, then fat, by contrast, has a more ambiguous significance.

Beuys had used fat and its cousins before, and would use them again after *zeige deine Wunde*. It already appeared in drawings from the late 1950s, such as in *Fettige Wolke löst sich aus dem Meer* (Greasy cloud emerging from the sea), in which an oily blob saturates its cardboard support (plate 6).[39] There are more ambiguous possible uses of fat from a year or two earlier, although these are difficult to confirm in the absence of technical analysis; notably, at least three of his *Plastische Bilder* (plastic or sculptural pictures, a term that Beuys used for relief-like early works) dating from 1957–58 appear to include stearin, a derivative of animal fat.[40] An early outlier is an untitled work bearing the parenthetical label *Junge Frau und zwei spielende Kinder* (Young woman and two playing children), dated 1949; according to its cataloging information, its materials include a "Fettfleck" or "spot of fat."[41] The material's grand debut, however, came in 1963, with the *Stuhl mit Fett* (Chair with fat) of that year—almost contemporaneously with the artist's emergence into broader public visibility with the first of his public actions (fig. 12). In the same year, the artist had his first solo gallery show, with Block in Berlin, at which he presented the action *DER CHEF THE CHIEF. Fluxus Gesang* (Fluxus song) (fig. 13).[42] These remain among the artist's most recognizable works. They established the metaphoric baseline for his subsequent use of fat and its cognates. *DER CHEF* incorporated smeared fat applied to the corners of the room in which it was performed. As for the intention behind this gesture, I think that historian Annie Suquet is on the right track: "By drawing or marking a space with fat, Beuys subtracted it from the deadly 'appropriating mastery' of the right angle: fat, as

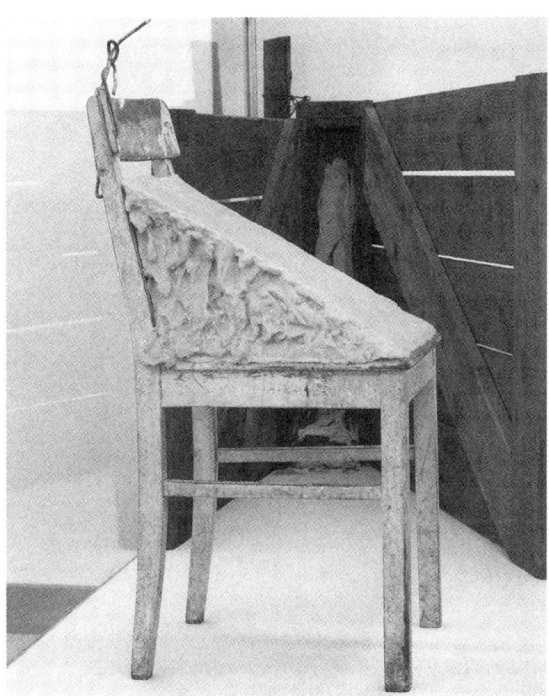

**Fig. 12.**
Joseph Beuys, *Stuhl mit Fett*,
1963. Wood, wax, and metal.
39⅜ × 18½ × 16½ in. (100 ×
47 × 42 cm). Hessisches
Landesmuseum, Darmstadt.

unstable matter, can shift from the liquid (warm) to the solid (cold) state and compensates, through its very reversibility, the motionless rigidity of architectures."[43]

Fat had also been part of his first action altogether, *FLUXUS Sibirische Symphonie 1. Satz* (FLUXUS Siberian symphony first movement), which he had performed at a Fluxus festival at the Kunstakademie Düsseldorf the previous year.[44] As the full title of the piece indicates, fat was also present in Beuys's action *Kukei, Akopee—Nein!, Braunkreuz—Fettecken—Modellfettecken* (Kukei, Akopee—no!, brown cross—fat corners—model fat corners), which took place at the aforementioned Festival der Neuen Kunst in Aachen on July 20, 1964. Beuys here melted a small amount of fat on an electric hot plate. *Stuhl mit Fett*, however, is not the first instance of the use of fat in Beuys's sculptural oeuvre. Buchloh gives the curiously imprecise date of "1960–1963?" for a *Fettecke* (Fat corner) in his article "Twilight of the Idol," which I have introduced above.[45] In this he follows art critic Caroline Tisdall's catalog for the artist's retrospective at the Guggenheim. Buchloh mentions this inconsistency, in a footnote, as

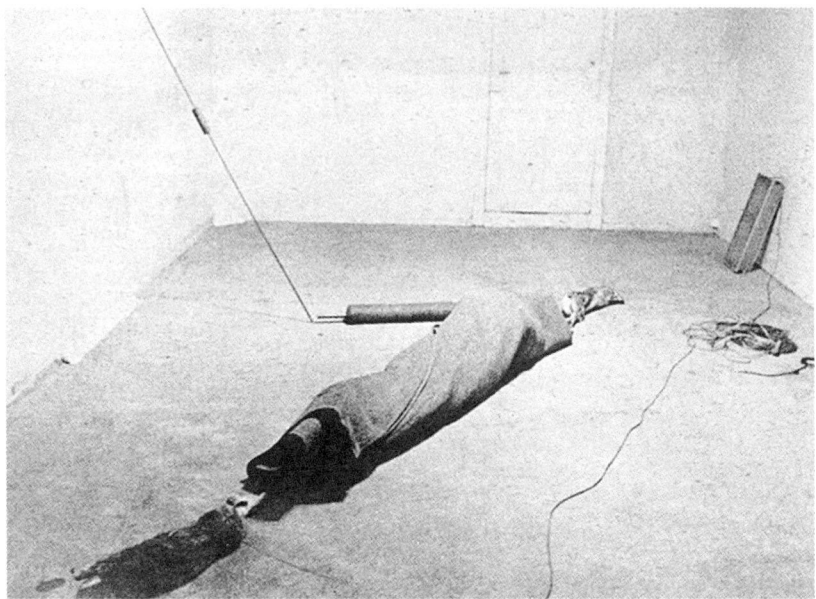

**Fig. 13.** Joseph Beuys, *DER CHEF THE CHIEF. Fluxus Gesang* (THE CHIEF. Fluxus song), action, Galerie René Block, Berlin, December 1, 1964.

evidence of Beuys's looseness with the truth. In any case, the earlier date seems erroneous. The preponderance of reliable sources suggest that fat only became a major sculptural material for Beuys in 1963 in works such as a *Fettbatterie* (Fat battery), now in the collection of the Tate in London, although there may be isolated instances of its use from approximately a decade before. In this murky early phase of Beuys's career, secure dating is near to impossible. According to one source, the substance used in *Fettbatterie* is coconut oil.[46] It seems that Beuys more frequently used commercial margarine. Most descriptions of the artist's works incorporating fat do not further specify the exact nature of the material.

It would be interesting to know how many works use animal as opposed to vegetable-based fats as well as the number of instances in which "fat" actually designates wax, paraffin, stearin, and so on, or some compound thereof. This is an issue in determining the initial dates for Beuys's use of a given material. He seems to have begun employing beeswax no later than around 1952, for example, and perhaps as early as 1947, if the dating of the sculpture *Bienenkönigin I* (Queen Bee I) in Tisdall's 1979 catalog can be

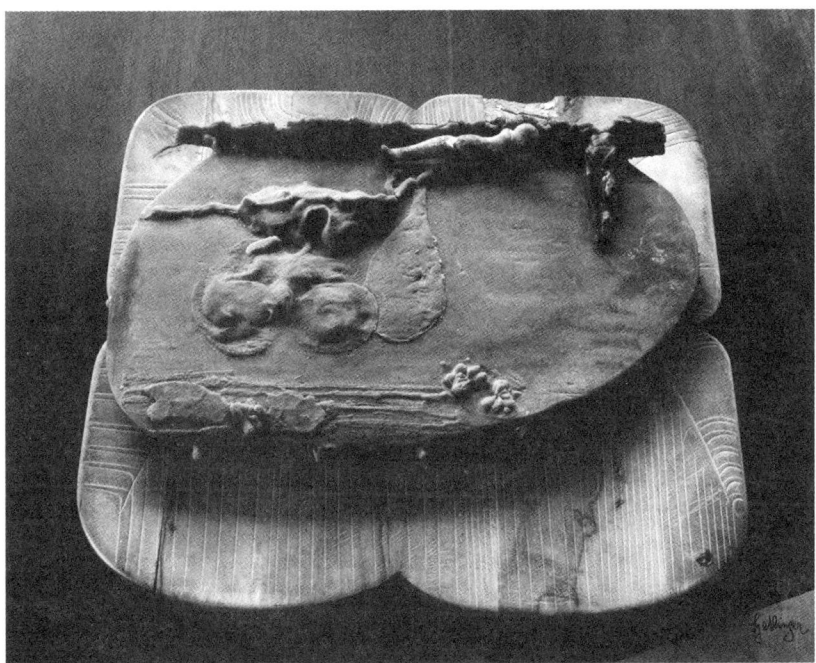

Fig. 14. Joseph Beuys, *Bienenkönigin I* (Queen bee I), 1952. Boxwood, wax, and fired clay. 13½ × 13¾ × 3 in. (34.3 × 34.9 × 7.5 cm). Schenkung Lothar Schirmer, Städtische Galerie im Lenbachhaus, Munich.

trusted (fig. 14).[47] Like fat, wax is malleable, sensitive to heat, and organic. It may have been the first step along the way to the other material's eventual preeminence. That wax seems to precede fat in Beuys's production is a strike against the notion that the latter substance bears a direct, deeply personal relation to the originary moment of the future artist's experience in Crimea. It appears, rather, that he was interested in a continuum of materials that share similar properties, such as greasiness, sensitivity to heat, and plasticity. In other words, Beuys behaved like most artists. His use of materials was experimental, fluid, and not fixed once and for all by symbolic associations.

Fat itself seems to make its appearance no later than 1953, which is the given date for a *Fettgefäß* (Fat vessel) now in the *Block Beuys* installation at the Hessisches Landesmuseum Darmstadt.[48] This work evidently consists of a crudely formed wax goblet-like shape filled with pure white fat; it therefore combines the two related materials. Tisdall's 1979 catalog also illustrates a work there captioned *Fat Sculpture* and erroneously dated 1952.[49] In fact, it is *Fettplastik (transponiert) Wachs* (Fat sculpture [transposed] wax), now dated 1964, also in the *Block Beuys*.[50] This work does indeed appear to be composed of wax rather than fat, though whether the form was somehow "transposed" from an earlier or contemporaneous model in fat remains unclear. On the next page, Tisdall illustrates a work captioned *Wax Sculpture* that she dates to 1953; it too is now in the *Block Beuys*, where it is instead assigned to 1952.[51] In Beuys's first biography, published in 1973, the same sculpture is again reproduced, but is designated *Fat Sculpture*, 1952, which is also the title for which the Hessisches Landesmuseum has opted.[52] A different photograph of the same piece, labeled "*Fat Sculpture* 1952," is included in panel 30 of a complex work that I will discuss later in this book: *Arena—Dove sarei arrivato se fossi stato intelligente!* (Arena—Where would I have got if I had been intelligent!), 1970–72.[53] It appears that this *Fat Sculpture* is in fact made of wax as opposed to fat, in which case Tisdall's title, although perhaps not her date, would be correct.

Beuys's first use of fat thus occurred in 1952 or 1953–that is, if all the objects described as being made of "fat" are not wax after all, and if we bracket the status of the *Fettfleck* in the drawing *Junge Frau und zwei spielende Kinder*, dated 1949. (Beuys sometimes modified earlier drawings, such as by adding his *Haupstrom* or "Mainstream" stamp.) Only *Fettgefäß* unquestionably incorporates the material named in its title, although even here it is possible that the wax vessel was made in 1953 or thereabouts, and its filling added at some other time. Fat only returns as an important medium for his sculpture about a decade later, at the moment of *Stuhl mit Fett*. The intervening years were marked instead by the predominance of more traditional sculptural materials: wood, plaster, and bronze. Fat does not make an appearance in the drawings until around 1959. Wax appears just before the initial fat sculptures in the early 1950s or perhaps even as early as 1949—that is, once more, if the dates for works in either medium can be relied on.[54] Wax's role in bronze casting, with which Beuys was involved during this period, perhaps suggested its independent use as a sculptural material. There may of course be minor or lost instances of the artist's use of these materials dating from earlier in his career. Though pointedly unclassical, the use of nonstandard media such as wax or fat would not necessarily be antimodernist. It features in Edgar Degas's *Little Dancer of Fourteen*, from 1876, as well as in the work of Medardo Rosso (Buchloh mentions both artists in relation to Beuys).[55] I can find no evidence that either of these precedents made an impact on Beuys, however, or even that he knew them at all in this early stage of his postwar development. To all appearances, he arrived at his characteristic materials independently. Moreover, it seems that he only arrived at fat rather late—at the earliest, nearly a decade after his plane crash in 1944. His initial sculptures and drawings, which date from around the time he enrolled in the Kunstakademie Düsseldorf in 1946, do not employ unconventional substances.

## 5.

Why fuss about these minutiae? Because the transitivity of Beuys's use of materials is important. It would appear to be a central axiom in the Beuysian system that there is such a thing as an innate significance that attaches to the artist's recurrent materials, of which fat is for now my example. This claim is rhetorical. It elides the potentially arbitrary nature of the association through the reiterated consistency of the work's symbolic arsenal. Fat *means* something whenever Beuys uses it. Basically, it has to do with healing, trauma, and the body, as its connection with the Tatar legend makes clear. Yet when we look to his actual practice, what we see instead is slippage. Iconographic desiderata are secured just as well by displacement and deferral as opposed to direct relay between a given work's material composition and its semiotics.

So far, we have been considering small, early objects. But the dynamic could play out on an immense scale as well. With *Unschlitt/Tallow*, made for the first instance of the exhibition *Skulptur Projekte* in Münster in 1977, the artist had intended to pour tons of beeswax into the space beneath a pedestrian ramp on a newly constructed building that was part of the city's university (fig. 6). This space suggests the scene of *zeige deine Wunde*'s installation the year before. Both installations testify to a fleeting engagement with the interstices of modern urban space.[56] Beuys settled for beef suet mixed with paraffin and stearin when the cost of beeswax turned out to be prohibitive, in an ironically literal instance of economic determinism in the artist's work.[57] The symbolic content of wax was evidently transferrable to a near but not exact substitute.

This was not the only act of transference in the work's production. Accounts of the piece often convey the impression that it was cast directly

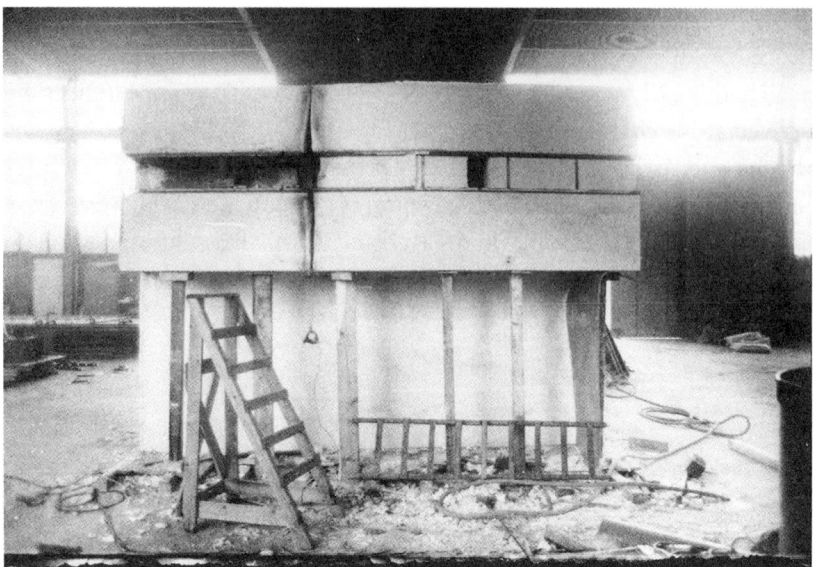

**Fig. 15.** Cast used in the production of *Unschlitt/Tallow*, Hermann Borchard Betonwerk, Münster-Roxel, 1977. Photograph by Ute Klophaus.

from the unprepossessing nonspace on the University of Münster campus, photographs of which have been reproduced in catalogs.[58] Such was not the case. As a result of insurmountable technical difficulties, the work was instead poured into a replica of this form that was constructed in a nearby warehouse under the supervision of Beuys's assistant Heiner Bastian (fig. 15). It is the traces of *this* contraption that we see on the sculpture's surface, not those of an architectural readymade. Descriptions of the work sometimes elide the discontinuity between the two sites. The catalog of the 1979 Guggenheim retrospective, for example, cites an article by art critic Laszlo Glozer in the *Süddeutsche Zeitung* that correctly notes that the work was cast from a replica of the space. Yet Glozer says that Beuys "had an exact mold of the corner filled with tallow."[59] It could not literally have been an exact mold of the architectural space since the form was built out of plywood and wood framing; presumably, it was constructed according to measurements taken either from the real underpass or perhaps from plans of the building. Icon and index are confounded. The work was thus a simulacrum before it was ever displayed, and indeed doubly so. Made neither in the location nor out of the material originally intended, the work

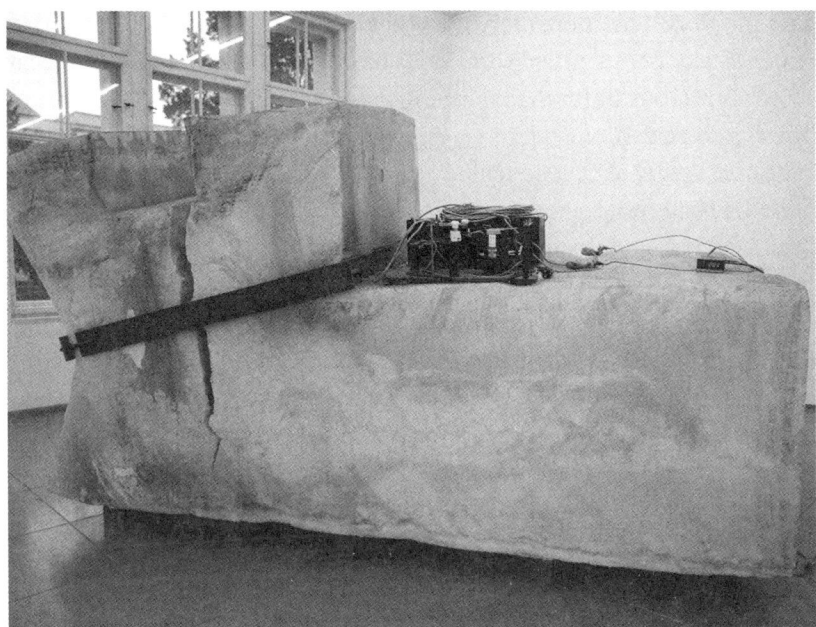

**Fig. 16.** Joseph Beuys, *Unschlitt/Tallow (Wärmeskulptur auf Zeit hin angelegt)* (Unschlitt/tallow [heat sculpture designed for long-term use]), 1977 (detail). Beef suet, paraffin (?), stearin, steel, and electric elements. Cut from a cast measuring 76⅘ × 376 × 120½ in. (195 × 955 × 306 cm). Dimensions variable as installed. Sammlung Marx, Berlin, on long-term loan to the Staatliche Museen zu Berlin, Hamburger Bahnhof–Museum für Gegenwart.

as it eventually came to be undermines the logics both of the index (the cast) and a (post)minimalist straightforwardness with respect to materials (compare Serra's sculptures in lead and iron, which do not claim to be other than what they appear to be). The cast was then cut up into six blocks and exhibited in the atrium of the Landesmuseum in Münster.

Beuys subtitled *Unschlitt/Tallow* "sculpture that does not want to become cold." As if to confirm that desire, its organic matter eventually gained a supplement of wires, an AC adapter, a voltmeter, and some unnerving equipment that captions blandly describe as "thermal elements" (fig. 16). The work's subtitle is quite literal. Long after the work's initial casting, its interior is said to have remained liquid and warm. The thermometer that penetrates to the interior of one of the six blocks, as if stuck into a half-baked turkey—it is still visible in the sculpture's current installation at the Hamburger Bahnhof in Berlin—seems to remain functional and consistently displays a temperature that is higher than that of the surrounding air. Long after the work's creation, there was still a danger that it might break apart, which is why Beuys girded some of its blocks with metal stays that are far more obtrusively bulky than normal conservation practice would allow.[60] This is a work that one might say approaches the condition of a living organism as nearly as a static sculpture can, or at any rate, more nearly than does the *Fond* series. If so, however, it looks to be an organism in dubious health—bandaged, its temperature taken, held together by jury-rigged prostheses. It, too, shows its wound.

Fat is suited to Beuys's purposes because it is a material that does a great deal of metaphoric work on its own.[61] The connection between fat and the body is nearly inescapable. Fat insulates bodies; when available commercially it is, in many instances, derived from animal bodies, as in the cases of lard and suet. Only slightly further afield are a set of connotations that arise from the substance's calorific properties. Fat stores energy and then is burned to expend it, whether in muscles or lamps. It suggests metabolism, and this in turn summons other metaphors—perhaps, for example, the labor-mediated "metabolism [*Stoffwechsel*] between man and nature" that Marx described as an "eternal natural necessity" of human life.[62]

As opposed to the elaborate and frequently opaque network of references that Beuys embedded in his verbal self-explications, the properties of his materials are a sort of commons. They augment intentionality or even replace it. As Beuys put it, "In this concert of objects it is not I who speak, but rather the things have their own inner language."[63] But that inner language is hard not to read as Beuys's own since it only partly coincides with either scientific knowledge or shared cultural assumptions. While insulation and fuel are natural associations, as it were, that of fat and felt with healing is more of the artist's own making; the plane crash story secures his iconography of materials. Of course, the circumstance that fat is a salve and felt keeps bodies warm is the condition of possibility for such work on myth. Myth is another commons to the extent it isn't only individual. (Whether "individual myth" is even conceivable is dubious; the term may make no more sense than "private language.") Social and natural history bleed into one another. As the example of *Unschlitt/Tallow* demonstrates, Beuys's way of working allowed for a degree of metaphoric elasticity between matter and meaning—a degree of transitivity or play that allows tallow to stand for beeswax, which itself is intermediary between fat and honey.

Another property of tallow is that it melts, as do all varieties of fat and wax. It changes form. As we have seen, *Unschlitt/Tallow* did not at first, or perhaps ever, completely solidify; it remained and perhaps still remains thermodynamically active. Even when that process of change is arrested, such materials retain a sense of plasticity unlike that of stone or bronze. Beuys played on these associations. Sculpture in its expanded sense was for him a matter of energy, changes of state, and transit between binary pairs. He made this clear in a statement printed in the catalog for his Guggenheim retrospective in winter 1979–80, where *Unschlitt/Tallow* was installed on the floor of the museum's rotunda. In one column are the words "chaos undetermined organic warm expansion"; in the other, "order determined crystalline cold contraction." Between the two columns is the word "movement."[64] This is not aesthetic theory so much as cosmology.

## 6.

Before returning to *Unschlitt/Tallow*, let's continue with the problem of fat and wax, but now from another point of view: neither art nor cosmology, but philosophy. René Descartes had an interest in beeswax. In a passage from his *Meditations on First Philosophy*, published in 1641, Descartes takes leave of the main course of his argument in order to consider an empirical situation. I will quote at length, as the whole of the passage illuminates Beuys:

> Let us consider the things which people commonly think they understand most distinctly of all; that is, the bodies which we touch and see. I do not mean bodies in general—for general perceptions are apt to be somewhat more confused—but one particular body. Let us take, for example, this piece of wax. It has just been taken from the honeycomb; it has not yet quite lost the taste of honey; it retains some of the scent of the flowers from which it was gathered; its colour, shape, and size are plain to see; it is hard, cold and can be handled without difficulty; if you rap it with your knuckle it makes a sound. In short, it has everything which appears necessary to enable a body to be known as distinctly as possible. But even as I speak, I put the wax by the fire, and look: the residual taste is eliminated, the smell goes away, the colour changes,

the shape is lost, the size increases; it becomes liquid and hot; you can hardly touch it, and if you strike it, it no longer makes a sound. But does the same wax remain? It must be admitted that it does; no one denies it, no one thinks otherwise. So what was it in the wax that I understood with such distinctness? Evidently none of the features which I arrived at by means of the senses; for whatever came under taste, smell, sight, touch or hearing has now altered—yet the wax remains.

Perhaps the answer lies in the thought which now comes to my mind; namely, the wax was not after all the sweetness of the honey, or the fragrance of the flowers, or the whiteness, or the shape, or the sound, but was rather a body which presented itself to me in these various forms a little while ago, but which now exhibits different ones. But what exactly is it that I am now imagining? Let us concentrate, take away everything which does not belong to the wax, and see what is left: merely something extended, flexible and changeable. But what is meant here by "flexible" and "changeable"? Is it what I picture in my imagination: that this piece of wax is capable of changing from a round shape to a square shape, or from a square shape to a triangular shape? Not at all; for I can grasp that the wax is capable of countless changes of this kind, yet I am unable to run through this immeasurable number of changes in my imagination, from which it follows that it is not the faculty of imagination that gives me my grasp of the wax as flexible and changeable. And what is meant by "extended"? Is the extension of the wax also unknown? For it increases if the wax melts, increases again if it boils, and is greater still if the heat is increased. I would not be making a correct judgment about the nature of the wax unless I believed it capable of being extended in many more different ways than I will ever encompass in my imagination. I must therefore admit that the nature of this piece of wax is in no way revealed by my imagination, but is perceived by the mind alone. (I am speaking of this particular piece of wax; the point is even clearer with regard to wax in general.) But what is this wax which is perceived by the mind alone? It is of course the same wax which I see, which I touch, which I picture in my imagination, in short the same wax which I thought it to be from the start. And yet, and here is the point, the perception I have of it is a case not of vision or touch or imagination—nor has it ever been, despite previous appearances—but of purely mental scrutiny; and this can be imperfect and confused, as it was before, or clear and distinct as it is now, depending on how carefully I concentrate on what the wax consists in.[65]

Descartes finds that the variousness of sensory experience throws him back to rationalism. The passage I have just quoted is immediately followed by a section in which Descartes says that the men he sees when looking down from his window might as well be clothed automatons based on the evidence of the senses alone and therefore it is the mind that judges them instead to be men. Strictly empirical observation proves unable to confirm the identity of bodies, such as the melting piece of wax, which we know to perdure even though we cannot offer an account of all of their qualities or visualize all of their possible metamorphoses. Such is the poverty of the imagination, by which Descartes means the faculty that produces mental images. Imagination is distinct from the pure exercise of thought. Only the mind is capable of showing that what we are describing is a single quantity of wax in two different states as opposed to two heterogeneous bodies appearing one after the other, though we gain this realization only after a detour through experience. An exception proves the rule, then, while also recognizing the system's outside. Mere perceived matter remains nonrational, a rush of confused sensations without the certainty of the cogito.

If Beuys is like Descartes, it is because he seems to reinstate a distinction between qualities known and qualities sensed in things. In a certain philosophical vocabulary—that of John Locke, rather than Descartes, although Descartes anticipates its terms here—these are respectively called primary and secondary qualities. *Unschlitt/Tallow* is, on the one hand, nothing but extension. We recognize it, or are able to do so after reading its description, as the imprint of a certain bounded space. (We have seen that the work equivocates over the nature of the relation between its forms and its site-specific referent.) In the gallery, the work presents this space again, reconfigured. The objects take up a certain volume, they do not move, and there are six of them. These are primary qualities. They are also yellowing with age, in some places even black or rusty brown, and we infer that they are soft to the touch, at least relative to more usual sculptural materials such as stone or bronze, except perhaps for those parts that have crusted dry. (Early photographs of the work show that its color was at first a warmer, buttery off-white.) If we could move close enough, we might even find that they have a scent. These are secondary qualities. They are aspects of the object known by sensory perception rather than by being held in the mind, according to Locke's schema. The work's primary qualities, by contrast, could be understood with no sensory intuition whatsoever, such as if we knew only *Unschlitt/Tallow*'s dimensions without having the work or an image of it before us. What moves between primary and secondary qualities is thought, which encompasses known form as well as the contingencies of observation.

Minimalist art also trades on this distinction between "the known constant and the experienced variable," as artist Robert Morris put it.[66] Yet it is clear that these two epistemological modes do not exhaust what we know about *Unschlitt/Tallow*—that is, if we have at least a passing familiarity with Beuys's work. We also know what Beuys intended us to know. We know his art's use of fat, to which the work's paraffin-stearin-suet mixture is close enough to pass. The work is defined by displacement, yet its rhetoric depends on a claim to immediacy. This sculpture is indeed one of the most extreme statements of its maker's faith that mere accumulation of a given symbolic material, or its analog or simulacrum, is sufficient to amplify its resonance; a transition occurs from quantity to quality. *Unschlitt/Tallow* thus adopts the same logic as the *Fond* series. The literal mass of Beuys's sculptures has sometimes presented challenges to their exhibition. In a letter dated October 1, 1978, addressed to Bastian, Guggenheim curator Linda Shearer notes that the weight of *Fond IV/4* was so great that it could only be placed in a single location in the museum's galleries during the artist's 1979 retrospective; otherwise, it could damage the architecture.[67] As in the case of the shift in *Unschlitt/Tallow*'s ingredients, this instance of prosaic material determination has potentially important effects on the work's meaning. Given that the roughly chronological sequence of "stations" so much impressed the exhibition's visitors—it suggested a hidden logic or even narrative, as we will see closer to the end of my book—what does it mean that at least one placement was dictated by nothing more profound than the need to preserve the structural integrity of Frank Lloyd Wright's building?

Something therefore comes undone once we consider the impact of contingency on the work of symbolization. Yet in the case of *Unschlitt/Tallow* at least, this has not seemed to issue in a lasting semiotic crisis; once we accept Beuys's mythology, a reading presents itself almost as a matter of course. As a German exhibition catalog puts it, "The production of this sculpture ... resembled a healing process that saved a cold and wounded site."[68] (But which site? And what exactly is the healing substance?) Similar interpretations could be adduced. Once the significance of the work as an act of healing becomes self-evident, though, we have to ask in turn why the site is wounded, what violence or trauma or lack could have led to a need for the artist's healing, just as *zeige deine Wunde*'s command leaves us unsure of how and where we are supposed to be hurt. It is perhaps the designation itself that creates the injury. Or else brings it into view.[69]

The displacement of the work's site of production from its supposed index (from the walkway at the University of Münster to a wooden framework constructed in a warehouse) only makes the question more urgent. A different yet related question arises in the case of *zeige deine Wunde*. At its first installation in a large, lonely subterranean passageway in Munich, the ensemble's various components were separated by an appreciable distance and thus constituted effectively self-contained objects of attention, the relation of which to each other could only have been synthesized, gradually, by a peripatetic viewer. The version of the work that ended up in Munich's Lenbachhaus, however, is compact almost to the point of claustrophobia. Here, viewers look into a room that remains off-limits to any but optical perception. Its staging resembles that of a shop window and hence precludes the mobile, extended viewing experience that must have been key to the work's inaugural manifestation. There is simply a wall at the back of the Lenbachhaus version. By contrast, the original installation was located in a passageway—a site of transit and circulation. Given these differences between the two installations, does it make sense to speak of the "same" piece of art at all? Descartes would say yes: its components persist, although they have been subject to a transformation perhaps not wholly unlike that undergone by the philosopher's piece of wax (or the reverse, from an expanded to a more compact form).

If there is indeed a constant in *zeige deine Wunde*, though, it would seem to be more securely founded on a set of metaphoric rather than strictly abstract, conceptual identities. The presence of the same objects represents a continuity, needless to say. Still, if the work is essentially the "same" in its two versions, as Beuys implied by keeping the same title and overseeing its transfer to the Lenbachhaus, this surely has much to do with the symbolic resonance of those objects—their suggestions of bodiliness, mortality, and resurrection. These motifs ensure a baseline of meaning even across a drastic shift in the work's phenomenological coordinates.

The same is true of *Unschlitt/Tallow*'s link to the notion of healing, which persists even as the indexical link to the sculpture's primal scene reveals itself to have been a matter of mediation and representation—iconicity versus indexicality—all along (as was the plane crash narrative, which exists only in its retellings). The so to speak "official" reading of the work has likewise persisted in its move from its first installation in the courtyard of the Westfälisches Landesmuseum to its present home in the Hamburger Bahnhof around 250 miles away.

Descartes could not be sure that seeing (or feeling, smelling, or imagining) an object such as his piece of wax could ever be sufficient to know it. With *Unschlitt/Tallow*, too, knowledge of both material and origin are unsettled. But here Descartes took flight to reason. Beuys, by contrast, takes flight to myth. If the work's metaphorics, iconography, or in short, meaning derive so much from an indexicality that is not truly there, then to what exactly does the rhetoric of healing refer? A sympathetic magic is conceivably at work. What is done to the representation is done to reality ("a healing process that saved a cold and wounded site"). But then, the status of the material traces of this act of magical transference (that is, the several tons of fatty compound now in Berlin) is left hanging since the work's substance was never in physical contact with the site of the "wound." The sculpture's dismemberment into six pieces as well as its displacement from the site of production to a museum courtyard, both of which already vitiate its quality as a site-specific index, find a double in the near subterfuge of its well-advertised but only notional relation to the nonspace of the University of Münster walkway. In this, *Unschlitt/Tallow* differs from the model of the Non-Site developed by Beuys's contemporary, the artist Robert Smithson, to which it might otherwise seem proximate. Non-Site works typically consist of a sample of material taken from a given site paired with a photo-reproduced element on the wall that represents that site. Few question whether the materials in a Smithson Non-Site really come from the location Smithson said they did, nor does it seem particularly important if they do or don't. Like the insignificant ramp in Münster, the places from which Smithson sourced his rocks, gravel, and so on have little preexisting resonance. The identification of a site as "wounded," however, makes its specificity important since a wound cannot be cured by proxy—not without magical thinking, anyway. There is no vicariousness of wounding, as there is no vicariousness (so far as we can tell) of somatic reactions such as nausea. (The possibility of a "vicariousness of vomit" is, though, important to Derrida in his essay "Economimesis," so we will return to this.) If the cast is not really from the wound, the entire symbolic edifice threatens to crumble. Beuys thus again introduces an element of bad faith.

# 7.

What if "bad faith" were essential to Beuys's kind of art making, though—essential to his art's fictionality, which as we have already seen, runs counter to the metaphoroclastic drive that characterized much art of the twentieth century (Buchloh's "formalist tradition" and "work growing out of it")? In *Unschlitt/Tallow*, the wound was never there. Or maybe it will turn out to have been elsewhere, just as in *zeige deine Wunde*, it is unclear whether the damage has been done to Beuys, the viewer, or society at large, and as it is unclear in *Fond III/3* how or to what purpose "energy" is being accumulated.

Like the *Fond* series, *Unschlitt/Tallow* belongs to a subset of Beuys's sculptural oeuvre that seems particularly engaged with contemporaneous minimalist sculpture from the United States. As with the treatment of Descartes above, a comparison may help to clarify similarities and differences. Over the past few decades, it has been common to link Beuys with Morris, another contemporary. They became acquainted while Morris was staying with the dancer Yvonne Rainer at gallerist Schmela's Düsseldorf apartment in early 1964. Later that year, Beuys asked Morris to perform a version of his action *DER CHEF* in New York City simultaneously with its presentation at Galerie René Block in Berlin. The piece involved Beuys wrapping his body in felt and making inhuman moans into a microphone over the course of eight hours. Morris did not follow through, for reasons that remain obscure; perhaps he simply did not find the prospect appealing. There is a letter from Morris to Beuys, dated January 21, 1965, in which the former apologizes for not writing sooner and explains that he still hopes to perform the action.[70] Morris's epochal show at the Green Gallery, New York, in late 1964 contained, among other works, a *Corner Piece* that bears a resemblance to a *Filzecke* (Felt corner) that Beuys had made in 1963.[71] Morris's subsequent adoption of felt as the medium for some of his "Anti Form" works in the late 1960s again echoes Beuys's precedent.[72]

The point of divergence is clear, however. Missing from these works, at least on any intentional level, is the assumption that materials have an inherent significance. Felt in a Morris piece has nothing to do with healing unless we bring that idea to it. A Morris Anti Form sculpture remains agnostic with respect to these suggestions if it does not actively ward them off. Its perceptual contingencies—its secondary qualities—are quarantined from possible conceptual supplements; there is not, or at least there is not supposed to be, a second rationality hiding behind the perceptual encounter. Another way to put this is that Beuys's second degree of signification—this phrase being critic Roland Barthes's technical definition of myth—does not exist in the US artist's production, though of course it would be foolish to assume that minimalism was without mythologies of its own.[73] The difference is that in Beuys, the mythology is put there on purpose.

To be sure, Beuys himself occasionally asserted the nonsymbolic nature of his art. Consider a statement from 1981: "My work is not symbolic. It is practical, never symbolic. I have always chosen the corresponding forms, quantities, materials that in my opinion illuminate the energy-context [*Energiezusammenhang*] ... because it is always the forms themselves, the materials, that immediately represent the energy-context, not the symbols."[74] Beuys must have taken this line because he felt that many of the motifs that his interpreters took to be symbols were no such thing. Rather, these apparent "symbols" were operative. For Beuys, a substance such as fat or honey illuminates the "energy-context" at stake in a given situation by its nature, not because it stands for something else. This is another reason why I have said that understanding the artist seems to force his interpreters to take metaphors literally—that is, if we stay with the immanence of his structures of meaning. We have no other choice if we want to work out the logic of those structures. As historians, however, we need not accept this premise of immediacy. Such meanings may have been self-evident to Beuys; they rarely are for the unprepared viewer. Taking these claims at face value would involve pseudoscience or occultism. Ultimately, I will propose another way to maintain critical immanence by untangling his art's mimesis to a slightly less hermetic kind of signification: economic value. Myth and capital have a common ground.

For now, though, compare Morris's *Untitled (3 Ls)* of 1965 with the six irregular blocks of *Unschlitt/Tallow*, to which they bear a limited formal resemblance (fig. 17). Morris painted his plywood forms a neutral and evidently nonsignifying gray. Their material is hard to guess from perceptual

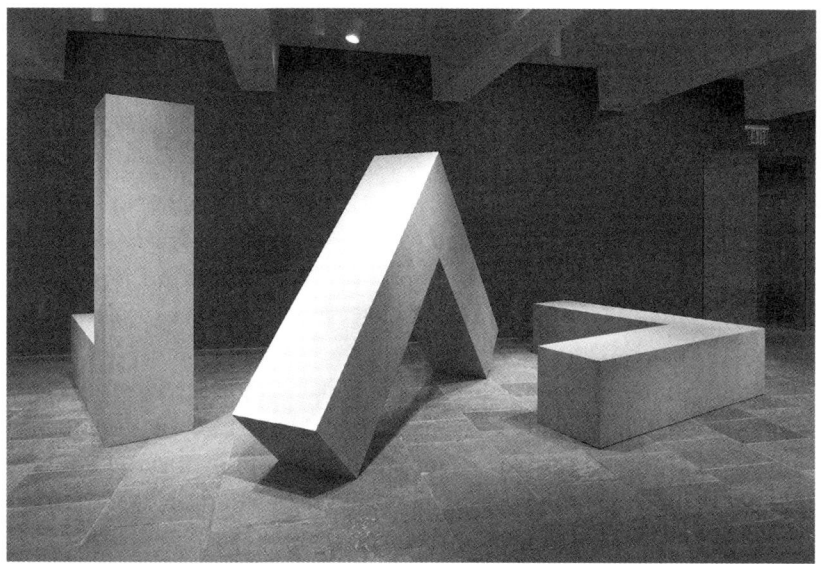

**Fig. 17.** Robert Morris, *Untitled (3 Ls)*, 1965, refabricated 1970. Stainless steel. Dimensions variable. Whitney Museum of American Art, 76.29a–c.

data alone. But they do not pretend to be made of something they are not; if anything, they pretend to be made of nothing. They are also hollow, and thus disavow the weight, solidity, and substance that are crucial to the German artist's work. If they suggest a kind of bodiliness nonetheless, it is on the more general level of phenomenological presence and is not freighted with mortality except to the extent that any invocation of human corporeality is (which is to say, potentially very much so). Beuys imports a vast apparatus of the spiritual to avoid such metaphoroclastic clarity. Myth is the work's a priori. It takes over the role of the Cartesian cogito in that it ensures the coherence of the work's signifying structure, as the mind "knows" the persistence of a piece of wax by synthesizing the data of perception. Myth transposes that synthesis, that guarantee of consistency, to a point external to the viewing subject, at the same time, however, as it naturalizes a fraught relay between interior and exterior. There is nothing in the material form of the work to bind it to the concept of "healing." Multiton blocks of hardened fat do not especially suggest that idea. The suggestion depends on a displaced, discursive reference, as opposed to the relatively straightforward, if also still iterative and deferred, logic of the index.[75] *Unschlitt/Tallow* is more like a traditional sculpture and less like a photograph than is a minimalist artwork. This is because the mold from which it was made was already a kind of sculpture, a kind of representation in its own right. The elision of the real site of making with its referent is rhetorical or at least figurative; it phenomenalizes a content that is most likely social or political to the extent that the idea of healing, in Beuys, is never only personal, as seems clear enough from a sampling of his verbal statements. (Hence the second-person address in *zeige deine Wunde.*) In this case, the sculpture "heals" a public site, specifically one of learning—a walkway on a university campus. Healing for Beuys is always social and therefore the significance of the motif ought by rights to be universally intelligible. Yet this content has to be conveyed by means that are "extra-aesthetic," so to speak, insofar as it is hard to derive the proper significance from immediate aesthesis, or immediate sensory perception. The presence of the work's intended meaning cannot be assumed in the phenomenolog-ical encounter; it cannot be assumed to emerge in the spectator without a kind of nudging. That nudging is myth.

Myth, in *Unschlitt/Tallow*, thus can be defined more precisely as the ele-ment of the work's conceptuality that does not belong to the viewer: an ex-cess or supplement of meaning. This is a kind of "objective" conceptuality that is, from the beholder's perspective, groundless inasmuch as it must be brought in from a locus that remains inaccessible to experience or rational evaluation (Beuys's lipocentric origin myth, in this case; in the *Fond* series, the mythical notion is that of the battery, which did not have the same intensely personal associations as did the materials of fat and felt). When myth becomes form, we call it iconography. Myth adds a conceptual con-tent that is not reducible to primary and secondary qualities—to rational knowledge and the phenomenological encounter, respectively—but rather is historical since it had to be constructed before it could be communicated. We have not yet considered what the ground of that content may be, other than a personal iconography of healing. And if it is only the latter, then it is hard to see why anyone should care about it. "Personal iconography" is perhaps as senseless as "private language" since iconography as understood in the methodology of the history of art manifests shared narratives and values, even if the community involved in the language game is extremely small. The work, in fact, might be better without it—might succeed as sculpture even if it fails as myth. But that would make Beuys into a mini-malist, a metaphoroclast, which he was not.

*Unschlitt/Tallow* goes almost all the way toward the noncomposition and indexicality that are said to mark certain important practices of the same period, Morris's included, only to pull back and reinstate another model entirely. With a different cogito in hand, then, we can again ask Descartes's question: "What then did I know so distinctly in this piece of wax?"—or in this case, in *Unschlitt/Tallow*'s several tons of fat. It turns out that I knew what I had been told. Familiarity with the artist's other works, statements, and theories along with repetition of the latter in wall labels, exhibition catalogs, and a stack of art historical studies had primed me to understand fat not merely as substance but as an element of a conceptual system too. Descartes *knows* that the people he sees are people rather than automatons because his mind is capable of such a judgment, although the mind's sovereignty is grounded in radical doubt of anything but the subject's capacity to think. On the other hand, the viewer of Beuys's art knows that fat signifies healing because an association in the artist's mind has been successfully communicated, largely, if not entirely, in words. The viewer's certainty is off-loaded to an external signifying system that is impervious to critique. Myth holds together the material and conceptual aspects of the work, making its unitary meaning transmissible. It does so even when the material "ground" itself threatens to give way. The bond is tight. And yet the two moments can be separated. The work's claim to an immediate transit between substance and meaning is precarious, not least because of the instability of its material status. If fat can really be wax, and wax can really be paraffin, suet, or what have you, what is left of this iconography of materials at all? A work like *Unschlitt/Tallow* is in constant danger of slipping out of the Beuysian synthesis, of decomposing into filthy, meaningless stuff, on the one hand, and concepts without a bearer, on the other. Correlation of aspects A and B is the task of the artist's labor. He holds together the work's conceptual identity with makeshift theory, much as a threatening physical crack in one of its elements is stayed by a set of ungainly metal braces.

There are at least two registers of metaphor here, one with personal meaning grounded in trauma (healing of the individual), and another that constitutes a broader social, political, and/or economic metaphor (the healing of urban space or maybe the entire world). Although the leap in scale between these two registers is dizzying—and has the potential to involve Beuys in a questionable sort of representational politics inasmuch as the world's healing could seem to depend on a single man's trauma and recovery—the association is at least plausible because each dynamic is homologous.[76] To heal one is to foretell the healing of all. Still, the leap from personal and to some degree fictional experience to a universalist doctrine of redemption, which is in turn, somehow, to be attached to the physicality of his art, only makes sense if we suspend disbelief. Artistic fictions or virtualities generally present themselves in the mode of the as if, so there is nothing extraordinary about that. It is, however, unusual for an artwork in the modern era to propose fictions that are not really meant to be fictions, metaphors or virtualities that are to be taken literally; since the Renaissance, it would seem that the very notion of what it means to be a sophisticated maker or viewer of art depends on segregating reality from mere representation, with the latter now corralled into the neutralized zone of the aesthetic.[77] The form that art historian Carrie Lambert-Beatty has named "parafiction" is also distinct from Beuysian fiction because its practitioners know the difference between the real and the fake (they are not true believers in their own myths); at some point, in theory at least, they let the viewer in on the difference too.[78] In parafiction, deception is involved only as long as dramatic irony persists, before the actual situation is unveiled and fiction dissipates. This moment never arrives in Beuys's fictions, if fictions is what they are. (Of course, it bears mentioning that a successfully duplicitous artwork would never be recognized as such; that is, it would not be subject to the persistent bouts of debunking that have marked Beuys's reception.) I have more tendentiously been using the word "myth" to name this aspect of his practice, to differentiate it from kinds of fictionality that historians and critics find easier to digest. If the Beuysian socioplastic transit between unalike categories requires either suspension of disbelief, which would seem to betray the more serious (that is, nonrepresentational, nonsymbolic) stakes of socioplastic effectivity in favor of a gentler fiction, or crediting magical causality—a regression that we ought not to countenance—then the entire project may be incoherent.

## 8.

The remaining chapters of this book are intended to show that the Beuysian system does after all hang together to the extent that it takes up a mimetic stance toward the "objective conceptuality" of a binding social relation, namely capital. That is, there is already a social relation that produces a nonidentity of things with themselves in a manner that furnished Beuys with a mimetic object. The value of a commodity has nothing more to do with its substance than does that of *Unschlitt/Tallow* with the notion of healing. The *Fond* series adumbrates most of the key issues in its condensation of metaphors: battery, financial instrument, healing substance, and accumulation versus expense. To move forward, it will be necessary to take one more metaphor literally: Kunst = Kapital (art equals capital). In the chapter that follows, I leave the *Fond* series and *Unschlitt/Tallow* behind while mostly staying with major sculptural works from the 1970s. I read these projects in terms of their metaphoric structure, which I argue constitutes an inverse and image of the value abstraction. In aiming to resist, overcome, or absorb capitalism, Beuys also mapped it. More strangely still, his art reproduced its logic, not in the register of iconic resemblance, but in the convergence of its metaphoric structure with moments in the actual circuit of value accumulation.

To put it simply, the systematicity of Beuys's oeuvre does not belong to Beuys. It belongs to capitalism. I will therefore contend that the "totalizing" dynamic in the work is extrinsic to Beuys. The artist is rather an agent of *dis*order in his very attempt to master a totality. His system produces the surplus materiality that it would seem to want to reduce, sometimes violently, to an airtight iconography (to equations such as "fat equals healing"). But this in turn points to the contradiction at the heart of capital's totality: that between use value and exchange value. Materiality and significance are at odds in his work in a way they ought not to be, per standard modern aesthetics, because his art tries to exempt itself from modern art's foundational exemption from instrumentality. In claiming social instrumentality (socioplasticity)—in trying to heal a place, himself, or the world, for example—Beuysian art seeks to occupy the role of a general social mediator. Capital already plays that role all too well. Without these preliminary clarifications, the questions that now result, and that will occupy the remaining pages of this book, might seem little short of nonsensical: How is art like or unlike capital? How totalizing can art get without ceasing to be art? And since capitalism itself is at once a totality, a unity in separation, and a mass of insuperable conflicts, what does that do to our sense of the coherence of an aesthetic system that takes capital as its image or horizon?

Hence the concept of unity or systematicity at work here is different from what is usually at stake in accounts of the artist. It is unnecessary to stress either the supposedly totalitarian closure or conceptual incoherence of the artist's system. Both moments are immanent to it. Indeed, they are immanent to particular works, such as *Fond III/3*, when its "meaning" alternates between sheer material presence and an economic, scientific, or perhaps even social or political metaphor on a potentially gigantic scale. This is a heteronomous systematicity; it has its coherence in a moving contradiction.[79]

So far, we have established that Beuys's work involves a structure of signification that differs from the metaphoroclastic austerity of some of his contemporaries because it generates a dissonance between indexicality ("this form is a trace of its making") and discursive, quasipropositional content ("this substance heals something"). The latter constitutes what I have been calling myth. Beuysian myth is thin, as I have said. But that is ordinary. Blumenberg describes myth as a human strategy to reduce the "absolutism of reality."[80] Myth does not explain things, primarily. Beuys certainly did not need to explain how metabolism or thermodynamics work. His science, as art and film critic Annette Michelson once noted, is nineteenth-century at best: "When I came home from the exhibition [the artist's 1979 retrospective at the Guggenheim], I looked up in a couple of books something about the history of our knowledge of electricity. Beuys stops around 1830, I would say, just after Faraday."[81] Science did mythic work for the artist, as did his plane crash. Instead of making a real battery, Beuys constructed a metaphor out of felt and copper. Myth opens a zone in which humans can maneuver against necessity, according to Blumenberg. Myth is not strictly separate from enlightenment, nor is the relation between the two inevitably a catastrophic dialectic.[82] Both are instead interrelated modes of addressing the fact of human fragility in the world. Blumenberg further distinguishes work "on" myth from the work "of" myth. The latter generates the materials out of which myth is originally made, while the former is the constantly creative process whereby myth is transformed over time and thus made usable again in new historical conjunctures. Blumenberg's point in titling one of his major books *Work on Myth* was to underscore that it is not really a culture's myth*making* that tells us about its sense of reality. Myths are almost never cut out of whole cloth. It is rather the transformations to which a store of mythical topoi (for example, the Promethean revolt against the gods; the trope of palingenesis or triumphant rebirth) are subject over the course of history that do the real work of making a world.[83] Beuys originated little in the way of new mythical substance, or at least not much that has stuck in the wider culture. The association of felt and fat with healing, for instance, remains entirely his own. His work *on* what he borrowed—the legend of the coyote; the Tatars with their felt and fat—was prodigious, though.

What absolutism was Beuys up against? What kind of reality did his work on myth mediate and possibly resist? And finally, why insist on "myth" as a name for what Beuys was doing rather than, say, allegory, since in either case the key dynamic seems to be the alignment of arbitrary material signifiers that require a label to make sense? Of the two terms, allegory has the better modern pedigree. For critics such as Walter Benjamin and Paul de Man, allegory insists on the materiality and historicity of signification, as opposed to its transhistorical necessity. The difference is this: whereas allegory, in the body of literature to which I have just alluded, is usually taken to be a *de*naturalizing technique that foregrounds its arbitrariness, Beuys's work is at pains to naturalize its meanings. Hence the "allegory" of *Unschlitt/Tallow* presents itself as an immediately comprehensible statement as opposed to a contingent code: fat heals a wounded space. The equation has to be produced, but once produced, it is meant to be more than contingent. To put it differently, *Unschlitt/Tallow* is meant to fuse form and content. Paradoxically, the strategy that Beuys adopted to do so was to accumulate mute, nearly abject matter on such a scale that the sculpture's nonidentity with its assigned meaning becomes impossible to ignore. In the presence of the work, I have never felt the healing effect that Beuys claimed for it. It is, instead, unpleasantly dirty seeming, if impressive.

So there is a tension between the rhetoric that Beuys deployed in the cause of his art and his art's effect, even though the antimetaphoric strain in his rhetoric would seem to have no point other than to suppress this tension in favor of identity between form and content. In the terms of the canonical opposition that has been extracted from early Romantic aesthetics, Beuys is thus a partisan of the symbol, not of allegory. In early Romanticism, this doctrine of the symbol is explicitly linked to a revival of myth (for example, in the mysterious *Oldest Systematic Program of German Idealism* from about 1796–97). This is a problem only if one accepts that the task of art in the modern age is essentially that of its own demystification, its disenchantment: metaphoroclasm. Beuys's original sin, from a metaphoroclastic point of view, is to have ignored the discovery of the signifier, which is supposed to have been a crucial step toward a rational theory of meaning. He regresses instead to a mystified view of the process of signification as essentially *un*problematic, although this is a point on which the work is visibly anxious. It is not the case that Beuys relies on the self-evidence of his meanings. Otherwise, he would not have spent so much of his time explaining them.

The above may push things too far or set expectations that will be difficult to meet. Fully immanent, self-grounding (or at least self-reflexive) aesthetic or formal systems are the exception rather than the rule in the history of art; they may not even exist at all. It is also unclear whether anyone would choose to live in such a sober world. Even the most austere modernist devices—such as the grid, as art historian Rosalind Krauss has shown—turn out to be mythological. The grid is a way to have things both ways: it delivers both blunt, material immanence as well as transcendent infinity.[84] Beuys is distinct in two respects, however. First, his art depends on naturalizing its structure of meaning even as it foregrounds its own contingency, especially its contingency on the artist's personal history, real or invented. And second, the weight that rests on this mythological structure is immense because Beuys's art is redemptive. His oeuvre is indeed an especially extreme instance of the "culture of redemption," as Bersani once named the tendency to valorize art as a compensation for reality's imperfectness.[85] It is not entirely an exaggeration say that it was meant to save the world. Formal gestures are therefore never only formal gestures in Beuys, since they point to a limit that abuts religion. To shore up this structure, Beuys needed a totalizing principle.

The one that he chose sometime in the late 1960s, at the latest, is the doctrine that he called "social sculpture" (Soziale Plastik). In the briefest summary, "social sculpture" means that everyone should act as artists do, everywhere and all the time, not only in the production of art. Or rather, social practice in general ought to be reconceived *as* art, thereby as creative and autonomous; everything ought to be an end in itself. This practice of universalized artistic production would then shape not only the material environment but also, more important, social relations, including such things as money and the state. If realized, this process would be equivalent to the artistic "shaping" (Gestaltung) of society itself, which would thus become a work of art. At the same time, Beuys's iconography, preeminently that of his materials, was to naturalize and as such guarantee the functioning of this system as a unified set of meanings, of which the most significant, or at least the most prominent of those we have encountered so far, is that of social and individual healing. It remains to be considered why, exactly, the universalization of art as a practice would require a universal semiotic too. Indeed, there does not on the face of it seem to be a reason why a world of artists couldn't proliferate countless incommensurable, even incommunicable "personal mythologies." Beuys's insistence on making his own meanings understood is, then, maybe a little puzzling. (Conversely, the fact that his meanings were so often *not* understood—that much of his art remains hermetic—suggests that a tension between proselytizing discourse and material enigma was inherent to his practice, maybe consciously so.)

A particular idea of totality is at stake here. This program is not unique to Beuys, though. It is part of the legacy of Romanticism. Beuys's revolution took the form of a totalization of certain Romantic and modernist understandings of creativity as freedom—the German poet Novalis's demand to "romanticize the world," for example. This seems to be the meaning of Beuys's "expanded concept of art" (*erweiterter Kunstbegriff*) as well as the related proposition that *jeder Mensch ist ein Künstler*—"everyone is an artist." The point is not that everyone would *make* art in the limited sense with which we are familiar. Everyone would not become a maker of art objects (art commodities). Rather, the making of everything, every relation, material or otherwise, would become "artistic"—free, autotelic, unalienated: "Even the act of peeling a potato can be a work of art if it is a conscious act."[86]

In the twentieth century, though, there existed, as there still exists, another, more real totality than that of art's imagined omnipresence. It was on this structure that Beuys's art came to lean. I intend to show that this other structure—capitalism—provides a key to Beuysian semiotics and hence also a solution to (or more modestly, a better account of) the problem of meaning that has been developed so far. The peculiarity of the capitalist system is that it is not exactly an ideology (it is not discursive), even if it arguably requires ideology to survive. Capital is an "automatic subject" that behaves as if nobody is really in the driver's seat.[87] In what follows, I will argue that the point of Beuys's peculiar economics is to secure his peculiar structure of meaning and vice versa. The latter discourse had to explain the former, yet it relied on a (naturalized) version of economics for its legitimacy. And although he was nominally an anticapitalist, Beuys's system identified art and capital, quite literally.

It is also in Beuys's discourse that a curious fact about his iconography of materials comes to the fore. My presentation of works such as *zeige deine Wunde*, the *Fond* sculptures, and *Unschlitt/Tallow* has so far been more or less devoid of temporality. I have written as if these works simply "are" and "mean" whatever I claim they do (or fail at it), without much concerning myself with how ontology and semiotics might be subject to becoming and negation, which is to say, history. This is not an effect solely of presentation. The crystalline, eternal aspect of the works is important, but it is only part of the system. To move on, it will now be useful to consider the opposite pole. Though evidently static and ahistorical, from one point of view, the system of meanings that Beuys constructed is also permeated with notions of change, from the most basic physical changes of state to the revolutionary transformation of society as a whole. It is at this conjunction of the always the same and always changing that we can locate the mimetic relation between Beuys's art and the circulation of value.

# Chapter 2. Circulatory Systems

## 1.

It is perhaps odd that Beuys chose honey as his circulatory material par excellence. In nature, honey does not circulate. It accumulates. "Honey is flowing in all directions" was nonetheless one of the artist's talismanic slogans in the 1970s. The phrase, in English, is screen printed onto a yellow vinyl sheet in a multiple that Beuys produced for Edition Staeck, his publisher, in 1974 (plate 7).[1] This work takes the form of a postcard, with the title on one side and ancillary information on the other. Since the sheet is translucent, the inscriptions on both sides are visible simultaneously, producing an effect not unlike an alternating boustrophedon script. The multiple thus literally activates a process of circulation or flow in its perception. This was three years before Beuys's most spectacular realization of the concept: the *Honigpumpe*, or honey pump, that he installed in the basement of Kassel's Fridericianum at *documenta 6* in 1977, and that pumped honey in transparent plastic tubes strung throughout the building's halls for the duration of the exhibition (figs. 18 and 19)[2] It is primarily in relation to *Honigpumpe* that I will build this chapter's argument, which is that Beuys's totalization of an aesthetic of Gestaltung here parallels even as it contests the logic of postwar capitalism.

I have described the work briefly in this book's introduction, so I can proceed efficiently. The honey's movement was powered by an electric pump lodged in a semicircular space on the museum's bottom floor. This space lay beneath the actual exhibition rooms at the base of a stairwell that extended to the building's upper stories. The room was off-limits to visitors during the exhibition. The work's infrastructure was therefore visible, though not physically accessible, to the museum's patrons as they ascended

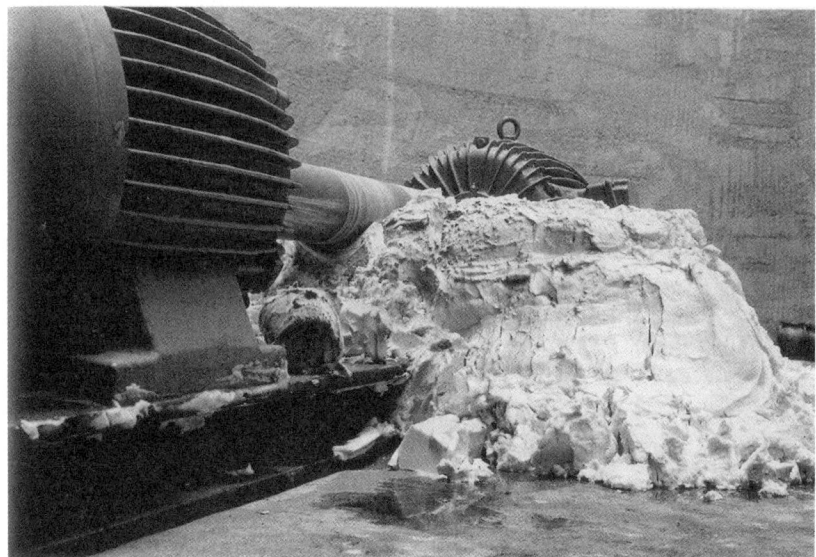

**Fig. 18.** Joseph Beuys, *Honigpumpe am Arbeitsplatz* (Honey pump at the workplace), 1977 (detail). Installation with two electric motors, copper shaft, stainless steel container, galvanized metal pipe, plastic tubing, honey, margarine, and three ceramic pots. Dimensions variable. Installation view at *documenta 6*, Fridericianum, Kassel, 1977. Elements now in the collection of the Louisiana Museum of Modern Art, Humlebæk, Denmark.

and descended from one gallery to another. Near to the pumps was a large rotating copper shaft, powered by another motor and heaped round with fat—or to be specific, with about a hundred kilograms of yellowish margarine. Ever mindful of opportunities for recycling, Beuys would sell portions of this fat and honey sealed in Mason jars and tin cans, respectively, in a multiple that he produced in an edition of sixteen in 1978 (fig. 20).[3]

In a later silk screen connected with the installation—it was included in a multiple published in 1985, also titled *Honigpumpe*—the copper shaft is labeled *Wille* (will), whereas the two motors are each labeled *Wirtschaft* (economy) (fig. 5).[4] Above, the words "heart," "capital," "law" (or "right" [*Recht*]), and "labor" can be made out. At the top of the drawing, the exhibition spaces to which the tubes carrying honey finally made their way are labeled "head" and "spirit" (or "mind" [Geist]). The "heart" evidently corresponds to a stainless steel container that lay next to the pump apparatus, where excess honey pooled before reentering circulation. Another element of the work was a galvanized metal pole, or rather a thin pipe, that

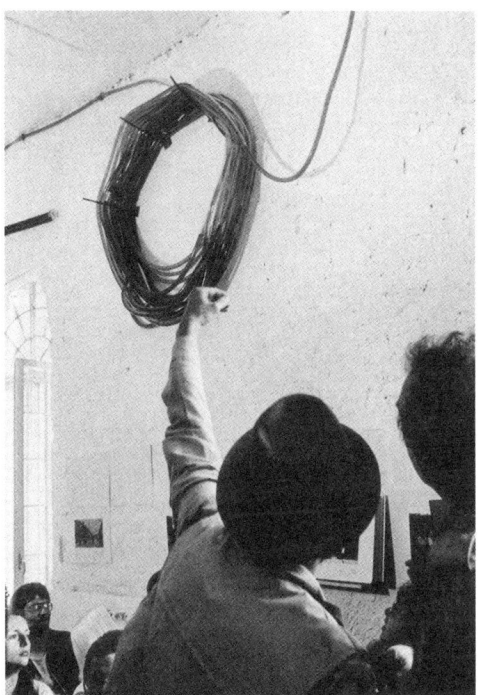

**Fig. 19.**
Joseph Beuys, *Honigpumpe am Arbeitsplatz* (Honey Pump at the Workplace), 1977 (detail). Installation with two electric motors, copper shaft, stainless steel container, galvanized metal pipe, plastic tubing, honey, margarine, and three ceramic pots. Dimensions variable. Installation view at *documenta 6*, Fridericianum, Kassel, 1977. Elements now in the collection of the Louisiana Museum of Modern Art, Humblebaek.

was set upright in the stairwell. This object functioned as a rigid double of the plastic honey tube that hung parallel to it. Or more precisely, this rod did *not* function since it had no practical purpose. Neither did the copper shaft, it seems. Photographs taken at Kassel reveal a power cord connected to the device, but not any mechanism to transmit its rotation; neither is it linked up to any of the plastic tubes carrying honey.[5] Finally, Beuys placed three unassuming ceramic pots in a corner of the room. They resemble and in fact probably are the vessels that Beuys had already used in Edinburgh in *Three Pots Action*, which I discussed in chapter 1.[6] Although physically at the center of the Fridericianum, the work's ambiguous nature seems to have made it difficult to apprehend as art or perhaps even notice. Several high-profile reviews of the exhibition do not mention the honey pump at all.[7]

Honey, like fat, was one of the artist's recurrent symbolic materials and indeed is related to fat through the intermediary substance of beeswax, the intended original medium of *Unschlitt/Tallow*, a work that was on view concurrently in Münster in summer and early fall 1977. Beuys had previously

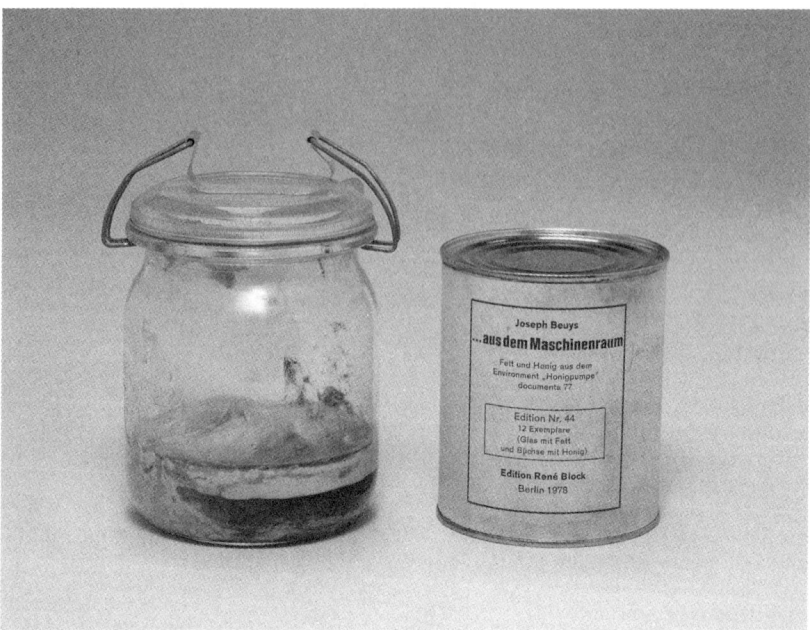

**Fig. 20.** Joseph Beuys, … *aus dem Maschinenraum* (… from the machine room), 1978. Glass canning jar with fat, tin can with honey, printed label, and inscribed in graphite. Jar: 6¹¹⁄₁₆ × 4⁵⁄₁₆ × 4⁵⁄₁₆ in. (17 × 11 × 11 cm). Can: 4¾ × 3¹⁵⁄₁₆ × 3¹⁵⁄₁₆ in. (12 × 10 × 10 cm). Edition of twelve plus four artist's proofs. Harvard Art Museums, Cambridge, 1996.53.

used honey to affix gold leaf to his face during the 1965 performance *wie man dem toten Hasen die Bilder erklärt* (How to explain pictures to a dead hare) (fig. 21).[8] There, it already signified collective effort and non- or extrahuman intelligence. At Kassel, the flow of honey was by contrast clearly analogized to the flow of knowledge among human beings. Beuys's other primary activity at the show was to organize a series of panel discussions and seminars under the aegis of the FIU (fig. 22). The incorporation of pedagogical elements into artworks became strongly associated with Beuys in the late 1960s and 1970s. The strategy was not exclusively his even within the close-knit Rhineland art scene, though. In the late 1960s, his students Jörg Immendorff and Chris Reinecke founded a "LIDL Academy" that clearly drew from Beuys's example and to some extent even proceeded under his patronage; meanwhile, artist Bazon Brock (who taught at the Hochschule für Bildende Künste in Hamburg from 1965 to 1976) staged versions of his *Besucherschule* (visitor's school) at four successive iterations

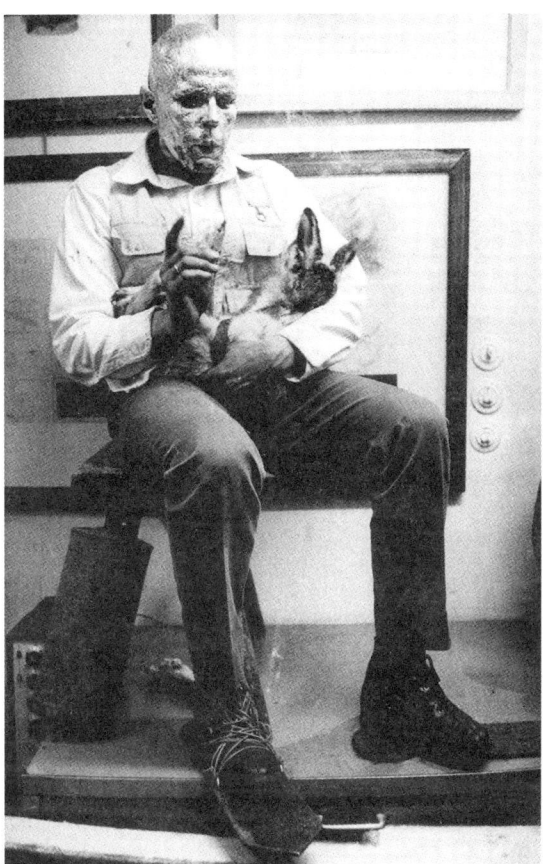

**Fig. 21.**
Joseph Beuys, *Wie man dem toten Hasen die Bilder erklärt* (How to explain pictures to a dead hare), action, Galerie Schmela, Düsseldorf, November 26, 1965.

of *documenta* between 1968 and 1982.[9] The full schedule of FIU workshops at *documenta 6* can be found in a number of flyers and posters that were distributed at the time, now preserved in the Beuys archive at Museum Schloss Moyland, among other sites.[10] Themes included human rights, nuclear power, unemployment, the media, and "alternative forms of life." Anarchist publishers Helga Weber and Wolfgang Zucht also conducted a three-day seminar on "nonviolent revolution."

*Honigpumpe* was a reworking, indeed a spectacularization, of ideas about teaching and the production of knowledge that Beuys had developed over course of the 1960s. It seems evident that his later public pedagogy built on practices that he had developed in the *Ringgespräche* (group discussions) that were a defining feature of the *Beuysklasse* at the Kunstakademie

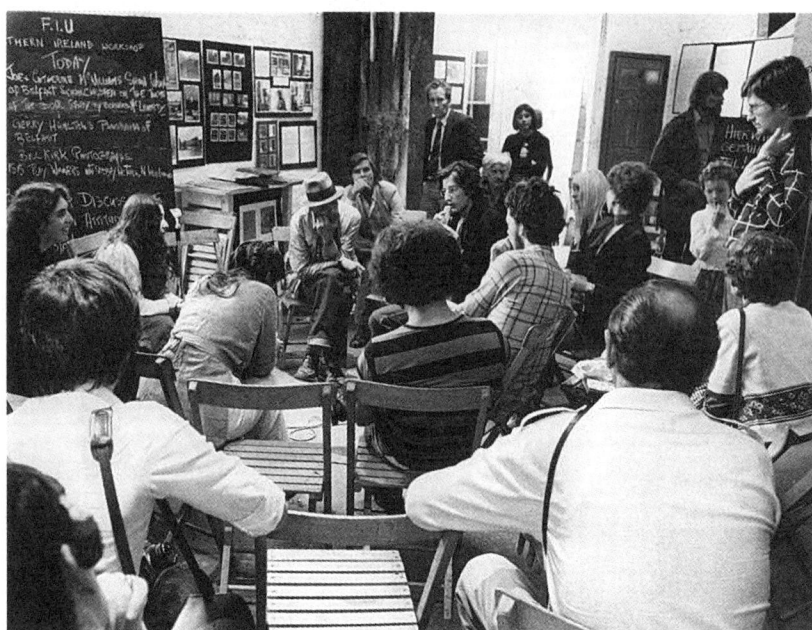

**Fig. 22.** Free International University workshop at *documenta 6*, Fridericianum, Kassel, 1977.

Düsseldorf from an early date. Rather than traditional art school critiques, the *Ringgespräche* were open-ended, wide-ranging conversations during which Beuys would hold forth on his philosophy, or provoke his students by presenting enigmatic objects, propositions, or gestures.

When translated from the relatively intimate setting of the Kunstakademie to the public sphere, the contours of Beuysian pedagogy sometimes became blurred. It was often unclear whether an institution such as the FIU was meant to function as an actual school or something more like a conceptual front for Beuys's various interventions. On March 3, 1985, for example (thus near the end of his life), Beuys had to write to a perspective applicant, a certain Dominique Quentin, to explain the true nature of the FIU: "One cannot enroll in the FIU. ... In reality it has to do with a social model [*Gesellschaftsentwurf*] beyond capitalism and communism."[11] This suggests that the "university" in the group's title was more aspirational than otherwise, by that time at least. Nonetheless, it is undoubtedly the case that Beuys initially envisioned a much more literal kind of school, complete with a permanent building, as the minutes of several mid-1970s FIU membership meetings attest.[12] Funding was sought from an array of governmental as well as private sources both within and outside West Germany.

The FIU was pointedly international, with an emphasis on the "periphery of Europe." A typewritten document on the organization's stationery dating from 1977, for instance, details actions in Dublin, Northern Ireland, Glasgow, Sicily, Bologna, Wales, and London.[13] Many of these "branches," however, seem to have consisted of little more than small groups of friends or acquaintances who were deputized from afar. Outside Germany, the organization only had a lasting presence in Great Britain and Ireland, thanks in large part to Tisdall's initiatives. Successor branches of the FIU would eventually spring up in the Netherlands, Belgium, and a number of German cities outside the Rhineland, where they were led for the most part by Beuys's students. As the prospect of establishing an actual academy faded in the mid- to late 1970s, the FIU became increasingly metaphorical. The *Honigpumpe* project, by contrast, was indeed realized according to plan, though Beuys and his collaborators still had to grub financial support where they could get it: the *documenta* administration denied Block's request for a contribution, for example.[14] The FIU produced certificates to record donations. One exemplar, now held in the Beuys archive at Museum Schloss Moyland, records a contribution of three hundred deutsche mark (equivalent to around US$130 at the time) from Cologne's DuMont publishing house, dated April 28, 1977.[15] If nothing else, these records indicate that the FIU was not simply funded out of Beuys's by then respectable private income. It was meant to be a serious, self-sufficient entity.

*Honigpumpe* was the apotheosis of the FIU. But in another sense, it was opposed to its very principle. The activities of the FIU at *documenta 6* consisted of human activity and discourse. As with his contribution to the previous iteration of *documenta* in 1972—where Beuys had installed his *Büro für direkte Demokratie* (Office for direct democracy), but did not submit any physical artworks—the central elements of his contribution were, first of all, the artist's physical presence, and second, the discussions that this presence occasioned. In 1977, the latter aspect of the program was more ambitious than it had been five years before. Beuys not only engaged with the general public himself but also staged a series of workshops and panel discussions involving a range of guest speakers, some established and some obscure. This was a logical extrapolation given the development of his career since *documenta 5*. The FIU itself had been founded in the interim; whereas the *Organisation für direkte Demokratie durch Volksabstimmung*

(Organization for Direct Democracy through Referendum) had been, at least nominally, a political group and nothing more, pedagogy was in the FIU's DNA. Take the *documenta 5* discussions, add the notion of a "university," and what you get, more or less, is what actually emerged at *documenta 6*: a counterpublic sphere, as Beuys's contemporaries Oskar Negt and Alexander Kluge might have called it, adjacent to and yet independent from mainstream academia.[16]

The discontinuity here is rather the honey pump itself. *Honigpumpe* is a thing—a sculpture, though of an untraditional kind. It has an objective presence that does not evaporate into pure sociality, as did the discussions at *documenta 5*.[17] The allegory involved in the sculpture's presence clearly has something to do with the idea as well as the actual fact of circulation. But "circulation" has at least two referents. In the 1985 lithograph that Beuys would eventually use to explain the piece (and in his verbal explanations too; we will get to these soon), the words "capital" and "economy" are near to "heart," "head," and "mind." Blood circulates, and so do ideas. But so does money. *Honigpumpe* (I am now referring to the entire work complex, including the pedagogical activities that occurred over the hundred days of the exhibition) was at once school, biological system, and economic model, more or less metaphorically in each instance. The circulatory motif is the key to all three topoi. But how do we make sense of their overlapping?

## 2.

Circulation is a biological metaphor that introduces dynamism into Beuys's table of meanings at the same time as it stabilizes it. To circulate, after all, is only to end up in the same place. Its logic is not unlike that of feedback. What travels returns to the sender with added force. Hence the importance of the word "movement" that intervenes between the two columns of Beuys's chart in the 1979 Guggenheim catalog. "Movement," it seems, is among other things a name for the primal force of creativity that Beuys wanted to liberate in all humanity. Honey symbolizes creativity. The biological suggestion of circulation, however (of blood, bodily fluids, or more generally any of the processes by which an organism or ecology maintains homeostasis), renaturalizes what was in fact a hyperactive practice of signification. Beuys's presence at Kassel in 1977, even more than in

1972, was marked by endless talking, discussion, and debate. The many square feet of blackboards that Beuys filled with cryptic diagrams and inscriptions over the course of his various public actions—they were much in evidence at *documenta 6*—bear witness to the artist's logorrheic drive as well as its collapse into nonmeaning.[18] Few of them are immediately coherent, even to scholars of the work; they were activated in the course of performance, and although they remain auratic objects, there is rarely much to be learned from them. If their symbolism *is* decoded, it usually turns out to be a series of catchphrases with which we might as easily have become familiar through Beuys's interviews and written statements. Whatever pedagogical purpose the blackboards have thus seems to be oddly self-defeating. Contrary to a surface reading of his practice, it is therefore uncertain whether Beuys's efforts to explain himself reterritorialize what had been rendered unstable in the physical oeuvre, or if indeed the objectivity of the latter called forth, as its inverse, a radically self-undermining discursive apparatus.[19]

In the previous chapter, I unearthed one of Beuys's most important semiotic dyads: the link between the substance of fat and its declared significance, the concept of healing. In what follows, I will turn to another such dyad, although a more complex one. This is the artist's pairing of the substance of honey (or on a more general level, the motif of the beehive) with various of his ideas about economics and social transformation. My shift in attention follows a shift in Beuys's practice. The metaphoric complex of the beehive and its circulating substance is not static. It requires activation in order to function; change therefore enters the system. Hence the pedagogical supplement in *Honigpumpe*. Fat, by contrast, "means" what it means in Beuys more or less just by being what it evidently, if not always physically, is. (We have seen that the work sometimes occludes its material composition.) When Beuys invoked the motif of the circulation of honey, however, blackboards, diagrams, and verbal explanations were rarely far behind. The beehive needed people. Most pointedly, it needed the artist himself, though without an engaged audience, too, a work such as *Honigpumpe* would have been incomplete, if not inconceivable. Here we see the concrete labor of pedagogy that Beuys's art necessitated, or that *was* his art, to a large and increasing extent in the years after 1968. His activities became a kind of endless seminar, or interminable analysis, with the aim not of resolving but at least making manageable his art's aporetic structure: to work through its contradictions, over and over again. Beuys was aware that his art needed labor. This is clear enough from the full title of his installation in Kassel: *Honigpumpe am Arbeitsplatz* (Honey pump at the workplace).

It takes work, then, to mediate concept and matter—with "matter" here standing on some level for the objective world as a whole. There is no need in this context to determine philosophically or scientifically what "matter" is, any more than there is a need to do the same for "concept" or "meaning." The significance of an idea will emerge immanently in the way Beuys articulates it with its contraries. Indeed, it is to this practice, to the work of articulating mind with substance, that I draw attention. One name for this work is dialectic, or the labor of the negative. Beuys had more trouble with negativity because his message was essentially redemptive. His key concepts and slogans—"social sculpture," "everyone is an artist," and so forth—project a sense of reconciled unity: the *Gesamtkunstwerk* as the freedom of all and each. Perhaps he failed properly to recognize the concrete antagonisms that would stand in the way of the dream's realization. The point has been argued either way, and we will return to it.[20] Yet his engagement with politics required that he sometimes look the negative in the face and tarry with it. From this perspective, the difference between *Stuhl mit Fett* (Chair with fat) and *Unschlitt/Tallow* is the difference between 1964 and 1977, a pair of dates that bookend epochal changes for Beuys and West German society alike. By 1977, the work had become larger, more emphatically public, and more concerned with a notion of healing that is collective rather than personal, since after all it is now the fabric of the city itself to which Beuys applies (or instead, pretends to apply) the salve.

This is typical of the artist's work around this period. Another large-scale installation, *Straßenbahnhaltestelle / Tram Stop / Fermata del Tram, 1961–1976, A Monument to the Future*, his installation at the 1976 Venice Biennale, has a similar tone of public address; it was, moreover, one of the clearest signs to date of his ambition to speak to the darker moments of European history (fig. 23). The work incorporates a railroad tie as well as a sculpted head bearing an expression of what seems to be pain. (This iron head is said to represent Anacharsis Cloots, a Kleve-born French-German revolutionary who was a role model for Beuys; it seems that the head was originally a plaster work that Beuys's student Beatrix Sassen made in 1962).[21] The German Pavilion at the Venice Biennale is housed in a structure that was thoroughly renovated during the Nazi period. Given its motifs, *Straßenbahnhaltestelle* has suggested to many of its viewers a

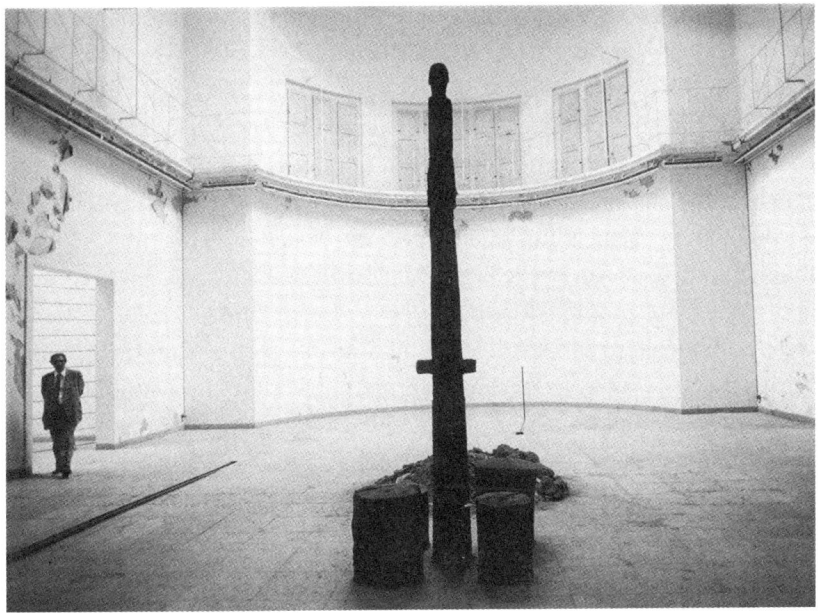

**Fig. 23.** Joseph Beuys, *Straßenbahnhaltestelle / Tram Stop / Fermata del Tram, 1961–1976,*
*A Monument to the Future*, 1976. Iron. Dimensions variable. Installation view, thirty-seventh
*Biennale di Venezia*, Venice, 1976. Components now in the collection of the Kröller Müller
Museum, Otterlo.

reference to the traumas of Germany's twentieth century, or more specifically to the Holocaust.[22] Beuys had made a proposal for an Auschwitz
memorial in 1957. Objects and drawings related to this design are now in
the *Auschwitz Demonstration* vitrine housed in the *Block Beuys* installation
in Darmstadt. The memorial was unrealized, however, and thus it seems
legitimate to consider *Straßenbahnhaltestelle* as the first truly monumental
public manifestation of Beuys's engagement with the Holocaust. As I will
observe in my book's third chapter, however, this association does not
seem to have been much noticed at the time of its initial exhibition and
may not have been intended at all. Which leaves us with the following
question: If such a reference is in fact present, even if ambiguously, is
Beuys's approach to it defensible? Would its very ambiguity suggest that
it isn't? And what does the public, political, and memorial function of
such a work have to do with the equally public and political, but not in any
obvious way memorial, function of the biological-cum-pedagogical and
economic metaphor in *Honigpumpe*? Figuring this out will require some

thinking about history; it will require articulating the National Socialist period with its legacies in the capitalist Federal Republic of Germany some twenty or thirty years later.

History means change. My discussion of *Unschlitt/Tallow* approached the relation between conceptual content and its material substrate in a synchronic manner. In anthropologist Claude Lévi-Strauss's structuralist account, mythical meaning is generated out of fixed associations of a fundamentally ahistorical or cyclic kind. But to read Beuys's works in such terms is to elide their public address. *Unschlitt/Tallow* and *zeige deine Wunde* were both meant to be seen at large, high-profile group exhibitions, which means that they were, in Buchloh's terms, entries into the symbolic order. *Honigpumpe* and especially *Straßenbahnhaltestelle* make the issue of history along with its taking place in public ineluctable. With *Honigpumpe*, the structure of a mythology becomes the stuff of a process in which matter and meaning are metabolized, together, but not necessarily smoothly, in public—specifically, by means of the public's active participation. In a private, hermetic practice, meaning can be imposed by fiat. Work with social ambitions needs a more universal claim to validity.

In the 1970s, Beuys's expanded concept of art evidently required a new kind of practice in which models of communication, transmission, circulation, and accumulation, though already present in the 1960s, took on new form and significance. I have already said, in abstract, that over the course of Beuys's attempt to totalize his art as the basis of a new social order, the work became a mimesis of the forces that it was attempting to negate. In this chapter and the next, I will make a case that in the 1970s, the center of gravity of Beuys's project shifted from a relatively private mythology of healing toward a project that aimed to mediate the twentieth century's vexed transit between value accumulation and the desire called socialism.[23] The key issues are capital, money, and Beuys's ambition to subordinate both to the principle of conscious human shaping, or Gestaltung.

## 3.

*Honigpumpe* is an exceptionally suggestive work in part because it leans on an existing trope rather than one of the artist's own invention. In Blumenberg's terms, it is another example of the work *on* myth rather than the work *of* myth. The Attic rhetorician Isocrates, in the fourth century

BC, advised his young friend Demonicus to seek wisdom in many places: "For just as we see the bee settling on all the flowers, and sipping the best from each, so also those who aspire to culture ought not to leave anything untasted, but should gather useful knowledge from every source."[24] Isocrates is an early instance of the trope, which may simply have been a commonplace. It recurs in several other classical authors. Three hundred years later, Lucretius, in the paean that begins the third book of *De Rerum Natura*, likens those who delve into the works of the great Epicurus to "bees that sip of all in flowery wolds."[25] Seneca the Younger then echoes both Isocrates and Lucretius in one of his *Moral Letters to Lucilius*: "We should follow, men say, the example of the bees, who flit about and cull the flowers that are suitable for producing honey, and then arrange and assort in their cells all that they have brought in. … We also, I say, ought to copy these bees, and sift whatever we have gathered from a varied course of reading, for such things are better preserved if they are kept separate; then, by applying the supervising care with which our nature has endowed us,—in other words, our natural gifts,—we should so blend those several flavours into one delicious compound that, even though it betrays its origin, yet it nevertheless is clearly a different thing from that whence it came."[26] Virgil in turn dedicated part of the fourth book of his *Georgics* to the qualities of bees. "They alone," he says, "have children in common, hold the dwellings of their city jointly, and pass their life under the majesty of law."[27]

The communalist emphasis follows a venerable precedent. In the *Phaedo*, perhaps the most influential of ancient texts on the immortality of the soul, Plato has Socrates speculate that those who have practiced "the social and civil virtues which are called moderation and justice" are likely to be reincarnated into "some such social and gentle species as that of bees or of wasps or ants."[28] These three insects are the most sociable of animals. In the Western literary and philosophical tradition, they accordingly often serve as a model for human intercourse—bees in particular, because unlike wasps and ants, they also produce a tangible good (honey) that is likewise of use to humans. This has been the mainstream of apian commentary since the time of the Greeks. But the nature of the allegory changes. Philosopher Bernard Mandeville's *Fable of the Bees: or, Private Vices, Publick Benefits*, 1714, was, in its time, a scandalous turn on the idea.[29] His bees are not altruistic. Rather, they maintain their commonwealth through the pursuit of individual, amoral self-interest, which however redounds to the advantage of all: "Thus every part was full of vice, / Yet the whole mass a paradise."[30]

When selfishness and sin are eradicated from the hive by a literal act of God, commercial activity grinds to a halt.

Mandeville's *Fable* is a primal scene of early liberal economics. The text would find an interested though critical reader in economist and philosopher Adam Smith, who discussed it in his *Theory of Moral Sentiments* of 1769. And with Smith we find ourselves on the threshold of the modern world. In this way the trope came down to Beuys, who gave it yet another valence. To what extent he was familiar with the literature on bees is uncertain. What is not is the duration and intensity of his interest. In the previous chapter, I referred to Beuys's three *Bienenkönigin* (Queen bee) sculptures, the first of which Tisdall dates to 1947–52 in her Guggenheim catalog.[31] Given the book's shaky chronology, it is not advisable to put too much stock in the precise year; in any case, the rather formless wax sculptures resemble bees only in a vague way. Other works are more firmly attested from the beginning of the 1950s. There is, for example, a drawing from 1952 titled *Aus dem Leben der Bienen* (From the life of bees)—a phrase borrowed from the title of a book by ethologist Karl von Frisch.[32] (Frisch was the first scientist to interpret correctly the "waggle dance" of bees.) The title returns in a number of later works, such as a drawing dated 1954, now in the Tate / National Galleries of Scotland collection, and in a lithograph that Beuys produced after this drawing in 1978.[33] There are also several works from the 1950s that share the title *Bienenkönigin*, in addition to the three sculptures mentioned above.

Starting around 1952, works with other bee-related titles start to pop up. In the collection of the artist's widow, Eva Beuys, there exist, for example, drawings titled *Bienenflug* (Bee flight) and *Bienen und Metamorphose* (Bees and metamorphosis), both inscribed "Beuys 52." The catalog of Beuys's first public presentation of his work—a showing in 1961 of drawings, watercolors, oil paintings, and "plastic images" (*plastische Bilder*) belonging to the van der Grinten brothers—features its first bee-related title in 1954 (*Aus dem Leben der Bienen*); there are no earlier works so designated.[34] A drawing dated 1947 bears the inscription *Bienenkönigin* on its verso, but since to all appearances the pencil and watercolor renderings on both the recto and verso depict humanoid as opposed to insectoid forms, it is questionable whether the title was contemporaneous with the work's production or instead retrospective.[35] The first public expression of Beuys's preoccupation with bees and the substance of honey evidently came in a TV interview conducted in 1964 on the occasion of *documenta 3*, in which the three *Bienenkönigin* sculptures were exhibited. Beuys here mentions an association between what he calls the *Wärmeprinzip* (principle of warmth) and honey.[36]

Last but not least, Beuys's father-in-law, Hermann Wurmbach, was a zoologist who, in 1965, became the director of the Institut für Landwirtschaftliche Zoologie und Bienenkunde (Institute for Agricultural Zoology and Apiology) at the University of Bonn.[37] Beuys married Eva in 1959. Since it appears that his first bee-related works date from as early as 1952 (unless they were either retrospectively backdated and/or retitled), it is implausible to claim that Hermann's scientific vocation was their initial impetus, although this happenstance may later have encouraged the artist's continued preoccupation with the motif. The record, at any rate, suggests that the artist's preoccupation with these useful insects was more or less contemporaneous with his first uses of fat as a material, from which the bee motif differs, however, in lacking a retrospectively validated autobiographical association such as that of fat and felt with the Tatar legend.

In his engagement with the theme, Beuys almost certainly also had in mind the lectures on bees that Steiner delivered in 1923 to the workers building his Goetheanum—the headquarters of the Anthroposophical Society—in Dornach, Switzerland. These texts were first published in 1929.[38] Steiner is fully in line with the usual interpretation of the trope in outline, if not always in detail. The beehive is, for him, the image of a well-ordered, spiritually healthy society. In fact, though, it is more than an image since for Steiner, these representational linkages between the natural and human worlds are not a mere conceit but rather quite real, to the extent that they indicate the relatedness of all creation: "Looking at things in a properly natural way, we can see in all the processes of nature, symbols and representations of those things that occur in human life."[39] Beuys's own metaphysics are not far away.[40]

The bees themselves are absent from *Honigpumpe*. Only their product remains. At Kassel, as we have seen, honey was meant to flow, yet accumulate too—not itself, but the spiritual or mental energy generated by discussion. This was the artist's concept of "social sculpture" at its fullest. Metaphors lay heavily one atop the other. Beuys explained it thus:

> With Honey pump [*sic*] I am expressing the principle of the Free International University working in the bloodstream of society. Flowing in and out of the heart organ—the steel honey container—are the main arteries through which honey is pumped out of the engine room with a

pulsing sound, circulates round the Free International University area, and returns to the heart. The whole thing is only complete with people in the space round which the honey artery flows.[41]

Beuys discussed the nature of *Honigpumpe* on a number of other occasions. In a later, book-length interview with writer (and later priest) Volker Harlan, for example, he asserts that *Honigpumpe* "is not thinkable only as a thing, only as a machine or as a sculpture. Human beings are actually a part of it [*Die Menschen gehören eigentlich dazu*]."[42]

The mechanism that Beuys describes works something like this. Honey travels from the heart that is the museum's basement to its head, the exhibition spaces above. Work, specifically pedagogical work, then mediates the metabolism of matter and significance. The dynamic of social sculpture is reciprocal. It is not only the case that the substance of human existence (bodies and discourse) makes up an element of the work. Social existence in turn is also aestheticized, reshaped, even if only implicitly, under the influence of the honey metaphor, which relies on the antique trope of the beehive for much of its utopian force. Beuys picks up on many strands in the tradition: the Isocratean simile in the notion that it is knowledge that is being collected; the more widely disseminated idea that the society of bees is a model for the society of humans; and perhaps even Mandeville's heresy in the installation's suggestions of circulation and efficient exchange. Myth is a commons. It reinforces a conceptual apparatus that otherwise might appear insuperably willful. In fact, it sets and keeps that apparatus in motion. The system is economical enough to disturb any critic of aesthetic ideology.[43] But it is an economy in a more restricted sense as well. The mechanism by which honey flows and purportedly extracts creative energy is clearly analogous to the process of capital's accumulation of value.

## 4.

Beuys was not reluctant to make this association himself. Kunst = Kapital (art = capital) was one his ubiquitous slogans in the 1970s and 1980s. I have already said, in abstract, what I take to be the basic metaphoric structure of Beuys's work in the period now under consideration. It is that of a mimesis of the circulation of value—in other words, a mimesis of the fundamental mediating dynamic of capitalist society. This mimetic relationship will then explain much about the puzzling structures of meaning that were my object of analysis in the previous chapter. *Honigpumpe* offers the clearest demonstration of the claim's validity. No hermeneutic of suspicion is necessary here; Beuys openly said that the monetary topos is what his iconography of circulation was about, or at least part of what it was about. Now it is time to follow his lead. But it is here, in moving from Beuys's discourse back to his material oeuvre, that we come across a crucial problem. This mediating dynamic—the circulation of value—does not lend itself to sensuous presentation, in art or any other form of representation (including language). It is too vast, too totalizing, and at times too immaterial for any directly representational practice easily to capture. *Honigpumpe* is an image of the economy (or some economy), real or not. But at first glance, it may not be an image that tells us very much.

Art most plausibly approaches the totality of the capitalist social metabolism by way of allegorical fragmentation, metaphor, or metonymy. *Honigpumpe* seems to draw on the second and third of these tropes especially: it is both a metaphor for circulation and a part that stands for a whole. (Beuys, as I have noted, takes his distance from at least the postmodernist, secularizing mode of allegory, as it was to be theorized in texts that only slightly postdate *documenta 6* and the artist's retrospective at the Guggenheim two years later.)[44] The horizon of the mode of production is sublime because it defeats any individual's attempts to perceive the whole of it. Oblique stratagems are required to get capital into representation. It seems that the most common point of entry for such allegorical approaches to the representation of the capitalist absolute, at least in the visual art of the twentieth and twenty-first centuries, has been the commodity form. This is because the commodity is a tangible thing that promises to decode the whole of capitalism from its smallest perceptible element, which thus works as a sort of metonym; Marx, after all, begins *Capital* in this manner. Artworks can represent commodities, or they can mimetically aim to be or impersonate commodities, in a way that they cannot easily represent or mimic immaterial financial instruments, for example, let alone a totalizing system. We have seen something of this in the *Fond* sculptures. A work such as *Fond III/3* is meant to be a "battery" as well as a kind of financial device. Yet the latter notion is even more tenuous than the first. Easier to comprehend, one imagines, would be a strategy that takes not the abstract accumulation of value as its object but rather some concrete thing, some product—in other words, some commodity. Such gestures are common in the history of modern art, from Duchamp to Warhol to Jeff Koons (to invoke painfully obvious names).

Beuys, however, is different. His object really is the totality of capital. *Honigpumpe* contains no analog to the discrete commodity. Instead, it is an image of the total circuit of money's transit through society. And although *Honigpumpe* demonstrates this point more clearly than any of his other works (and for this reason is my privileged case study), I also want to show that this logic is true of his practice at large, at least as it took shape in response to the upheavals of the later 1960s. Capital is his object of representation, mimesis, and critique all at once. The link between Beuys's art and what I claim is its most fundamental object therefore cannot be one of straightforward representation, as might be the case of artworks that thematize the commodity form alone.

To say more precisely what all of this means, I will now attempt to reconstruct the logic of Beuysian economics. Although this may seem like a tangent, it follows from the course of the argument so far. The previous chapter introduced the problem of meaning, in its most general sense, in Beuys's work and questioned the nature of his yoking of meaning to matter. Economics would appear to be a distant topic. Economics, though, is a structure of meaning in its own right, even if of a reduced and only precariously discursive kind. It assigns a meaning called "value" to things. It was by contending with economics that Beuys's work most powerfully formalized the question of how it might be possible to represent capital in art. The point of this operation, moreover, was not merely to represent capital but rather to mediate and modify it—in short, to change the capitalist world by submitting it to a more totalizing principle, the "expanded concept of art." Magical thinking was involved here, no doubt—but not only that. The stake of the following pages is thus to show that Beuys's economics (which I will describe on the basis not only of his spoken and written statements but also in terms of the metaphors materially embedded in works such as *Honigpumpe*) amount to an attempt to solve the problem that I already named in my first chapter: finding a ground for the association between certain of Beuys's social or political desiderata, such as "healing," and the stuff of his art, to which these ideas often seem only dubiously related. His economics were an essential part of his aesthetic practice. Value was an epistemology—one that Beuys could use. But its side effects were dangerous. Nearer to the end of my book, I will in turn emphasize this practice's fractures and fatality, which emerge in its most utopian moments.

# 5.

Beuys made numerous statements on economic topics. They are not always clear, but in sum they do suggest a consistent attitude, if not exactly a consistent theory. I begin with one of the last. It comes from a lecture that Beuys delivered in Munich on November 20, 1985, shortly before his death:

> CAPITAL is at present the work-sustaining ability. Money is not an economic value though. The two genuine economic values involve the connection between ability (creativity) and product. That explains the formula presenting the expanded concept of art: ART = CAPITAL. Products we really need are now possible. We do not need all that we are meant to buy today to satisfy profit-based private capitalism. You already know what we do not need. We should stop everything that prevents us from affirming our inner natures. We would then have economic laws which make clear the function of money since the liberation of money is the precondition for the liberation of work. That liberation, which surmounts money's function as a commodity and means of exchange, making it into the functional basis of law and even of human rights, then brings about the democratisation of financial processes. Sham democracy for veiling the power of money then becomes real democracy.[45]

This is strange enough if viewed from any mainstream economic perspective. But Beuys had made perhaps even stranger claims in a short address that he presented in Halifax on receiving an honorary doctorate from the Nova Scotia College of Art and Design in 1976. He delivered this talk in his idiosyncratic English:

> The most important thing is to organize, and now appears the idea of organization as the idea of sculpture, as the idea of design, as the idea of molding and sculpturing the society. To regulate these processes, to have the means to regulate and to care for a structure in law necessitates a constitution. A law appears as a sculptural good of the people. It means it has to be done by the people. Therefore it now becomes a problem of basic questions. It will not be the practice of the future that only a minority with a special interest have the full political power to sculpture or to induce laws. And you will find that this law structure could work

in the field of economics, that there would be a law for the money, because the money is the most important sculpture as a regulating means of all creative processes. Since money regulates in all fields, in all the bloodstream of the society, it therefore has to have the character of a bloodstream. It has therefore to be described as a law-money, a bill of rights, while now it is only standing in a money-economics. The character of this money-economics will be metamorphized and will form an ability-society or spiritual-society.[46]

Much of Beuys is condensed here. I will try to unravel some of it. First, note that the metaphor of the bloodstream has returned, now explicitly in connection with the concept of money. Money is to society as blood is to the body. It is what makes possible any sort of metabolism and thus life itself. Blood of course requires a heart to pump it. In another public presentation, a lecture with the suggestive title "Society as a Work of Art" (*Die Gesellschaft als Kunstwerk*) that he delivered at an anthroposophical conference in the tiny southern German town of Achberg in 1974, Beuys described his hypothetical "money-distributing committees [*Gremien*]" of the future as the "actual heart-organ" charged with nourishing the new self-managed institutions that he hoped would finally make it possible to liberate human creativity from its subjection to capitalism and the state.[47]

The heart in *Honigpumpe* was the steel honey container in the basement of the Fridericianum—the apparatus that fed honey into the pump and to which were attached the "arteries" that are the transparent plastic tubes.[48] The association between money and the bloodstream recurs frequently in Beuys's economic pronouncements of the 1970s and 1980s. We have seen that Beuys in turn analogizes honey to blood. By the principle that if A = B and B = C, then A = C, it would appear legitimate to claim that the work equates honey not only with blood but with money too. In the flyer distributed at *documenta 6* (cited above), Beuys was quite explicit in connecting *Honigpumpe* to the circulation of money. The text offers a succinct résumé of the economic doctrines that I am exploring: the importance of a new concept of money and the need to transform money into a legal document akin to a contract. This conflation may have been operative as early as the action *wie man dem toten Hasen die Bilder erklärt*, from 1965, in which Beuys affixed gold leaf to his face using honey. In German, *Gold* (gold) and *Geld* (money) are near homophones, although the felicitous proximity between "honey" and "money" is of course absent in the language. Thus *Honigpumpe* conjures a trio of closely related concepts—honey, money, and blood—all of which, for Beuys, also had associations with the principle of universal human creativity that is condensed in the proposition that "everyone is an artist."

This is *Honigpumpe*'s conceptual force field. What remains is to clarify some points of its economics. In the 1985 lecture I have quoted above, Beuys asserts that money is not an "economic value" (*Wirtschaftswert*).[49] Economic values instead "involve the connection between ability (creativity) and product"; as he explains elsewhere in the same text, "Economic value entails employment of human ability in work and the resultant product: a good sculpture, a marvelous picture, an environmentally acceptable car, a tasty and healthy potato, or a healthy fish caught in the sea rather than something poisoned."[50] In another terminology, we could rephrase this to say that economic values are whatever facilitates the successful encounter between labor power and the process of production. They may be goods involved either in the production process itself or the reproduction of labor power. Beuys thinks that money, at least in its current form, fulfills neither function. Versions of these claims date to the early 1970s at the latest. They were part of Beuys's mental furniture—so omnipresent that to explain them fully often struck him as superfluous, it seems.

Nonetheless, there do exist a few relatively programmatic statements. Beuys laid out his monetary theories in some detail in a manifesto-like essay, "Aufruf zur Alternative" (Appeal for an alternative), that he published in the *Frankfurter Rundschau*, at that time a major national newspaper, on December 23, 1978. The relevant passages deliver nothing less than a vision of social transformation founded on a shift in the nature of money. I will quote at length in order to make more visible the concatenation of his ideas:

> What has led to the transformation in the function of money, which has been ignored up to now? This transformation commenced with the appearance of central banks in the modern development of money. Money emerged from the world of economic values, where it had previously served as a universal means of exchange.
>
> This new way of issuing and managing money through the institution of the central bank led to the development of a circulatory system in the social organism, through which, in a manner comparable to the evolutionary advance in the biosphere from a lower to a higher organism, the social whole assumed a more complex form of existence. Money was

constituted as a new functional system. It became the legal regulator [*Rechtsregulativ*] for all creative and consumptive processes.

On the side of production, enterprises [*Unternehmen*] require money for the fulfillment of their tasks. They receive it from the banking system in the form of credit (interest, which is now coupled with the concept of credit, comes from an understanding of money that is opposed to its essence!).

In the hands of enterprises, money = productive capital is a legal document [*Rechtsdokument*]. It commits enterprises to the deployment of the capabilities of their employees through labor.

When money, as income, enters into the control of those who are active [*Tätigen*], it changes its legal meaning. As consumption capital it entitles its user to acquire consumption values.

With this, money flows back into the realm of production and changes its meaning one last time. Now money has no relationship to any economic value. As such it entitles the enterprises that receive it to nothing at all. Therefore all credits are dissolved, the accounts of the enterprises balance those of the credit banks. Because many enterprises— as for example schools and universities—demand no price for their services, the accounts of the various enterprises amongst each other must be balanced in connection with associative banks, to the extent that some have surpluses and others deficits.

Once it has been raised to such a level of social evolution, this concept of money has sweeping consequences. It solves the problem of power, insofar as this has arisen from the side of money. Because it was not recognized that the money-order is not part of economic life, but had rather become an independent functional system in the legal sphere [*Rechtsbereich*], it was possible unreservedly to retain the old Roman idea of private property. In this way the categories of "profit" and "loss" were able to come into effect. The unrestrained appropriation of everything connected with the sites of production remained legal.

Without a single state-bureaucratic measure or acrobatic tax policy the recognition of the changed concept of money leads to the abolition of both the property principle and the profit principle in the productive sphere.[51]

Of this text, it is first worth pointing out that Beuys has an antimaterialist (that is, idealist) view of economic transformation. The function of money has already changed in reality. The change, however, remains unrecognized, and for this reason, certain old arrangements—private property as well as the phenomena of profit and loss—remain in effect.[52] To abolish this obsolete economy, it is necessary to disseminate knowledge of the true nature of money and capital. Transformation comes from within; earlier in the essay, Beuys says that we must overcome the "frivolous prejudice" against the position that real change can proceed from a change in concepts (or rather, concepts alone). "Concepts," he says, "are always bound to a far-reaching practice, and the manner in which one thinks about a situation is decisive for how one interacts with that situation."[53] This concept-forward position differentiates Beuys from the Marxist Left, with its emphasis on the material basis of society's conceptual superstructure. The artist's critique of materialism does not spare its would-be revolutionary manifestations. As he once put it, evidently in a note to himself, "Marxism is nonbelief in the human."[54]

In another lecture that he delivered in Achberg, this time in 1973 (thus a year before the lecture I have already quoted; it was the first of these conferences), Beuys was evidently candid in saying as much. No manuscript or recording remains from this event, and hence we are reliant on notes by Anki Dieterle, an attendee, for the gist of the presentation. In Dieterle's abbreviated transcript, Beuys asks, rhetorically perhaps, whether "the worker in the *Marxian* sense can still be found" and if the workers are class conscious. Immediately thereafter we read this: "The point of departure for the new revolution is creative life: the artist will initiate the next phase of the revolution." He then explains what he means:

> The revolution is a radical metamorphosis, a transformation into a higher level. The artist leads out of the world of the mechanic-dead [*Mechanisch-Toten*]: a new concept of art. He defines creativity. He says to people that they are all artists, the manager as much as the doctor. They are all artists. Thus, they abandon the idea that only a few can make art.[55]

I bring on this obscure document, however, not because it is a fine literary specimen but rather because of its reference to what Beuys, or his amanuensis, calls the *Mechanisch-Toten*—the "mechanically dead" or "mechanic-dead."[56] (In German, the adjectival and adverbial forms are indistinguishable; in any case, the two words have been conjoined into a single compound substantive, as the fact that they are both capitalized indicates.)

This phrase recalls certain important philosophemes of the mid-century. I am thinking for instance of Jean-Paul Sartre's "practico-inert." This is a term that Sartre develops in his *Critique of Dialectical Reason*, which was published in French in 1960 and in German translation in 1967.[57] The practico-inert is, for Sartre, the sediment of Marx's "metabolism between man and nature." It is whatever has been produced, thus objectified, in human practice, but that then becomes a barrier to the subject's free activity. Institutions, for example, are practico-inert. They form in the heat of struggle, but in its aftermath they all too often become a brake on further progress. Beuys's attitude toward money is not wholly dissimilar. Though it was, once, an "economic value"—a term we could gloss as referring to any material good that is conducive to human flourishing and more particularly to the flourishing of creative production—it has long since ceased to be so and now only impedes the unfolding of creativity. Hence the social machine needs a reboot. Money can function as the lifeblood of society only once it has been redefined as a legal document, as a "sculptural good of the people."

This may seem an odd proposition given that money is already definitionally a legal document. As we know it, at least (if not as cryptocurrency utopians may dream), money is nothing but a promise backed by the credit of a given state. But for Beuys this purely consensual, legal function of money had been obscured by its further status as a commodity. Rescuing money from this distortion—which facilitates private profit—requires acknowledging that money is an arrangement between people that falsely takes on the appearance of an independent substance with its own occult powers. In Steiner's terminology, it is necessary to shift money out of the realm of *Wirtschaftsleben* and into the realm of *Rechtsleben*: from the economy into the realm of politics and law. What then takes money's place in economic life is art: universalized creativity, the bearer of which is the artist as everyone. At his 1978 Achberg lecture, Beuys asserted the logical consequence: "The *expanded concept of art* is therefore identical with the *expanded concept of the economy*."[58] And as such, Kunst = Kapital.

This is, again, economical in the double sense of the word. The game of musical chairs seems to go smoothly enough. As soon as money vacates economics in order to assume its rightful position in the domain of law, art steps in to take its place; the transition is therefore, simultaneously, from economics to law (money becomes sculpture) and from art to economics (art becomes capital). But there are loose ends here. There is, of course, the obvious point that the dynamic does not come full circle. Gestaltung remains the master term here—the category that subsumes and is not subsumed by others—which is perhaps why Beuys chose to continue calling himself artist at all rather than becoming exclusively an economist or politician. If creativity moves into the economy, it is not the case that it thereby abandons the terrain of art, nor does it seem that on the other end of things, Rechtsleben (law or politics) displaces the aesthetic, though perhaps in some convoluted way this is what Beuys meant by referring to law as a "sculptural good of the people." These questions may ultimately be imponderable. There are others, however, that will be of more use in moving us forward.

What, for example, did Beuys intend by describing money as a Rechts-dokument or legal document? In the example of central lending, which he explores in the *Frankfurter Rundschau* article, it seems to mean, simply, that when money takes the form of credit, it is no longer a commodity: instead, it represents a contract between two or more parties. (His objection to interest may have been founded on the circumstance that it is only interest that makes debt viable as a commodity; there would hardly be a market for debt securities if only the principal were ever at stake.) As credit relations increasingly define the productive sphere, central banking binds society into an ever more complex and closely interrelated totality. Since, Beuys reasons, all money eventually returns to the productive enterprises from which workers buy their means of subsistence (that is, with wages that those same enterprises previously advanced), and hence money remains in the same closed system regardless of individual profit and loss, it would be more reasonable to wipe the books—to balance all debts and credits, and therefore complete what seemed to him the logical evolution of money from commodity money and means of exchange to a pure money of account. What is more, profit is illegitimate since as soon as money is extracted from the productive circuit (pocketed by the capitalist class or state-capitalist bureaucracy), it then ceases to be an "economic value" and thereby loses whatever raison d'être it has in the circulation of the economic bloodstream. It is thus necessary to liquidate profit just as much as the commodity status of currency. Once this is accomplished, money could then become a legal rather than an economic document, as it would no longer exchange in the anarchy of the market (to use Marx's term) but would instead in every case be subject to conscious command. As such, it could authorize the fully democratic allocation of resources. Legal documents are, in Beuys's language, a "sculptural" good, meaning something amenable to human shaping or formation—the more adequate German word is Gestaltung.[59] As in the revolutionary socialist perspective, it is this achievement of conscious, democratic control that is then supposed to unleash the forces of production, though Beuys conceives of these forces in terms of individual human creativity rather than technological mastery over nature. The achieved revolution is equivalent to the universalization of self-management, or *Selbstverwaltung* (a term that Beuys sometimes used in the 1970s, such as in the 1974 Achberg lecture that I have already quoted). Yet there is no talk here of expropriating the means of production. Indeed, questions of ownership are conspicuously absent in the artist's disquisitions on free democratic socialism.

Beuys adopted many of these ideas from the anthroposophical economist Wilhelm Schmundt, with whom he was on friendly terms.[60] I will not try to argue whether all of this constitutes good or bad economics. It does, at least, constitute a system, and tracing its implications will allow us to say something about Beuys's art, of which his "economics" are an integral component. For certainly not the least striking aspect of the texts that I have been discussing is the extreme fluidity they seem to propose in the relation between aesthetic and economic categories. It should now be evident, for example, that Beuys's concept of money centered on an opposition between the "sculptural" principle of shaping (or Gestaltung) and the automatism of the *Mechanisch-Toten*. To the latter would belong the invisible hand of the market as well as the more direct manipulations of the totalitarian state (whether state socialist or fascist); the result in either case is heteronomy for the masses and autonomy for the elite, or perhaps merely the autonomy of the practico-inert as embodied in the forms and institutions of the economic sphere. Freedom, by contrast, would mean taking the conditions of one's life into one's own hands, shaping them much as a sculptor shapes their material. Liberation from the deadweight of mainstream economics, whether capitalist or communist, was for Beuys equivalent to a wholesale translation of artistic categories into economic ones.

What can it mean, though, to say that money is a "sculpture," except that money is a plastic form, hence potentially alterable by humans? But then, what can it mean that the new money founded on the aesthetic principle of form making—totalized Gestaltung, achieved socioplasticity—must appear in the guise of the circulation of blood, except that conscious control over social mediation must in turn be renaturalized, made necessary rather than contingent? In the 1976 Halifax lecture, this perplexity comes to a head in Beuys's completely unmediated transition between the claim that money must function like a bloodstream and the following assertion that "it has therefore to be described as a law-money, a bill of rights."[61] Few things, it would seem, are more unlike each other than legal documents and the flow of bodily fluids. The latter is organic, common to all animals, continuous, and automatic; the former are, by contrast, artificial, specific to human beings, discrete, and come into effect only by an act of decision or consensus. A simple (surely too simple) way to describe the opposition would be to say that one belongs to nature and the other to culture. These are two contradictory moments in Beuys's concept of money. Its circulation is meant to be at once as natural and automatic as the flow of bodily fluids, and as subject to human command as the making of a work of art. The two propositions are difficult to reconcile without the aid of myth.

## 6.

It is here, at the threshold of conscious intention, that Marx draws the line between human and nonhuman, using bees as an example, as it happens. Since money is a thing that is entirely social (that is, human) in origin yet functions in the manner of an autonomous and thus natural force, we ought to pay attention to this boundary:

> A spider conducts operations which resemble those of the weaver, and a bee would put many a human architect to shame by the construction of its honeycomb cells. But what distinguishes the worst architect from the best of bees is that the architect builds the cell in his mind before he constructs it in wax. At the end of every labor process, a result emerges which had already been conceived by the worker at the beginning, hence already existed ideally.[62]

The trope did not originate with Marx. In section 43 of the *Critique of Judgment*, Kant writes this: "By right we should not call anything art except a production through freedom, i.e., through a power of choice that bases its acts on reason. For though we like to call the product that bees make (the regularly constructed honeycombs) a work of art, we do so only by virtue of an analogy with art; for as soon as we recall that their labor is not based on any rational deliberation on their part, we say at once that the product is a product of their nature (namely, of instinct), and it is only to their creator that we ascribe it as art."[63] Marx interestingly transfers the comparison to human labor in general rather than artistic production in particular, though he remains within the expanded realm of the applied arts: weaving and architecture. Apart from that, Marx's argument differs little from Kant's. Bees seem to be the inescapable species in either case. Derrida, commenting on the *Critique of Judgment* in his essay "Economimesis," notes the curious insistence of this comparison:

> What can be glimpsed in this inexhaustible reiteration of the humanist theme, of the ontology bound up with it as well, in this obscurantist buzzing that always treats animality *in general,* under the purview of one or two scholastic examples, as if there only a single "animal" structure that could be opposed to the human (inalienably endowed with reason, freedom, sociality, laughter, language, law, the symbolic, with consciousness, or an unconscious, etc.), is that the concept of art is also constructed with just such a guarantee in view. It is there to raise man up [*ériger l'homme*], that is, always to erect a man-god, to avoid contamination from "below," and to mark an incontrovertible limit of anthropological domesticity. The whole of economimesis (Aristotle: only man is capable of *mimesis*) is represented in this gesture.[64]

The real existence of something analogous to the generic "animal" will soon be of importance. Beuys introduces a twist in the economimetic tradition, though. It is for the sake of providing an image of conscious Gestaltung (building in the mind before building in reality) that the artist paradoxically draws on the trope of the beehive, the classical figure of *un*conscious, instinctive collectivity. This fold of the heteronomous into autonomy, or as it may turn out, autonomy back into heteronomy, is the fundamental operation of Beuysian economics. It is also parallel to his conflation of labor with capital in the "expanded concept of art." In both instances, he accomplishes this at least in part by moving the goalposts. Given that Kunst = Kapital and that the artist is a kind of worker, there is no longer an opposition between capital and labor since both can be reduced to the faculty of creative production. This is indeed a short-circuit in Derrida's deconstruction of economimesis: whereas the latter ideologically separates "free" art from the "mercenary" realm of economics (while nonetheless covertly depending on an analogy between the two), Beuys simply collapses the two realms by basing economy on art rather than vice versa.

It then stands to reason that Beuys's solution to the related nature/culture polarity, which he inherited from apian myth, would be to show that these two forms of "creativity"—nature's unconscious generation of forms and humans' conscious generation of the same—are not so different after all. Indeed, it turns out that the beehive was not, for Beuys, an entirely natural phenomenon. He devoted some of his most complicated work on myth to this revision of the old topos. In an interview he gave to the *Rheinische Bienenzeitung* (Rhineland bee magazine) in 1975, he observes that the regular form of the beehive is

> in a certain sense a cultural good [*Kulturgut*]. The entire beehive as we know it is a form cultivated by humans [*eine Zuchtform des Menschen*]. Wild bees work like wasps, rather anarchically. The beehive as we know it today is an immemorial cultural form [*eine uralte Kulturform*], that is, it is derived from a wild form belonging to wasps that live in plants, or most often in trees.

> And it has actually been cultivated that way. That is already in itself a profoundly plastic understanding.

Beekeeping is literally sculpture, and it is social because the substance it shapes is an insect society. In the same interview, Beuys describes socialism as a "bee cult" (*Apiskult*). It is not coincidental, he says, that members of the Jura Federation of the Chaux-de-Fonds watchmaking industry— where geographer Peter Kropotkin underwent his definitive conversion to anarchism—"symbolized their concept of socialism through bees." He is quite aware of the potentially dystopian shadings of the analogy too. Nonetheless, he denies that the "bee state" (*Bienenstaat*) is "something terrifyingly perfect, the perfect autonomous state without humanity." Despite this caveat, some alarming remarks do follow. Beuys goes on to say that "the bee state is indeed not a state that consists of individuals, as our state consists of living individuals; rather the single bee has no individual function but is only an appendage [*Gliedmaße*], has only this function of an appendage. That is to say, a bee would correspond to a little hair on my body. Seen in this way, my body is also a state that functions perfectly." Bees are therefore more like cells in a larger organism than people with their own autonomy: "And the drones that are superfluous, that's not murdering individual existences, rather it's an elimination [*Ausscheiden*] of cells that are needed at some point to maintain the process, and which keep coming back, but then keep getting withdrawn again, while other groups of cells [*Zellverbände*] have a longer life." Near to the close of this meditation, Beuys tips into language that is not distant from more recent posthumanist theory: "Thus, the human being is, practically speaking, also a swarm of bees, a beehive … the whole indeed has the character of a group-sense [*das ganze hat ja Gruppensinn-Charakter*], the whole is a unity."[65]

This is a complicated argument. While Beuys acknowledges that bee society is unlike human society, on further elaboration he claims, first, that the former is a perfectly functioning state, and second, that the human body is analogous to this bee state. As his highlighting of the socialist attraction to the bee analogy makes clear, however, the beehive certainly is a model for Beuys's free democratic socialism, whatever caveats he may add (*Honigpumpe* would be incomprehensible if this were not the case). So, too, is the human body. Recall that in the *Honigpumpe* screen print, discussed at the beginning of this chapter, Beuys reterritorializes the Fridericianum installation as a body complete with a "heart," "head," "spirit," and "will," in addition to "capital," "economy," and "law." Metaphors are again laid atop one another. Specifically, the two organicist metaphors in play, those of the human body and beehive, both symbolize the same thing: modes of human (self-)organization.

## 7.

At this point, though, it may be evident that a piece has dropped out of the puzzle. The *Rheinische Bienenzeitung* interview addresses neither the function of money in general nor the analogy between honey and money that Beuys would monumentalize in Kassel two years later. Money adds further complications to the structure of metaphors we are dealing with because it presents an especially vexing indeterminacy between (human) autonomy and (natural or mechanical) automatism. For the same reason, it lies at the core of problems of signification in the modern age.[66] Money's qualities are exceedingly odd.

In a capitalist system, money functions as the universal medium of exchange and universal equivalent of all other commodities. It is an abstraction, but we nonetheless always take for granted its real existence.[67] For this to work smoothly, any given amount of money has to be equivalent to any other given amount of money of the same numerical value, regardless of whether it happens to take the form of coins, bills, or integers in a database. Money's value is exclusively quantitative, not qualitative. Money therefore abstracts from all concrete particulars, but in so doing it facilitates the exchange of other commodities—commodities that in a Marxian terminology represent use values for their buyers (or in Beuys's language, "economic values") as well as exchange values for their sellers. Money eliminates the cumbersome apparatus of barter, thus making large-scale market economies much more feasible. Only its abstract universality allows money to play this role. It is patently absurd to imagine two banknotes of the same issue and face value behaving as nonequivalents in the market, such that one of them would fetch a much greater or smaller quantity of goods in exchange, or be available for use only in certain kinds of transactions and not others. A dollar bill is a dollar bill regardless of what you spend it on. Unless, that is, our hypothetical banknote were to be modified in some way that removes it from the company of its fellows, and instead shifts it into another social or cultural realm—that of art, for instance.[68]

This is exactly what Beuys did in a series of autographed banknotes from 1979, all of which are entitled *Kunst = Capital* (plate 8).[69] On a certain level, the works are the most literal possible demonstration of the claim embedded in their collective title. The act of inscribing the notes with the artist's signature, plus one of his better-known slogans, vastly increased their worth, as they now exchange for much more than their nominal value. (Indeed, given that the notes are the discontinued deutsche mark, their nominal value is now zero.) Art—moreover, art reduced to the barest Duchampian gesture of inscription—here would seem to valorize its material ground in an entirely real way, thereby proving Beuys's point that art is identical to capital. It is even superior to the usual monetary understanding of capital since no other form of human activity could possibly have increased the exchange value of these bills. This is true enough. The trouble arises when we attempt to generalize the lesson of this simple demonstration. For it is obvious that the elevated value of these works, whether framed in monetary or other terms, has to do with the fact that it was not just anyone who signed them but rather Beuys. His signature in effect supersedes that of the president of the Bundesbank (the West German central bank), which is still visible in much smaller script underneath the artist's. Art may in theory be capable of stepping into the role of capital. But the effect of doing so is not what Beuys's own rhetoric suggests. The "expanded concept of art," at least in its earlier phase, paradoxically reinforces the privilege of the unique, named artist as opposed to diluting it. It vastly increases the artist's power by projecting his authority into realms where it previously had no standing.

Perhaps this was meant to be the case only so long as the artist remains in the vanguard, as the "leader" who initiates the "next phase of the revolution." Like the socialist state after the seizure of power, one might expect the artist's charismatic authority to wither away as ever greater masses of humanity come to grasp their innate creative powers. Even if we imagine Beuys's gesture as universalized, however, things are not much better. And it is worth imagining this situation, even though the *Kunst = Kapital* bills are obviously not realistic economic propositions but instead artworks; Beuys's conceits best reveal their meaning when taken most literally, which is to say, when taken to extremes. We need to take the metaphors literally, once again. It is immediately evident that if everyone were to take up Beuys's call to become an artist and, like him, begin issuing their own signed banknotes, one of three things would happen: the notes would become worthless, or they would find an equilibrium among each other and thus function in no way differently from the old centrally issued money, or else inequalities of value would arise on the basis of real differences in power, credibility, fame, and so forth—much as would already be the case in the comparison between a banknote signed by Beuys and one signed by, let us say, Daniel Spaulding. If the responsibility for issuing such particularized variants of the currency were to fall to democratic organizations of some kind (Beuys's *Gremien*) rather than individual artists, the same contradiction between the particular and universal would still undoubtedly emerge sooner or later. Either a single overarching and potentially totalitarian entity would have to arbitrate the exchange rates between individualized currencies, or else they would not be exchangeable at all except through haphazard, piecemeal negotiations, which could take place either democratically (through consensus or voting) or by means of the market (though if that market were to become large enough, it would be as good as indistinguishable from money markets such as already exist).

My analysis of Beuys's monetary theory in the above paragraph bears a relation to Marx's criticism of labor-money schemes in a section of the *Grundrisse*, his first draft of *Capital*.[70] Among other things, Marx points out that a system based on the distribution of chits corresponding to actual labor hours would necessitate a monstrously bloated bureaucracy to function. Beuys did not propose to install labor time chits, however. His idea of replacing commodity money with legal documents dispenses with the correlation between labor time and value altogether. If I am properly interpreting his somewhat ambiguous presentations of the doctrine, monetary values would be entirely conventional, or in fact political, in the sense that the allocation of money would be determined through democratic deliberation as opposed to a market mechanism. In any case, the contradiction at issue is broadly the same: both the Beuysian Rechtsdokument and the labor chit system aim to replace the current form of money, which operates more or less automatically (though of course with incessant central bank fine-tuning of supply), with another form that is more particularized, concrete, and responsive to voluntary modification—yet without wanting to do away with the universal function of money as such that historically led to the predominance of the more abstract value form to begin with. Fundamentally, this translates to maintaining a link between an abstract measure of value (whether directly or indirectly keyed to actual labor time) and access to the social store—in other words, to goods and services (or to means of the reproduction of labor power, when goods and services are consumed by workers). So long as this link obtains, the basic function of money has not in fact been overcome. Since the universal form of money that actually obtains in the modern world is the most efficient in accomplishing the tasks given it—whether those tasks would exist at all in a better world is a separate question—any more particularized form of currency will eventually tend to fold back into it or simply disappear. Various alternative currencies may work on a small scale, at least for a time, but thought experiments such as the one I have just briefly run through reveal why they are unlikely to succeed if the attempt is made to generalize them. If I can be blunt about it: in the modern world, either you have money in your society or you do not. Any middle ground (or "third way," as Beuys called it) is likely to be a will-o'-the-wisp.

These were matters that Beuys did not consider, though admittedly the persistence of various labor-based alternative monetary schemes down to the present indicates that he is not alone in this. Another question—and a more serious one—that Beuys never seems to have adequately addressed is why money would be necessary at all in his future society. It would seem more logical simply to decide on the allocation of resources directly without the need for any abstract mediating form. If profit and loss as well as the market have already been liquidated, it is hard to know exactly what money would do. The classic justification for markets is that they deliver price signals that result in the most efficient allocation of resources. In a society in which all such decisions are to be made by democratic deliberation, this function would become obsolete. Perhaps Beuys's attachment to the metaphor of circulation (and its various correlates: blood, honey, and so forth) was so strong that he never seriously considered this problem; he took it as axiomatic that *some* all-pervasive substance would be needed to lubricate society's reproduction, whether it be money, art, or something else.

## 8.

Of course, it isn't fair to insist on so literal a reading of the *Kunst = Kapital* banknotes. If the signed bills are suggestive as pieces of art, rather than as serious economic propositions, it is because the work they do is not exactly propositional; it is metaphoric and associative. This metaphoric condensation attempts to reconcile two counterposed impulses. On the one hand, Beuys wants to retain the idea of circulation. The equivalence between art and money (as between honey, money, and blood in *Honigpumpe*) operates as it should only so long as the aesthetico-economic substance that results from it retains the liquidity proper to capital in the usual, more restricted sense. If art as capital is to unleash the forces of (artistic) production, it follows that it must be as universal—as all-pervasive and fungible—as the form of value. In capitalism, value is the general social relation that mediates between all concrete acts of production and consumption; it is what makes all commodities commensurable with each other (the commodity of labor power included). There is, in capitalist society, no other model for an equivalently totalizing yet dynamic mediating form.

Beuys hardly concealed the fact that his art bore a mimetic relation to capital, though he did attempt to turn the tables. Art in its totalized or "expanded" sense just *is* capital for Beuys. Capital is accumulated value and the ultimate necessity in our mode of production. In the modern world, art more usually tries to maintain its autonomy by distancing itself from that form of necessity; for this reason, it also often represents a promise of freedom (art is the concrete form of at least one beyond or other to capital, however illusory). In the *Kunst = Kapital* multiples, Beuys chose a different strategy. Instead of retreating either into the autonomous enclave of art's nonidentity with the value form or a mimetic relation to the commodity as an allegorical figure for the unrepresentable totality of value's metabolism, he attempted to subsume value to art—to make value a subset of art's totality rather than vice versa. I think this is the meaning of the claim that art equals capital. The claim is not a statement of fact. It is a socioplastic and economimetic program of the highest ambition, of which the signed banknotes are only the most unsubtle manifestation. It is hard to imagine how anything could take on this function without also falling prey to the extreme abstraction that is the value form's most salient attribute. This is likewise a contradictory program since socioplasticity and economimesis are usually opposed. Beuysian socioplasticity asserts the receptivity of social abstractions to sculptural "shaping," whereas economimesis assimilates aesthetic form to existing abstractions (those we conventionally call economic). Value is the preeminent instance of the latter. Value is indifferent to the qualities of the things it mediates. Money is this social abstraction made concrete.

Marx expressed the point in a memorable analogy: "It is as if, in addition to lions, tigers, hares and all other really existing animals which together constitute the various families, species, sub-species, etc. of the animal kingdom, *the animal* would also exist, the individual incarnation of the entire animal kingdom."[71] Philosopher Samo Tomšič usefully glosses this passage in terms of the Freudian theory of fetishism:

> The Animal is first presented as an abstract universality, contained in every animal, and then as a concrete abstract universality (sensual suprasensual thing), an element of the animal kingdom and its limit. Because the universality of the commodity world can be held in hands, money is the privileged object of fetishism. The space of values is curved, and this internal torsion supports the apparition of generality in the form of particularity. Fetishisation of the general equivalent becomes a particular case of fetishism and a universal model.... The

general equivalent raises the same logical and topological problem as the phallus in the universe of signifiers. The Phallus is the Animal, the general equivalent of *jouissance*.[72]

In other words, money is the privileged fetish object in the capitalist system because it materializes and particularizes the (nonexistent) universal signifier, value, much as the fetish in Lacanian psychoanalysis both discloses and compensates for the absence of the phallus, or master signifier. This evidently paradoxical structure of causation accounts for many of the difficulties of value theory. Value as such does not exist, but as a structural relation, the autonomy of value (like the autonomy of the signifier in Lacan) determines actual phenomena. It also possesses a concrete material representation in the form of money just as the absent phallus is represented in both the penis and fetish. The causality of value, and by extension, that of capital, like that of the signifier, is structural and relational. Or as Marx put it, "Capital is not a thing, it is a definite social relation of production pertaining to a particular historical social formation, which simply takes the form of a thing and gives this thing a specific social character."[73]

Marx's metaphoric *animal* is a relation become an object. Beuys's "expanded concept of art" is *the animal* translated to the aesthetic. It designates a universal: art as such, or more precisely, the activity of making art or capacity to do so; we could also call it the generic faculty of human creation.[74] Or rather Gestaltung. The slippage here is symptomatic. Beuys collapses the "capital" or currency that enables creation with creation itself. The artistic faculty is in turn something like the capacity to labor that lies at the basis of all societies, according to Marx. Beuys meant for it to become the fundamental, inexhaustible energy source that would fuel all other social dynamics. Recall, though, that Beuys defines capital as "work-sustaining ability" in his lecture of November 20, 1985. This phrasing leaves it unclear whether Beuys is here referring to a capacity within the individual (which would then be analogous to labor power), or on the contrary, to a form of sustenance that comes to the labor process from somewhere else (in which case it would be analogous to capital in the standard, extra-Beuysian construal). If art equals capital, then art, in the expanded sense, would consequently be both the "work-sustaining ability" and work proper—at once capital and labor. The implication we can draw from this is that the expanded concept of art therefore supersedes the antagonism between capital and labor since it encompasses both in a higher unity. The *erweiterter Kunstbegriff* was the truth; it was the surface level of economic appearance that was telling lies. Money, after all, is not an economic value.

# 9.

It should be evident that the "expanded concept of art" has now been stretched thin. It is equivalent to the "expanded concept of the economy"; it has subsumed the creative faculty and that of labor power (the two of which are moreover identical), together with capital, value, and money. It may well have subsumed society as a whole. Remember that the title of the 1974 Achberg lecture is "Society as a Work of Art." This, in turn, is a variant of another of Beuys's grand concepts, or catchphrases, that emerged in the 1970s: "social sculpture." The term cuts two ways. Social sculpture means both of the following: if, on the one hand, sculpture is henceforth supposed to be made out of the stuff of society (out of people), it is no less the case that society is to become sculptural; social relations must submit to the principle of aesthetic formation and thus be made as plastic as the raw materials of art. If everyone is indeed an artist, that may be harmless enough. As Beuys put it near his death, "The slogan 'Everyone is an artist,' which generated a great deal of excitement and is still misunderstood, refers to re-shaping of the social body in which every single person both can and even must participate so that we bring about that transformation as quickly as possible."[75] Everyone would then participate equally in the Gestaltung of collective worlds and hence the principle of democracy would be left immaculate; it simply finds itself redescribed in socioplastic terms. But the idea has an unsavory provenance.

At the beginning of his book *The Cult of Art in Nazi Germany*, which was published in French in 1996, art historian Éric Michaud cites a few lines from a novel by Hitler's propaganda minister, Joseph Goebbels: "A statesman is also an artist. For him, the people is merely what stone is for a sculptor. The Führer with the masses poses no more of a problem than does a painter with color."[76] Michaud argues that the metaphor of the statesman as artist and thus society as a work of art was fundamental to Nazi ideology. In an essay published in the journal *October* in 1988, Michaud extracts the most unsettling aspects of Beuys's practice: his apparent belief in the special redemptive mission of the German people, his all-devouring model of Gestaltung, and the blood-and-soil connotations of his rhetoric. It is, once again, an account of the artist that rests overwhelmingly on words as opposed to artworks. Michaud notes that Beuys, for all of his emphasis on the plasticity of artistic form, in fact repeatedly asserted the supremacy of language over the matter of art and the more intractable processes involved in any act of making it: "It is on this naïve certainty of an absolute transparency between form and matter and the 'idea' that Beuys's system is constructed. It offers the immense advantage of allowing the artist to create as if in flashes of lightning in which the opacity of (the) work in process is eluded, in which form is always adequate to the idea." What Michaud then writes about Gestaltung converges with some of what I have proposed:

> But what is this *Gestaltung*, this productive and transformative energy, if not this power that, in its affirmation and its exhibition, makes of every object in the world simply the instrument or means of its activity—to the point of making itself the instrument of its own perpetuation? What is it if not artistic activity itself? Beuys identified his artistic activity with human labor in general: in so doing, he made of it the law to be adopted by man so as to attain the highest freedom, or absolute autonomy. But his "social sculpture" can, I believe, mean only the subjugation of the real world and real men, which it reduces to the mere instruments of its free exercise. In identifying itself with human labor in its generality, the "expanded concept of art" makes of activity both means and ends: thus, there is no way for it "to render the concept of politics void" or to blend with it without at the same time identifying itself with this self-propaganda and this self-propagation that was, more than all else, the emblem of the Nazi regime—identifying its political action with artistic activity.[77]

This is, of course, a strong claim. Michaud is not only saying that Beuys at times used terminology that recalls fascist ideas. Rather, the very principle of his practice (social Gestaltung) is homologous to the Nazi conception of politics. This is as much to say that socioplasticity is inherently irredeemable.

It may be circular first to derive fascist politics from art and then to condemn art for being fascist. But since there are alternatives—kinds of art that reject the model of Gestaltung and mastery that the Nazis appropriated wholesale from the nineteenth century; modern art of the kind that Michaud presumably approves; in short, metaphoroclastic art—this observation does not get us off the hook. I will not try to defend Beuys

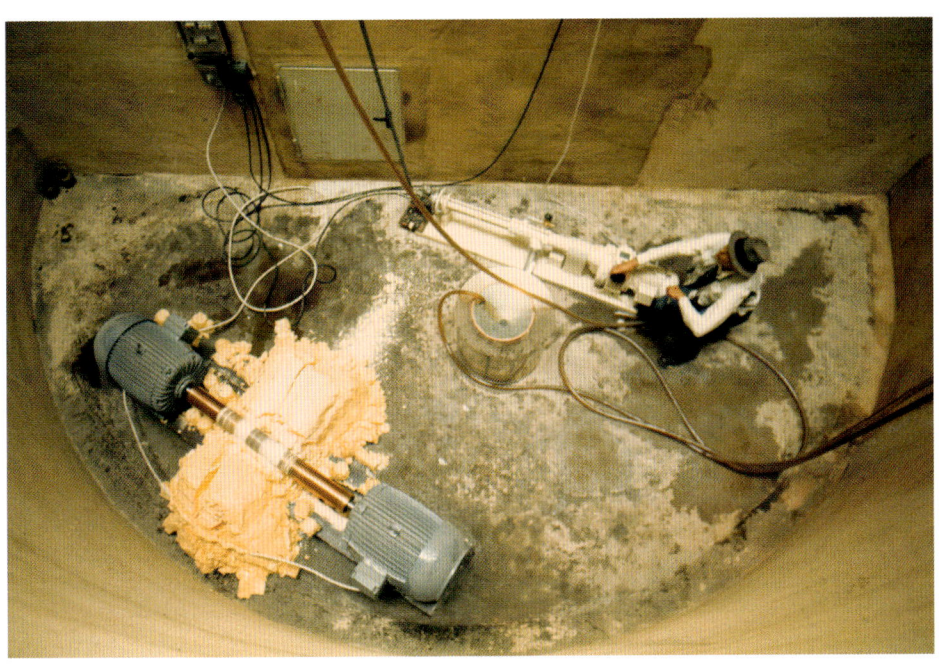

**Plate 1.** Joseph Beuys, *Honigpumpe am Arbeitsplatz* (Honey pump at the workplace), 1977. Installation with two electric motors, copper shaft, stainless steel container, galvanized metal pipe, plastic tubing, honey, margarine, and three ceramic pots. Dimensions variable. Installation view at *documenta 6*, Fridericianum, Kassel, 1977. Elements now in the collection of the Louisiana Museum of Modern Art, Humlebæk, Denmark.

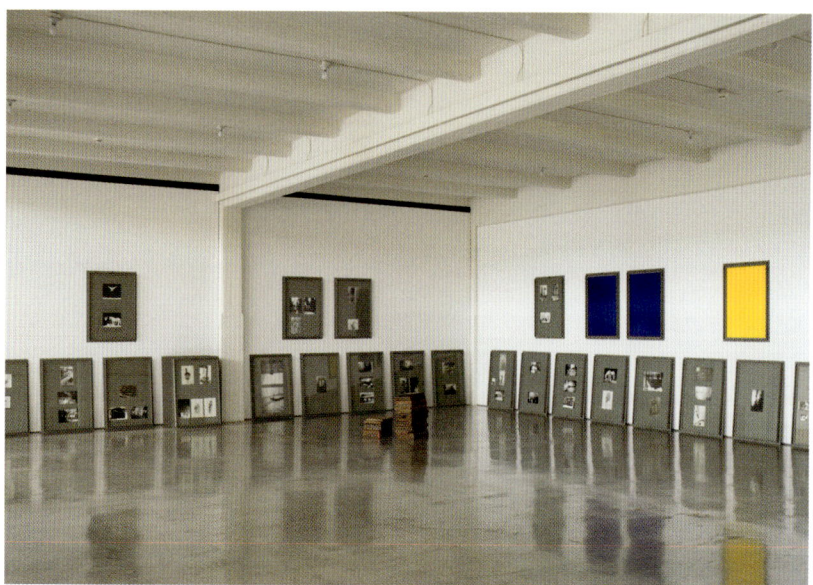

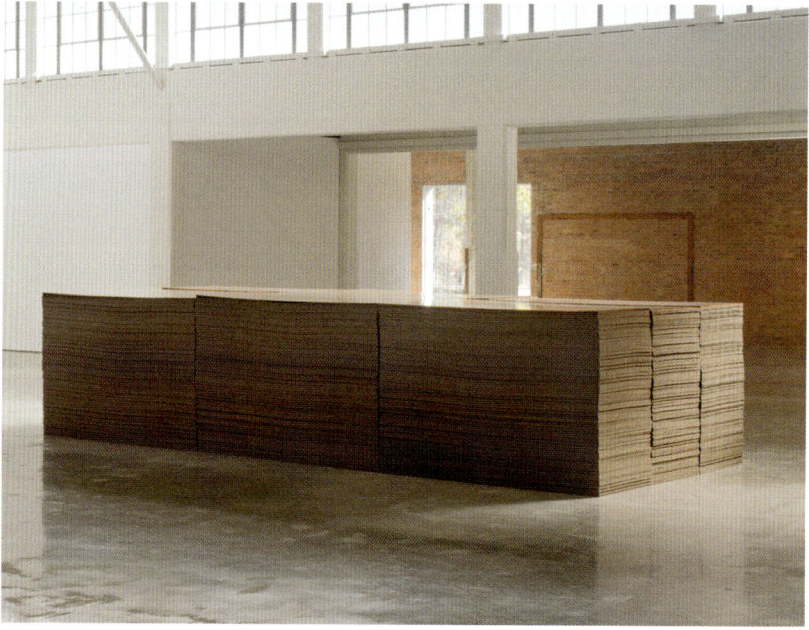

**Plate 2.** (top) Joseph Beuys, *Arena—Dove sarei arrivato se fossi stato intelligenti!* (Arena—Where would I have got if I had been intelligent!), 1970–72. Photographs with wax, paint, and acid in aluminum and glass frames, fat, wax, copper, iron, and oil can. Dimensions variable. Dia Art Foundation, New York, 1980.054.

**Plate 3.** (bottom) Joseph Beuys, *Fond III/3*, 1979. Nine hundred felt sheets, each 78¾ × 39⅜ in. (200 × 100 cm), nine copper sheets, each 78¾ × 39⅜ in. (200 × 100 cm), total dimensions approximately 39¹³/₁₆ × 236¼ × 118⅛ in. (152 × 600 × 300 cm). Dia Art Foundation, New York, 1980.526.1-.1008.

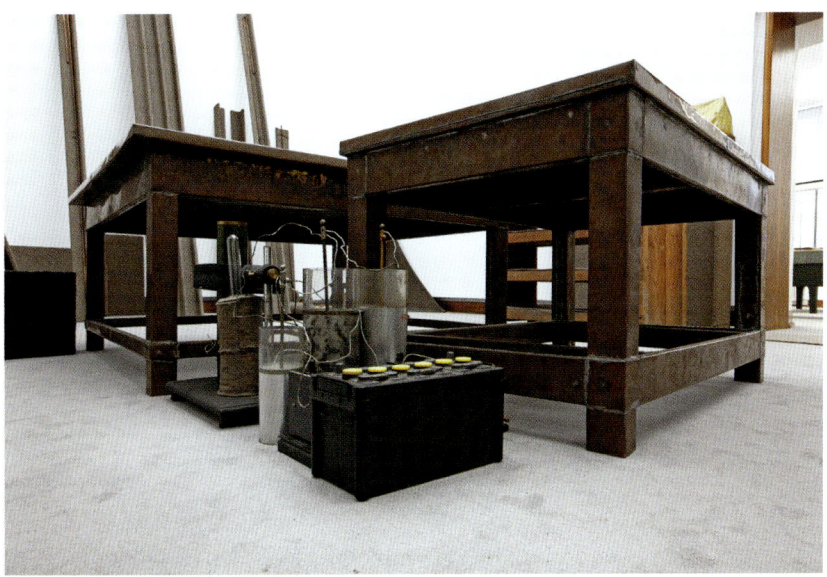

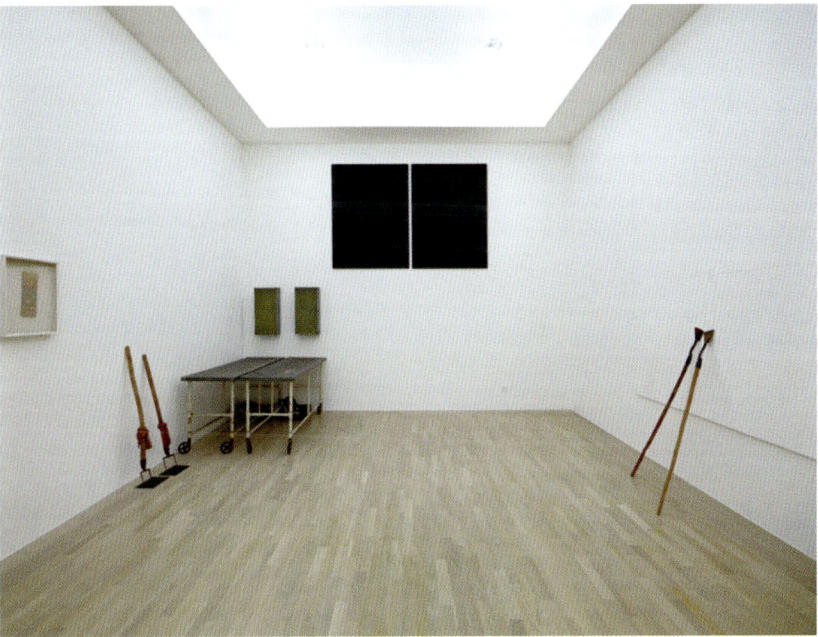

**Plate 4.** (top) Joseph Beuys, *Fond II*, 1968. Two tables, copperplate, and electric generator. Dimensions variable. Hessisches Landesmuseum, Darmstadt.

**Plate 5.** (bottom) Joseph Beuys, *zeige deine Wunde*, 1974–75. Two work tools, two white panels, two pitchforks with cloth, two small blackboards, two large backboards with chalk, two metal and wood stretchers, two empty zinc boxes, two zinc boxes with fat and gauze, thermometer, reagent glass with bird skull, two preserving jars with gauze, and two copies of the newspaper *Lotta Continua*. Approximately 500 × 800 × 580 cm. Städtische Galerie im Lenbachhaus, Munich.

**Plate 6.** Joseph Beuys, *Fettige Wolke löst sich aus dem Meer* (Greasy cloud emerging from the sea), 1959. Watercolor and fat on cardboard. 32.2 × 25.4 cm. Aeneas Bastian collection, on long-term loan to the Staatliche Kunstsammlungen Dresden, Kupferstichkabinett, DLN Bastian 59.05.

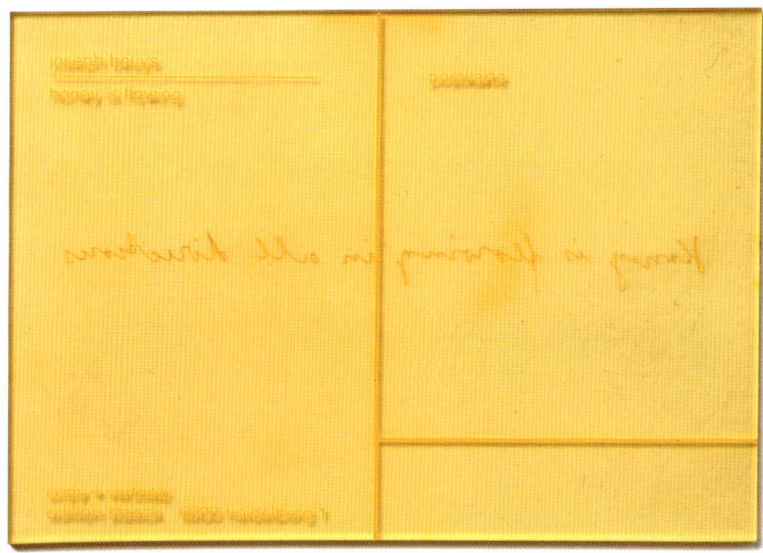

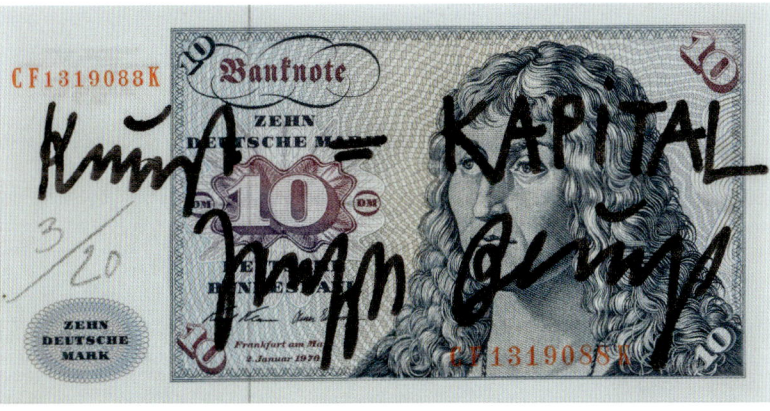

**Plate 7.** (top) Joseph Beuys, *Honey Is Flowing*, 1974. Silk screen on vinyl. 7¹⁄₁₆ × 4¹⁵⁄₁₆ × 2³⁄₈ in. (18 × 12.5 × 6 cm). Harvard Art Museums, 1995.295.1.

**Plate 8.** (bottom) Joseph Beuys, *Kunst = Kapital*, 1979. Banknote with handwritten addition. 2½ × 5⅛ in. (6.35 × 13.02 cm). Edition of twenty plus ten artist's proofs. Publisher: Edition Staeck, Heidelberg. The Broad, Los Angeles, F-BEUYS-106.303.

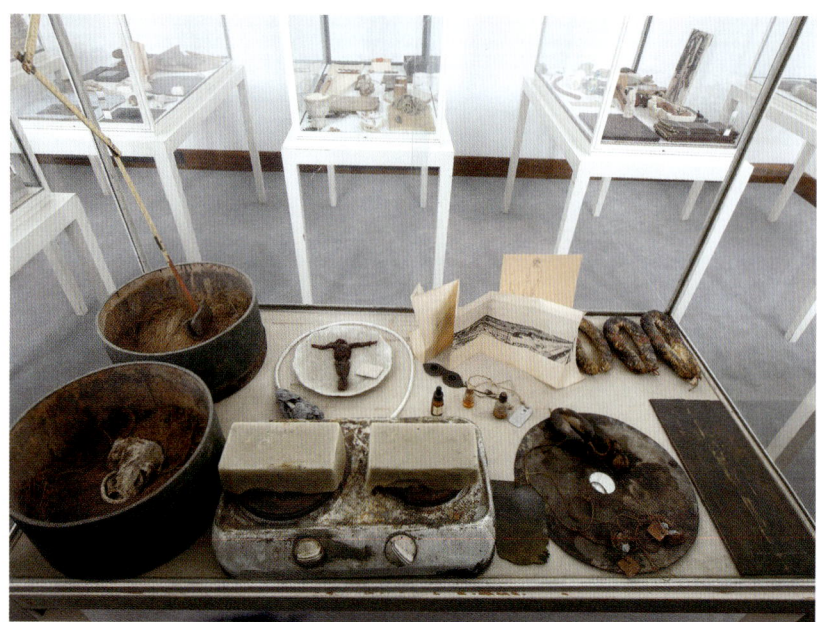

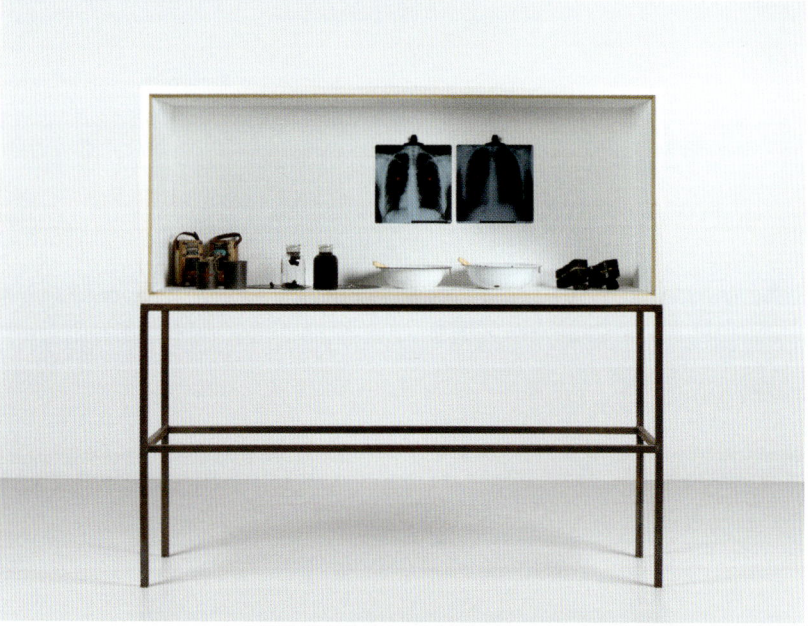

**Plate 9.** (top) Joseph Beuys, *Auschwitz Demonstration*, 1956–64. Glass and metal vitrine with two metal pots, hot plate, fat, sausages, paper, and other objects. Dimensions unknown. Hessisches Landesmuseum, Darmstadt.

**Plate 10.** (bottom) Joseph Beuys, *Doppelobjekte* 1974–79. Glass and metal vitrine with objects including two x-ray prints with oil paint, two batteries, charcoal briquettes, butter, coal, two enameled bowls with soap, two glass bottles with oil paint, metal brackets, two vinyl records, bones. 205.7 × 220 × 49.5 cm. Collection of Marguerite and Robert Hoffman.

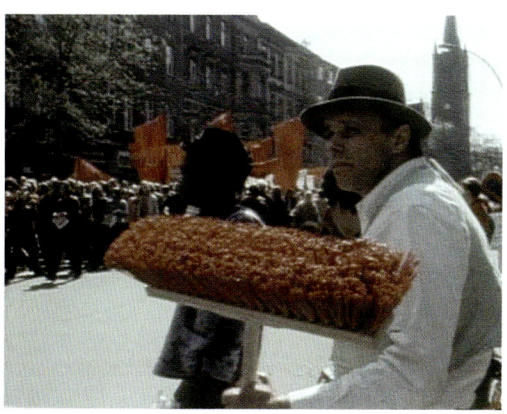

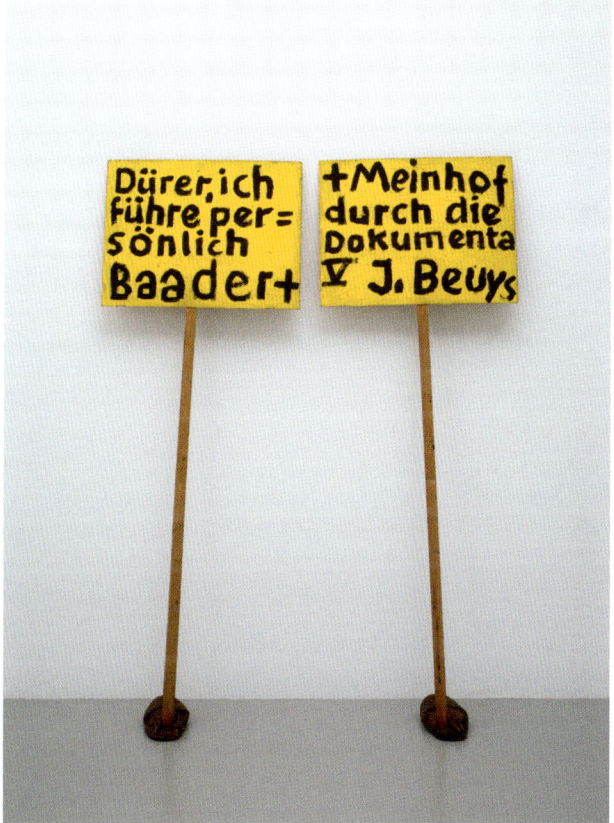

**Plate 11.** (top) Joseph Beuys, *Ausfgegen* (Sweeping up), 1972. Action, Karl-Marx-Platz, Berlin. Film still.

**Plate 12.** (bottom) Joseph Beuys and Thomas Peiter, *Dürer ich führe Baader + Meinhof persönlich durch die Documenta V*, 1972. Two masonite boards, wood, felt, fat, rose twigs, and shoes. Approximately 200 × 200 × 40 cm. Sammlung Viehof, Mönchengladbach.

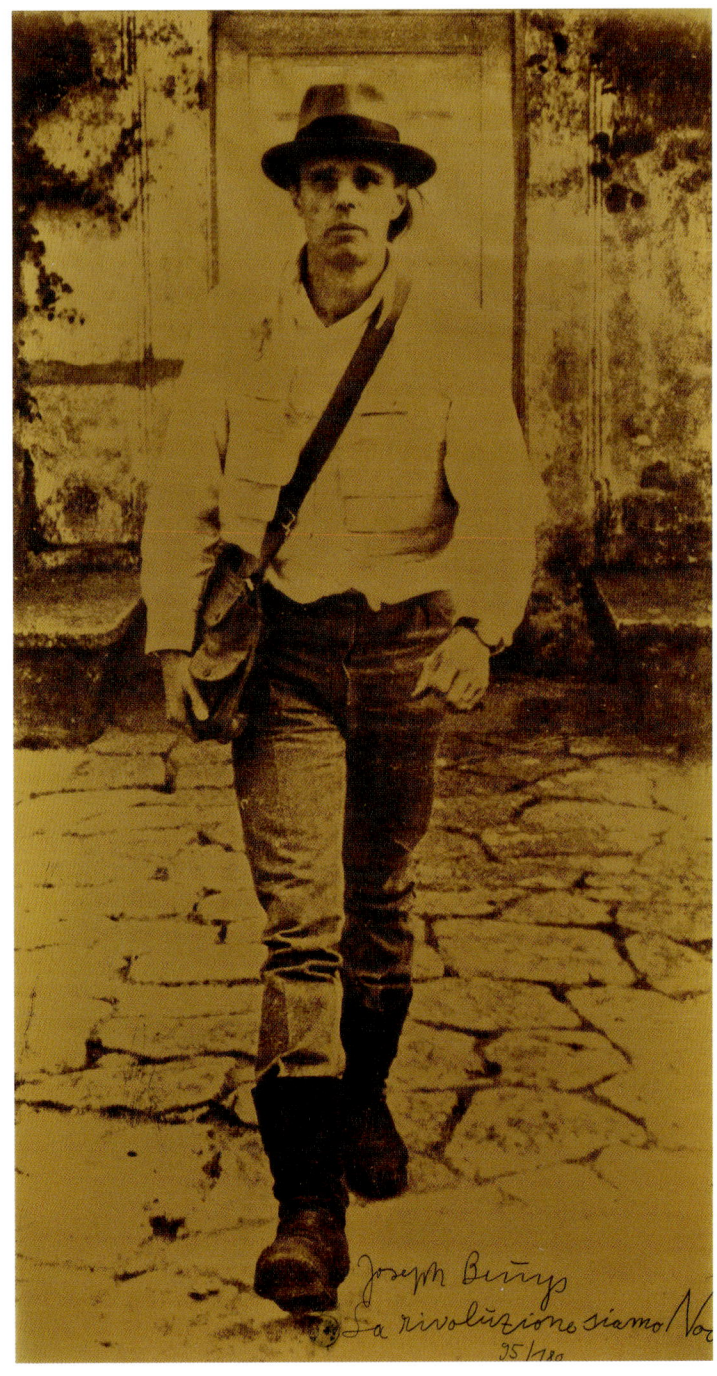

**Plate 13.** Joseph Beuys, *La Rivoluzione siamo Noi* (We are the revolution), 1972. Phototype on polyester sheet with handwritten text; stamped. Framed: 77 × 41¼ × 1¹⁄₁₈ in. (195.58 × 104.78 × 2.86 cm). The Broad, Los Angeles, F-BEUYS-106.044.

from Michaud. If one were inclined to do so, however, one might start by pointing out that a fascist work of art is perhaps only effectively such if it meets a fascist reception. There are reasons to be suspicious of Beuys's following. It has generated little or nothing, however, that can be construed even loosely as instantiating a fascist politics. So far as the present author can tell, Beuys has, since his death, left actual right-wingers unmoved—in Germany or elsewhere. That said, in his biography of the artist, H. P. Riegel draws attention to Beuys's personal connections to individuals on the political Right, some of whom he knew through reunions of war veterans that he attended. In its early years, the German Green Party, of which Beuys was a founding member, also had a right-wing faction that identified with a tradition of conservative ecological thinking with *völkisch* overtones.[78]

Beuys's use of the term *Volk*, which Michaud stresses, nonetheless cannot be reduced to its racialist implications. In part the issue is a matter of translation. Whereas in the anglophone world, as in many other countries, one presumes, the term *Volk* and its cognates understandably tend to be associated with Nazi rhetoric, in Germany the word is quite ordinary and does not necessarily evoke right-wing connotations unless those are specifically brought to the fore in the context. There are countless everyday usages that have no such resonance. Indeed, in the lecture from 1985 on which Michaud bases much of his argument, Beuys goes out of his way to emphasize that "a people is not a race."[79] This caveat, though, may have been a late, self-conscious addendum to the text. An envelope covered in handwritten notes dating from 1985 contains what seems to be an outline for this lecture. Beuys here turns to the problem of *Volkstum* (folklore or folk traditions—a keyword in the German *völkisch* movement of the early twentieth century). Among other things, he reminds himself to define the concept of *Volk* (*Begriff* -> *Volk definieren*). Below, Beuys clarifies that "a people is not a race" (*Ein Volk ist keine Rasse*).[80] This is the same phrase that occurs in the lecture, but the fact that it appears to be the sole mark on the sheet in pencil rather than ink suggests that it was made at a different time than the other notations. At some point, perhaps a belated one, Beuys therefore clearly became aware of the possibility that his remarks could be perceived as racially tinged and sought to assure his audience that they were not. This evidence perhaps suggests an attitude neither of total obliviousness as to the *völkisch* connotations of his terminology nor of intentional cryptofascist coding, but perhaps instead a self-conscious, if stumbling, attempt to formulate a nonfascist populism. The notion of the "people" has after all fueled any number of left-wing populisms as well as hybrid phenomena of an ambiguous political stripe. We will return to some of these proposals for a "third way" in what follows.

Beuys's reliance on Rudolf Steiner's teachings further complicates the issue. Steiner was unquestionably a racist. Beuys's appropriations of Steiner, however, cannot so easily be interpreted as expressions of white supremacy. His development of the concept of the "Eurasian," for example, has resonances with an early twentieth-century discourse on Germanic identity that intersected with, but cannot be reduced to, Nazi racial theories from two or more decades later. A widespread idea in the early twentieth century was that "Aryan" peoples descended from the nomadic tribes of the Central Asian steppes, and as such, had more in common with the spirituality and culture of the East than with the classical heritage of the Mediterranean world.[81] I have not found evidence that Beuys was much aware of these earlier debates when developing his ideology, which instead seems to be based quite closely, perhaps even exclusively, on anthroposophical sources. Since the end of the Cold War, Russocentric Eurasianism has seen a revival among far-right circles; Russian political philosopher Aleksandr Dugin formed a "Eurasia Party" in 2002, for example. Because of these echoes, I should make it clear that I consider Beuys's racial theories wholly unusable, regardless of the artist's intentions.[82]

What is more consequential here is that the idea of social Gestaltung has had proponents other than the Nazis. (A corollary is that laissez-faire has had proponents other than benign liberals.) It is also entrenched in the leftist tradition; think of the glorification of the plan—the rational administration of society's productive forces—by the twentieth century's socialist and communist parties. There are further echoes in the more immediate context of Beuys's postwar artistic career, not only his youth under fascism. Michaud's point is that the National Socialist political machine took up the metaphor of artistic creation in order to autonomize itself, thereby subordinating individual human beings and society as a whole to its self-perpetuation. Beuys then reverses the metaphor, or indeed, returns it to its origins. If the Nazis conceived of their political activity as having been modeled on art, Beuys in turn models his "social sculpture" on a form of aestheticized politics. In either case, it seems that the authority of the "sculptor" remains supreme, over and against the human material that they shape. Yet it is difficult to separate this supposed hypostatization of means over ends from the adoption of these same means to other ends. And it is also hard to be so sure of the distinction between the "sculptor" and their social material. Beuys's point, after all, was that *everyone* should be an artist, not in the sense that everyone should make objects institutionally recognized as "art," but that the doing and making of everything, from the design of financial institutions to peeling a potato, ought to be creative and free, as is, ideally, the making of a sculpture or painting. Everyone should partake of the same practice of Gestaltung. Buchloh's objection to Beuys can be boiled down to the observation that such freedom is illusory. Modern political and economic pressures drastically restrict options for autonomous art. As we have seen in the example of the *Kunst = Kapital* banknotes, the authority of the charismatic artist is also not so easily disposed of.

The notion that politics and artistic Gestaltung bear an affinity goes back to the very origins of Western political philosophy. As philosopher Philippe Lacoue-Labarthe puts it:

> The political (the City) belongs to a form of *plastic art*, formation and information, *fiction* in the strictest sense. This is a deep theme which derives from Plato's politico-pedagogic writings (especially *The Republic*) and reappears in the guise of such concepts as *Gestaltung* (configuration, fashioning) or *Bildung*, a term with a revealingly polysemic character (formation, constitution, organization, education, culture, etc.). The fact that the political is a form of plastic art in no way means that the *polis* is an artificial or conventional formation, but that the political belongs to the sphere of *technē* in the highest sense of the term, that is to say in the sense in which *technē* is conceived as the accomplishment and revelation of *physis* itself. This is why the *polis* is also "natural": it is the "beautiful formation" that has spontaneously sprung up from the "genius of a people" (the Greek genius) according to the modern—but in fact very ancient—interpretation of Aristotelian mimetology.[83]

Note here that the Greeks anticipate Beuys's naturalizing maneuver. The polis is a product of *technē*, or craft, and thus is artificial. But at the same time, it is a natural outgrowth of a given people's "genius." These matters would not cease to be relevant two thousand years later.

## 10.

The question of social Gestaltung has never been primarily a question of ideas. In the twentieth century, it was rather a practical issue of interests and power, the management of class conflict, and control over modernizing

economic development; its adherents belonged to both the labor movement and the fascist reaction that was its enemy. It therefore was an objective problem, not solely an ideological one, worldwide and throughout
Beuys's lifetime. It will now be helpful to consider this broader historical
field. One of my aims is to describe the impact of the Nazi past on Beuys's
postwar production, but in a manner that does not reduce this relation
to a framework of trauma, repression, and symptomatic repetition. Or
rather, if these are indeed terms at stake in his art, I hope to show that
their temporality is not that of a simple relay from the National Socialist
period straight to what was, then, the present. (This question will find a
more complete treatment in this book's third and final chapter.) A second
aim is to demonstrate that the discourse and reality of postwar "planning"
complicates any reduction of the so-called *Wirtschaftswunder* (economic
miracle) to an unambiguous triumph of consumerism. Instead, to some
West Germans, the abundance of the era suggested the possibility of a
more purposive management of their nation's new wealth. These are the
conditions in which Beuys emerged as an artist. It was in response to a crisis
in this order that his practice of the 1970s then took shape.

Nazi leaders may have understood statecraft as akin to the activity of an
artist. This autocratic parsing of the analogy was of course discredited after
the fall of the regime. Yet the question of the Gestaltung of the devastated
nation did not thereby disappear—not even for those who had the greatest
interest in reasserting the "natural" mechanisms of the capitalist market. It
is notable, for example, that the strain of liberalism that was ascendant in
Germany in the period following the currency reform of 1948 and founding
of the Federal Republic the next year was not categorically opposed to state
intervention. West Germany's new leaders still had an interest in shaping
the broader contours of the new capitalist society. Postwar neoliberalism
(as it was dubbed; it also became known as ordoliberalism, after *Ordo—
Jahrbuch für die Ordnung von Wirtschaft und Gesellschaft*, the tendency's
major scholarly journal) was willing to countenance a degree of top-down
control that the neoliberal movement's own later ideologues would come
to find embarrassing.[84] Recent scholarship has indeed emphasized the role
of state power in such thinking.[85]

The new government's shibboleth was the "social market economy"
(*soziale Marktwirtschaft*). This was a slogan as much as a concept; it was
calibrated to suggest that there would be neither a return to the laissez-faire
attitude of the pre-Depression era nor a command economy as was then

taking shape in the Soviet-occupied sector of the formerly united country. (It also indicated a relaxation of the omnipresent price controls that had been established at the end of the war.)[86] Even if the social market was to provide for the material needs of West Germans, however—and soon it largely did, thanks to the upswing of the so-called economic miracle in the 1950s—pressing issues of political legitimacy nonetheless remained unsettled in the early postwar years. Economic policy was key. The new chancellor, Konrad Adenauer, knew that his personal popularity as well as that of the government and even the democratic constitution depended on whether it would be possible to follow through on the improvement in living standards that resulted from the introduction of the deutsche mark in 1948. This reform had ambiguous effects. Though a flood of previously hoarded commodities suddenly appeared on the nation's shelves, the arrival of the new currency decimated personal savings, while its benefits were widely perceived as accruing to the wealthy alone. A massive strike wave in the US and British occupation zones that same year indicated that the Western industrial districts on which the nation depended for its export-led recovery were not yet immune from working-class discontent.[87] In a poll conducted in the Western zones in March 1949, only 35 percent of respondents approved of the recent currency reform. By contrast, 32 percent approved of monetary policy in the Soviet-occupied sector.[88]

In these circumstances, it behooved proponents of the free market to highlight the "social" side of the *soziale Marktwirtschaft*. But in doing so, they sometimes said things that were more familiar than the rhetoric of the post-1945 *Stunde Null* (zero hour) would suggest. This had been the case from the beginning of the reconstruction period. In November 1945, for instance, the newly founded Free Democratic Party—the most outspokenly liberal and promarket of the nation's emerging democratic forces—drafted a program that marked a clear distance from classical laissez-faire doctrines, including those of its own predecessors before 1933; as it reads at one point, "The economy is there for the people and not the people for the economy."[89] Innocuous enough, except that this is close to a paraphrase of Adolf Hitler's memorandum on the Four Year Plan of 1936. There, the Führer made his economic priorities plain: "The nation does not live for the economy, for economic leaders, or for economic and financial theories: on the contrary, it is finance and the economy, economic leaders and theories, which all owe an unqualified service in this struggle for the self-assertion of our nation."[90] The trouble for the Free Democrats, as for other German liberals, was to find a way to articulate the communalistic aspect of their social vision without either giving too much ground to a possible *völkisch* resurgence or betraying their procapitalist convictions. At the same time, it was imperative not to press too strongly for a deregulated market. The free market indeed remained widely unpopular, not to say incomprehensible, for much of the German populace. It was too strongly associated with the disasters of the Weimar Republic and Depression.

Alexander Rüstow, one of the leading neoliberal economists of the postwar era, explained this conundrum in a statement he made in 1950:

> It is an undoubted and powerful advantage for the planned economy that its principles can be enthusiastically understood within ten minutes by the simple layman—and indeed they will particularly appeal to him. On the other hand, even a full university training in economics may not be enough to enable one to understand the invisible and complicated mechanisms of the market.[91]

This passage may strike twenty-first century readers as an inversion of our common sense. From the 1970s onward, the market was naturalized to such an extent that it is economic planning that looks to be artificial, morally dubious, and inefficient, though perhaps necessary in moments of crisis (these instincts persisted even after unprecedentedly massive interventions to stem the financial meltdown of 2008–9, as the subsequent imposition of austerity across much of Europe shows; the revival of industrial policy and neomercantilism over the past decade can perhaps only now be said to mark a real break with the neoliberal model). Such was not the case in Germany in the late 1940s and even beyond. The prestige of ambitious projects of economic intervention within a more or less capitalist framework— the New Deal in the United States and the Keynesian policies enacted by Clement Atlee's 1945 Labour government in the United Kingdom—was still untarnished in the eyes of many. Moreover, there existed right next door the living example of an alternative economic order: the socialist command economy of the Soviet Union along with vast swathes of Eastern Europe, including East Germany (known as the *Deutsche Demokratische Republik,* or German Democratic Republic, after 1949), that had fallen under its hegemony. No one in 1945 could have taken liberal democracy and the free market for granted.

The economy of the *Bundesrepublik Deutschland* (Federal Republic of Germany, or BRD) as it took shape in the 1950s and 1960s was far from being a capitalist free-for-all. Organized labor was strong. But the government, together with large concerns such as automobile manufacturers, largely succeeded in clipping its political wings. The Communist Party of Germany was banned in 1956. It had been tiny in any case; more consequential was the trajectory of the German Social Democratic Party (SPD), which relinquished more and more of its anticapitalist platform over the course of the 1950s. This process culminated in the party's Godesberg conference of 1959. Here, the SPD formally abandoned the aim of deposing capitalism as well as its once ambitious program of nationalizations, along with its very character as a working-class party.[92] It would henceforth designate itself a *Volkspartei* (people's party), which in the German context means a party intended to represent the whole of the electorate rather than a particular interest. By 1966, the SPD had enough common ground with the Christian Democrats to enter into a federal "Grand Coalition" that would govern the country until the party took undisputed command in a new alliance with the much smaller Free Democrats in 1969.

In tandem with this retreat from political polarization, a new contract between labor and capital emerged in these years. Nationalization was now out of the question; in recompense, however, German firms surrendered ground on the doctrine of so-called *Mitbestimmung*, or codetermination. This translated into more extensive rights for workers to decide on the policies of the enterprises that employed them—within limits, since management ultimately was always to remain in the same hands. A closely related concept was that of the so-called *Mitgestaltungsrecht*: a neologism that has been translated as the "right to participate" in social, economic, and political decisions, though this rendering occludes the crucial presence of the root word "Gestaltung" at the center of the compound. Along with these new rights came regular and highly formalized wage negotiations.[93] As a pair of economic historians have put it,

> The German economy in fact remained tightly regulated, both absolutely and relative to more slowly-growing economies like Britain. The postwar model of Rhenish capitalism drew heavily on a regulatory model established in the early and mid-1930s, complemented by an improved version of the corporatist wage bargaining that had prevailed in the Weimar republic before 1933.[94]

Welfare protections also steadily expanded over the Federal Republic's first two decades, reaching something like their final state under the Social

Democratic chancellorship of Willy Brandt in the early 1970s. At the same time, government economic policy consistently focused on controlling domestic demand in order to prevent higher wages from depressing international competitiveness, as the nation's postwar economic prosperity was based on industrial production for export.[95] In the early years of the BRD, this policy also involved keeping rents, coal, and other basic necessities artificially cheap, which in turn lowered the pressure for wage increases. At the same time, the government stimulated investment in heavy industry, utilities, and transportation in order to rebuild productive capacity.

Hence it is somewhat paradoxical that postwar West Germany is so frequently characterized as a consumer society. It was, rather, very much a society founded on production. The growth of individual consumption was premised on and unimaginable without the astounding success of highly capitalized industry. In 1970, the industrial sector employed 48.7 percent of the workforce in the BRD. This was the highest ratio for any advanced capitalist economy; in the same year, the figure for the United States was only 31.7 percent, for example (just slightly higher, it bears mentioning, than Germany's industrial employment today). Approximately ten million people in the Federal Republic then worked in manufacturing as opposed to just over twenty million in the United States, a nation with more than two and a half times the population and twice the per capita GDP.[96] Crucial to the success of German capitalism was the labor peace that employers and their allies in government bought with continuously expanding social services. So long as business was good, the price was not too high to pay.

One could argue that the economic and political structure that emerged in the BRD during the crucial years of Beuys's development as an artist was thus already on the road to a "third way" such as he was later to propose, though it was a compromise still geared toward the accumulation of capital.[97] It was only the spectacular recovery of West Germany's capitalist economy, and in particular the manufacturing sector, that allowed for the broad expansion of welfare provisions that made up the "social" component of Adenauer's *soziale Marktwirtschaft*. In the absence of a fundamental shift in property relations, there was no basis for this redistributionist policy other than the continued profitability of capitalist enterprise. Indeed, so long as profitability remained high, all seemed more or less well. Workers and the mass of the West German population enjoyed rising standards of living at the same time as capitalists could rest secure in the knowledge that there would be no serious challenge to the rights of private property.

High profits, high taxes, and high social spending went hand in hand. Despite the political upheavals of the 1960s and 1970s, this general consensus on the shape of postwar West German society proved quite durable. It remained fundamentally intact even as the United States under President Ronald Reagan and Britain under Prime Minister Margaret Thatcher—among other countries—slipped into the long right-wing reaction of the 1980s. Ironically, it was to be an SPD chancellor, Gerhard Schröder, who pushed through the first real assault on Germany's social state in the early 2000s, causing a left-wing split from the party.

Ludwig Erhard, the primary architect of the BRD's economy after 1949, hit on a slogan to augment the idea of the *soziale Marktwirtschaft* during his unsuccessful reelection campaign for the chancellorship in 1966.[98] It was a term that Erhard's adviser, conservative intellectual Rüdiger Altmann, had invented shortly before. This was the concept of the *formierte Gesellschaft*, or "formed society."[99] Altmann argued that traditional social antagonisms had by then all but ceased to exist and hence the real threat to the BRD was an excess of "pluralism." The formed society was the response to what Altmann, and Erhard after him, perceived as the increasing power that special interest groups such as monopolistic cartels were then exercising at the expense of the nation's common good. To curb egoism and social atomization, it was necessary to insist on a strong, centralized state capable of subordinating partial interests to those of society as a whole. This hardly meant that Erhard was turning his back on the market. The formed society, like the *soziale Marktwirtschaft* before it, was rather to guarantee the principle of fair competition within a capitalist framework, although under the guidance of paternalistic state control. The point of government intervention into the economy, for example, was to level the playing field by breaking up concentrations of power; it was not, however, to attack capitalism per se. Erhard's emphasis was clearly on social cohesion over and above egalitarianism. The slogan expressed, in his own words, a "wish for a stabilization of life and at the same time for a sensibly structured society that gives a sense of security to the individual and to the community, even if it is not wholly comprehensible."[100]

As such, the *formierte Gesellschaft* might be understood as a conservative analog to President Lyndon Baines Johnson's contemporaneous "Great Society" initiative—a set of broad reformist measures that had been introduced to the United States in 1964–65. Both were among the last ambitious postwar programs for overall social remodeling. Where

Johnson focused on poverty and civil rights, though, Erhard's vision was more resolutely tied to an ideal of social order. Society was, exactly, to be *formiert*, "formed." The verb *formieren* has militaristic associations; it can mean "to deploy" or "muster up" (an army, for example), but also to *re*form or *re*align, especially when used in the phrase *neu formieren*. It is not a particularly common word in German. Nor does it apply, as does its English cognate, to processes of artistic or, more generally, plastic formation. For these the verb is *gestalten*, from which Gestaltung is derived. The phrase *"formierte Gesellschaft"* nonetheless belongs to a constellation of terms that came to prominence in the postwar era as ways to describe the unprecedented interpenetration of planning and laissez-faire, government intervention and the persistence of the market, that came to define the economic and political order of the nonsocialist world. As it turned out, the *formierte Gesellschaft* failed as a slogan. It was almost instantly ridiculed as out of touch, latently authoritarian, and unrealistic—or in the paraphrase of a later writer, a "petty-bourgeois dream of a conflict-free society."[101]

Yet oddly enough, it was a dream, or maybe nightmare, that had its leftist versions too. That the enmeshment of state and economy had proceeded almost up to or even beyond the point of eliminating all classical social antagonisms was an axiom in Adorno's description of the "administered world" as well as in philosopher Herbert Marcuse's concept of "one-dimensional man."[102] Some years earlier, some Frankfurt School critics, notably Max Horkheimer, had accepted the thesis of the so-called liquidation of the sphere of circulation (that is, the market) practically as an a priori.[103] The rise of monopoly capital and state-led direction of the economy supposedly meant that nineteenth-century liberalism had become obsolete, and with it all theories of the autonomy of the economic sphere. Hence from this perspective, the border between economic rationality and directly political administration had come to be all but imperceptible over the first half of the twentieth century.[104] Where the German neoliberals sought to preserve the market in the face of state and monopoly control, even by means of state intervention, the BRD's left-wing critics by contrast viewed the passing of classical competitive capitalism as more or less a fait accompli. The postulate of the liquidation of the sphere of circulation was also widespread in German leftist circles of the late 1960s. Neither the proponents nor the critics of the *soziale Marktwirtschaft* seem to have anticipated the vigorous reassertion of market fundamentals that would increasingly characterize global economic discourse from the 1980s onward.

If the thesis of the liquidation of competitive capitalism has a familiar ring to it in the present context, it is perhaps because Beuys's vision of economic transformation in "Aufruf zur Alternative" and elsewhere shares some of its tenets. It has been worth considering postwar German economic theory and practice in detail because it is necessary to have some understanding of this particular relation between the capitalist market and notions of rational planning if we are to parse Beuys's economic propositions in their historical context. To simplify, one might say that this economic discourse of the post-1945 period and indeed the welfare state itself constituted the work's raw material. Beuys, too, claimed that advanced capitalism had outstripped the nineteenth-century model. Profit was for him only a vestige of an earlier stage of spiritual development; it represented an illegitimate extraction from a productive circuit that was not monetary at all but instead founded on the principle of human creativity. These propositions are phrased in a vocabulary that is different from that of the Marxist New Left, of course, but some of their content is not so drastically different. In fact, the conclusion must be that Beuys aimed to appropriate the *same* content—or at least to address the same problems— for the purposes of his own ideological construct, the "expanded concept of art." This was a conscious process; he knew enough about Marxism to get what he needed from it. By the same measure, it is worth pointing out that the Marxist Left perhaps had more in common with its adversaries than it may have seemed at the time.

In a text from 1968, for example, Hans-Jürgen Krahl—one of the most radical theorists of the Socialist German Student League (Sozialistischer Deutscher Studentenbund, or SDS), the largest and most influential group involved in the West German student movement of the late 1960s—wrote of the "liquidation of the sphere of circulation by the monopolistic market controls of centralized authoritarian production."[105] This was a phenomenon that he seems to have perceived as occurring in the nominally capitalist West just as much as in the socialist East. Though Krahl would have resented the comparison, it bears pointing out that Erhard was talking about much the same thing in his various presentations of the *formierte Gesellschaft*. In his reflections on the closed circuit of the credit economy, Beuys also had a broadly similar intuition as to the passing of classical market mechanisms: money had ceased to be a simple means of exchange in the market, becoming instead become a "legal" document and thus an object of essentially political decisions. For Beuys as much as for Krahl, this putative supersession of the market represented capitalism's "naturally produced historical terminus" and hence opened the possibility of capitalism's final overcoming.[106] So long as control remained in the hands of the state and private monopolies, however, no liberation could follow. As such, Beuys and Krahl had the same enemies too.

Beuys often repeated the claim that socialism was his political goal. I hope to have indicated that this was not purely misdirection. But neither was his brand of socialism identical to that of Krahl or other Marxists (though in the late 1970s, Beuys was eventually to have a working relationship with Rudi Dutschke, Krahl's closest ally in the SDS as well as the most visible figurehead of the previous decade's West German student and youth revolt).[107] His free democratic socialism is better seen as yet another response, this time couched in the idiosyncratic vocabulary of "social sculpture," to a situation that was broadly perceived to represent a critical juncture in the BRD's history. This sense that an earlier phase of competitive, liberal capitalism had come to an end in the postwar era alarmed commentators across the political spectrum. Many Germans on both the Left and Right—from student radicals to ordoliberal theorists to Erhard himself—might have approved Beuys's indictment of monopoly interest and the oligarchic political system. As we have seen, his stress on the Gestaltung of society likewise has points in common with a broad range of positions. One is that of Nazi ideology; in this Michaud is correct. But Beuys's conceptual apparatus was also a reflection, in however complexly mediated a form, on what was arguably the most important problem in conceptualizing the BRD's postwar development—namely, the problem of how capitalism might coexist with planning. (For "planning," read some or all of the following: social cohesion and security; the avoidance of Weimar-like crisis situations; the rational or at least equitable allocation of resources; and the nonviolent management of social conflict—in short, peace between capital and labor on the basis of shared prosperity along with a reasonable degree of egalitarianism.) Could this cohabitation of the lawlessness of the market and rational planning continue at all, or would it reach a tipping point? And if the latter, what would be its result? Krahl and his comrades had an unambiguous answer: proletarian revolution and the advent of socialism. But it was not the only answer, nor did its conciseness necessarily resolve the challenge of crisis and transition. If state and economy had indeed fused into an impenetrable whole, in which the old liberties of the free market, such as they were, had long since ceased to be operative, what might then happen in the event of what philosopher and sociologist Jürgen Habermas, writing in the early 1970s, called a "legitimation crisis": a crisis that "cannot be resolved within the range of possibility that is circumscribed by the organizational principle of the society"?[108] Where would the chain reaction end? And what new organizational principle, if any, might then take the place of the *soziale Marktwirtschaft?*

## 11.

To sum up, it seems irrefutable to me that the real basis for Beuys's work on the metaphor of a new principle of economic organization was the emergence of a West German welfare state in the 1950s and 1960s. It was this long event that provided Beuys with terms that had some traction on the shifting tectonic plates of postwar economic and political reconstruction; they were the material of economimesis. The problem of Gestaltung was real. It was the problem of ordering society itself. Adenauer and Erhard were trying to answer the same questions.

Beuys's cross-pollination of economics, politics, and aesthetics took shape, however, not in the full bloom of the "economic miracle" but rather in the period of change that marked its end.[109] The works in which Beuys made his transition from an implicit thematics of circulation, accumulation, and so forth, to an explicit thematization of money, capital, and labor, date from the years immediately following the recession of 1966–67 (the first obvious indication of trouble with the boom) and in particular the onset of the more profound economic slowdown of the early 1970s. This is one difference between *wie man dem toten Hasen die Bilder erklärt* (How to explain pictures to a dead hare) and *Honigpumpe.* Whereas in the earlier work, the economic connotation was embedded deep within the texture of a personal mythology, in the latter it has been brought fully to the surface. The economic theme is now the manifest content of the piece. But at the same time, the economic sphere has come to be infected with a complex of metaphoric associations.

This might have happened at least in part because the smooth functioning of the real monetary economy to which *Honigpumpe* assumes a mimetic relation had in the interim been profoundly disturbed. With President Richard Nixon's abolition of the Bretton Woods system in 1971, the international monetary order ceased to be based on the US dollar's convertibility to gold at a fixed rate of thirty-five dollars per ounce. The new system would be based instead on floating fiat currencies.[110] The world went off the gold standard, once and for all. The substance that had been so crucial to *wie man dem toten Hasen die Bilder erklärt* then lost its primary economic function. Nixon had left its metaphoric associations high and dry, so to speak.[111] The resonance between the displacement of gold's economic significance and that of *Unschlitt/Tallow*'s deferred material poetics bears keeping in mind. It could be argued that there is something distinctively "post–Bretton Woods" about the latter sculpture's deferred structure of meaning. The artist's final important work—the installation *Palazzo Regale*, 1985—in turn features seven "gold" panels that are in fact made out of brass with a powdered gold plating. This slippage between materials again seems indicative of something more than cost cutting. It may be that Beuys consciously or unconsciously played with acts of counterfeiting, perhaps even as a reflection on his own persona as a suspected charlatan. With the rise of the financialization that characterized the post–Bretton Woods system, though, money—the fundamental signifier in a capitalist mode of production—likewise came to be increasingly unmoored from any physical anchor.

Meanwhile, the BRD lumbered into a new economic universe. The oil crisis of 1973 and the intractable phenomenon of stagflation, or inflation combined with stagnant growth, followed soon after the so-called Nixon shock. The Bundesbank's response was initially indecisive. After floating a number of contradictory policies over the 1970s, the West German authorities finally chose a monetarist course that prioritized inflation control over full employment.[112] In this period, the nation indeed saw jobless numbers rise to levels unknown since the lean days of the early postwar period. A generation of West Germans (those younger than Beuys) then confronted, for the first time, the fragility of the order in which they had come of age. Yet even so, the nation's welfare state did not come under serious threat; in fact, it grew. This was thanks in part to the strength of the social movements that had emerged at the end of the previous decade—few politicians were bold enough to take away benefits that their predecessors had already granted—and partly to the continued overall strength of the West German economy vis-à-vis its competitors, an unshakable component of which was, by this time, the highly skilled, highly organized industrial working class. The German crisis was therefore peculiar from an international perspective. The capitalist system and welfare state that it had tolerated as a condition of political peace remained viable even in the midst of upheaval and uncertainty. So-called *Modell Deutschland* was thus frequently held up as a beacon of prosperity in the doldrums of the global 1970s.

The question is how to articulate Beuys's doctrine of free democratic socialism in relation to both the postwar welfare state as well as the political and economic challenges it faced from the late 1960s onward. The present book is not a contextual history that aims to reduce aesthetic phenomena to another level of reality; everything has its autonomous consistency. Yet Beuys clearly made art about economy and politics during this period. We are obligated to think about economy and politics in relation to Beuys as we are obligated to think about Protestant theology in relation to German painting in the sixteenth century. Beuys's art is reflexively economimetic. It is also the case that economy sometimes appears in its own, mostly unmetaphoric guise at points in the artist's trajectory.

Take, for example, the money-distributing organizations that Beuys envisioned in his "Aufruf zur Alternative." These are perhaps not terribly different from West Germany's real mechanisms of social welfare, except that the state has somehow been removed from the picture. The significance of that distinction is worth pondering in light of what has happened in the decades since. For most artists and nonprofit organizations, autonomy from state funding is surely no longer a goal toward which to strive so much as an unavoidable condition. Things become especially pointed when concrete problems of institution building arise. In an interview with publicist Friedrich Wolfram Heubach on the topic of the "ideal academy," published in the second issue of his journal *Interfunktionen* in 1969, Beuys conspicuously avoids answering his interlocutor's question about funding. Beuys also mentions that he sees "his party" (the German Student Party) as a "new academy," thereby leaving the status of already existing academies— such as the one he was then teaching at in Düsseldorf—up in the air.[113] Though his organizations gained adherents over the coming decade, money remained a thorny issue. In 1976, Tisdall wrote up a detailed report, addressed to the European Economic Community, on the prospects for establishing an FIU outpost in Dublin. Although Tisdall provides a detailed budget, her section on "financing" is only slightly less vague than Beuys's statements to Heubach several years earlier; she proposes that funds may be sought from the European Economic Community itself, the European Cultural Foundation, and the Gulbenkian Foundation (a charitable organization based in Portugal).[114] One questions whether funds derived from

European rather than national bodies, or from private sources, would really safeguard Beuys's desired independence, let alone his grander program. At such moments, Beusyian ideology thuds down to earth. *Honigpumpe* emerged amid this search for cash as the FIU's most spectacular realization to date. It colonized an art institution as the premonition of a pedagogical community that was never, indeed, to find secure footing.

The metaphoric relay from honey to money to blood that is at play in *Honigpumpe* is utopian, then, but it is shadowed by the disruption of the real economic circuit to which the work refers, or more accurately, that serves as its model and through which it obtains its structure. If the horizon of planning and a "third way" between laissez-faire capitalism and state socialism in the 1950s and 1960s provided Beuys with the economimetic raw material for his approach to socioplasticity (or totalized Gestaltung), it was by contrast the specter of a breakdown in this feedback loop between capitalist development and expanded social welfare in the decade following 1966–67 that was the immediate context for the installation's work on the metaphor of the beehive (a prime example of Blumenberg's "work on myth"). This sense of crisis had multiple valences. It was in the work's interest to keep all of them in the air: the immediate travails of the FIU; recession and political crisis in West Germany; and world historical, if not cosmic cataclysm. The model that the ancient trope of the beehive suggests is not wholly unlike the *formierte Gesellschaft* or any other fantasy of a nonconflictual social order.[115] But the *formierte Gesellschaft* failed, whereas Beuys hoped that social sculpture would succeed. *Honigpumpe* is not only an image of the West German economy. It is a proposal for how to fix it.

# 12.

Beuys's extremism often seems to be explicable only as a symptom. But artworks do not simply duplicate their conditions of possibility; they formalize and work on them. I am offering a reading of one artwork along these lines. *Honigpumpe* reflects on the economic difficulties of its era. The installation's utopianism is a counterimage to the precarity of the economic situation in West Germany during the period in which it was made. The work models itself on this real situation, only to reflect that economy back to its audience as something more sanguine than it actually was (if I can be forgiven the pun). Here the double-edged quality of

Beuysian economimesis will be evident. If *Honigpumpe* is, on the one hand, utopian—it is a proposal for an economy that has never yet existed—on the other hand, the fact that the work submits itself to a mimesis of the accumulation of capital (that is, the social form that stands in the way of liberation) threatens to debase art through its too literal identification with the fundamental mediating structure of the capitalist economy.

My claim is that we can best interpret the articulation of the economic and aesthetic in works such as *Honigpumpe* as a reflection on the specific historical circumstances to which its forms were a response. The broad post–World War II problematic of planning, social Gestaltung, and the persistence of capitalism, though perhaps an illiberal and noncompetitive version thereof, set the parameters for the artist's political imagination, which was from the start engaged in work on myth (a set of old organicist tropes). Or to put it more precisely, Beuys's old philosophy of nature took on new allegorical significance as social, political, and economic concerns became newly prominent in his work and thinking during the 1960s. The crisis of the 1970s then posed a challenge to the coherence of this politico-aesthetic discourse, even as it also seems to have prompted Beuys to ratchet up its intensity to unprecedented levels. The strange fact is that Beuys in many ways seems to anticipate the restructuring of the global capitalist economy along neoliberal lines since the 1970s. His identification of capital with creativity is practically a calling card of recent bourgeois ideology. Part of its legacy is every "disruptive" start-up CEO who claims to think like an artist. Yet at the same time, Beuys's doctrine of "social sculpture" preserved, in the most ambitious fashion possible, the ideological chimera that neoliberalism doggedly snuffed out: the hope that capitalist production might be subordinated to a new, more rational, and more democratic order—to free democratic socialism. It is this fact that bears explanation. I will suggest that the circle could *not* be squared. This failure accounts for the oeuvre's otherwise discrepant negativity, to which chapter 3 will turn.

There is another way to talk about *Honigpumpe*, though, and it deserves a hearing before we move on. Beuys's installation was a sculpture in a more or less traditional sense (it was a set of objects in three-dimensional space). It was also a social sculpture: an aesthetic situation of which human minds and bodies were a part. It was furthermore, as we have seen in some detail now, a materialized metaphor of two apparently very different things: a natural circulatory system and a human economy. This *dispositif* was operative. Neither the physical pump nor discursive practice alone made up the whole of the piece; as we have already quoted the artist as saying, *Honigpumpe* "is not thinkable only as a thing, only as a machine or as a sculpture. Human beings are actually a part of it." In short, it was a system. It had inputs and outputs. So did other of his projects. *I Like America and America Likes Me* had two key elements: Beuys and the coyote (two mammals in a room). By locking himself in with the coyote, Beuys constituted a system that relied on inputs to maintain its homeostasis (food, water, straw for bedding, and a felt blanket for warmth) and that produced outputs as well: feces and semiosis (the ponderous symbolism of the "psychological trauma point of the United States' energy constellation," as Beuys put it, but also a less easily paraphrased—which is to say, more poetic—exchange between human and animal ways of being in the world). *I Like America* was an ecology.

Ecologies may exist on practically any scale. A room is a small one. As the totalizing horizon of his "expanded concept of art" suggests, however, Beuysian art could produce or appropriate grandiosely immense ecologies, as he did in declaring the entire city of Hamburg a *Gesamtkunstwerk* in 1983, for instance. At this point, Duchamp's gesture of nominating objects as readymades expands to such an extent that it becomes almost self-parody. The Italian artist Piero Manzoni indeed already took the logical next step as early as 1961: with his *Socle du monde*, he put the entire Earth on an upside-down pedestal, thus implying that the planet itself was now the artwork and his sculpture merely the base for it. At this point—at this imaginary moment of the subsumption of the entire planet to the status of art, which Manzoni ironizes and Beuys's practice seems to tend toward, without ever reaching it—the economic or semiotic exchange between art and nonart would cease because the art system would no longer have any exterior; it would no longer have any nonart material from which it could draw sustenance. Another way to put it would be to say that *Socle du monde* is an imagined sublation of the parergon, absorbing the entire work into its "inessential" supplement and by the same measure making everything except the work into the work. A total ecology of this sort would just be the Earth's ecology as it is (including, of course, all of its anthropogenic malaise). That is, a totalized artwork would no longer really be an artwork at all but instead reality as such. The Hamburg project is less dizzying than this, but only just. It is gratuitously provocative, if not megalomaniacal, to declare a city not only a work of art but specifically one by Joseph Beuys. (It is also rather megalomaniacal to sign a banknote.) Yet the *Gesamtkunstwerk Freie- und Hansestadt Hamburg* was subtler than this. His proposal

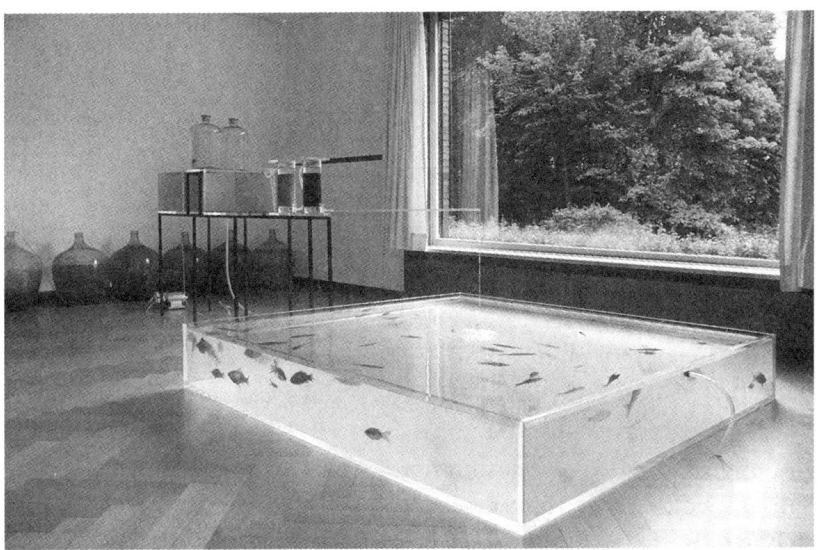

**Fig. 24.** Hans Haacke, *Rheinwasseraufbereitungsanlage* (Rhine water purification plant), 1972. Installation view, Museum Haus Lange, Krefeld, 1972. Glass, acrylic, water pump, water, tubing, filters, chemicals, and goldfish. Dimensions variable.

was to rehabilitate old dumping grounds on the site of a former village in the city's harbor area by using plant species to treat chemically polluted mud displaced in the dredging of the Elbe River, thereby reflecting on the industrial history of a major northern German city.[116] Although it was never realized, thanks to a veto by the mayor of Hamburg, it remains an interesting project for its sheer ambition and scale. Totalized art was, once again, collateral for trying to achieve something else, at the same time as it was the alpha and omega of Beuys's efforts.

It also happens to be an idea that recalls an earlier work by a German contemporary of his, Hans Haacke, who in 1972 set up a filtration plant to clean a small amount of polluted water that he diverted from the Rhine into a gallery of the Museum Haus Lange, which happens to be located in Beuys's hometown, the city of Krefeld (fig. 24). After filtration, the water flowed out another tube back into the river. Putting these two projects in contact is useful for clarifying the different approaches of Haacke and Beuys (a comparison that will return in a more agonistic key in this book's coda). Haacke's project is an extraction from a larger system or, interpreted differently, constitutes a minisystem of its own within the art institution. Beuys instead seeks to subsume an entire real system to another category: art. (The same thing happens in the relation between economy and Gestaltung.) In Haacke's piece, water exits an exterior ecological system—the river with all of its tributaries and thermodynamic inputs, together with the animal, plant, and human systems that interact with it—which then temporarily becomes part of a social system called the museum, or more broadly, the contemporary art institution.[117] In the *Gesamtkunstwerk Hamburg*, Beuys, by contrast, does two more ambitious things. First, he proposes not a symbolic extraction from a larger system (or a kind of temporary capture of an ecology by the category of the aesthetic) but rather aims to work directly in natural and social reality by expanding the concept of art to absorb technical as well as political activity, such as the installation of large-scale filtration systems in public space. Second, he subsumes the entire natural, social, and technical system called "the city of Hamburg" to the status of a readymade artwork.

Art and nonart elements thus pass through these two projects in quite different ways—as they do in a comparison between Haacke's filtration plant and *I Like America*, to which the former work does not bear an obvious visual similarity. (Haacke's tubes do, by contrast, look a bit like *Honigpumpe*.) Much as in Haacke's piece, though, Beuys here rerouted something from outside the anthropogenic world—in his case, a wild animal—in order to bring it inside the physical and social institution of art (more concretely, a commercial gallery). Just as the water in Haacke's installation was pumped back into the Rhine after the artist's intervention had modified it, the coyote was released after its experience of living with Beuys. The action would become foundational for Beuysian mythmaking; its long-term impact on the coyote is harder to guess. For the duration of the performance, the exhibition space of Galerie René Block was a closed system. Beuys, it bears mentioning, transgressed neither the boundary between the gallery's public-facing side and its infrastructure, as did his US counterpart Michael Asher, nor that between its physical inside and outside, as conceptual artist Daniel Buren did at another New York gallery in nearly the same moment.[118] The piece does not, then, seem especially to criticize or even thematize the historically specific convention of the "white cube." Beuys and the coyote were both locked within the space, and whatever happened between them happened within that closed system. In that sense, *I Like America* can also be compared with slightly earlier systems aesthetics works by Haacke, such as his *Condensation Cube*, which is a sealed, clear, plexiglass container with a small amount of water in it. As the temperature of the surrounding gallery changes, the water in Haacke's cube either evaporates or condenses. It therefore operates as a closed system that nonetheless registers its larger environment, somewhat like a thermometer. In the coyote performance, Block's gallery is equivalent to the plexiglass cube. Whatever happens inside it constitutes a closed system involving two main variables: a human being and an animal. But their interaction indexes larger systems outside the gallery's restricted ecology, among which are the ideological functions of a pointedly "mythical" creature.

In this work, there is an ecological aesthetic that goes beyond that somewhat naively environmentalist idea of, for instance, planting trees to make an urban space more pleasant, which is the substance of his most famous ecological project, *7000 Eichen* (7,000 oaks) (fig. 25). What is involved, rather, is a series of inputs and outputs that effect an exchange between material and semiotic systems. The coyote moves between two different semiotic conditions at the same time as it moves in and out of the gallery. It changes from being a wild animal to being the stuff of an artwork, as does the body of the artist. This is a kind of economy. The coyote as well as the human body take on a different value once they are processed through the art system, or to put it slightly differently, through the art institution— in this case, a gallery. If we return to the *Gesamtkunstwerk Hamburg*, we see that there is potentially a final horizon for this process. That horizon would be the total work of art as literally everything: the subsumption of all material, social, and semiotic systems to the master category of art. If a city can become an artwork signed "Joseph Beuys," then anything can. This is the same power that discloses the exact day on which capitalism will end.

Now consider *Honigpumpe* one more time. Its system—its ecology—is neither exactly open nor closed. It is both at once. The circulation of honey is closed. Although there seems to have been some seepage (publisher Gerhard Steidl's photographs suggest as much), and although the steel pooling container introduced an element of latency and accumulation at odds with the motor's dynamism, the honey never escaped its circulatory system because it never escaped its plastic tubing. Yet it was, metaphorically, also somehow meant to absorb the mental or spiritual energy of the work's other notable component: the collective sociality of knowledge production. The latter system was open because it had inputs (living participants at *documenta*) as well as outputs (new ideas, blackboards filled with bullet points and arrows, and the bodies of the same participants after leaving

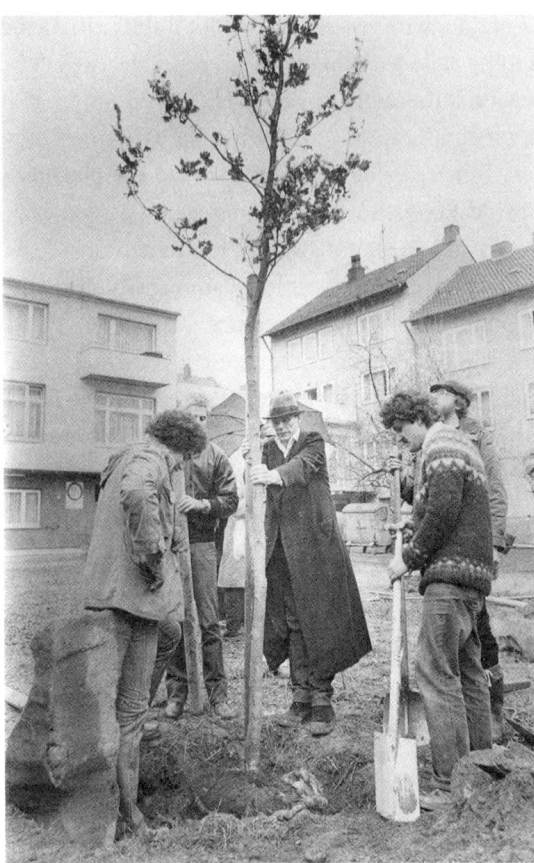

**Fig. 25.**
Joseph Beuys, *7000 Eichen*
(7,000 oaks), 1982. Photo-
lithograph. $5^{13/16} \times 4^{1/8}$ in.
(14.7 × 10.4 cm).

the Fridericianum) that were not permanent parts of the installation but
rather variables that entered and exited its more restricted ecology over
the course of the exhibition's hundred days.

One can easily imagine the hot topic of cybernetics popping up during
some of the *documenta* discussions, even if no trace remains in the archives.
Beuys is not usually thought of in connection with the transit between
systems-theoretical analysis and twentieth-century art, or if so, his work
stands for a romantic reaction against those trends. A more proximate point
of reference, though, is philosopher Max Bense, whom Beuys engaged in a
heated discussion at the Werner-von-Siemens-Schule, Düsseldorf, in 1970.
Bense was an important conduit for the spread of both semiotics and systems theory to the German-speaking world. Claus Pias, a media theorist,

has narrated this encounter as one between late modernist rationality and postmodern irrationalism.[119] This opposition is too straightforward. *I Like America* and *Honigpumpe* were "systems" artworks too, and over the past few paragraphs, I have shown (without even especially belaboring the point) that one can describe them quite readily in the cybernetic language of inputs, outputs, and feedback mechanisms. They were real ecologies and social situations, and at the same time metaphors of things beyond: economies and political orders. Beuysian ecology involves all of this.

Haacke is the more modest artist in this comparison because he limits his interventions to what art or the aesthetic can reasonably do. The aesthetic can extract things from larger systems or constitute an autonomous, closed system of its own (which may, of course, model other, larger ones as a form of representation). But to go beyond this—to posit that art can absorb everything—is to step into dangerous territory. Art's autonomy in the modern age was a hard-won zone of freedom, or at least something mimicking it. From a certain, powerfully influential point of view, that mimesis of freedom is art's only politics. To subsume everything to art is also, simultaneously, to expose art to the danger of being subsumed to something else. Something more powerful and more violent. To make sociality part of an ecology of which the extraction of surplus value is another aspect is to reinscribe capitalism's logic. At least potentially.

# Chapter 3. The Shape of History

## 1.

In what follows, the center of gravity shifts from economics to politics, with the latter understood as the collective production of history. Germany's political and economic development after 1945 was unique among the Western European nations for reasons that are not hard to decipher: the heavy weight of the Nazi past along with the subsequent occupation and partition of the country. One result of this partition was the absence of a mass communist party in the BRD. Though it had an outpost in West Berlin, East Germany's ruling Socialist Unity Party (Sozialistische Einheitspartei Deutschlands) never made much headway in the Federal Republic, and the national Communist Party that would have been its natural ally disappeared in 1956—or rather, was banned, albeit without much fanfare. This was in contrast to Italy and France, where communist parties marshaled formidable voting blocs throughout the postwar era. The dynamics of state planning, free or semifree markets, and revolutionary opposition outlined in the previous chapter necessarily looked different in those contexts.

Italy exerted a particular fascination on Beuys from the time of his first visit as an established artist in 1971.[1] Characteristically, he attributed this attraction at least in part to a seminal moment in his youth. As a soldier in 1943, he had been stationed at Foggia in the southern region of Puglia. Many years later, he would claim that this short period was the basis for his "deep relationship to those forces that are in present in Italy."[2] In a letter to his parents dated February 8, 1943, Beuys wrote that the country is "wonderfully beautiful," but that the area where he is stationed is a "frightfully barren area, where in summer the heat is 70 degrees and already [that is, in early February] during the day it is 30 degrees." We may doubt his figures; 70 degrees Celsius is 158 degrees Fahrenheit. Nonetheless, his enthusiasm for the "colorfulness and vibrancy of this landscape" seems genuine.[3]

In the same letter, Beuys notes that his passage through Italy proceeded over the Brenner Pass, followed by stops in Verona, Florence, Rome, and Naples. His itinerary closely tracks Goethe's *Italienische Reise* a century and a half before—the most famous of all German pilgrimages to the south. This may have been a happenstance of military logistics. Less likely to be fortuitous, however, is his invocation of that same journey in a major work that took shape over the years 1970–72: *Arena—Dove sarei arrivato se fossi stato intelligente!* (Arena—Where would I have got if I had been intelligent!) (plate 2).[4] The core of the piece is a set of one hundred rectangular panels onto each of which are mounted between one and six black-and-white photographs of actions, sculptures, or drawings that Beuys had realized since the 1950s. A small number of these photographs are further enhanced by the application of either yellow paint or Braunkreuz (Beuys's brown oil-based pigment). There are three exceptions to the rule. First, there are two identical monochrome blue panels and one monochrome yellow panel that do not contain photographs. And second, there is a single panel (number 13) that contains a photograph that does not depict either Beuys or one of his works. The subject is instead the Roman amphitheater (or arena) in the city of Verona, from which the entire complex seems to have taken its name. Beuys assembled the first version of the work for the exhibition *Strategy: Get Arts* at the Edinburgh College of Arts in 1970.[5] At that time, the photographs were mounted on humble poster board, and the installation did not yet include the yellow and blue monochromes. Nor had it acquired its Italian subtitle.

In Edinburgh, most of the panels were simply propped up against the bottom of the gallery wall, although a few were hung at eye level in a more usual fashion. The work functioned here as something like a photographic retrospective of Beuys's oeuvre. The collection could not yet have been complete since some of the snapshots that would end up in the final version of the work date from later than 1970. (Panel 24, for example, captures an awkward-looking Beuys celebrating his fiftieth birthday at the Kunstakademie Düsseldorf in 1971.) The installation attracted little attention in the press at the time. Far more widely remarked on were Beuys's two other contributions to the show: *The Pack (das Rudel)*, 1969, and the first iteration of *Celtic*, his collaborative action with composer Henning Christiansen, which was here titled, in full, *Celtic (Kinloch Rannoch) Scottish Symphony*.[6] The panels only acquired their metal and glass frames in summer 1972, when the installation was reworked for exhibition at gallerist Lucio Amelio's Modern Art Agency in Naples, at which point the piece seems to have received its full-length Italian title. Here the photographic panels were further supplemented with two piles of wax and fat layered with sheets of iron and copper as well as an oil can. These props were used in an action titled *Vitex agnus castus* that Beuys performed at the show's opening on June 15 of that year.[7]

Curator Lynne Cooke notes that in choosing the Verona amphitheater as the work's namesake as well as its single photographic outlier, Beuys almost certainly would have had in mind the structure's memorable appearance in Goethe's *Italian Journey*.[8] It was, Goethe writes, "the first great monument of the ancient world I have seen." For Goethe, the ruins in Verona were impressive not in the first order as architecture but rather as an image of vanished collectivity:

> When I entered it, and even more when I wandered about on its highest rim, I had the peculiar feeling that, grand as it was, I was looking at nothing. It ought not to be seen empty but packed with human beings.... But only in ancient times, when a people were more of a people than today, can it have made its full effect. Such an amphitheatre, in fact, is properly designed to impress the people with itself, to make them feel at their best.
>
> When something worth seeing is taking place on level ground and everybody crowds forward to look, those in the rear find various ways of raising themselves to see over the heads of those in front: some stand on benches, some roll up barrels, some bring carts on which they lay planks crosswise, some occupy a neighboring hill. In this way in no time they form a crater. Should the spectacle be often repeated on the same spot, makeshift stands are put up for those who can pay, and the rest manage as best they can. To satisfy this universal need is the architect's task. By his art he creates as plain a crater as possible and the public itself supplies its decoration. Crowded together, its members are astonished at themselves. They are accustomed at other times to seeing each other running hither and thither in confusion, bustling about without order or discipline. Now this many-headed, many-minded, fickle, blundering

monster suddenly sees itself united as one noble assembly, welded into a mass, a single body animated by a single spirit.[9]

What we are reading in this passage is an organicist metaphor of society of the kind that disturbs Éric Michaud. From here it may not be far to Goebbels's notion of society as an artwork. The crucial difference is that Goebbels refers to a "sculptor" who shapes the human mass, whereas it seems that Goethe imagines his socius as emerging immanently within and as the crowd itself.[10] Specular collectivism without a sovereign is different from what either Goebbels or Michaud has in mind. If Beuys indeed meant for the collective presence of his hundred panels to evoke Goethe's "noble assembly," then the political interpretation of that gesture hangs on whether he follows one or the other of these two models. This in turn would seem to depend on the role of the "social sculptor" and thus finally on Beuys himself.

There are two problems with mapping Goethe's social vision directly onto Beuys's *Arena*. The first is that in some ways, Beuys's installation does not appear to be social at all since the photographs (with the exception of that of the arena) depict either Beuys's body or his works as opposed to a well-rounded community. Other human figures turn up here and there, but only as spectators, or at best, assistants. The second problem is that the dynamics of mutual recognition that are so crucial to Goethe's scenario likewise seem absent given that the collection of photographs suggests not exchange but rather accumulation—that is, not a community so much as a storehouse. The work functioned exactly in this way. In its definitive Naples showing in 1972, not all of the panels were visibly on display. Many were instead sandwiched between and behind others in stacks that leaned against the gallery walls. In its third installation, at the 1973 exhibition *Contemporanea* in Rome, Beuys "unpacked" the panels and displayed them as pictures on the wall of a subterranean parking lot under the Villa Borghese.[11] In this instance, the work's mode of presentation was conventional, but its site was not. A parking lot is after all a kind of storage facility more akin to a museum's depot than to its public galleries. Finally, the panels were stacked up once again for Beuys's 1979 Guggenheim retrospective. They sat on the museum's rotunda in proximity to *Unschlitt/Tallow* and *Straßenbahnhaltestelle*. This was *Arena*'s most condensed presentation. Only three of the one hundred panels here turned their front sides to the exhibition's spectators. The rest lay dormant behind them.

The wax and metal stacks that Beuys added to the work for its Naples debut bear a clear relationship to the *Fond* sculptures that I discussed in my first chapter. *Arena*'s invisible panels too, at least in some of the work's incarnations, seem to play a role akin to these piles of felt and copper. Perhaps they are also "batteries" standing in reserve. Like the *Fond* series, *Arena* is characterized by a logic of accumulation that plays out in both material and metaphoric registers. Recall that the photographs embedded in the work date from the course of at least a decade and picture nearly the whole breadth of Beuys's production—in other words, his (artistic) labor. Beuys was not a photographer.[12] The pictures used in *Arena* must have belonged to Beuys, but they were the product of collective creativity; the artist amalgamated these images into a new, concentrated arrangement. Photographs are a kind of storage device. They "capture" a moment in time. Barthes associated this quality with death.[13] *Arena* literally accumulates, re-presents, and refigures Beuys's work. In this it has something in common with other projects from the period. His massive album of drawings, *The Secret Block for a Secret Person in Ireland*, dates from 1974, for example.[14]

*Honigpumpe*, as I have said, collapses multiple temporalities into its socioeconomic metaphor. The work is an image of present and future. It is an image of the existing capitalist welfare state, a response to a crisis within that order, and finally a revelation of a new order to come. It also echoes past attempts at the Gestaltung of society. The trouble is in sorting out how these temporalities intersect. *Honigpumpe* stands for collectivity, thanks to the trope of the beehive. *Arena* represents collectivity too, but it stands, more clearly than does *Honigpumpe*, for a principle of mute, maybe deathly accumulation. There was no motorized circulation here. In this it resembles the *Fond* sculptures and thus belongs to the "cold," crystalline pole of the artist's production. Photographs of actions and artworks, once performed or made by living bodies, are now entombed in metal cases. They are hidden from view and powerful only as a gathering potential, like the "noble assembly" before it recognizes itself—but also like money piling up in a vault. *Arena* superimposes a metaphor of accumulation atop one of sociality. If what is being accumulated is, in fact, past labor—artistic performances and artworks transfixed in the spectral medium of the photograph—then we quickly find ourselves amid the gothic rhetoric to which Marx was drawn as he sought to describe the parasitic relationship between "living" and "dead" labor. This is perhaps the only way in which sociality, or rather social labor, really can accumulate in capitalism:

as capital. If that is the message of *Arena*, then we will have to take another look at *Honigpumpe* too.

Now that the tropes of accumulation and circulation have brushed against capital and death, we are better poised to take stock of things. This book's argument so far has been the following. In the first chapter, I elucidated the transit between concept and material form in Beuys's sculptures of the 1970s, and tried to say how it is that what I call "myth" aimed to stabilize that relation. In the second chapter, I reconstructed Beuys's economics, which offer a partial solution to the problem of meaning through mimesis of the form of value. The process of value accumulation was the anchor that prevented his myth from floating off into the ether. But it also raised stubborn problems. In particular, my analysis brought to the fore two related contradictions in Beuys's claim that "art = capital": first, the contradiction between the automatism of economic circulation and the principle of conscious control (or Gestaltung), and second, that between the particularity of material artworks and the abstract universality of money. These divergent metaphors make for contradictions rather than antagonisms because they are manifest in the *same* works of art. The stake of the analysis, then, is to show how or whether these opposed impulses have something to do with each other, despite appearances. Later in the same chapter, I described the historical conditions under which this project took shape and perhaps made a kind of sense—namely, the postwar development of a welfare state, in the context of which capital accumulation occurred alongside a massive expansion of social protections and therefore continued state intervention into the economy.

I have noted the problem that *Arena* raises for Beuys's socioeconomic logic. The installation layers a metaphor of human collectivity atop a metaphor of accumulation to which the first trope would seem to be opposed. *Honigpumpe* does so as well, but in a less perspicuous way, since honey does continue to circulate in a closed loop; nothing is either added or subtracted. The "accumulated" substance in this case is immaterial collective knowledge. *Arena*, by contrast, stills past action into dead and, in most iterations of the piece, largely invisible form. This is a contradiction analogous to Beuys's claim that money at once has to be a legal document and a naturally circulating substance like blood. The one is a human construct, and the other something that occurs whether humans will it or not. The problem again is that of the relation between freedom and necessity.

The present chapter starts to bring the argument to its close. Here we return to fracture, crisis, and trauma in the context of a break in the postwar political, economic, and social order of the BRD in the late 1960s and 1970s. I will describe Beuys's navigation of this state of affairs, which put the "personal" ideology that he had developed in the 1950s and early 1960s to the test of public scrutiny. It was in proposing an alternative to other, less conciliatory responses to the problems of his era that socioplasticity came into its own. But his solution had a remainder. That remainder was negativity, or in the last instance, death. The particular form that death took in Beuys's work is a consequence of, or at least is correlated with, his art's economimesis and turns on the place of negativity in an ecological practice that never resolved a conflict between its models: the infinitude of capital accumulation as opposed to the closed loop of a sustainable homeostatic (eco)system. (This was the thrust of the contrast between Haacke and Beuys that I developed at the end of the previous chapter.) Just prior to concluding, I will try to drive this conflict to its extreme by advancing a totalizing—but only possible, not definitive—reading of the artist's 1979 installation of his work at the Guggenheim, which I suggest can be interpreted as implying a horrific equivalence between the Nazi economy of death and postwar capitalism. Before getting to these more abstract and disturbing ideas, though, I will start with a device that has so far not received much attention in my analysis—namely, Beuys's use of glass vitrines. These works pose the question of value in another way.

## 2.

A vitrine sculpture accumulates objects within a standard museological display mechanism. They have this in common with the glassed frames of *Arena* and hence evoke related problems. Beuys's vitrine sculptures tend to bear dates that reflect a loose sense of their entire process of gestation, such as 1956–64 for the *Auschwitz Demonstration* vitrine (now in the *Block Beuys* in Darmstadt) (plate 9) or 1960–72 for *Untitled (Phytolacca americana)*, an austere assemblage named after a species of North American weed.[15] As a rule, the initial year in a given vitrine's date seems to refer to the point at which Beuys created or appropriated the earliest of the objects contained within the piece, whereas the latest refers either to the date of the last discrete object that it encases, or the year in which Beuys sealed and thus completed the finished work. Regardless of the actual timing of their production, it appears that Beuys first exhibited vitrines around 1968.[16] Hence it was the last of the artist's major forms to be developed, some years after the "action" and sculptural installation—both of which emerged in the early 1960s—as well as the multiple (1965).[17] Drawing and sculpture proper had been central to Beuys's practice from its origins in the late 1940s.[18]

The syntax of the vitrines is difficult to parse for the same reason that an installation such as *zeige deine Wunde* flickers between modes of interpretation. Any object in such an arrangement may mean something specific, a multiplicity of things, or perhaps nothing at all. The vitrines foreground a problem that emerges whenever viewers assess the ontological status of Beuys's art. Objects in these works are frequently related to actions that the artist had performed either in close association with the production of the vitrine itself or in some cases a good while before. Other assemblages in the format, by contrast, seem nearer to the *Fond* series in both materials and strategy. They incorporate piles or rolls of felt, copper canes, brooms, drawings, other items daubed with Braunkreuz, preexisting multiples, and so forth—that is, objects and substances that occupy legible positions within the Beuysian symbolic cosmos. Like the *Fond* sculptures and *Arena*, they rely on a logic of accumulation.

Finally, there is a third category of materials that is present in the vitrines, though it overlaps with both of the above. This category consists of forms of matter that are perishable (such as foodstuffs, or the remnants of animals and plants) as well as other objects that are off-putting in one way or another, even if they do not literally induce nausea, as might the decaying masses of sausage or dead rabbits found in some of the artist's works. Consider the wax *Mundplastik* (Mouth sculpture) impressions today found in the eighth vitrine in the fifth room of the *Block Beuys* installation in Darmstadt, which the artist produced by biting pieces of wax in the course of his action *Hauptstrom Fluxus* (Mainstream Fluxus) in 1967.[19] These wax objects are indexical marks of the body and thus perhaps can be related to contemporaneous developments in US performance art, such as Vito Acconci's *Trademarks*, 1971, in which the artist bit every part of his body that his teeth could reach and then made prints from the indentations. The *Mundplastik* works convey the visceral suggestion of human saliva, regardless of how clean they may be.

A useful word to describe this stomach-turning quality is surely "abject." Such things are degraded. Yet many of these objects, perhaps all of them, simultaneously function as relics, or as something like relics, indeed in a manner close to the religious sense of the term.[20] The *Mundplastik* sculptures have come into contact with the artist's body in a particularly intimate way, and artists are unusual humans. Beuys's body was a locus of even greater charismatic power thanks to his persona as shaman and healer. We have noted this in connection with the *Kunst = Kapital* banknotes, which are literally valorized by their contact with the artist's touch (in this case, his signature, which is a conventional emblem of artistic authenticity). The "relics" in the vitrines would thus also seem to bear a meaning that transcends their material abjection, as do the bones and bits of flesh in Christian reliquaries. Beuys's relics are emissaries of the divine power of creativity. By contact with that power, they become sacralized. The dynamic should be familiar by now. It is not dissimilar to what I have said about *Unschlitt/Tallow*'s equivocation between mute literalness and the metaphor of healing, or *zeige deine Wunde*'s suggestions of both mortality and mortality's opposite. The important point is the ambiguity that such works exude between great worth and worthlessness. This is the characteristically Beuysian tension between the status of the relic and that of abject refuse.

It is not just that the vitrines often resemble buildups of trash, however. They also frequently suggest injury, death, or disease. Take, for example, *Doppelobjekte* (Double objects), 1974–79, which is close in its iconography and mode of presentation to *zeige deine Wunde* (plate 10). Among other things on display in this work (such as a pair of enamel bowls) are two X-ray photographs of a human chest. It is perhaps, though not necessarily, the artist's own. This reminder of human weakness sits uneasily with the metaphorics of the work's presentation. The deployment of the vitrine is a musealizing gesture, although vitrines are more likely to be found in museums of anthropology, archaeology, or natural history than of art. Vitrines call into question the distinction between artworks and other kinds of objects, natural or human-made. What they do not inherently question is the specialness of whatever happens to be inside. Things are usually only put into vitrines because they are valuable and require protection. By convention, the format separates what it contains from the rest of the world and most immediately from the viewer's touch. The device therefore allows a "staging of the abject" that is simultaneously a form of distancing from it, as theater scholar Barbara Gronau has pointed out.[21] Yet it may be that the abject is not so easily kept at bay. The *Block Beuys*, especially, remains a difficult work to appraise in a mood of disinterested contemplation. The excessive nearness of its organic matter within the densely packed installation allows its viewers few chances to establish a properly "aesthetic" remove. (Which is not to say that the works accordingly elude the aesthetic altogether; here it is appropriate to mention that Derrida's essay "Economimesis" develops a theory of disgust, or more particularly, the immanence of disgust to the system of the beautiful as the parergon of the aesthetic.[22] The immanence of excreta such as vomit to aesthetic totalization will return as a matter of interest in the coda that follows the present chapter.) *Doppelobjekte* also conveys an effect of simultaneous fascination and repulsion. X-ray transparencies are by their nature forensic objects. They are made to be seen. Yet the vitrine enforces a certain distance. Viewers are physically unable to approach close enough to make the prints medically useful. If one could, there is always the potential that what will be discovered will turn out to be pathological. The vitrine enables a staging of this encounter that would not be possible had the X-rays simply been hung on the wall.

Finally, Beuys's use of vitrines is borrowed not only from museums but from the techniques of advertising and commercial display. The incorporation of multiples into some of these works (such as vitrine seven in room seven of the *Block Beuys*, which encloses no less than four of them) strengthens the association, since editioned multiples really are commodities produced for the market.[23] When encountering a vitrine, one can never be sure, at first, whether the things inside will turn out to be art, relics, commodities, or a bit of all three. In this sense, they revert to the ambiguity that accounts for the fascination of early modern cabinets of curiosities—an association that comes perhaps too easily to art historians writing on vitrines in contemporary art. Or at least this would be the case if it were possible to bracket the institutional context of the device (its placement in a museum or department store). This is true of vitrines in general. The possibility that the objects might also be trash seems to be Beuys's distinctive contribution to the repertoire. Some works, such as the *Hasengrab* (Hare's grave) case now in a private collection, go out of their way to pile up the most inconsequential materials possible.[24]

Beuys thus desublimates the vitrine, even as he relies on the form's suggestion of preciousness to designate the enclosed objects as "art" or perhaps even something higher—as the fetishes of a cult. Beuys's claim to distinctiveness in this regard is admittedly open to challenge. In "Beuys:

The Twilight of the Idol," Buchloh stresses the continuity between Beuys's use of vitrines and French artist Arman's "Accumulations" and "Poubelles" (Trash bins), the first examples of which date from around 1960. The German artist's works evoke many of the same issues, such as postwar commodity culture and the advent of disposable products. Still, I think the imbrication of the commodity with the negative with which I am concerned is less evident in Arman, though it is certainly there too. The very act of "entombing" objects within cases has a deathly aspect and hence it is no surprise that similar associations have occurred to viewers of Arman's work. I do not believe that Beuys's adoption of the vitrine can be attributed straightforwardly to Arman's influence, although Arman's solo exhibition at Galerie Schmela, Düsseldorf, in summer 1960 certainly attracted attention in the local art world. In the 1960s, however, vitrines could also be found in the work of the US artists Claes Oldenburg and Paul Thek, among others. The use of the device seems like a natural outgrowth of Fluxus presentation strategies, especially the modular box or "Fluxkit." It is a short step from box to vitrine; the main difference is that the latter emphasizes passive spectatorship more than tactile activation. It might therefore be plausible to consider the vitrine as something like an emergent period device that suggested itself to a number of artists in response to similar artistic and extra-artistic circumstances.[25]

An example will clarify what nevertheless make Beuys a little different. The vitrine titled *Ausfegen* (Sweeping up) is one of the most literal demonstrations of the maneuver. The work's "filling" consists of a broom as well as the sundry materials that this very broom presumably was used to sweep up from Karl-Marx-Platz in West Berlin during an action that Beuys performed in the wake of a large political demonstration on May 1, 1972 (plate 11). The *Ausfegen* vitrine thus contains literal rubbish, a large amount of which consists of crumpled left-wing flyers. There would seem to be no reason to conserve waste in such an ostentatious manner. The performance that resulted in the *Ausfegen* vitrine took place during a critical moment of transformation within the West German Left. May 1972 was the peak of the Red Army Faction's first round of violent activity. Beuys's reactions to leftist militancy will receive greater notice in my book's coda. What is important here is that this fact of chronology itself indicates one locus for the issue of "trauma" in Beuys's oeuvre. The sculpture bears witness to the existence of conflict within the postwar European welfare state, as do the paired copies of the communist newspaper *Lotta Continua* in *zeige deine Wunde*.

To trash and trauma, then, we should add "politics" as a third term in play in a work such as this. How do these various ingredients—the abject use of materials in much of Beuys's art; that same work's evident reference to trauma or wounding (in Greek, *trauma* simply means wound), and finally its engagement with radical politics—add up to something coherent? Do they at all?

## 3.

An easy answer is at hand. Beuys's trauma was his experience in the Second World War, which he made stand for the traumas of modernity writ large. Yet our understanding of that experience is the product of unreliable narration. Hence the aura that such objects radiate may turn out to be based on displacement and fiction rather than indexical immediacy. *Unschlitt/ Tallow*'s connotations of healing and injury were subject to a related displacement. The traumatic relic promises unquestionable meaning. Beuys evokes that promise only to undermine it. This occurs so often in his work that it seems less subterfuge than strategy. Despite their seeming metonymic immediacy, religious relics in the proper sense can also be subject to displacement along replicatory chains. Art historian Christopher S. Wood has argued that in the context of the "premodern substitutional paradigm" for religious images—which in medieval Christianity were frequently themselves treated as miracle-working relics—a replication of an object could be considered just as "original" as the lost object that it replaced as long as certain guarantees of accuracy were observed.[26] The discursive supplement that secures the link between, for example, the substance of fat and its narrative point of origin in the Tatar legend serves as mythical metadata somewhat as does a label informing us that an otherwise unidentifiable finger bone is that of a given saint. Benjaminian auratic authenticity thus emerges here as a metadiscursive effect subject to tropological displacement.[27]

If that is the case, the exact register of Beuysian "trauma" becomes difficult to specify. Slippage is integral rather than extraneous to the logic of trauma, though. This is after all how Sigmund Freud explains the *Wiederholungszwang*, or repetition compulsion, which has its art historical manifestations too. In the 1990s, art critic Hal Foster borrowed from Freud to posit *Nachträglichkeit*, or delayed action, as the master term for the relation between the "historical" or pre–World War II avant-garde and its postwar (neo-avant-garde) successors.[28] In Freud's account, traumatic events do not necessarily have immediate effects. They produce symptoms later on that register not so much the event as a disavowal of it. These symptoms require decoding because their operation is to conceal and yet also acknowledge what has happened. In effect, trauma does not really occur until it is repeated in a symptom that simultaneously effaces the original event. Hence Freud's never resolved uncertainty about whether it matters if a given infantile scene happened at all (for example, whether the "Wolf Man" really saw his parents engaged in coitus a tergo).[29] Foster claims that the historical avant-garde marked a rupture in the history of art and culture. This rupture was then (partially) repressed in the twentieth century's various returns to order. The neo-avant-garde is consequently the return of the repressed—and paradoxically this return itself in some sense constitutes its own traumatic origin. One of the neo-avant-garde's most characteristic effects or strategies is what Foster elsewhere calls "traumatic realism"—phenomena of pathological repetition and discontinuity that indicate a history of repression.[30]

Condensation and displacement are operative in the formation of symptoms just as much as in that of dream images. But condensation and displacement are *un*conscious processes, whereas Beuys's work presumably entailed at least a modicum of conscious control. Similarly, in Foster's presentation of the concept, it is sometimes ambiguous whether traumatic realism is an unconscious reaction, in which case it truly would be a variant of the Freudian symptom, or whether it is an aesthetic strategy that artists consciously pursue. This ambiguity is not necessarily external to the art. How is it possible to claim, irrefutably, that a given form is an instance of one or the other modality? How is it possible to say that one "traumatic" reference is a piece of belabored, if not arbitrary, symbolism, whereas another is involuntary and thus in some way irrefutably motivated? Can trauma be cultivated as an effect without losing its peculiar legitimacy? These questions are relevant to Beuys.

The example of *Ausfegen* points in one direction. The major trauma at stake in German art after 1945 was, naturally, that of the Second World War.[31] *Ausfegen*, however, makes no direct reference to Nazism or the war, whereas it does, by contrast, clearly refer to Beuys's attempts to position himself with respect to contemporaneous leftist politics. This relation was always fraught, especially where his own colleagues and students were concerned. Such conditions perhaps contribute to the "traumatic" quality of Beuys's art, along with the legacy of the Nazi era. Or rather, the two phenomena become overdetermined, condensed. This still may not be adequate to explain the deathliness of some of the pieces that I have already brought into the discussion. *Zeige deine Wunde*, for example, will likely strike some viewers as over the top in its invocations of death and debility, even as the piece—like *Ausfegen* and most, though not all, of the vitrines—lacks explicit allusions to Nazi atrocities. Either personal or political trauma might account for some of the work's morbidity, but in what measure? And finally, why did Beuys's process of formalizing his response to trauma take this particular path, characterized as it is not only by a distinctly morbid iconography (the stretchers from the morgue; the X-rays in *Doppelobjekte*) but also, in *zeige deine Wunde* and a significant number of other works, by a strict principle of doubling, which is perhaps an inherently uncanny motif? To understand Beuys, it is imperative to give reasons for the most extreme and unsettling manifestations of the artist's practice—those that most urgently seem to call for a language of pathology.

To start with, these might be a straightforward expression of unease. It need not have been unease in an existential or world historical register but rather such as pertained to the artist's insecure institutional status during the years under consideration. This counterfactual is worth pursuing if only to block the interpretative shortcut that would relate every aspect of his production to a single primal scene. If the plane crash only became an operative myth in the 1960s, then to what concrete needs, to what sense of reality, did the artist's *work* on myth correspond? Surely to the emergence of a German *Erinnerungskultur* (culture of remembrance). But this new style of coming to terms with the past was not distinct from the political earthquake of these years. Already around forty as the decade began, Beuys effectively belonged to the *Tätergeneration* (perpetrators' generation) of his students' parents, even as he aimed to position himself as a model for their burgeoning radicalism. This awkward position placed special demands on an experimental artist, especially one lacking the exculpating circumstances of either a prewar modernist practice, "inner migration," or exile.

It does not seem that Beuys had a readymade response to the eruption of social conflict and economic instability that emerged at the end of the 1960s. His attempts to engage with and at times appropriate the politics of a younger, radicalized generation—that of his students at the Kunstakademie Düsseldorf—bear the marks of improvisation rather than masterful command. *Ausfegen* was one manifestation of this process; his pedagogical strategies were another. Eyewitness accounts of the *Beuysklasse* circa 1968 to 1972 leave the reader with the impression of a maelstrom. Beuys was at its center, but it is demonstrably not the case that all of his pupils were under the spell of the master's charismatic authority. Decades later, art historian Petra Richter was to conduct interviews with many such former students.[32] These are studded with instances of self-positioning with respect to Beuys. While the interviewees frequently note the overwhelming force of their teacher's personality as well as the sometimes devastating effects of his criticism, others claim to have had a more distanced or autonomous relationship. Some were even explicitly antagonistic. Comments often emphasize that although Beuys's personality may have been dominant in the classroom, his actual artistic production was hardly known even to his most loyal students until he began exhibiting more widely in the late 1960s. Beuys was, if anything, astonishingly permissive vis-à-vis his students. Some of what they made resembles his work; much of it, however, does not—perhaps because few of them had seen it. In the case of Imi Knoebel and Imi Giese, Beuys handed over the keys to an entire classroom (room nineteen) at the Kunstakademie, where the pair effectively had free reign. Here they created one of the landmark sculptural installations of the era.[33] Although there were certainly acolytes, such as Johannes Stüttgen, other students were indifferent or oblivious to the elaborate cosmology behind their professor's actions.

Moreover, toward the end of Beuys's tenure at the Kunstakademie, his classes overflowed with an alphabet soup of political groupings that competed for a share of attention with his own German Student Party, Organization for Nonvoters, and Organization for Direct Democracy through Referendum.[34] At the beginning of the 1970s, these included the Kommunistischer Studentenverband (Communist Student League, an organ of the Maoist Kommunistische Partei Deutschlands—Aufbauorganisation, sometimes translated as Communist Party of Germany—Organizational Structure), Rote Zelle Kunst (Red Cell Art, founded by artists Erinna König and Henning Brandis in room thirteen of the Beuysklasse; it was one of many "Red Cells" established at universities across the nation), Marxistischer Studentenbund Spartakus (Marxist Student League Spartacus, an outgrowth of the pro-Soviet Deutsche Kommunistische Partei, or the German Communist Party), artists Jörg Immendorff and Chris Reinecke's LIDL group, and finally the antiauthoritarian YIUP group, which actively disrupted Beuys's presentations and even went so far as to steal his signature hat during a television shoot in 1971. (YIUP gave him five tinfoil dunce caps in exchange.)[35] It may be, then, that the edifice of Beuysian myth was intended to assert control over a situation that was not under control at all. In this context, the more or less automatic legitimacy effect of trauma may have been appealing insofar as it could ground an infallibly meaningful artistic practice. How could Beuys's authority, at least in matters pertaining to the significance of his own art, ever be questioned if it arose from something as primal as his rescue on the steppes of Crimea? Thus it is perhaps no coincidence that the solidification of Beuys's socioplastic terminology in the late 1960s and early 1970s occurred at the same moment as difficulties with the administration of the Kunstakademie that resulted in a highly publicized dismissal from that institution in 1972, nominally for refusing to cap enrollment in his courses. Beuys then found a new role in the public eye after the loss of his former home base. That his firing turned the artist into a cause célèbre was crucial to his reorientation in the 1970s. This crisis situation at once pushed the old metaphors into the limelight and put them under exceptional pressure.[36]

Here, then, is trauma in an immediate and literal sense. Political upheaval represented a challenge to the coherence of the practice and theory that Beuys had developed over the previous decade. Whereas in the earlier 1960s he was able to occupy the role of the avant-gardist operating well ahead of the culture at large, the emergence of the student movement exposed him to the risk of lagging behind a newly radicalized vanguard.[37] While making clear his opposition to Marxist materialism, Beuys allowed his classrooms to breed subversion. Contemporary attacks launched in the orbit of the Kunstakademie Düsseldorf circa 1968–72 indeed tended to imply that there was something fascistic about this tolerance itself. Beuys was supposed to have encouraged his disciples to antiauthoritarian displays—for the sake of building his own cult of personality. In a curious fashion, it was the antiauthoritarian art students, and by extension their purported ringleader, Beuys, who thereby came to be designated as "antidemocratic and super-authoritarian," as Kunstakademie faculty member Gerhard Hoehme put it in a letter to the academy's director, Eduard Trier, on February 2, 1969.[38] This was likewise the argument of an open letter signed by a large contingent of the Kunstakademie's faculty and administration (including Trier as well as Hoehme and a number of other professors) that was published in the high-profile *Süddeutsche Zeitung* on November 30, 1968. Such accusations were something of a period style.

In 1967, Habermas coined the phrase "left-wing fascism" to criticize the German extraparliamentary opposition. Although he would walk back the term as soon as 1968, by then it had already taken root in German politics and media.[39] It was in this discursive ambience that the Beuys conflict took shape. Internal documents of the Kunstakademie, however, reveal a more complicated picture than the *Süddeutsche* open letter would suggest. Beuys had supporters within and without the school, not all of whom can plausibly be accused of having fallen under the artist's charismatic influence. Moreover, these disputes took place amid intense conflict over a proposed new charter (*Verfassung*) for the Kunstakademie as well as struggles between factions within the school's *Allgemeiner Studentenausschuss*, or general student council; in these years, such councils tended to be dominated by student radicals and especially SDS members. Finally, it was at exactly this moment that a highly public controversy erupted over Immendorff and Reinecke's LIDL activities, which culminated in a brief occupation of the Kunstakademie building—on Beuys's invitation—from May 5 to 7, 1969. Police soon evicted the occupation at Trier's request.[40]

It thus appears that charges of authoritarianism have their classic site, if not their origin, in a power struggle within the Kunstakademie, in the course of which both sides (if there were, indeed, only two of them) frequently turned to the press to advance their claims. Beuys's eventual firing in 1972 likewise resulted from an interinstitutional conflict in which he was alleged to have abused his privileges in a paradoxically "authoritarian" manner. The immediate cause was his rejection of the Kunstkademie's *numerus clausus* policy, which limited the number of students who could be admitted each term. Beuys instead preferred to allow as many people as were interested to attend his classes, regardless of whether they were formally enrolled. Defiance of the school's administration came to be framed as demagoguery. Beuys's supporters were later to mount a fierce and ultimately successful counterattack on the Kunstakademie's own turf. Beuys returned to his studio on campus after winning a lawsuit against the state of Nordrhein-Westfalen on April 7, 1978.[41]

## 4.

Beuys *was* under attack, and from more than one side. The point bears emphasizing especially now as these conflicts recede from living memory.

In fact, the events of 1968–72 were only a culmination of conflicts that had emerged several years earlier. Beuys probably first met public opposition during his action *Kukei, Akopee—Nein!* at the *Festival der Neuen Kunst* (festival of new art) that took place at the Technische Hochschule Aachen on July 20, 1964. This date was the twentieth anniversary of army officer Claus von Stauffenberg's attempt to assassinate Hitler. Indeed, the festival had to be presented to the university as a commemoration of this event in order to be approved at all. Prior to Beuys's entrance, his colleague Bazon Brock had already provoked the audience by playing Goebbels's notorious 1943 "total war" speech over a loudspeaker in the stairwell leading to the auditorium. A common though only circumstantially supported claim in the Beuys literature is that some of the infuriated students visible in documentation of the festival—one of whom struck Beuys in the face—belonged to the far right. During his performance, Beuys inadvertently spilled acid onto a student's clothes, leading the student to attack him. A photograph of Beuys, nose bloodied, with a crucifix in his left hand and his right hand raised at an angle that suggests the Nazi salute, quickly became an iconic image of the artist, although the exact significance of his gesture remains difficult to interpret. The first organized *leftist* protest against Beuys, as far as I can surmise, took place during *Ich versuche dich freizulassen (machen)* (I am trying to set [make] you free), an action that took place at the Akademie der Künste, Berlin, on February 27, 1969. The proceedings were disrupted by students who took the stage and distributed a flyer that criticized "great magicians and ideological quacks."[42] There were good reasons why the artist might have found these years stressful.

Of course, this may still strike readers as an impoverished approach to the issues of trauma and history in his work, which after all involve problems of wider import than intra-academic tussles or leftist pranks. I am thinking of arguments such as art theorist Gene Ray's in his essay "Joseph Beuys and the After-Auschwitz Sublime."[43] Beuys, Ray claims, initiated a "project of mourning" in the aftermath of the Holocaust—the first in German art.[44] Buchloh in turn credits Beuys as the "first artist to address the history of fascism."[45] If so, it was a project that he pursued obliquely rather than in full public view. Unless one includes grave monuments, Beuys only completed a single public memorial, in 1958–59: a set of doors and a crucifix-like hanging sculpture installed in a ruined medieval church tower in the Büderich neighborhood of the town of Meerbusch, which is located between Düsseldorf and Krefeld, the artist's birthplace. The work is somewhat vaguely titled *Memorial to the Dead of the World Wars*. The names incised into the work are those of Büderich's German war dead, not those of deportees.[46] Beuys's use of Christian iconography in works that implicitly or explicitly reference the Holocaust has not gone unnoticed. Art historian Mario Kramer, for instance, finds the incorporation of a crucifix in the *Auschwitz Demonstration* vitrine to be "irritating": "It claims the presence of the mystery of Golgotha in Auschwitz. An alienating idea for Christians as well as Jews."[47] With the Büderich memorial, it may be the case that no such reference was even intended. Aside from his early proposal for a memorial at Auschwitz (materials related to which later found their way into the *Auschwitz Demonstration* vitrine, now housed in the *Block Beuys* installation at the Hessisches Landesmuseum in Darmstadt), direct references to the Nazi period are rare in his work (plate 9). In an interview with artist Max Reithmann in 1982, Beuys tried to explain why: Auschwitz could not be "represented in an image"; hence he would instead attempt to remember it through its "positive counter image."[48]

What does that mean? Presumably Beuys intended for his positive artistic project to redeem historical suffering. He once claimed that his postwar realization of the true extent of Nazi crimes was "my primary experience, my fundamental experience, which led me to begin to really go into art."[49] He thus reversed Adorno's claim that it is barbaric to write poetry after Auschwitz.[50] For Beuys, it was the artist's duty to speak, not to remain silent. This had been the substance of his assertion that "the silence of Marcel Duchamp is overrated," which he first made public during a televised performance in 1964.[51] The notion of silence also figures in perhaps the most outrageous of the artist's statements on the Holocaust: "The human condition is Auschwitz, and the principle of Auschwitz finds its perpetuation in our understanding of science and political systems, in the delegation of responsibility to groups of specialists and in the silence of intellectuals and artists."[52]

Is this massive generalization of the "after-Auschwitz" condition more than an evasion of personal and collective responsibility? And if this is the horizon of Beuysian redemption, then what practice could live up to it? To make another Adornian point, any art that attempts directly to instantiate utopia within wrong life cannot avoid affirming the conditions that deny reconciliation and therefore will betray its own utopian content.[53] Or perhaps it is rather that through its contact with historical disaster, utopia becomes instructively debased. Perhaps in Beuys's time, utopia could only be figured in the dirty fragments of the *Block Beuys* or *zeige deine Wunde*'s macabre mise-en-scène. In which case the contradiction between the material work's negativity and its maker's doctrine would turn out to be its saving grace. This is a problem that art historian Armin Zweite, one of the artist's most persistent interpreters, has attempted to parse by differentiating Beuys's verbal statements, which emphasize healing and reconciliation, from his art, which stresses pain and trauma. In effect, the material oeuvre constitutes a diagnosis and its verbal commentary a prescription, or course of therapy.[54] But things do not seem so clear-cut to me. His discourse is not so unfailingly Pollyannaish; in 1973, he told an interviewer that "death keeps me awake," for example.[55] The place of the negative has not yet been settled, then.

The issues at stake should in any case be recognizable from the preceding discussion of the vitrine sculptures. Those works preserve and present objects that are at once precious (relics or valuable artifacts) and decrepit, or even disgusting. They stand for life and death at once. Doubleness carries through to the larger installations as well. The utopia of *Honigpumpe* is, among other things, a "positive counterimage" of the camps. It seeks to model a society that is the opposite of hell on earth. Yet as any number of commentators have noted—Ray is the most thorough in doing so— Beuys's utopian art is nonetheless permeated with unsublimated traces of mortality, death, and decay. *Honigpumpe* itself is not insulated from these associations, even though it is far from being the most morbid of the artist's works. The whirring of the device in the basement of the museum and its panoply of transparent tubes, which perhaps have surgical connotations, might suggest a grotesque medical apparatus, much like the brace and "thermal elements" in *Unschlitt/Tallow*. If the installation is territorialized by the metaphor of the circulation of blood, which thus makes the Fridericianum into an immense body, it is a body that nevertheless plays host to a blatantly unnatural machinery. It is a body open to the threat of breakdown. If the pump were to have stopped functioning during the exhibition, the piece would have ground to a metaphoric as well as literal halt, with potentially disastrous effects for its socioplastic allegory. (Beuys had suffered a heart attack in 1975, as you will remember.) Moreover, Beuys heaped the base of the pump with a generous helping of fat. Although the artist's statements on the material invariably stress its healing properties, his interpreters have long noted its more unsettling connotations. As a formless remnant of otherwise absent bodies, fat carries with it its possible history of violence. More particularly—at least according to some reports, widely circulated in the postwar era—fat was extracted from the bodies of victims in the Nazi death camps in order to produce soap.[56]

Beuys's art was thus anything but only positive. The deepest scandal of his oeuvre is surely this: that his insistently optimistic vision found material expression in works of art that just as insistently evoke colossal atrocities. But what is perhaps even more difficult to untangle in the Beuysian complex is the multiplicity of its potential referents—such that in the works we have seen in this chapter so far, it is hard to disengage personal registers of trauma either from a broader reflection on German history or contemporaneous political developments. In negotiating the upheavals of the 1960s and 1970s, Beuys was responding to (or rather, helping to create) a new culture of remembrance. This culture was in turn inflected by that very experience of political unrest. Scholarship on the German New Left has drawn attention to the problematic or indeed often appalling ways in which the student movement and extraparliamentary opposition instrumentalized the Holocaust for their political aims. Student activists and hippie communards both compared themselves to Jews being sent to the gas chambers, often without seeming to grasp how this rhetorical maneuver might be profoundly offensive.[57] Similar issues arise in the case of Beuys. How could he speak of "the wound" without speaking much more clearly than he ever did about Germany's annihilation of millions of human beings? But perhaps this shared difficulty in maintaining what, some years later, were to look like necessary boundaries between the memory of the Holocaust and other, less singular events indicates that there was something essential as opposed to contingent about this contagion between different historical and political experiences.[58] It may only have been possible for Germans to develop a belated "memory" of the genocide by processing it through their own immediate political context, which in the period here under examination meant the clash between the nation's leftist counterculture and its conservative establishment.

Hence the issue of Beuys's response to the increasingly radical stances of many of his students is not separate from his response to the aftermath of World War II and the Holocaust. They were sides of the same process. Yet in scholarship on the artist, these two themes—the legacy of World War II and political activism—usually remain separated from each other. They are moreover unequally weighted. Attention to the former aspect of Beuys's production grew steadily from the 1980s onward in tandem with the emergence of a popular and academic discourse on the Holocaust, whereas interest in his relations with the New Left has waxed and waned according to the political climate of the day.[59] Earlier viewers, however, were not unaware of the nexus between Beuys's art and historical catastrophe; as we will see in my book's conclusion, Marcel Broodthaers, for one, picked up on it as early as 1968.[60]

There are two points that I wish to emphasize here. The first is that the relation between Beuys's utopian ambitions and his art's apparent references to the Holocaust is still in need of adequate explanation. (I do not claim to offer such an explanation here, nor do I necessarily think it *can* be offered.) The second point is that it is only infrequently possible to isolate a direct relay in Beuys's oeuvre from the one historical moment to the other—from the 1940s to the 1960s, 1970s, or 1980s. Instead, the referents of his art's traumatic symptoms more often seem ambiguous and multilayered. Beuys was not alone in this respect. The emergence of a German *Erinnerungskultur* among the 1968 generation was indeed widely marked by such temporal displacements. Historian Dagmar Herzog describes this phenomenon in her work on the legacy of the Holocaust in West German New Left sexual politics:

> Beginning to get at this complicated and in obvious ways so deeply freighted set of problems involves drawing not merely on the formative and programmatic texts of the 68ers, though those sources are crucial. It also means trying to make sense of the outpouring of autobiographical memory-essays about their adolescences in the fifties and their sexual comings-of-age in the sixties, written by ex-68ers in the late seventies and early eighties, as their faith in their own ability to sustain both a political and a sexual revolution broke down. This is where attention to the multiplicity and complexity of memory's "layerings" becomes especially important. For what is going on in these memory-texts is an attempt to reconstruct the fifties' interpretations of the thirties and forties within the context of the seventies' and eighties' struggle with the meaning of the sixties.[61]

Matters are different in the case of Beuys, if only by reason of his earlier birth and participation in World War II. He belonged to the generation of many of his students' fathers, but chose to position himself—with some difficulty—in the context of the 1960s' youth revolt. This explains, among other things, the curious time warp of a forty-six-year-old man founding a "German Student Party" in 1967. The aim of such gestures was arguably no less than to pry Beuys loose from generational belonging, which in postwar Germany was treacherous as nowhere else.

We have obviously strayed from where this chapter began, with two superimpositions in Beuys's work: accumulation on sociality in *Arena* and abjection on preciousness in the vitrines. But it only took a few short steps to get here. There is a negativity in Beuys's art that is difficult to make sense of without recourse to the context in which his practice developed. Without indulging in groundless psychological speculation, we perhaps can at least posit that some of the strangeness of his work and persona derives from having attempted to occupy roles at cross-purposes with each other: master and rebel, teacher and student, perpetrator and revolutionary. After the previous chapter, it will not come as a surprise that another of the factors at stake here turns out to be the dominance of value as a social logic in capitalist society. What *may* be surprising is that I invoke this in such proximity to a discussion of the Holocaust and wartime destruction, when for the most part the topics of Nazi-era trauma and the postwar boom have run along separate tracks in scholarship on the artist. Indeed, to transgress this divide may court dangerous relativization. Value, though, is not an "economic" theme that intrudes on the problematic of historical violence from the outside. In Beuys's practice, economics were rather bound up with violence from the start, though the morphology of this relation changes in the shift from the more private iconography of his early work to the public interventions of the late 1960s and 1970s. There was something about terror and value that pushed toward their collision. To see how this happened, we must ask after the several combined yet discretely analyzable elements that account for the work's articulation of the negative. It is necessary to ask, again, Where is the wound?

## 5.

Consider once more the ghoulishness of *zeige deine Wunde*. The installation resembles a morgue, complete with twin metal stretchers laid out for bodies that are, mercifully, absent, although there is a suggestion that their residue persists in the fat-filled containers below. The disquieting sag in the middle of each stretcher, like that left by a body in a mattress, is more evident in person than in photographs. I have noted that the work was exhibited in the aftermath of a heart attack that the artist suffered in 1975. The mortality at stake, then, would seem to be Beuys's own. Yet the installation does not speak in the first person. Its title—inscribed on the doubled blackboards—is an imperative presumably directed at the viewer, but the identity of its speaker is indeterminate. There are no direct references to Beuys himself, much less to the specifics of his health. The use of readymade elements such as the stretchers and agricultural implements reinforces this sense of relative anonymity. Where autobiography might have been expected, Beuys instead points toward a more general human condition. Everyone *has* a wound, the work implies, but *zeige deine Wunde* does not tell us where it is or came from; it only tells us that the wound is not the artist's property alone. The use of the second person imperative suggests that Beuys here occupies the role of the physician, not the patient.

Elsewhere the reverse happens: autobiography intrudes where history had seemed to hold court. This is true, for example, of his installation at the 1976 Venice Biennale, *Straßenbahnhaltestelle* (Tram stop), a work to which I have referred already in the previous chapter (fig. 23). Beuys's inclusion of a railway tie and iron sculpture of a human head contorted into what seems to be an expression of pain are not difficult to interpret as allusions to modern European history, or perhaps more specifically to the deportation of European Jews—the more so given that the work was originally shown in the Venice Biennale's German Pavilion, the current form of which dates to a renovation in 1938 that brought the structure into line with Hitler's classicist taste. Yet Beuys insisted on the installation's more personal iconography. Tisdall's entry on it in the catalog for the artist's 1979 Guggenheim retrospective adduces Beuys's childhood experience of waiting at a tram stop in Kleve next to a decaying memorial column from the seventeenth century.[62] The text implies that this was one of the artist-to-be's earliest encounters with the sculptural principle: "The forms interested him, not the details."[63] Another element of the work was a metal rod sunk into a hole drilled twenty-four meters below the surface level of the pavilion, thus into the groundwater of the Venetian Lagoon. The rubble left from this excavation is part of the work.[64] On its reinstallation at his Guggenheim retrospective in 1979, Beuys lowered the cannon/column and disassembled the metal rod so that they both lie horizontally on the floor. The original version of *Straßenbahnhaltestelle* is now in the Kröller-Müller

Museum, Otterlo, while a second version is in Berlin's Hamburger Bahnhof; both opt for the "deactivated" horizontal arrangement. Note, however, that the section of railroad tie in the Berlin version is in fact a split, not a single straight tie as in the original. This considerably alters the work's metaphorics; instead of an inevitable delivery from point A to point B, the second version alludes to a possible divergence between two futures. Given the work's widely perceived reference to the Holocaust, this is not necessarily a trivial change.

Such connotations do not seem to have been much noticed at the time, however. In an essay published in 1980 on the occasion of the work's installation at Berlin's Nationalgalerie, Heiner Bastian discusses the theme of "memory," again entirely in reference to the artist's childhood in Kleve. Like Tisdall, Bastian emphasizes the awakening of Beuys's sculptural sense in early childhood. The ruined memorial column "was nothing more than indeterminate, striking forms that were actually nothing, yet someone must have made them, somebody must have also seen another power, another purpose in them. The experience that one could make forms without a recognizable meaning is one of the key experiences in Joseph Beuys's childhood."[65] These and similar comments from close associates of the artist are so consistent that it is reasonable to assume that they paraphrase Beuys himself; they are, so to speak, "official" statements, like those that reiterate the Tatar legend. The association of railways with the Holocaust did not become a common trope until after the release of Claude Lanzmann's film *Shoah* in 1985 (although as we will see, it was an association that already occurred to one reviewer of Beuys's retrospective at the Guggenheim). Hence the failure of these commentators to mention it is not as surprising as it might appear from a later perspective. There may nonetheless have been a historical unconscious of sorts at work in Beuys's choice of motif and materials. As an always already ruined antimonument that, moreover, has been exhibited in horizontal and thus metaphorically toppled form ever since it was removed from the Venice Biennale, *Straßenbahnhaltestelle* could not have escaped at least an oblique discourse on postfascist memory. This is true even if the artist deflected from such a reading.

The imposition of autobiographical content onto the work shuts down its metaphoric mobility in favor of a single, direct reference, at the same time as it opens the piece toward the artist's mythologized personal history. This is not unlike the way in which Beuys delimited yet simultaneously relied on the wider connotations of materials such as fat. His autobiographical mythology was a way to triage historical reference. The use of fat in *zeige deine Wunde* is another instance of such controlled polysemy. Given the medical connotations of the stretchers, it is hard not to read the material as human, even though it certainly is not. But fat carries with it as well the complex of specifically Beuysian metaphors, especially the symbolism of healing, that we have already considered at length, the connotations of which are positive rather than morbid as far as their manifest content goes. Works of this sort would hardly be so arresting if they could not rely on a conflict between the two suggestions. We are told "healing"; we see death. Myth accordingly functions here not as a final grounding of a work's meaning but instead as an inflection of a larger semiotic economy. This raises again the specter of bad faith. The artist authorizes certain meanings while maintaining plausible deniability with respect to others.

Viewers need not be so restricted, however. Let us try, then, a "third" meaning for *zeige deine Wunde* in order to see how the work's formal strategies may or may not relate to the general dynamics of modern society. Doubling is the installation's principle, as noted before. Like any such primal trope, doubling invites a leap from one interpretative register to another.[66] In effect, it invites a leap into allegory, seemingly an unavoidable mode of interpretation given the rebus-like character of the piece (which it shares with the vitrine sculptures). A no less striking form of doubling characterizes capitalist society. Things, or more specifically commodities, are what they are, in material terms, at the same time as they bear something called value, which is "immaterial" yet nonetheless socially effective and indeed coercive. This doubling results from the subsumption of concrete, material labor to the accumulation of an abstract, immaterial, yet objectively real (because socially validated) "substance": value. Capitalism's separation of incommensurable spheres that nevertheless overlap in the same objects might be taken as this mode of production's fundamental characteristic. Marx's *Capital* is a detailed phenomenology of this divided world, starting with the immediate appearance of society's wealth as an "immense accumulation of commodities" in the first sentence of volume 1 and concluding with the "trinity formula" (land–ground rent; labor–wages; capital–interest) in the incomplete manuscripts that Friedrich Engels would eventually assemble into volume 3.[67]

Strange things happen to the material world when an abstract form comes to determine it. Marx sometimes uses the word *Verdopplung*, or doubling, when writing about this distinctive splitness of bourgeois society.

In his early writings of the 1840s, the idea is anthropological and linked to alienation. Bourgeois men are split between their identities as private persons and citizens, just as society itself is split between the private and public spheres, or civil society and the state (at the time, women, racialized populations, and the working classes would have been largely barred from Europe's officially sanctioned public and political realms altogether). The worker is analogously separated from the product of labor, which is alienated in the commodity. In his mature critique of political economy, though, Marx uses the term otherwise. Here the commodity is split too, along with its producers and consumers. Commodity exchange, he writes, "produces a doubling of the commodity into commodity and money, an external opposition in which they represent their immanent opposition of use-value and value."[68] Commodity and money are the hypostatized forms of a contradiction that is always already contained within the commodity inasmuch as it participates in the metabolism of generalized exchange. Adorno's student Hans-Georg Backhaus interpreted this aspect of Marx's theory as follows in an essay published in 1969:

> "All the magic and hubbub which befogs the products of labour on the basis of commodity production" manifests itself in the paradoxical relation in which the commodity is itself and at the same time its other: money. It is therefore the identity of identity and non-identity. The commodity is equal in essence to money and at the same time different from it. . . . *The commodity-money equation is the economic dissolution (Aufhebung) of the Principle of Identity.*[69]

Another reading of some of the works we have seen now presents itself. We know that *zeige deine Wunde* doubles nearly all of its components. There is an interpretation of this fact readymade in the literature. As so often in writings on Beuys, it was suggested by the artist's own words. I quote from a German exhibition catalog: "The striking doubling of the objects, a principle of form that Beuys often used, here recalls the threshold of death that is thematically addressed—the two funeral biers from the pathology department place the theme of death at the center—as the doubling of the human being into the outer and inner person and thus as the doubled perception of the same as a world of material and of spiritual reality."[70] This may be true; it is probably what Beuys intended or something like it. Yet we have also now seen that there is a real social form that accomplishes a doubling of material and nonperceptible reality in a less mystical way. Anyone unable to make nearly constant, if rough, calculations of an abstract, exclusively social property of things—their value—will not get far in the capitalist world. We can sometimes sense the spirit moving in the flesh. But we are more likely to be aware of the movement of value through its perceptible manifestations: commodity, money, and labor.

The elements of *zeige deine Wunde* seem to reflect properties of this movement. The old agricultural tools—so old and obsolete that their names and functions are difficult to track down—evoke living labor performed in some indeterminate past; decontextualized, they have lost their use values and become enigmatically charged artifacts. According to one source, the spade-like objects on the right are called *Schepser* and are used to remove bark from trees, while the objects on the left are pitchforks meant to secure gravel under train tracks.[71] Beuys evidently removed the central tine from each of the pitchforks, leaving them two- versus three-pronged, again reinforcing the dualistic motif. Furthermore, as explained in the same source, the rags tied around the shafts of the two pitchforks are made from the clothes of railway workers.[72] These items could thus stand for a precapitalist labor process now either subsumed to the accumulation of value or simply made obsolete. The containers of fat likewise suggest the laboring body since this substance stores calories expended in work. The energetic properties of fat are crucial to the material's function in the Beuysian system. At the same time, this metabolism of accumulation and expense points to the self-movement of capital, which throws itself into its negation, the labor process, to valorize itself—as, maybe, fat is valorized or spiritualized in its movement from the tins to the windowpanes via the membrane of the mortal body. Finally, one might perhaps relate the light shed by the two metaphoric lamps to the immaterial circulation of money in finance capital, which in the modern era need not be physical at all.

## 6.

This interpretation is allegorical and speculative, of course, but not more so than others that have been advanced in the literature. Moreover, allegoresis here is reflexive. It is possible to interpret doubling in light of Marxian value theory because the commodity itself is "allegorical" in structure, as Benjamin recognized. In allegory, one meaning is read through another. In the commodity, an abstract and universal social form is read through material contingency.[73] This mode of signification, though mandatory in an exchange economy, has a contingency that is distinct from the naturalization of semiosis that I have called "myth." Myth in its Beuysian shape attempts to secure a one-to-one correspondence of qualitative, material iconography to its meaning, in contrast to the "real abstraction" of quantitative equivalency and its indifference to qualitative specifics. As I have noted elsewhere, the term "real abstraction" originates in Marx, but was developed most fully in the work of economist and philosopher Alfred Sohn-Rethel; it designates the practical abstraction that occurs in commodity exchange as opposed to the mental formation of concepts, or for that matter, mythical symbolization. The artworks with which I have been preoccupied stage a tension between myth and capital's allegoresis, demonstrating in the process what happens to myth when the commodity becomes the world's dominant "symbolic form."[74] In a similar manner, the vitrines pointedly confuse reliquaries with the aesthetics of the shop window.

It is worth pursuing the implications of this reading further. That every object in *zeige deine Wunde* is doubled means that each is identical and not identical with its counterpart: formally the same, but physically distinct. Rather than being an open series, however, there are only two of everything. The work is dualist in a way consistent with any number of Platonisms or mystical philosophies, not to mention Descartes's cogito, but also just as much with the social ontology of capital. The work does not distinguish between these modes of dualism and that is part of its meaning. The same is true of *Honigpumpe*. Here, too, spiritual and economic values are conflated willy-nilly. The installation's metaphor of circulation applies equally to the dialogic production of knowledge and the movement of capital. The work in fact seems to want the two circuits to be or become one and the same. This confusion is likewise characteristic of the *Fond* sculptures that we encountered in chapter 1. These objects are metaphorized as immense batteries as well as financial instruments given the near homophony between *Fond* and *Fonds*, with the latter term, as we have seen, being a cognate of the English "fund." The works "accumulate" energy of an unspecified yet supposedly spiritual kind. But since that spiritual energy is itself "capital" (in the sense that Kunst = Kapital), the *Fond* pieces are by the same measure concentrations of economic value. They are monumentalized bank accounts or hedge funds made material. Finally, the vitrines are likewise characterized by this double signification. The objects they contain are trash and treasure at once—as value is indifferent to the material particulars of the commodities that are, at the same time, the indispensable means of value's accumulation. Capital thus exalts things and makes them superfluous in the same process. Capitalism generates heaps of commodities that are only means as opposed to ends. As soon as commodities have been instrumentalized for capital's expanded reproduction—after they have been sold—they become disposable. At its most fetishized extreme, capital even likes to pretend that it can do without commodities altogether, including the commodity of labor power (from capital's perspective, human beings are both essential and disposable, just like the things they make). This is the horizon of finance, which aims to abridge the formula M-C-M' (or money-commodity-more money) into M-M': money that breeds money apparently without the mediation of commodities or workers at all.

The point is not that a reading of these artworks from the perspective of value theory is more persuasive than any other but rather that the oeuvre leaves itself open to such a reading in a way that is symptomatic of its structure. The openness of the metaphor is an openness to its colonization by capital. That the value theoretical reading is even possible indicates that something has happened to ontology in the modern age; something about an opposition as primordial as that between spirit and matter has come to be a moment in the circuit of capital's accumulation.[75] It is not *only* that, but Beuys's persistent recourse to economic metaphors—on top of or even melting into his anthroposophical and ecological tropes—leaves little doubt that the association is relevant. Works such as *Honigpumpe* then complicate matters yet further by involving another object of mimesis: nature. If the circulation of honey in this work figures not only the circulation of money but also blood, thereby figuring, by extension, all the homeostatic, cyclic processes that characterize organisms and ecosystems, then Beuysian economimetic allegoresis absorbs ecology as well. Which is as much to say that the ecological impetus of his work does not simply alter the modern autonomy of the aesthetic by submitting art to a mimesis of nature; it also mimetically infects the concept of nature with the naturalized (but still, hardly natural) dynamics of capital accumulation.

These matters have continuing political stakes beyond the more limited sphere of German crime and guilt. For one thing, the immanence of nature to capital and vice versa has become a bone of contention in recent ecosocialist debates, with some theorists asserting the untenability of the nature/society dichotomy and others upholding it. Andreas Malm, for instance, has argued that fellow Marxist ecologist Jason W. Moore's insistence that capital does not *have* an ecological regime but instead *is* an ecological regime amounts to an abdication of responsibility since it is only by distinguishing human agency from nonagential nature that we can hope to fight climate change.[76] It would be out of place to adjudicate such disagreements here. What is important is that Beuys's work on myth poses questions to which these debates pertain. It remains hard to tell whether Beuys naturalizes capitalism or capitalizes nature—just as it is hard to tell whether the negativity of *zeige deine Wunde* resists capitalist abstraction or reproduces it.

We can now grasp why it is so hard to say what the objects under consideration in this book really are. On the one hand, Beuys's artworks seem to be ends in themselves. If they were not, they would hardly be "art" at all, at least as art has been understood since Kant; it is also in being teleological that they resemble organisms. (Kant after all devoted the second part of the *Critique of Judgment* to teleological judgment—in other words, our perception of ends in nature; organisms are for him "natural purposes.") Yet on the other hand, Beuys's works are vanishing mediators on the path to a more total social/natural metabolism. Once this breakthrough has been achieved, the category of "art" as a separate sphere of human activity would fade away, one may presume. Or what is perhaps the same, "art" would subsume everything. Absolute art is the end of art. Every art-like activity—every conceivable form of Gestaltung, whether "aesthetic," social, or economic—would then simply *be* everyday life and vice versa. This exchange between the totalization and dissolution of art, specifically sculpture, accounts for the instability of Beuys's work in the 1970s. If the horizon of his practice was the direct Gestaltung of social relations, then the material results of the shaping process might seem merely accessory—only a means to free democratic socialism. Much of his sculptural output does indeed look to be the by-product of other and conceivably more significant processes—namely, the artist's "actions" and pedagogical endeavors, both of which were meant to demonstrate the proposition that "everyone is an artist" and hence that the Gestaltung of society could be universalized as general socioplasticity. Yet Beuys at the same time made sculpture the model for all of his activities and never abandoned it as a practice. In either case—social as well as more traditional sculpture—the artist's work is that of formalization. What was unformed becomes formed, if only to dissolve again in the metabolism of a fully aestheticized everyday life. In totalizing the concept of art, though, Beuys left the fate of his individual, material artworks up in the air.

The paradox is again that of Marx's *animal*: the universal incarnated in the particular. Given that Beuys wanted to replace all hitherto existing economic arrangements with the proposition that art equals capital (and its corollary, that money is a legal or rather political form, but at the same time also somehow a "sculpture"), it is even the case that his "expanded concept of art" takes on the specific role of the *animal* in Marx's definition—that is, the role of money, which is the concrete manifestation of the abstract, universal form that mediates all social processes. Yet money is, by its nature, a "particular" impressed through and through with its character of universality. A dollar bill is a dollar bill. Discrete pieces of money are "particular" only in a trivial sense by virtue of their facticity (and of course, most money in the twenty-first century never becomes material even in this way, but instead exists exclusively as digital code). Money is fungible or it ceases to be money. Artworks, on the contrary, would seem to be nothing if not individual, idiosyncratic, and irreplaceable.

We have met this contradiction in the *Kunst = Kapital* banknotes. What I suggest now is that the contradiction is not particular to those works but rather a general property of Beuys's practice at large. His aim of universalizing creativity as a homogeneous substance of social mediation—*Honigpumpe*'s utopia—conflicts with the particularity of his artworks. And it confronts, too, the real existence of another social form that already mediates everything. Within the economy of matter and concept described over the preceding two chapters, this means that material particularity comes to be laden with an especially acute finitude since its counterpart is the infinitude of the equation "art = capital" (a short way of saying that human creativity is infinitely productive).[77] And the epitome of finitude is death.

At this point, the metaphysical question about the status of the Beuysian artwork has come to be articulated with, if not nestled within, a question about Beuysian economics. We can identify borderline cases and metaphors at cross-purposes in the oeuvre that make a straightforward resolution of the problem impossible. (As in *Arena*, a suggestion of pure sociality clashes with a suggestion of material and implicitly economic accumulation; or as in *Honigpumpe*, natural/economic automatism and

Gestaltung are equally operative though incompatible terms.) To review, quickly, the argument of the preceding few pages, Beuys's artworks undergo a split because they aspire to incarnate the value abstraction (in its transfigured artistic or "spiritual" guise) even as they remain particular, nonfungible things. Perhaps this was only to be a temporary phase. But the overcoming of the separation of aesthetic practice never arrived, for reasons having to do with the structure of capitalist modernity; as long as commodities remain commodities, art must remain art (a commodity too, but an exceptional one). Thus Beuys's assimilation of art to value remained arrested at a stage of incomplete or analogical mimesis rather than identity. Derrida's notion of economimesis is again useful here. In Kant's likening of the productivity of art to *natura naturans* and the productivity of God, as Derrida observes,

> A certain *quasi*, a certain *als ob* re-establishes analogical *mimesis* at the point where it appears detached. The works of the Fine-Arts must have the appearance of nature and precisely in so far as they are productions (fashionings) of freedom. They must resemble *effects* of natural *action* at the very moment when they, most purely, are works [*opera*] of artistic confection.[78]

This applies directly to Beuys. Where his work most insists on agential Gestaltung, it most thoroughly mimics natural processes, as when *Honigpumpe* mimics both the society of bees and the circulation of blood. The circulation of honey is in turn only *like* the circulation of money, and even so only in some respects. Had the fusion been complete, it is hard to imagine what purpose these artworks would have retained qua material artifacts. Indeed even on the work's own terms, the necessity of physically installing a motor in the basement of the Fridericianum needs explaining, if we assume that *Honigpumpe*'s payoff, so to speak, is not its existence as sculpture but instead its prefiguring of free democratic socialism in the shape of collective knowledge production (though of course we are also free to read another ruse of history in Beuys's anticipation not of a new type of socialism but rather a "cognitive capitalism" or "semio-capitalism" that posits artistic labor as a model for labor in general).[79] One might then argue that the failure of Beuys's wider socioplastic project rescues his works from their anticipated obsolescence. They persist as charged, ambiguous objects open to readings on disjunct levels, such as in the equivocation between relic and refuse in the vitrines. If, on the one hand, we are meant to take these pieces of art seriously in terms of form—as products of intentional Gestaltung—on the other hand, they constitute moves in a game of discursive redefinition as well as the testing of the boundaries between art and other, potentially more total phenomena: politics, economics, and nature.

Beuysian economimesis is therefore a modality of socioplasticity. It attempts a mimetic subsumption that is the inverse of capital's subsumption of the production process.[80] This would undo capitalist modernity. In its resistance to metaphoroclasm, Beuys's work tries to subsume the "real" metaphor (or social allegoresis) that is capital's forced equivalency of unlike things in the exchange relation (real abstraction) to a contrary principle of generalized social and material Gestaltung. The latter would abolish the distinction between art making and general social practice, and with it the problem, as T. J. Clark once described it, of modern art's "lack of grounding in some (any) specific practice of representation, which would be linked in turn to other social practices—embedded in them, constrained by them," since art would then have no outside; it would be universal.[81] But the only real universal in capitalism is capital itself.

# 7.

The above has been abstract. A return to objects will be useful. We may now be in a position to attempt a more complete mapping of Beuys's practice in the 1970s. His Guggenheim retrospective at the end of the decade provides a convenient unit of analysis; it was a self-conscious presentation of Beuys as something like a finished product for US consumption (fig. 26). Here, *Straßenbahnhaltestelle* was the twenty-second of twenty-four roughly chronological "stations" running from the top of the museum's spiraling rotunda to its floor.[82] Immediately following it was *Unschlitt/Tallow*. After that, concluding the retrospective, was a version of *Honigpumpe*, or more precisely, its disassembled components. A relatively modest presentation of *Arena* stood nearby. For whatever reason, the latter was neither designated as a "station" nor was it included in the exhibition's catalog (although the book does contain two photographs of the work's 1973 showing in Rome).[83]

Along with the *Fond* sculptures, examples of which were to be found in stations sixteen and seventeen, these were the artist's four most ambitious sculptural projects of the 1970s.[84] Their proximity might therefore only be

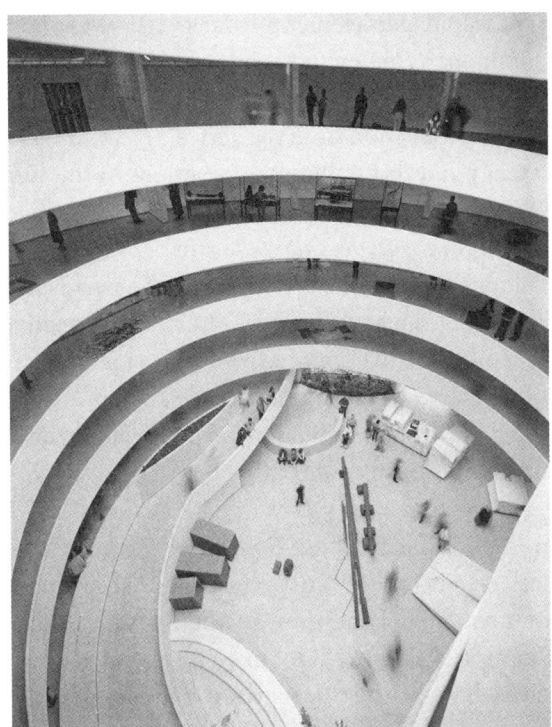

**Fig. 26.**
*Joseph Beuys*, exhibition,
Solomon R. Guggenheim
Museum, New York, 1979.

a matter of summing up. The differences between the works merit attention, however. Where *Straßenbahnhaltestelle* draws on the vocabulary of monumental sculpture, even to the point of including a figurative element, *Unschlitt/Tallow* instead announces a principle of near formless accumulation. To the exhibition's New York audience, this would have suggested commonalities with recent art from the United States (that of Morris or Serra, for example), even if these resemblances are ultimately limited in ways we have seen in chapter 1. *Honigpumpe* and *Arena* shift the focus from the material to the social aspect of Soziale Plastik. In its Guggenheim installation, though, *Honigpumpe* lay inertly on the floor of the museum as opposed to actively pumping away as it had in Kassel. Thus the community it conjured was more inoperative than otherwise. *Arena* was likewise shown in a state of latency, as only a tiny fraction of its panels—three out of one hundred—turned their front sides to the exhibition's viewers; the rest were stacked back-to-back on the museum's floor. The related gesture of "deactivating" a sculpture after its initial exhibition, and then subsequently repositioning its elements from a vertical to a horizontal posture, is in turn common to *Honigpumpe* and *Straßenbahnhaltestelle*. This tactic is in effect the large-scale equivalent of sealing objects within the vitrine sculptures; it marks a transition from the active, warm, and circulating pole to a state of latency and "crystalline" contraction. At the Guggenheim, *Honigpumpe*'s and *Arena*'s elements slipped back toward the category of sculpture, to which *Straßenbahnhaltestelle* and *Unschlitt/Tallow* more unambiguously belonged from the start. The lack of a performative or pedagogical component in the artist's Guggenheim retrospective likely distorted his US reception by overemphasizing this side of his production. At the time, these works were generally read as sculpture or installation, not through the more process-oriented and politically attuned optic that had emerged in the European context.[85]

If the four works converge on this level, they part ways again in their metaphoric penumbrae. *Straßenbahnhaltestelle* combines an autobiographical reference to the artist's childhood in Kleve with allusions to the tradition of monumental sculpture and perhaps the disasters of Europe's twentieth century. *Unschlitt/Tallow* likewise assumes a public scale and mode of address, but its rhetoric is keyed to a more impersonal notion of healing. The material itself, rather than the artist's shamanic contact, is what putatively repairs the urban site from which the sculpture was not, in fact, cast. As we have seen, the absence of a physical link to the site is a further complication in the work's signifying structure; it displaces the work's iconography of "healing" from indexical self-evidence to an iconography that relies on a more precarious interaction between matter and meaning. *Arena*, in turn, anticipates *Unschlitt/Tallow*'s principle of accumulation, but juxtaposes this metaphor with an invocation of human community through its reference to Goethe's "noble body," which is supposed to have recognized itself in Verona's Roman amphitheater.

*Honigpumpe*, finally, is a social, political, and economic allegory of Beuys's coming utopia. It is the most totalizing of the four works. This installation draws on a venerable trope: the beehive as society. Nonetheless, in contrast to *Arena*, the work's effect was meant to be wholly present and perhaps real versus only metaphoric to the extent that it not only figured but also literally materialized Beuys's community of fellow artists as everyone. Or it would have done so, had it been activated as it was at *documenta* two years before. Like many of Beuys's relics, its status is unclear once removed from its performative context. Are the pump, plastic tubes, and so forth valid sculptural objects of their own, or mere indexes of a past event? And if the latter, do they still bear their utopian potential? The question concerns the basic status of most of what remains of the artist's oeuvre. The historian Annie Suquet, for one, comes down squarely on the side of viewing Beuys's objects as essentially linked to their quasi-ritualistic function and thus inert without it: "The aesthetic appreciation of these objects ...—due largely to their museum exhibition—overshadows their primary vocation and annihilates it."[86] But this interpretation begs the question of why Beuys was willing to exhibit his sculptural work in museum settings at all; had this staging really been a betrayal of the work's "primary vocation," Beuys presumably would never have agreed to a retrospective. Drawing on sociologist Bruno Latour's actor-network theory, Gronau has for her part suggested that Beuys's sculptures function as "actants"—that is, "something that acts or to which activity is granted by others."[87] This account, though, runs into the problem of how literally to take Beuys's claims for the nonsymbolic agency of his materials and motifs. Even if we grant the thing or object its rights, there are probably few scholars willing to say that a *Fond* sculpture literally *is* a spiritual battery or that fat literally *is* a healing substance. Hence my recourse to metaphorology rather than new materialism. Our sense of the coherence of the Guggenheim installation surely depends on whether metaphoric totalization happens at all. And to the extent there is metaphor, there is no finality of "proper" meaning.[88]

We can nonetheless risk a metaphoric totalization of the Guggenheim show (as indeed any art reviewer would do). A kind of progress may be discernible here. Whereas *Arena* summoned Goethe's noble body only through figuration—in the work's community of photographic relics, which "store" time in a way that can be related both to the accumulative logic of works such as the *Fond* series as well as to the process of capital accumulation—*Honigpumpe* brought that community into being, albeit only in Kassel and not in New York. Yet Beuys did not thereafter abandon sculptural objectivity in favor of immediate, communal presence. To the contrary, these modalities developed along parallel lines from the late 1960s to the end of his life. In this continued allegiance to Gestaltung, Beuys differs from a number of contemporaneous practices with which he otherwise has some points in common—for example, US artist Allan Kaprow's happenings, which paradigmatically, if not always in practice, leave no physical residue behind; or the resurrection of ritual in the work of the Viennese Actionists, who tended to subsume participants and (abject) materials to the production of shared ecstatic, transgressive experiences.[89]What is distinctive about Beuys is that his "sculptural" principle is not exhausted in the production of new forms of community or experience but instead persists in the tension between immediate presence and the traces or relics that remain as indexes of the event.[90] The status of such relics is uncertain given that these objects are neither straightforward commodities produced for the market nor fully disposable props. *Honigpumpe* as it currently exists brings these issues to a head since as sculpture, the objects in the Louisiana Museum are decidedly unprepossessing.

The above analysis of the final four stations at the 1979 Guggenheim retrospective amounts to a table of structural possibilities that were latent in Beuys's "expanded" practice of art. The continuum runs from the monument to immediate sociality, or from a traditional notion of sculpture to its dissolution into a form of community that nevertheless preserves the principle of Gestaltung on a general social rather than a specifically aesthetic level.[91] These stages did not succeed one another but rather coexisted. Remember that apart from *Arena*, which dates from 1970–72, the works just named were all made in 1976–77. The fact that Beuys's art is structured as a continuum along which various works may occupy more than one position at a time helps to explain the work's slippage between meaningful sign (whether relic, "healing" substance, or bearer of economic value) and inert matter. Art can be everything or it can be nothing. It can be a means or an end, depending on how one looks at it—namely, whether one sees free democratic socialism as itself a work of art to which everything else must be subsumed, or an order beyond or after art, meaning something that would render superfluous art's separation from other practices and kinds of object. Socioplasticity wants to have it both ways.

## 8.

The epitome of finitude is death. If one pole of the Beuysian system—general socioplasticity—amounts to a horizon of infinite productivity, thanks to its reconciliation of art and labor, then it stands to reason that we will find death elsewhere. Art historian Thierry de Duve has argued that Beuys meant to identify with the mythic figure of the proletarian, "a term that transcodes *the bohemian* as a social type that excludes *the bourgeois* but includes all the rest of humanity suffering from industrial capitalism."[92]

This is incomplete. The Beuysian "expanded concept of art" is labor and capital simultaneously—both mediated substance and mediating form. By identifying the broken halves of the capitalist mode of production in a single infinitely self-mediating production, Beuys thereby notionally canceled both labor's negativity with respect to capital and capital's negativity with respect to labor—but only notionally, since as we have seen, deathliness is not so easily disposed of. Real negativity could not very well end up in either free democratic socialism or—what is the same—the infinitely productive identity of art, capital, and labor, at least not without introducing dissonance into Beuys's concepts themselves (which of course seems to have happened).[93] As such, it ended up in the material work, which sacrificially assumed the burden of finitude. Given that Beuys was corporeally involved in so much of his art—that so much of it was embodied in his actions and persona—this meant that nothing less than his life was on the line.

Before returning to an alternate reading of the Guggenheim retrospective, I want to locate negativity even more precisely in the apparatus or *dispositif* that is *Honigpumpe*. Let's return to it, almost but not quite for the last time. It will be noticed that in this work there is a caesura, not to say an opposition, between the living labor of knowledge production, of pedagogy, and the clanking machinery that is, however, paradoxically meant to take on the burden of metaphor and ineffability. It is this utterly material and inelegant mechanism that safeguards the plenitude of the system by giving it solid objectivity. The honey pump is in no way graceful or superior to human frailty; it does not constitute a higher degree of organization in any sense except the literally thermodynamic. The fact that Beuys assigned spiritualizing metaphoric duty to something so conspicuously unalive indicates that he grasped the material and historical contingency of his structure of meaning, even if unconsciously. It was a material system open to breakdown.

Why was it not sufficient to confine his intervention to the human activities above? Why the need for this mechanical supplement? I think that it stands for heterogeneity that is only just, or even not at all, at human command. It stands for dead, congealed labor. Fixed capital, in short. It figures the motor of the social process that keeps running whether we like it or not. In this it discloses the automatism of signification and links this to the automatism of value, which at its most fetishized appears to be an automatic subject independent from human beings. Beuys's advantage over later artists who submerged the aesthetic into social practice is to have risked objectification, and therefore to have dragged the will-o'-the-wisp of reconciliation through art back into the murk of its social, material, and historical coordinates—its inscription within capitalism. With this, finitude reenters the picture.

There is a flicker here between the work's late Romantic afflatus and the mere adequacy of its functioning. It is the latter quality that makes it worth talking about. The allegory of *Honigpumpe* is sinister, if we take it literally. And we should take it literally. It is as totalitarian as the artist's detractors would claim. I can only emphasize its provisional status. The pump is good enough—not menacing, not technocratic. The work is a model of how to live with the machine. It discloses the inhuman core of Beuys's machinery of signification, of his myth. Myth is a technique for orienting oneself in the world. It's a way to work on conditions that are given to one already and do not admit of rationalized control because their rationality lies outside the subject, whether in nature or the second nature that is society. By exteriorizing human reason to a sphere of superhuman necessity, myth, like a homeopathic remedy, at least promises to give its users a way to combat forms of necessity that otherwise are even more inscrutable. The danger of myth, of course, is that it will veil those conditions and make them less, not more, amenable to collective alteration. I don't wish to deny either the danger in the abstract or the insight that Beuys's particular version of mythic thought bears a structural affinity with the most horrific of all attempts to realize the conscious remaking of society. But there is another sense in which we can take the externalization of the work's "meaning." Its apparatus is effectively all supplement, all parergon, as Derrida would have called it; it constitutes a technical appendage to the spoken pedagogical Logos enacted in the seminar spaces above. Thus it would seem entirely superfluous to the work's logocentric fusion of voice, body, and ideology. Yet just the opposite is the case. Without its mechanical supplement, the installation is nothing. So there is indeed a terrible immanence here. Beuys inaugurates some sort of heterotopia nonetheless. The provisionality of *Honigumpe* is a way to think about being in common.

But is this too optimistic? Possibly. Probably. Something merely good enough, merely provisional, would not inherently need to evoke the more disturbing associations that Beuys certainly does. After all, the imbrication of utopianism with historical disaster is this book's theme. To end, consider an alternate reading of the final three "stations" at the 1979 Guggenheim retrospective. This will return us to a diachronic as opposed to a synchronic presentation of what I have called the table of structural possibilities available to the artist's practice during the period under consideration. As we have seen, *Straßenbahnhaltestelle* and *Unschlitt/Tallow* combine what seem like coded references to the Holocaust (the railroad tie and the material of fat, or rather something like it) with a message of social redemption (the power of the sculptural principle and the healing of an urban site). *Honigpumpe* in turn is an image of realized human community, though it also incorporates an ugly mechanical apparatus. The transit between these meanings is unresolved. They cohabit the same material artworks, at the same time. If the installation of these works is interpreted as sequential, however, a grim allegory suggests itself. Art critic Kim Levin reconstructed it in her review of the exhibition:

> There is a secret narrative in the work of Beuys, of which no one dares speak. Autobiography is by now an acceptable content for art; the atrocities of Nazi Germany are not. But with a little effort, the Stations—which are neither chronological nor exhibited in numerical order—are decipherable in terms of what is now euphemistically called the Holocaust. Station 22, *Tram Stop*, is an iron track alongside a rusty cannon. Besides the purely autobiographical childhood memories mentioned in the catalogue, *Tram Stop*—with a head protruding from the end of the cannon—suggests the end of the line at the concentration camps. Unraveling this hidden narrative backward, Station 21, *Hearth II*, is a large pile of felt suits: the clothing the victims stripped off. And although Station 23, *Tallow*, seems the culmination of the show there is also Station 24, *Honey Pump*, with its tubes full of honey, vats of honey and fat, and generators. Beuys calls the *Honey Pump* "the bloodstream of society" and says it is "only complete with people." In its metaphor of regenerated energies and transformation, there is a curious echo of Nazi concepts of the New Man. Hitler, who also saw himself as a messiah, spoke of the "bloodstream of our people" and thought he was restoring his people to "racial health." It makes us look at the iconography of Beuys in a new light: a suffering bathtub may be referring less to Duchamp's urinal than to the gas showers.[94]

Whether every detail of Levin's decoding is convincing is beside the point. In outline, the story is plausible. What can it mean, though, that this appalling allegory of Germany's past is layered atop another and seemingly unrelated allegory (or indeed more than one)? We know that these works incarnate metaphors of the circulation and accumulation of an indeterminate "spiritual" substance analogous to capital, even as they gesture toward a postcapitalist future. Beuys's artworks represent capital in order to overcome it. Yet if we follow Levin, they also represent the consumption of human beings in the death camps. Temporalities overlap. The Guggenheim installation reverberated with echoes of the Nazi era, even as it was an image of the capitalist economy of its own day, the 1970s, and a vision of an order yet to come.

It therefore seems that there are at least three ways to construe Beuys's metaphor of social metabolism. Either this process generates a common existence—socialism—or it accumulates a substance on the model of capital, or else, finally, it consumes without remainder the human material that is funneled into it, as did the Nazi death machine. The first would represent the making of a shared world, the second a ratification of Germany's real postwar economy, and the third a literal consumption of human bodies in an economy of death. The fact that the cycles are nearly congruent is telling. The circuits are nearly alike, as are the twinned objects of *zeige deine Wunde*.

The darkest interpretation of these works that I am able to conceive is accordingly the following. I do not mean to argue that this interpretation is correct or even necessarily admissible. Nonetheless, one can posit it on the premises developed so far. There simply *is* no irreducible difference between the reduction of human bodies to residue in the Holocaust and the reduction of human labor to abstract value in the postwar era. Accumulation proceeds in both instances by the violent leveling of particularity. In the one case, it is death that piles up; in the other, capital. The *Wirtschaftswunder* (economic miracle) of the 1950s was built atop the immense destruction not only of means of production but also of human life in war and genocide. These were the conditions of postwar accumulation. It was this ruin that cleared the field of noncompetitive capital and offered unprecedented occasions for profit to those with the resources to cash in. And it was the spectacular recovery of capitalism that in turn seemed to provide the material basis for schemes of rationally administered abundance, whether those of Erhard, Krahl, or Beuys. The machinery that arose in disaster's wake to transfigure death into life (*Honigpumpe*; the social market economy) was not death's negation but rather its triumph under the mask of prosperity. *Honigpumpe* is uncanny because the utopia it figures is soaked through with death's stench. I don't mean to convince the reader of every aspect of this interpretation. It *ought* to be repellent. I present it as a limit case that makes clear the stakes of what I have been writing about. That the metaphoric elasticity of Beuys's art leaves it conceivable at all is my point—as is the fact that merely stating these equivalencies in some sense reproduces their violence. The hypothesis that genocide, capital accumulation, and socioplastic community might not be distinct is its own violent leveling of particularity. But it seems to me that suggestions of these equivalencies, false or not, are built into the Beuysian complex and thus need to be stated plainly at least once.

This is also why Michaud's conflation of the Nazi art of politics with planning or social Gestaltung as such looks as convincing as it does. The continuities are real. Hence the question that I posed in chapter 1: Did Beuys have a "public"? (that is, Was there a form of reception that could have made of his mythology, as I have previously put it, "something that adds up to a totality of meaning held in common, or to a totality of practice, to a world"?)—may have an answer in the affirmative and be all the more terrifying for that. Our examples of modern utopia in action are not reassuring. Moreover, these circumstances explain much about the form that opposition to capitalism took in West Germany in the 1960s and 1970s. Legacies of the Nazi era were still nauseatingly present in the apparatus of capital accumulation. Many former Nazis were still in power, whether in government or corporations. This lent a particular urgency, even shrillness, to the rhetoric of West Germany's New Left, which saw itself tasked with the overcoming not only of capitalism but of a vestigial (or perhaps resurrected) fascism as well. It is probable, however, that the diagnosis of "fascism" in the BRD was a case of transference more than it was an accurate appraisal of then current political trends. This analysis—which was at times close to universally accepted in the German leftist milieu—derived from both recognition and insufficient understanding of the grounds of postwar capital accumulation in the preceding National Socialist era.[95] The terror that this imbrication of capitalism with fascism inspired lent added legitimacy to radical politics, even in the absence of objective conditions favorable to the success of violent revolution. It seemed to authorize acts of terror in response.

If *Honigpumpe* was one answer to these facts of the postwar era, the actions of the New Left were another. For a time, Beuys sought to align himself with—or even subsume or supersede—the politics of his students and their generation, and it was in this process that some of the "traumatic" effects of his art took form. Beuys and German Marxists alike presented themselves as antagonists to the order that had crystallized in the 1950s (that is, the economic miracle and social market economy). Both forms of practice, though, unfolded in the face of a crisis that had emerged in that order due almost entirely to factors other than themselves—to wit, the objective stumbling of the capitalist economy that began around 1966 in the BRD and then intensified globally in the early 1970s. The differences between the two projects ought to be clear enough by now, but aside from a few pages earlier in this chapter, I have not spent much time considering how they related to each other more concretely. I will thus devote some of this book's conclusion to a few telling moments in the dance between Beuys and his radicalized contemporaries.

# Coda. Terror and Its Double

I think about people eating and going to the bathroom all the
time, and I wonder why they don't have a tube up their behind
that takes all the stuff they eat and recycles it back to their mouth,
regenerating it, and then they'd never have to think about buy-
ing food or eating it. And they wouldn't even have to see it—it
wouldn't even be dirty. If they wanted to, they could artificially
color it on the way back in. Pink. (I got the idea from thinking
that bees shit honey, but then I found out that honey isn't bee-
shit, it's bee regurgitation, so the honeycombs aren't bee bath-
rooms as I had previously thought. The bees therefore must run
off somewhere else to do it.)

—ANDY WARHOL, THE PHILOSOPHY OF ANDY WARHOL

## 1.

Weigh this book against the example of Marcel Broodthaers, the Belgian
poet and artist who died in 1976. Although he was not personally close to
Beuys, Broodthaers was arguably his counterpart; his work likewise ranged
across media and was thoroughly political. He had many contacts in the
Rhineland art scene. The two have nonetheless come to be described as
something like antitheses in the literature of art history. Broodthaers stands
for a disillusioned, not to say cynical realism regarding the diminished
agency of art in late capitalism, and Beuys, of course, for undiminished
confidence in art's powers.[1] The process of their divergence can be read

most clearly in two "open letters" that Broodthaers addressed to Beuys over the course of four years. Below are excerpts from the first, from 1968. Broodthaers is responding to his colleague's work in *documenta 4*, which had just opened in Kassel:

My dear Beuys,

God, it was hard to say friend to a German when one was born on different soil. Beuys, you are a friend and Dutscke [*sic*] is a friend. Beautiful Germany is rising from the dead. [...]

Beuys, poet of the concentration camp, with your copper tables, your magic sparks, your felts full of cemeteries, your beds encircled by pestilence, with your new friends, South Americans, Jews, Yankees ...

Are we on the threshold of some new butchery? I can smell it rotting, in the distance, meat. But are we well informed? We don't know much here about your art, no more than in France. Our journalists are bizarre.

Here they're announcing the creation of a museum of modern art, in Brussels. Nobody believes it. [...]

Beuys, see you soon. Many people here are torn between analytic geometry and faith in an unbelievable god.[2]

Beuys had installed a *Raumskulptur* (spatial sculpture, or installation) at *documenta 4*, which was open to the public from June 27 to October 6, 1968. Among the works he displayed was *Lichamen*, 1967, a sculpture that resembles a mattress. The word *lichamen* is the plural of the Dutch word *lichaam*, or body; it is cognate with the German *Leichnam* (corpse). The letter is dated July 14: Bastille Day. "Dutscke" is Rudi Dutschke, the student leader who had been shot in the head by a right-wing attacker on April 11 of that year and was still recuperating at the time Broodthaers was writing. A decade later, Beuys and Dutschke would work together as co-founders of the German Green Party. They did not yet know each other in 1968. The Museum of Modern Art is Broodthaers's own. It was an elaborate pretense; no such museum existed outside his work. Unlike those of Beuys, the Belgian artist's fictions remain transparently understandable as such or at most playfully ambiguous. Beuys is ambiguous in a different way. For Broodthaers, it was axiomatic that Beuys was a "poet of the concentration camps." If Beuys, like Dutschke, was a friend, it must have been because he was on the side of a reawakening Germany that could, finally, confront its past. But if so, why the reek of the abattoir? These were the days of re-action in the wake of May 1968. Blood would flow, but whose? Was the art of Beuys premonition or memory? Where, in short, was the wound? The letter's final line does not resolve its opposition between "analytic geom-etry and faith in an unbelievable god." Reason and the remnants of myth would be a possible gloss; the writer takes no sides. (More proximately, "analytic geometry" might be a swipe at formalist art.)

Broodthaers had soured on his colleague by the time of his second open letter. This text is dated September 25, 1972, about a fortnight prior to both the closing of *documenta 5* and Beuys's ejection from the Kunstakademie Düsseldorf. The text was published in Düsseldorf's *Rheinische Post* under the title "Politics of Magic?" Broodthaers was then exhibiting versions of his *Musée d'Art Moderne* at *documenta* as well as at the Städtische Kuns-thalle in Düsseldorf. There was at least one concrete reason for tension. Both Beuys and Broodthaers had been invited to show at the Guggenheim in 1971, but the latter withdrew his contribution in protest of the museum's censorship of a work by Haacke, whom we met in chapter 2.[3] Beuys, how-ever, stayed on board and exhibited a sculpture as well as the program of his Organization for Direct Democracy. The open letter's conceit is that Broodthaers has discovered an unsent message from Jacques Offenbach to fellow composer Richard Wagner that he now transcribes for the benefit of his friend Beuys. Mock fragments of a damaged text invoke Wagner's essay *Art and Revolution*, the year 1848, and the word "Messiah":

To combat the degeneration of Art the musical drama would thus be the only form capable of uniting all the Arts. I can hardly agree with your position, and in any case I wish to express my disagreement if you include in your definition of art that of politics … magic? … My dear Wagner, our relations have become strained. And without doubt, this is the last message I will send to you. [ … ] King Ludwig II had Hans H. sent away from his castles. His Majesty prefers you to this specialist in compositions for the flute. I understand, if it is a matter of artistic choice. But is not the passion that His Majesty displays for you moti-vated by a political choice as well? I hope this question troubles you as much as it does me. What ends do you serve, Wagner? Why? How? Miserable artists that we are.

Vive la Musique.[4]

Beuys is Wagner and of course Hans H. is Haacke. So what has happened to Beuys between 1968 and 1972, as Broodthaers understands it? Some promise has been betrayed. Poetry of the concentration camp, though it may be the greatest barbarism, was nevertheless part of Germany's rebirth. The terror of the past had to be made speakable, and for that to happen violence had to be done to the present. Beuys's negativity did not, in the end, preempt its capture by the art world, though. His participation in compromised institutions had proven as much.

Broodthaers joined an occupation of the Musée des Beaux Arts, Brussels, in May 1968. By 1972, he was no longer on the barricades, but had found subtler ways to poke fun at the institution of the museum—by miming its rituals, exaggerating and exacerbating its pedagogical apparatus (a proliferation of signs and labels), and alluding to its complicities with capital and colonialism.[5] This is the strategy that was to become known as institutional critique.[6] Beuys, too, was critical of institutions, among them schools, political parties, and representative democracy itself—but in words. Meanwhile, his art continued to show up with clockwork regularity in major exhibitions of the period, without playing the explicitly self-reflexive moves that were by then increasingly popular among his international peers. (I have in mind not only Broodthaers's "museum fictions" but also projects such as conceptual artist Lawrence Weiner's *A 36" x 36" Removal to the Lathing or Support Wall of Plaster or Wallboard from a Wall*, realized at the Kunsthalle Berne in 1968, or Michael Asher's many rearrangements of gallery spaces to highlight the parameters of the so-called white cube.) I would say that even *Honigpumpe* does not critically intervene in the (infra)structure of the Fridericianum so much as reterritorialize it with a metaphor that fails to engage directly with the fact that it occupies a museum. For one thing, the propane motor that Beuys brought to Kassel was autonomous from the circuits of municipal water and electricity that would have been flowing through the building. The work constitutes a system within another system that it does not substantially disrupt.

So there is a chiasmus in the socioplastic trajectories of these two artists. Whereas Broodthaers had made a stab at revolution only then to retreat to wry fiddling with art's framing devices (whether this was the best or only option left after counterrevolution's triumph is not a question we can answer here), Beuys's ideology grew the more strident the more his output settled into an accommodation with art's institutions and markets. Beuys represented his politics (or myth), whereas Broodthaers aimed to burrow into modern art's conditions of possibility, thereby remaining true to the Kantian inheritance of critique. Neither strategy either exited from or directly attacked the system of which it was critical.

## 2.

This is bringing us to the topic of "Beuys and the Left." The point is not just to tell of frictions with contemporaries who likewise wanted to achieve something along the lines of free democratic socialism but rather to understand how his work's horizon of socioplastic Gestaltung implied a structural relation with the socialist shaping of history. While Beuys was in the Luftwaffe, Broodthaers served as a messenger for the Belgian resistance, joining the underground Communist Party in 1943 (he was expelled in 1951). He likely shared the suspicion of his German colleague's late-blooming radicalism that was widespread among contemporaries with deeper roots in politics.[7] By the time of his second letter, these differences had come to a head.

Other things of importance happened in 1972. Consider a work that I have already introduced: *Ausfegen* (Sweeping up), which was performed on May Day in that year (plate 11). For this action, Beuys followed crowds of radicals to Karl-Marx-Platz in Neukölln, a working-class neighborhood of West Berlin. Red flags are much in evidence in the film that documents the event. Beuys, though, carried only a broom. After the marches came to an end, he and two assistants swept up the trash in the square, not very subtly indicating that they were there to clean up the mess left by the Left.[8] The assistants were his students El Loko and Hiroshi Hirose, from Togo and Japan, respectively. In this way, Beuys gestured (perhaps clumsily) toward solidarity with a stratum of low-wage, largely immigrant labor that traditional working-class organizations had as yet failed properly to recognize. The trash was then packed into bags marked with a graphic stemming from Beuys's Organization for Nonvoters. Beuys dumped the resulting refuse in a gallery. Eventually it ended up in a vitrine, thus completing the metabolic cycle.[9]

Two months later, Beuys would stage a more charged confrontation with left-wing radicalism. It was at the opening of curator Harald Szeemann's *documenta 5*. During the show's initial press conference, discussion turned to the militant RAF, whose leaders Andreas Baader and Ulrike

Meinhof had been captured only days before. In the middle of the event, performance artist Thomas Peiter, costumed as the German Renaissance artist Albrecht Dürer, interrupted the proceedings with a satirical speech (its content does not seem to be well remembered). In response, Beuys called out, "Dürer, I will personally lead Baader and Meinhof through *documenta 5*, that will resocialize them."[10] Soon thereafter, Peiter made a pair of signs bearing the first part of this quotation (plate 12). Beuys and Peiter together marched the signs through the Fridericianum. Later the signs became sculptural objects in their own right, henceforth planted in a pair of felt shoes stuffed with fat and rosebush twigs. Over the course of a few days, the words, objects, and actions precipitated by this event therefore cycled through the rituals of the art institution, political debate, mock political protest, and back to the permanence of a potentially salable artwork. The shoes may remind viewers of the signs' previous mobility. As installed, however, they always point to the wall, as if to say that *this* protest is never going anywhere.

The chronology involved is worth bearing in mind. *Ausfegen* took place on May 1, 1972. A few days later, the RAF launched its "May Offensive," the most ambitious series of operations in its history. The first bombing, on May 11, killed a lieutenant colonel and wounded thirteen others at the US military headquarters in Frankfurt. A series of attacks in Munich, Augsburg, Karlsruhe, Hamburg, and Heidelberg followed over the next two weeks. Among the targets were a police building, another US Army base, and the right-wing Springer publishing house. In all, four people were killed and seventy-four wounded. A massive police response was immediately set in motion. Baader was arrested on June 1. All remaining members of the first generation of the RAF were in custody by the end of the month, with Meinhof captured on the fifteenth. The aim of the May Offensive had been to provoke the West German state into disproportionately repressive countermeasures, which the RAF then expected would lead the general population to rise in revolt.

Both its strategy and choice of targets led to intense debate within the West German Left, and it was surely in the margins of such a debate that Peiter's action took place in Kassel.[11] The nature of Beuys's subsequent walk through the Fridericianum is equivocal. Though it of course recalls a political demonstration, it might as well be a religious pilgrimage, or more suggestively, a penitents' procession. The artist puts his own body on the line for the sake of broader redemption. To resocialize Baader and

Meinhof would be to heal the wound that had opened over the previous two months. Yet we can ask again, Where was that wound? What had suffered injury here?

In part, it may have been the artist's own persona as a revolutionary, now put in the shade by more extreme actions. All the same, in the early 1970s, the RAF did not dissuade Beuys from adopting the trappings of radicalism. It was in 1971 that Beuys produced one of his most iconic self-images, the photograph that in the following year would become the basis for an editioned screen print titled *La rivoluzione siamo Noi* (The revolution is us) (plate 13). The work is based on a photo taken on the island of Capri. In it, Beuys strides toward the viewer, one hand grasping a shoulder bag, and the other clenched into a fist.[12] The title's slightly unusual syntax is notably close to that of another statement from 1972. After her arrest, Meinhof was kept in solitary confinement in conditions that sympathizers of the RAF claimed were inhumane. There she wrote theoretical texts on armed revolution. At the Summer Olympics in Munich a few months later, on September 5, the Palestinian liberation group Black September took eleven members of the Israeli national team hostage in an attempt to secure the release of comrades in prison, among them Baader and Meinhof. All eleven Israeli athletes were killed, two during the hostage taking and the remaining nine during a botched police raid on September 6. Members of the RAF had trained with Palestinian militants in 1970. Despite horror at the Munich events in the press, the group declared its solidarity. Meinhof accordingly set to work on an analysis of the action. She judged it favorably, and blamed the German and Israeli governments for the deaths. This subsequently notorious document is a wide-ranging treatise on the relation between struggles in advanced and underdeveloped countries. Meinhof wrote the following under a subheading titled "The Revolutionary Subject":

> If the people of the Third World are the vanguard of the anti-imperialist revolution, then that means that they objectively represent the greatest hope for people in the metropole to achieve their own freedom. If this is the case, then it is our duty to establish a connection between the liberation struggle of the peoples of the Third World and the longing for freedom in the metropole wherever it emerges. This means in grade schools, in high schools, in factories, in families, in prisons, in office cubicles, in hospitals, in head offices, in political parties, in unions—wherever.

Against everything that openly negates, suppresses, and destroys this connection: consumerism, the media, co-management [*Mitbestimmung*], opportunism, dogmatism, authority, paternalism, brutality, and alienation.

"This means us!" The revolutionary subject is us.

Whoever begins to struggle and to resist is one of us.[13]

The exclamation "This means us!" is in quotation marks, presumably indicating that it is spoken by a collective anyone in the metropole. The reader, too, is interpellated as a potential comrade. The next sentence, *Revolutionäres Subjekt sind wir*, is nearly identical to *La rivoluzione siamo noi*. But not quite. Meinhof says that we are the revolutionary *subject*, whereas Beuys says that we are the *revolution*.

It is a small but meaningful difference. *La rivoluzione siamo Noi* predates the Black September essay, which was at any rate only distributed clandestinely for some time after its writing, and it can hardly be suspected that Beuys influenced Meinhof. So the comparison is only a textual exercise. Without attempting to read too much into coincidence, let me say what I think constitutes the difference of perspective between Beuys and Meinhof. The difference between self-identifying, in the first-person plural, as the revolution as opposed to the revolutionary subject is that one thereby collapses the gap between agency and effect. If you *are* the revolution, there is no work left to be done—you only have to manifest yourself. If, on the other hand, you are the revolutionary subject, then you are likewise a tautology—you are nothing more or less than the subject who makes the revolution ("whoever begins to struggle and to resist"), but you are not the revolution itself. For revolution to take place, this subject must plunge into negativity, must meet resistance and accept conflict, to the death, if it comes to that, with other actors—with enemies, with antagonists met, in the last instance, as character masks of the totality's various moments. Such were Jürgen Ponto and Siegfried Buback, a banker and West Germany's attorney general, respectively, killed by RAF members a few months prior to the even bloodier events of the so-called German Autumn of 1977, which began to unfold just as Beuys was uninstalling his honey pump at *documenta 6*.

Beuys refused to countenance a gap between subject and object, as he refused to countenance the antagonism between capital and labor. This at once extracts him from a drive to violence and throws him on the shores of myth, which might be violent in its own, different way. The revolution that we are is a mythical personification. Beuys embodied it, as the photograph makes clear. He offers himself as an equivalent of Che Guevara or any other radical icon in whom action, image, and celebrity are one. And with his "we," he turns you, the viewer, into the same. Although it may not look like it at first, *La rivoluzione siamo noi* is thus also a loop: another system without an outside, another infinitely productive machine, another enactment of the closure of economimesis. The frontal photograph works like a mirror. In seeing Beuys, you see yourself, and you see the revolution that both of you are. Beuys's narcissism is yours too. A specular economy is at work.

## 3.

What happens to you as a viewer of Pasolini's film *Salò, or the 120 Days of Sodom*, his adaptation of the Marquis de Sade's unfinished novel? Most likely, you retch (fig. 7). Disgust would seem to be the opposite of mimetic identification with an image and thus the opposite of what Beuys invites in *La rivoluzione siamo Noi*. Pasolini's last film was released in 1975, three weeks after he was murdered on the beach at Ostia on November 2 (Beuys had suffered his heart attack in July). Its premise is that a group of powerful fascists in Mussolini's rump Italian Social Republic, also known as the Republic of Salò, have kidnapped a group of youths whom they rape, torture, and kill in a mansion. Its middle section is titled the "Circle of Shit," and its most notorious sequence features graphic (and thankfully, simulated) acts of coprophagia. The filmmaker had a concise allegory in mind. Asked what shit eating represents, he said, "Mainly this: that the producers, the manufacturers, force the consumer to eat excrement. All these industrial foods are worthless refuse."[14] On the evidence of this chapter's epigraph, Warhol—who was fond of junk food—would not have disagreed with Pasolini. As an aesthetic fact, the images seem too intense to justify so straightforward an interpretation, though.

Coprophagia closes the body's metabolic loop by making an output an input. In Beuys's *I Like America and America Likes Me*, from the previous year, bodily waste had been the only output from a sealed miniecosystem—an art gallery—apart from images and myth (fig. 10). The coyote's excrement was removed while food was brought in. There is a closed loop in *Honigpumpe*: that of the honey that circulates from the steel reservoir in the Fridericianum's basement up through the plastic tubing in the galleries and then back again. In this case a further input was involved, however. The pedagogical activity of Beuys and his collaborators was meant in a metaphoric sense to impregnate the circulating honey with human intellect, thereby making the system an instance not of simple but instead expanded reproduction in Marx's terms.[15]

Here is the difference between *Honigpumpe* and *I Like America*. It is in metaphor that the leap is made from homeostasis to accumulation. This might be fundamentally appropriate to how signification works. With metaphor, or polysemy in general, a semantic unit need not be tied to a single fixed meaning but rather can accumulate an infinite range of further connotations, thus enhancing its value. Beuys made his "expanded concept of art" (universalized Gestaltung) nearly a total metaphor, such that there were few aspects of existence that it could not in some manner subsume.[16] More generously, one might posit that the function of metaphor here is not to subsume distinct concepts but precisely to resist the closure of a conceptuality that would affirm the reified categories of modern capitalist society. The "deficiency of concepts" to which metaphor attests would thus consist not in their failure to conform to reality so much as in a historically conditioned flaw in reality itself (at bottom, the existence of classes) to which the concepts are indeed adequate, as, for example, mainstream economic concepts are adequate to the objective injustice of capitalism.[17] This is the field of socioplasticity, which in wanting to cover too much ground, constitutes an implicit critique of social relations that keep art separate from economics and politics. What is utopian about socioplasticity, then, is that it announces a realm of freedom that does not yet exist: an overcoming of class antagonism and the exploitation that depends on it. In Beuys's metaphoric economy, art or creativity stands for both labor and capital. Socioplasticity performs their reconciliation or even identification. The apparent antagonism between the two therefore becomes narcissistic mirroring—much as the viewer is mirrored in *La rivoluzione siamo Noi*, and also somewhat as the distinction between input and output (food and feces) is abolished in the coprophagic circle. This immanence is what honey's return to itself signifies in *Honigpumpe*. The outputs are not extracted as profit but rather pumped back into the same monetary "bloodstream." The honey presumably gets more and more intensely concentrated with Geist each time it passes through the circuit. Via Beuys's work on myth, we have hence arrived at Warhol's association of an imagined coprophagic loop with bees and honey.[18] (Warhol's thinking is not entirely rigorous here; aside from perhaps adding to the horror, it's unclear what advantage there is in the fact that "they could artificially color it [specifically pink] on the way back in" given that "they wouldn't even have to see it.") Moreover, we have now arrived, almost by accident, as it were, at the classically Freudian association of excrement with money. Warhol's recognition that honey "isn't bee-shit, it's bee regurgitation" is a point to which we will return.

Coprophagia is a bodily rather than a specular phenomenon. Much of what's shocking about *Salò*, however, has to do with the way that Pasolini stages these and other transgressive acts as rituals with an audience. Sadomasochism as such is a mimetic and specular dynamic. Or so argue Leo Bersani and Ulysse Dutoit in their interpretation of *Salò*. To start, Bersani here as elsewhere in his writings takes it as axiomatic that sexuality "might almost be thought of as a tautology for masochism."[19] Sexuality is a name for the enjoyment one feels on the "shattering" of the self. The sadist, though, cannot enjoy this self-shattering directly inasmuch as they retain a position of dominance. The sadist is obligated to remain a centered subject. Sadistic pleasure is, then, really the sadist's identificatory and mimetic enjoyment of the shattering they inflict on the victim. By the same measure, "*mimetic sexuality is essentially sadomasochistic sexuality.*"[20] The masochistic partner is a mirror. For this reason, "The most intense Sadean—and sadistic—sexuality depends on symmetry" (which is also why it is, for Sade, paradigmatically homosexual). Likewise because of this symmetry, "specular sadism" is "really a movement toward universal destruction"—a destruction that is "both a function and a consequence of mimetic orders" given that what the sadist seeks is their own destruction through the destruction of the other.[21] A malign feedback loop results. The consequences are dire if we extrapolate from this to a social level: "The Sadean argument which *Salò* implicitly makes is that if sexuality is intrinsically masochistic, it *requires* a Fascist state."[22]

Is there an alternative? What would a "convincing theory of nonmimetic sexuality" look like?[23] It turns out that Pasolini answers this too. The stylized action in *Salò*—whatever in it that most closely approximates a plot in conventional terms—is structured around the three forms of sexual deviance named in the "circles" of this inferno—namely, the "circle of manias," "circle of shit," and "circle of blood," which correspond respectively to fetishism, coprophagia, and murder, or more precisely erotophonophilia:

arousal derived from killing. Following Sade, though, Pasolini does not just illustrate each perversion straightforwardly but instead hangs the action around tales recounted by a set of three matron-like female storytellers. As the tales wind toward their ugly conclusions, the fascist overlords break off to enact the described crimes on living flesh. It is words, not bodies, that are the prime aphrodisiac. Thus although the term "erotophonophilia" contains a false cognate—the "phono" in the word is derived from the Greek *phoneúō*, to murder, not *phōné*, sound—the auditory association turns out to be fitting. The urge that fulfills itself in the "Sadean cult of mimetic violence" is an infatuation with narrativity, and it is sound rather than image that drives the sadists to (self-)destruction.[24] By extension—and here I am extrapolating from Bersani and Dutoit, not paraphrasing them—it is neither the anus nor the sexual organs that are the prime erogenous zone in *Salò*; it is the mouth. Coprophagia therefore takes on its singular appeal as defilement of the Logos itself.

But this is not where Pasolini lets matters stand. As Bersani and Dutoit observe, the film is packed with distracting, narratively superfluous incidents, such as the sequence in which the piano player, who throughout the rest of the film displays a "subversive passivity" as she accompanies the female storytellers, throws herself undramatically out of a window, thereby escaping in death the narrative drive that "sustains the glamor of historical violence."[25] In the movie's concluding scene, as the captors torture to death the remaining youths, Pasolini distances our view of the climactic action by having us watch from far above through binoculars. Amid the massacre, a pair of young soldiers dance with each other for no particular reason. These distancing effects do not register as anything so emphatic as resistance, which would only produce another mimetic, identificatory dynamic (much as Beuys produces an identification with his radical stance in *La rivoluzione siamo Noi*). The most direct act of resistance in the film—when a naked young man raises his fist in an antifascist salute, momentarily astonishing the quartet of torturers before they gun him down—is nonetheless made pointedly ambiguous since the episode has no effect on the plot (such as it is), and the death fails to be a martyrdom in the absence of witnesses or consequences. The viewer cannot determine whether the gesture is pointless vanity or something more. In contrast to more demonstrative actions, the furtive occurrences to which Bersani and Dutoit draw our attention duplicate the narrative and scopic drive, and precisely in duplicating it, produce a certain remove and indifference, a disinvestment from the isolation of each moment of violence as a libidinal/narrative climax that stands out as a figure from its putatively nonviolent ground.[26] As such, per Bersani and Dutoit, "Pasolini's brilliant trick in *Salò* is to use repetition and replication as distancing rather than imitative techniques."[27] The correct prophylactic against the violence inherent in sexuality, then, is not nonviolence, which is impossible, but instead a dispersal of ambient violence such that the figure/ground relation between narratively privileged climaxes and other, less intense moments loses its sharp contours.

This is all well and good. Bersani and Dutoit, however, perhaps downplay the repellent intensity of Pasolini's film, at least as most viewers seem to experience it. The following does not describe my reactions to *Salò* very well: "In a sense ... we never tire of being spectators; but it is the very limitlessness of our aestheticism which constitutes the moral perspective on sadism in *Salò*. The saving frivolity with which we simply go on looking creates a consciousness of looking as, first, part of our inescapable implication in the world's violence and, secondly, a promiscuous mobility thanks to which our mimetic appropriations of the world are constantly being continued *elsewhere* and therefore do not require the satisfyingly climactic destruction of any part of the world."[28] As I experience it, the film has a few moments in which this limitless aestheticism completely breaks down and one's gaze is arrested in revulsion—the shit-eating scenes above all. It may just be that we see killing and even torture so often in films that spectators don't register it as shocking (that is, as real). Though objectively less horrible, consuming excrement is also less quotidian. Bersani and Dutoit seem to recognize this too. On the essay's last page, they write, "Coprophagia in both Sade and *Salò* comes before what Pasolini aptly calls the Circle of Blood, but in a sense it is also after all the rest, the childish (re-) (per-) version which may be both our first retort and the last resort. In coprophagia, the Sadean libertine appropriates the dying which eludes him even in the *jouissance* of murder. The somber satisfaction of eating shit is that of eating death."[29] In other words, coprophagia is an absolute of sadomasochism in which mimetic enjoyment of the other's death, we may add, ceases to be specular and becomes somatic. For the viewer, this moment is a similar hinge. However much "frivolity" might hitherto shield us from mimetic identification with the cruelty that Pasolini depicts, it's in the stomach, throat, and mouth that we now unwillingly react. Nausea takes over.

So there is another potential "output" from this aesthetic/somatic circuit: not shit, but vomit, which even Sade's connoisseurs of perversion decline to ingest. Derrida suggests why this might be so. As he notes in his essay "Economimesis," the "examplorality" of Western logocentrism can get on rather well with exchanging mouth for anus. Both emit something. Vomit, though, is the substance that makes taste turn against itself in disgust. Vomit is autoaffection within the organ of examplorality, the mouth (*os* in Latin) from which pours forth the word (Logos in Greek). Yet because it is nothing other than taste's reaction against itself, vomit is also taste's proper other and indeed, nothing less than the parergon of the aesthetic, the edge on which the system depends. A true exit from the system would no longer involve vomit or disgust per se but rather something that exceeds the pairing of taste/disgust altogether: a hypothetical "vicariousness of vomit" that would no longer be located in the mouth. Hence even what seemed to be the absolute limit of logocentric aesthetics turns out to be a "parergic remedy": "The word *vomit* arrests the vicariousness of disgust; it puts the thing in the mouth; it substitutes, but only for example, oral for anal. It is determined by the system of the beautiful, 'the symbol of morality,' as *its* other; it is then for philosophy, still, an elixir, even in the very quintessence of its bad taste."[30] If this is so, we can perhaps hazard an interpretation of coprophagia in *Salò* as, in fact, a conservative motif—not because it signals the sadistic (that is, mimetic) consumption of death, as Bersani and Dutoit assert, but instead because it delineates the outer limit of the aesthetic "not in order to subvert it but in order to entrench it more firmly in its area of competence" (to borrow from a proclaimed Kantian, Clement Greenberg).[31] Like Broodthaers's institutional critique, then, Pasolini's shit eating remains critical in the Kantian sense. It demonstrates the lability of the aesthetic by going to the edge of what it can subsume.

Now remember that honey is bee regurgitation, as Warhol belatedly discovered. This aspect of apian biology does not seem to factor at all into Beuys's explanations of *Honigpumpe*. Nonetheless, the piece illustrates Derrida's point well. There is little about the installation that is recognizably "aesthetic" in any classical sense. The machine is ugly. It belongs more to technology than to art. It seems to lack even any distinction between the core of the work and its supplements, or parerga, since it sometimes includes human bodies (and minds) and sometimes is only the physical apparatus, or vice versa; sometimes the motor runs and sometimes it doesn't since the work can also be exhibited as it was at the Guggenheim in 1979—that is, inert. The seminars and discussions organized by Beuys's FIU would seem to belong to yet a third realm of human practice: paideia rather than either poiesis or techne. Yet the work is a totalizing allegory of aesthetic ideology. Why? Because of its economimetic analogy of infinite production to the creativity of the artist, which in turning back on itself in the manner of cybernetic feedback becomes not merely poiesis but instead autopoiesis. *Honigpumpe* allegorizes the "shaping" or Gestaltung of both aesthetic and social form as, at the same time, akin to nature's self-regulation. Gestaltung is *Bildung* too, the formation of the self. Socioplasticity is this model translated to a collective scale. Society becomes both the subject and object of its own shaping, somehow at once as natural as a tree and as artificial as a statue.

This is an elegant equation, but there are at least two discrepant remainders. First is the deadness of the machinery, which contradicts the work's core vitalist metaphor. Second is the fact that despite the analogy of both honey and blood to capital—and thus to a social form that valorizes and expands itself—the circulatory system that Beuys actually constructed is closed, with the quantity of honey in the system neither increasing nor decreasing so long as it remains contained in its tubing. It is, then, precisely as if Beuys had chosen to realize Warhol's erroneous conflation of bee shit with bee vomit. Honey here is a nourishing substance that travels ceaselessly in a closed circle. Yet it is also an excretion, an output from another biological system. He transported no living bees to Kassel. The quantity of honey introduced into the circuit was accordingly fixed. By feeding back into itself, as shit feeds back into mouths in *Salò*, the installation closes the circle of economimetic immanence, thereby amputating itself from the origin of its polysemic substance in another hybrid natural/human ecology. (Recall the artist's remarks in his interview with the *Rheinische Bienenzeitung* around two years earlier: beehives were for him a "sculptural" collaboration between insects and humans.) In the same way, Beuys imagined that all capital ought to feed back into production, thus forming the perfect loop of anthroposophical economics. This assertion severs his new understanding of capital from capital's historical origins in primitive accumulation and exploitation. In reality, capital comes into the world "dripping from head to foot, from every pore, with blood and dirt," as Marx puts it.[32] Beuys's system, by contrast, acknowledges no exterior, no precursor. It did, though, have an afterlife: on the one hand, the remnants of the device in the Louisiana Museum in Denmark, and on the other hand, the cans of honey and fat from the installation that he sold as editioned multiples (fig. 21). These latter art commodities were perhaps a coprophagic reminiscence of the cans of *Merda d'artista* that Manzoni had marketed a decade and a half earlier. Which is to say that honey's "exit" from the system of *Honigpumpe* simply threw it into its mimetic object: the wider capitalist economy. It would have been more utopian just to pour it down the drain.

I am being hard on Beuys, again in the spirit of taking metaphors literally. The immanence I have described is why *Honigpumpe*'s moments of negativity emerge within the system itself as opposed to being excluded as its other. We might observe the same of *zeige deine Wunde*, which is approximately contemporaneous with *Salò*. Amid the installation's neat symbolism of mortality and spiritual recuperation, the twinned copies of the radical newspaper *Lotta Continua* function as an index of class conflict—that is, of a real wound in capital's immanence versus a figurative one. As in *Dürer, ich führe*, Beuys here apparently subsumes violent social contestation to econommimetic metabolism. Yet the real persists as an irritant in the loop of spirit's return to itself. Neither could Beuys's intent have been to suppress traces of struggle altogether. For a time, he had a real commitment to the group Lotta Continua. In 1981, for example, the artist installed a sculpture titled *Terremoto* at a fundraising exhibition that Lotta Continua organized in Rome after a devastating earthquake in the south of Italy.[33] The group had by that point ceased to exist as a political organization, but was still publishing its newspaper. *Terremoto* indeed incorporates a typesetting machine that had previously been used to print *Lotta Continua* itself. The cassette tape that is also part of the installation plays a speech by Beuys's friend Checco Zotti, a Lotta Continua member who had arranged the show. By 1981—that is, after the kidnapping and murder of former Italian prime minister Aldo Moro and subsequent suppression of the Autonomia movement—echoes of Italy's so-called Years of Lead would already have had a retrospective cast. Not so, however, in the mid-1970s, when Lotta Continua was still a street-fighting militant organization. What energy, then, is the newspaper meant to radiate in *zeige deine Wunde*? Is it part of the injury or part of the healing process? Both, I am tempted to say. Lotta Continua stood for conflict in the social body as well as for the hope, or illusion, of overcoming it. It was dagger and bandage at once.[34]

Two things thus happen to aesthetic ideology in Beuys's torsion. On the one hand, it functions—unsurprisingly perhaps—as alibi. Lotta Continua in *zeige deine Wunde* is not Lotta Continua as a threat to capital and the state. On the other hand, aesthetic totalization finds itself ruptured here by the immanence of violence to the social totality that is the work's object of economimesis. That is, if art is everything, if Kunst = Kapital, then art can only repress and then no less ineluctably formalize capital's negativity. In *Honigpumpe*, the repressed term is "nausea," together with its product, "vomit," which is both present and absent here—present, because honey is literally bee regurgitation, per Warhol, and absent because it is exactly the chance of any fluid exiting its body-like circuit that the work's physical and discursive apparatus forecloses, as *zeige deine Wunde* cocoons the *Lotta Continua* newspaper in a spiritualizing gloss. It seems logical, then, to say that a recovery of *Honigpumpe*'s radicality depends on holding tight to Derrida's "vicariousness of vomit": the negative moments that the system neither succeeds in eliminating altogether nor recuperates as its properly disgusting parergon (as I think mostly happens to the abject yet also theologically precious matter in the artist's vitrines). Utopia is in the work's unplaceable queasiness, not its manifest ideology.

Here Beuys departs from Pasolini. The system that is *Salò* does, by contrast, have its proper finitude and exterior. It ends with "universal destruction." When there is nobody left to kill, the film simply peters out; there is nothing that even resembles a classical narrative denouement. For Bersani and Dutoit, whose modernist faith in form may be overoptimistic here, refusal of narrative closure is *Salò*'s saving grace.[35] Our gaze is scattered rather than mirrored. There is nothing like this in *Honigpumpe*, which is why, despite its upbeat agenda, the installation is the darker of these two artifacts of European late modernism. We need not even countenance Kim Levin's Holocaust allegory to say so. But the darkness is ours, since we inhabit the world it figures. The point is to find a way out—not in representation, but in practice.

# 4.

Does Beuys still need apologies? Does he even need attention? To both questions, I say yes. This is because Beuys has never been mourned. Per T. J. Clark, "Not being able to make a previous moment of high achievement part of the past—not to lose it and mourn it and if necessary revile it—is, for art under the circumstances of modernism, more or less synonymous with not being able to make art at all."[36] We probably no longer live and work "under the circumstances of modernism," and it seems contemporary art has been getting along just fine, at least if the market is any judge. Whether Beuys's oeuvre counts as "high achievement" is a matter for each reader's judgment. Still, I insist, at a minimum, that the problems Beuys makes properly unbearable have mostly been abandoned rather than worked through in the decades since his passing. We have lacked art that draws the full and terrible consequences of an aesthetic remaking of the cosmos. (As opposed to an abdication of will in favor of non- or posthuman agencies.) If we are going to imagine a role for art amid catastrophic anthropogenic climate change and a global resurgence of the far right, we ought to return to the biggest questions; any merely humane exit from the ongoing planetary crisis will require collective action on a scale that vastly surpasses that of the twentieth century's revolutionary movements. Such action is unlikely to be nonviolent. A corollary is that what does remain of Beuys as an influence on the art of our time reemerges for the most part in less unsettling guise. An artwork like *Honigpumpe* is not properly understood—an artwork like *zeige deine Wunde* is not understandable at all—if assimilated to the genealogy of social practice art, relational aesthetics, or the "material turn." These are not the work's entelechy but instead its sanitized aftershocks. The negative has an entirely different insistence in his art. It would, of course, be just as misguided to make of him an absolutely exceptional figure, as does much of the insular literature that continues to pour forth from the German Beuys industry. Reading such texts, it's easy to feel that Beuys inhabits a mental and aesthetic universe of his own that bears little connection to the rest of contemporary art (but no end of connections to Leonardo da Vinci, Dürer, or Jesus Christ himself, to drop just a few of the names in existing comparative studies). He did not inhabit a universe of his own. He inhabited capitalist modernity, as do we.

My aim in this book has accordingly been twofold. In attempting to trace mediations between the social and the aesthetic, I join the project of historicizing Beuys's practice that has been inaugurated by scholars who now take a certain distance from the polemics of previous decades. Yet I am also writing against the apparatus of historicization, in favor of unresolved difficulty. Beuys is a rupture. A future potential will be lost when the rupture heals. I want to postpone the onset of art history in order to hold open the wound.

# Acknowledgments

When I was writing this book, friends, comrades, and colleagues helped me in ways that are irreducible to debt. Hence the form of these acknowledgments. I would rather avoid making distinctions between kinds of help. It matters that everyone I acknowledge here has aided this project in direct or indirect ways, in some instances without knowing it. My thanks to the following (and apologies to those I forgot):

Anna Andrzejewski, Edgar Arceneaux, Carol Armstrong, Stephan Arntz, George Baker, Ian Balfour, Jacob Bard-Rosenberg, the late Hans Belting, Jasper Bernes, Roland Betancourt, Sam Blanco, Eugen Blume, Yve-Alain Bois, Anne Boyer, Michael Shane Boyle, Sebastian Brehmer, the staff of The Broad, Benjamin H. D. Buchloh, Craig Buckley, Andrea Buddensieg, Barbara "Suzy" Buenger, Linn Burchert, Nicholas Cahill, Jill Casid, Julio Cervantes, T. J. Clark, the late Joshua Clover, Luisa Lorenza Corna, Elizabeth Covington, Kari Coyle, Andrew Culp, Jonh J. Curley, Thomas Dale, David De La Torre, Eta Demby, Michael Denning, Jonathan Dentler, Zen Dochterman, the staff of the documenta archiv, Pablo Echaurren, Sebastian Egenhofer, Ken Ehrlich, Philipp Ekardt, the staff of Ennova Art Museum, Esteban Felix, Paul Fleming, Devin Fore, Hal Foster, Florian Fuchs, the staff of Galerie Crone, Jacopo Galimberti, Vladimir Gallegos, Paul Galvez, Izabel Gass, Aaron Gemmill, the staff of the Getty Research Institute, Romy Golan, Lauren Graber, Andrew Christopher Green, Rose-Anne Gush, Andrea Gyorody, Bruce Hainley, Stevie Cisneros Hanley, the staff of the Harvard Art Museums, Birgit Heuvelmann, Cara Jordan, David Joselit, Brandon Avery Joyce, Teddy Kaul, Shawon Kinew, Michelle Komie, Erinna König, Pamela Kort, Oliver Kretschmann, Colin Lang, Yuhang Li, Elisa Linn, Alexander Locascio, Megan R. Luke, Shana Lutker, John MacKay, Antje-Britt Mählmann, Ron Manheim, Jaleh

Mansoor, Daniel Marcus, Nancy Rose Marshall, Anita Martinez, Jeremy Melius, Cindy Milstein, Avigail Moss, Viren Murthy, the staff of Museum Schloss Moyland, Christian Nagel, the late Rainer Nägele, Jennifer Nelson, Rebecca Peabody, Pamela M. Potter, Alex Potts, Jennifer Pruitt, Marcia Reed, Jonathan Regier, Susanne Rennert, Kevin Repp, Petra Richter, Judith Rodenbeck, Max Rosenberg, Susanne Rübsam, Marta Ryczkowska, Sam Sackeroff, Michael Sanchez, Janet Sarbanes, Jaime Schwartz, Martha Schwendener, Victoria H. F. Scott, Benedict Seymour, Nizan Shaked, Sami Siegelbaum, Amanda Smith, Jason E. Smith, Luke Smythe, Sven Spieker, Joni Spigler, Kerstin Stakemeier, Trevor Stark, Jacob Stewart-Halevy, Allison Stielau, Barbara Strieder, Nicola Suthor, John Tain, Jordan Troeller, the late Marina Vishmidt, Anne Wagner, the staff of the Walker Art Center, Ruobing Wang, Ross Warren, Alison Weaver, Noura Wedell, Lara Weibgen, Andrew Weiner, Michael Werner, Gregory Williams, Kirsten Wolf, Lennart Wolff, Christopher S. Wood, Benjamin Young, Sebastian Zeidler, Wolfgang Zumdick,

and

Sharon Jones, Greg Spaulding, and Timothy Spaulding,

and especially,

Alana LaBeaf.

# Notes

## INTRODUCTION: ECONOMIMESIS

1 A closely related work is the multiple *Countdown 2000*, 1981. The piece consists of an offset lithograph reproducing a computer-generated calendar that enumerates all the days from January 1, 1980, to January 1, 2000 (with a correction to the calculation in the artist's handwriting).

2 See Manfred Kuttner et al., *Leben mit Pop: Eine Reproduktion des kapitalistischen Realismus* (Düsseldorf: Kunsthalle Düsseldorf, 2013). Cultural critic Mark Fisher reintroduced the term in his book *Capitalist Realism: Is There No Alternative?* (Winchester, UK: Zero Books, 2009).

3 Art historian Hal Foster has developed the idea of mimetic critique in relation to both the pre–World War II European avant-garde and more recent art. See especially Hal Foster, *Bad New Days: Art, Criticism, Emergency* (London: Verso, 2015).

4 Joseph Beuys, "'Death Keeps Me Awake': Interview with Achille Bonito Oliva," in *Energy Plan for the Western Man: Joseph Beuys in America: Writings by and Interviews with the Artist*, ed. Carin Kuoni (New York: Four Walls Eight Windows, 1990), 168–69.

5 Benjamin H. D. Buchloh, *Gerhard Richter: Painting after the Subject of History* (Cambridge, MA: MIT Press, 2022), 378.

6 As art historian David Adams notes in one of the earlier texts to make this point, "An approach to ecology worthy of the epithet 'radical' is one that does not limit its concerns to ecological systems within the natural world. Radical ecology also sees these in connection with larger patterns of human life: social forms; economic theories, practices, and interests; political and legislative history and method; control of information and communications media; and, indeed, the underlying philosophies and teleologies of Western civilization. By this definition, the German artist Joseph Beuys (1921–86) was not only a radical ecologist, but also the pioneer investigator of the role of art in forging radical ecological paradigms for the relationship between human beings and the natural environment." David Adams, "Joseph Beuys: Pioneer of a Radical Ecology," *Art Journal* 51, no. 2 (Summer 1992): 26.

7 Beuys's job title at the Staatliche Kunstakademie Düsseldorf (Düsseldorf State Art Academy) from 1961 to 1972 was "professor of monumental sculpture." He did in fact produce a handful of monuments or plans for monuments in the traditional sense. I will say more about these later.

8 On this point, compare Nicole Demby and Daniel Spaulding, "Art, Value, and the Freedom Fetish," *Mute*, May 28, 2015, https://www.metamute.org/editorial/articles/art-value-and-freedom-fetish-0; Dave Beech, *Art and Value: Art's Economic Exceptionalism in Classical, Neoclassical, and Marxist Economics* (Leiden: Brill, 2015).

9 Compare, for example, Luke Skrebowski, "On Pierre Huyghe's UUmweltanschauung: Art, Ecosystems Aesthetics, and General Ecology," *Grey Room* 77 (2019): 66–83.

10 Karl Marx, *Capital: A Critique of Political Economy*, trans. David Fernbach (London: Penguin Books, 1981), 3:949.

11 See, for example, Jason W. Moore, *Capitalism in the Web of Life: Ecology and the Accumulation of Capital* (London: Verso, 2015). For opposing viewpoints, see John Bellamy Foster, *Marx's Ecology: Materialism and Nature* (New York: Monthly Review Press, 2000); Andreas

Malm, *The Progress of This Storm: Nature and Society in a Warming World* (London: Verso, 2018). In recent years, the writings of Kohei Saito have also brought ecosocialist theory to an unexpectedly broad audience.

12 Hans Blumenberg, "Prospect for a Theory of Nonconceptuality," trans. Hannes Bajohr, in *History, Metaphor, Fables: A Hans Blumenberg Reader*, ed. Hannes Bajohr, Florian Fuchs, and Joe Paul Kroll (Ithaca, NY: Cornell University Press, 2020), 241 (emphasis in the original).

13 Capital's rhythms are out of sync with nature's and the body's. Compare E. P. Thompson, "Time, Work-Discipline, and Industrial Capitalism," *Past and Present* 38, no. 1 (December 1967): 56–97; Moishe Postone, *Time, Labor, and Social Domination: A Reinterpretation of Marx's Critical Theory* (Cambridge: Cambridge University Press, 1993). For an account of the emergence of the fossil fuel economy and thus anthropogenic climate change that stresses the subsumption of the labor process to the temporal exigencies of capitalist control over working-class bodies, see Andreas Malm, *Fossil Capital: The Rise of Steam Power and the Roots of Global Warming* (London: Verso, 2016).

14 Hans Blumenberg, "Observations Drawn from Metaphors," trans. Florian Fuchs, in *History, Metaphors, Fables: A Hans Blumenberg Reader*, ed. Hannes Bajohr, Florian Fuchs, and Joe Paul Kroll (Ithaca, NY: Cornell University Press, 2020), 232.

15 Jacques Derrida, "Economimesis," trans. R. Klein, *Diacritics* 11, no. 2 (Summer 1981): 2–25.

16 For a related approach to working with structural binaries, compare Daniel Spaulding, "A Scheme Transfer for Global Modernism," *October* 186 (Fall 2023): 163–96.

17 Theodor W. Adorno, "Reconciliation Under Duress," trans. Rodney Livingstone, in Ernst Bloch et al., *Aesthetics and Politics* (1961; repr., London: NLB, 1977), 151–76.

18 Paul de Man, *Aesthetic Ideology*, ed. Andrzej Warminski (Minneapolis: University of Minnesota Press, 1996).

19 Genealogies of such practices often play Beuys near the root. See Karen van den Berg, Cara M. Jordan, and Philipp Kleinmichel, eds., *The Art of Direct Action: Social Sculpture and Beyond* (Berlin: Sternberg Press, 2019).

20 György Lukács, *History and Class Consciousness: Studies in Marxist Dialectics*, trans. Rodney Livingstone (Cambridge, MA: MIT Press, 1971).

21 T. J. Clark, *Image of the People: Gustave Courbet and the 1848 Revolution* (London: Thames & Hudson, 1973), 12.

22 Moore, *Capitalism in the Web of Life*, 8.

23 "In [Carl] Einstein, art formalizes ontological stances towards the world from within it: just like all other human practices. And it does so autonomously: just like all other human practices. Autonomy is *Selbstgemäßheit*, the uniquely proper self-consistency of any such practice." Sebastian Zeidler, "Form as Revolt: Carl Einstein's Philosophy of the Real and the Work of Paul Klee," *Res: Anthropology and Aesthetics* 57–58 (Spring–Fall 2010): 243.

24 Compare Malm's "substance monism property dualism" approach, which "recognizes that everything is connected to everything else (the Alpha of ecological science) and that some parties behave disruptively within that web (the Omega)." Malm, *The Progress of This Storm*, 62.

25 This is the claim in Paul North, *Bizarre-Privileged Items in the Universe: The Logic of Likeness* (New York: Zone Books, 2021).

26 A term from poet Paul Valéry that Blumenberg made an important part of his aesthetics. See Hans Blumenberg, "The Essential Ambiguity of the Aesthetic Object," trans. Hannes Bajohr and Julia Pelta Feldman, in *History, Metaphors, Fables: A Hans Blumenberg Reader*, 441–48.

27 Compare Paul de Man, "Aesthetic Formalization: Kleist's *Über das Marionettentheater*," in *The Rhetoric of Romanticism* (New York: Columbia University Press, 1984), 263–90.

28 Derrida, "Economimesis," 4.

29 For a commentary on this idea, see Stewart Martin, "The Absolute Artwork Meets the Absolute Commodity," *Radical Philosophy* 146 (November–December 2007): 15–25.

30 Marina Vishmidt, "What Do We Mean by 'Autonomy' and 'Reproduction'?," in *Reproducing Autonomy: Work, Money, Crisis and Contemporary Art*, by Kerstin Stakemeier and Marina Vishmidt (London: Mute Publishing, 2016), 41, 43 (emphasis in the original).

31 For an account, see Robert Brenner, *The Economics of Global Turbulence: The Advanced Capitalist Economies from Long Boom to Long Downturn* (London: Verso, 2006).

32 Theodor W. Adorno, "The Idea of Natural History," trans. Robert Hullot-Kentor, *Telos* 60 (June 1984): 111–24.

33 The most thorough study is Ron Mannheim, *Beim Wort genommen. Joseph Beuys und der Nationalsozialismus* (Berlin: Neofelis, 2021). For another collection of Beuys's statements intended to highlight ideologically questionable content, see Hans Peter Riegel, *Beuys. Die Biographie*, vol. 4, *Verborgenes Reden* (Zurich: Riverside AG, 2021). Riegel particularly associates Beuys with the problematic racial doctrines of Austrian esotericist Rudolf Steiner, the founder of anthroposophy. Here, as in his biography of the artist, which I will cite elsewhere, Riegel oddly seems to be under the impression that mention of Beuys's anthroposophical leanings has been "taboo" among his followers, when in fact the influence of Steiner and anthroposophical thinking on his thought and practice has sustained a minor publishing industry since the 1980s.

34 A terminological note: In 1949, the former Allied occupation zones became the Federal Republic of Germany (Bundesrepublik Deutschland, or BRD) while the Soviet zone became the German Democratic Republic (Deutsche Demokratische Republik, or DDR). In English, the term "West Germany" tends to be used as a synonym for the BRD—a usage I have adopted in this book. Strictly speaking, this is not quite accurate since the BRD also contained West Berlin, located far to the geographic east of the formerly unified nation. During the Cold War period, Germans accordingly sometimes used the phrasing "the BRD and West Berlin" to refer to the nation as a whole, even though West Berlin was part of the BRD.

35 Jason W. Moore, ed., *Anthropocene or Capitalocene? Nature, History, and the Crisis of Capitalism* (Oakland, CA: PM Press, 2016).

36 There is no guarantee that a future ecosocialism would be less authoritarian than most of socialism's twentieth-century manifestations. This is the scenario somewhat cheekily called "Climate Mao" in Geoff Mann and Joel Wainwright, *Climate Leviathan: A Political Theory of Our Planetary Future* (London: Verso, 2018).

37 Hans Blumenberg, *Work on Myth*, trans. Robert M. Wallace (Cambridge, MA: MIT Press, 1985).

38 Leo Bersani and Ulysse Dutoit, "Merde Alors," *October* 13 (Summer 1980): 22–35.

39 Marx introduced the concept of real abstraction. For its most influential articulation, see Alfred Sohn-Rethel, *Intellectual and Manual Labour: A Critique of Epistemology*, trans. Ralph Mannheim (London: Macmillan, 1978).

40 The strongest negative readings have come from art historians Benjamin Buchloh and Éric Michaud. I respond to both in subsequent chapters. See Benjamin H. D. Buchloh, "Beuys: The Twilight of the Idol, Preliminary Notes for a Critique," in *Neo-Avantgarde and Culture Industry: Essays on European and American Art from 1955 to 1975* (1980; repr., Cambridge, MA: MIT Press, 2000), 41–64; Éric Michaud, "The Ends of Art according to Joseph Beuys," trans. Rosalind Krauss, *October* 45 (Summer 1988): 36–46.

## CHAPTER 1: THE MATTER OF MYTH

1 For a reading of this prior version of *Fond III*, see Carl-Peter Buschkühle, *Wärmezeit. Zur Kunst als Kunstpädagogik bei Joseph Beuys* (Frankfurt: P. Lang, 1997), 131–43.

2 Beuys oversaw the transfer of this material into the Hessisches Landesmuseum in 1970. On the *Block Beuys* installation, see Inge Lorenz, "Zur Gesamtinstallation des Block Beuys in Darmstadt," in *Vorträge zum Werk von Joseph Beuys*, ed. Arbeitskreis Block Beuys im Verein der Freunde und Förderer des Hessischen Landesmuseums in Darmstadt e.V. (Darmstadt: Häusser, 1995), 9–18; Barbara Gronau, *Theaterinstallationen. Performative Räume bei Beuys, Boltanski und Kabakov* (Munich: Wilhelm Fink, 2010), 97–129; Eva Beuys, Wenzel Beuys, and Jessyka Beuys, *Joseph Beuys. Block Beuys* (Munich: Schirmer/Mosel, 1990).

3 The form of this work is based on a basalt cross that Beuys had made in 1955–56, now in a private collection.

4 Quoted in Georg Jappe, "Fond III von Joseph Beuys," *Frankfurter Allgemeine Zeitung*, February 11, 1969, reprinted in Georg Jappe, *Beuys packen. Dokumente 1968–1996* (Regensburg: Lindinger + Schmid, 1996), 67–68. All translations in this book are my own unless otherwise noted.

5 Joseph Beuys-Archiv / Stiftung Museum Schloss Moyland, Inv.-Nr. JBA-B-0040804.

6 Another, earlier version of *Fond IV/4* (dated 1970–74) is in the Kaiser Wilhelm Museum in Krefeld. *Brasilienfond* derives its name from the fact that it was first exhibited at the fifteenth São Paulo Biennial in October–December 1979.

7 Jappe, *Beuys packen*, 67.

8  On Serra's "verb list" and its implications for a "general theory of transitive art," compare David Joselit, "What to Do with Pictures," *October* 138 (Fall 2011): 81–94. A transcription of the original text can be found in Richard Serra, *Writings/Interviews* (Chicago: University of Chicago Press, 1994), 3–4.

9  For methodological reasons, in this context I mostly remain faithful to the "tautological" self-interpretations that minimalist and postminimalist artists themselves tended to provide in the 1960s rather than delve into broader (that is to say, less literal) connotations of their work. For an alternate reading of the semiotics of minimalism, compare Georges Didi-Huberman, *Ce que nous voyons, ce qui nous regarde* (Paris: Éditions de Minuit, 1992).

10  Beuys's work was included in a section subtitled "Personal Mythologies" at the fifth installment of the exhibition *documenta*, curated by Szeemann in Kassel in 1972.

11  See Ulrike Bohnet et al., *Joseph Beuys und die Schamanen* (Bedburg-Hau: Stiftung Museum Schloss Moyland, 2021).

12  Beuys visited Edinburgh several times in the 1970s on the invitation of Demarco, a gallerist and curator. On their collaborations, see Richard Demarco and Joseph Beuys, *A Unique Partnership: Richard Demarco, Joseph Beuys* (Edinburgh: Luath Press Limited, 2016). *Three Pots Action* is documented in Uwe Schneede, *Joseph Beuys. Die Aktionen: Kommentiertes Werkverzeichnis mit fotografischen Dokumentationen* (Ostfildern-Ruit bei Stuttgart: G. Hatje, 1994), 354–59 (henceforth *Die Aktionen*).

13  Art critic Donald Kuspit's essay "Enchanting the Disenchanted: The Artist's Last Stand—Joseph Beuys," for example, only makes cursory reference to specific works in its footnotes. See Donald Kuspit, *The Cult of the Avant-Garde Artist* (Cambridge: Cambridge University Press, 1993), 83–99.

14  The first biography appeared in 1973: Götz Adriani, Winnifried Könitz, and Karin Thomas, *Joseph Beuys* (Cologne: DuMont Schauberg, 1973). This was the second book-length critical text on the artist, appearing shortly after Lothar Romain and Rolf Wedewer, *Über Beuys* (Düsseldorf: Droste, 1972).

15  There are now several biographies available. In addition to the work by Adriani, Könitz, and Thomas cited just above, compare Claudia Mesch, *Joseph Beuys* (London: Reaktion Books, 2017); Hans Peter Riegel, *Beuys: Die Biografie* (Berlin: Aufbau Verlag, 2013); Frank Gieseke, *Flieger, Filz und Vaterland. Eine erweiterte Beuys Biografie* (Berlin: Elefanten Press, 1996). The latter two are avowedly hostile to the artist.

16  "Richard Serra by David Seidner," *Bomb*, January 1, 1993, https://bombmagazine.org /articles/richard-serra/.

17  Compare Stanley Cavell, "Music Discomposed," in *Must We Mean What We Say? A Book of Essays*, by Stanley Cavell (New York: Scribner, 1969), 180–212. The trope of charlatanism gained critical mass around the moment of Beuys's 1979 retrospective at the Guggenheim Museum, which I will discuss elsewhere. The cover of the November 4, 1979, issue of *Der Spiegel* features a huge photo of Beuys's face paired with the caption "*Der Größte: Weltruhm für einen Scharlatan?*" (The greatest: World fame for a charlatan?). See also Bettina Funcke, *Pop or Populus: Art Between High and Low*, trans. Warren Niesłuchowski (Berlin: Sternberg Press, 2009), 112–27.

18  Suggestions along these lines can be found in Roland Barthes, *Mythologies*, trans. Annette Lavers (New York: Hill and Wang, 1972); Paul Veyne, *Did the Greeks Believe in Their Myths? An Essay on the Constitutive Imagination*, trans. Paula Wissing (Chicago: University of Chicago Press, 1988). See also Theodor W. Adorno and Max Horkheimer's various writings on the recrudescence of mythical thinking in modernity, of which their book *Dialectic of Enlightenment: Philosophical Fragments*, trans. Edmund Jephcott (Stanford, CA: Stanford University Press, 2002), is the most influential.

19  For the idea that artistic formalization works on and transforms ideological material, compare T. J. Clark, *Image of the People: Gustave Courbet and the 1848 Revolution* (London: Thames & Hudson, 1973), 13.

20  See Antje von Graevenitz, "Erlösungskunst oder Befreiungspolitik: Wagner und Beuys," in *Unsere Wagner: J. Beuys, H. Müller, K. Stockhausen, H. Jürgen Syberberg*, ed. Gabriele Förg (Frankfurt: Fischer Taschenbücher, 1984). On Beuys and the *Gesamtkunstwerk*, compare Manuela Göhner, *Rhetorische Ästhetik des Gesamtkunstwerks. Joseph Beuys: ein Beitrag zur Methode der Kunstkritik aus der Sicht der rhetorischen Anthropologie* (Oberhausen: Athena, 2000).

21  Early documentation of the work can be found in Caroline Tisdall, *Joseph Beuys Coyote* (Munich: Schirmer/Mosel, 1976). This text was written in English, but translated into German; an English version was not published until 2008. Caroline Tisdall, *Joseph Beuys: Coyote* (London: Thames & Hudson, 2008). *I Like America*

inaugurated a hiatus in the artists "actions" that would last until 1977, except for the *Three Pots Action* that I have described above, which he in fact performed on his way back from New York City after the conclusion of *I Like America.* The sole "action" of 1977 was a "potato planting" that occurred at Galerie René Block in Berlin that March. On the occasion of the death of Fluxus leader George Maciunas in May 1978, Beuys performed the first of a series of actions with Nam June Paik that would revive their Fluxus era collaborations from the 1960s. The modus operandi of the "action" never regained its preeminence in the last decade of Beuys's life.

22 The footage was shot by Helmut Wietz. An edited version with titles was released by Galerie René Block in 1978. On Beuys and film, see Ulf Jensen, *Film als Form. Joseph Beuys und das bewegte Bild* (Berlin: De Gruyter, 2016).

23 Joseph Beuys, "Coyote, I Like America and America Likes Me," in *Energy Plan for the Western Man: Joseph Beuys in America: Writings and Interviews with the Artist,* ed. Carin Kuoni (New York: Four Walls Eight Windows, 1990), 141. This passage is excerpted from a discussion with Tisdall originally published in the catalog that she edited for the artist's 1979 retrospective at the Guggenheim. Caroline Tisdall, *Joseph Beuys* (New York: Solomon R. Guggenheim Museum, 1979).

24 It is worth considering issues of cultural appropriation in this context. Art historian Steven M. Leuthold has proposed a critique along these lines: "Following from the whiteshamanist [*sic*] attitude, indigenous religious expressions are viewed as 'available' by members of non-native cultures to 'use' in inventing their own myths or traditions. . . . One must beware of 'inventing one's own myths' or rituals if they involve the appropriation of key symbols from other cultures that have been radically decontextualized. Beuys's appropriation of the coyote as a key symbol in the aforementioned piece [*I Like America and America Likes Me*] is an example of the radical decontextualization of an American Indian symbol." Steven M. Leuthold, *Cross-Cultural Issues in Art: Frames for Understanding* (Abindgon, UK: Routledge, 2011), 117.

25 On the relation of concepts of reality to aesthetics, see especially Hans Blumenberg, "The Concept of Reality and the Possibility of the Novel," in *History, Metaphors, Fables: A Hans Blumenberg Reader,* ed. Hannes Bajohr, Florian Fuchs, and Joe Paul Kroll (Ithaca, NY: Cornell University Press, 2020), 499–524.

26 Blumenberg analyzes Goethe's hymn *Prometheus* at length in Hans Blumenberg, *Work on Myth,* trans. Robert M. Wallace (Cambridge, MA: MIT Press, 1985).

27 Benjamin H. D. Buchloh, "Beuys: The Twilight of the Idol, Preliminary Notes for a Critique," in *Neo-Avantgarde and Culture Industry: Essays on European and American Art from 1955 to 1975* (Cambridge, MA: MIT Press, 2000), 41–64, originally published in *Artforum* 5, no. 18 (January 1980). For a slightly earlier critique of Beuys along somewhat similar lines (it was written in response to the same 1979 Guggenheim retrospective), see Werner Spies, "Von Filz und Fett zum Sonnenstaat? Joseph Beuys im Guggenheim-Museum in New York," *Frankfurter Allgemeine Zeitung,* November 13, 1979, 21.

28 Buchloh, "Beuys: The Twilight of the Idol," 59 (emphasis in the original).

29 This is a narrative that one can extract from the work of the critics and art historians associated with the journal *October.* See, for example, Rosalind Krauss, *Passages in Modern Sculpture* (New York: Viking Press, 1977); Benjamin H. D. Buchloh, "Conceptual Art 1962–1969: From the Aesthetic of Administration to the Critique of Institutions," *October* 55 (Winter 1990), 105–43; Hal Foster, "The Crux of Minimalism," in *The Return of the Real: The Avant-Garde at the End of the Century* (Cambridge, MA: MIT Press, 1996), 35–68. In Buchloh's writing, this trajectory is complicated by a recognition that resistance to modern instrumental rationality may sometimes involve forms of obsolescence that at first glance may look regressive, such as the German artist Gerhard Richter's reversion to the genres of premodernist painting (portrait, landscape, and still life), just as the apparently progressive disenchantment of art may only liquidate resistance to administrative and capitalist rationality.

30 Benjamin H. D. Buchloh, "Reconsidering Joseph Beuys: Once Again," in *Joseph Beuys: Mapping the Legacy,* ed. Gene Ray (New York: D.A.P., 2001), 89.

31 Compare Daniel Spaulding, "Legitimation Crisis: Notes on Benjamin Buchloh's Method," *Zeitschrift für Kunstgeschichte* 86, no. 3 (September 2023): 406–19.

32 On bricolage and myth, see Claude Lévi-Strauss, *The Savage Mind* (Chicago: University of Chicago Press, 1966), 16–34.

33 Buchloh, "Beuys: The Twilight of the Idol," 48.

34 I owe this suggestion to Daniel Marcus.

35 Blumenberg develops the notion of "absolute metaphor" in his book *Paradigms for a Metaphorology*, trans. Robert Savage (Ithaca, NY: Cornell University Press, 2010). Briefly, an absolute metaphor is one that cannot be further reduced to or translated into conceptuality but rather grounds the felt structure of a world in the first place prior to conceptual elaboration. The persistence of metaphor also indicates points at which conceptuality falters.

36 The work was produced for the city's *Kunstforum* exhibition of that year. It is now in the collection of the Städtische Galerie im Lenbachhaus, Munich, where it is housed in quarters drastically smaller than the site of its original installation. (Beuys oversaw the changes.) There are a number of treatments of the piece. Compare Eva Huttenlauch and Matthias Mühling, *Joseph Beuys. zeige deine Wunde* (Munich: Schirmer/Mosel, 2021); Gerald Schröder, *Schmerzensmänner. Trauma und Therapie in der westdeutschen und österreichischen Kunst der 1960er Jahre: Baselitz, Beuys, Brus, Schwarzkogler, Rainer* (Munich: Wilhem Fink, 2011), 231–48. Photographs by Ute Klophaus of the original 1976 installation in a subterranean pedestrian walkway at the corner of Maximilianstraße and the Altstadtring in Munich can be found in Joseph Beuys, *Zeige deine Wunde* (Munich: Schellmann & Klüser, 1976). For an expanded and reworked version of the above publication, see Armin Zweite and Joseph Beuys, *Joseph Beuys. Zeige deine Wunde*, vol. 1 (Munich: Schellmann & Klüser, 1980).

37 Tomas Schmit and Wolf Vostell, eds., *Actions, Agit-Prop, De-Collage, Happening, Events, Antiart, L'Autrisme, Art Total, Refluxus. Festival der Neuen Kunst, 20. Juli 1964, Aachen* (Mülheim: T. Schmit, 1964). See also Brigitte Franzen, Annette Lagler, and Myriam Kroll, eds., *Nie wieder störungsfrei! Aachen Avantgarde seit 1964* (Aachen: Ludwig Forum, 2011); Eva Beuys, *Atlantis. Joseph Beuys: 3 Aktionen, 1964–1965* (Düsseldorf: Joseph Beuys Medien-Archiv, 2008), 13–62.

38 Quoted in Annie Suquet, "Archaic Thought and Ritual in the Work of Joseph Beuys," *Res: Anthropology and Aesthetics* 28 (Fall 1995): 149.

39 On Beuys's drawings, see Ann Temkin and Bernice Rose, *Thinking Is Form: The Drawings of Joseph Beuys* (Philadelphia: Philadelphia Museum of Art, 1993). *Fettige Wolke* probably represents one of the earliest uses of fat in the artist's graphic work, as art historian Eva Huber dates the first fat drawings to 1959–60. See Peter Bürger et al, *Joseph Beuys. Die Materialien und ihre Botschaft*

(Bedburg-Hau: Museum Schloss Moyland, 2006), 76.

40 Museum Schloss Moyland, Raum 43 / Wand 3, Plastische Bilder, 18: *o.t.*, 1957; Museum Schloss Moyland, Raum 41 / Wand 4, Plastische Bilder, 12: Fuß-Aktion, 1958; Museum Schloss Moyland, Raum 41 / Wand 3, Plastische Bilder, 16: Weiblicher Torso, 1958.

41 Museum Schloss Moyland, Raum 30 / Wand 3, 38: *o.t. (Junge Frau und zwei spielende Kinder)*, 1949.

42 A less ambitious version of *DER CHEF* was first staged at a Fluxus festival in Copenhagen on August 30, 1964. Beuys repeated the action at René Block's gallery on December 1. I follow Schneede's catalogue raisonné for the orthography of this and other titles of actions; much of the Beuys literature forgoes the capitalization. Schneede, *Joseph Beuys*, 58.

43 Suquet, "Archaic Thought," 151.

44 *FESTUM FLUXORUM FLUXUS—Musik und Antimusik—Das instrumentale Theater* took place at the Kunstakademie Düsseldorf on February 2 and 3, 1963. Materials used in this action were later incorporated into the 1966 sculpture *Eurasia Sibirische Symphonie 1963* (Eurasia Siberian symphony 1963), now in the collection of the Museum of Modern Art, New York (213.2000.a-b).

45 Buchloh, *Neo-Avantgarde and Culture Industry*, 54.

46 Judith Nesbitt, ed., *Joseph Beuys: The Revolution Is Us* (Liverpool: Tate Gallery Liverpool, 1993), 21.

47 Another *Plastisches Bild* dated 1950 is described as being composed of wax and plaster. Museum Schloss Moyland, Raum 41 / Wand 5, Plastische Bilder, 6: Kreuz. As in other early instances, the use of these materials may be connected with bronze casting. There are three *Bienenkönigin* sculptures, all of which were exhibited at *documenta 3* in Kassel in 1964. For the catalog of the show, see Siegfried Hagen and Alfred Nemeczek, eds., *Documenta III: Kassel '64*, 3 vols. (Cologne: Verlag M. DuMont Schauberg, 1964). Each consists of a wax sculpture laid atop a carved wooden platter-like element. Hence they resemble table settings. Indeed, *Bienenkönigin II* is equipped with a wooden fork and spoon. Numbers one and two also incorporate small clay and wax figurines that recall prehistoric sculptures. *Bienenkönigin II* and *Bienenkönigin III* eventually found their way into the *Block Beuys* installation in the Hessisches Landesmuseum in Darmstadt, while the remaining work (*Bienenkönigin I*) is now housed in art

collector Lothar Schirmer's donation to the Städtische Galerie im Lenbachhaus in Munich, where *zeige deine Wunde* and *Badewanne* are located too. Helmut Friedel and Lothar Schirmer, eds., *Joseph Beuys im Lenbachhaus und Schenkung Lothar Schirmer* (Munich: Schirmer/Mosel and Lenbachhaus, 2013), cat. no. 3, 28–35. Of these works, only *Bienenkönigin III* displays clear morphological similarities to the creature named in its title or at least to some manner of insectoid form. (I will examine the apian motif in chapter 2.) The terminal date consistently given for all three works is 1952. Only the first in the series currently bears the initial date of 1947, which so far as I know seems to have been canonized by its inclusion in Tisdall's 1979 catalog—a text that is not always reliable. In the catalog of *documenta 3*, however, the work bears only the date 1952. Hagen and Nemeczek, *Documenta III*, 1:324.

48 For images and a description of this object, see Eva Beuys et al., *Joseph Beuys: Block Beuys*, 188–91, 359.

49 Tisdall, *Joseph Beuys* (1979), 48, ill. 77.

50 Eva Beuys et al., *Joseph Beuys: Block Beuys*, 352.

51 Tisdall, *Joseph Beuys* (1979), 49, ill. 81; Eva Beuys et al, *Joseph Beuys: Block Beuys*, 359, ill. 189. For an analysis of this work, which also incorporates a strip of film, see Ulf Jensen, *Film als Form: Joseph Beuys und das bewegte Bild* (Berlin: De Gruyter, 2016).

52 Götz Adriani, Winfried Konnertz, and Karin Thomas, *Joseph Beuys. Leben und Werk* (Cologne: DuMont, 1973), 54, ill. 24.

53 Lynne Cooke and Karen Kelly, *Joseph Beuys: Arena—Where Would I Have Got If I Had Been Intelligent!* (New York: Dia Center for the Arts, 1994), 124–25.

54 A rather formless thing titled *Grab (Fragment)* (Grave [fragment]) bears the date 1949–50 and is cataloged as incorporating wax. Museum Schloss Moyland, Raum 33 / Vitrine, 10: *Grab (Fragment)*.

55 Buchloh, "Beuys: The Twilight of the Idol," 64.

56 For background on the 1977 exhibition in Münster, see Rainer Schnettler, *Ausstellung von Skulptur im öffentlichen Raum. Konzeption, Vermittlung, Rezeption am Beispiel der "Skulptur" 1977 in Münster und der "Skulptur Projekte Münster 1987"* (Frankfurt: Peter Lang, 1991). On Beuys and architecture, compare Wolfgang Zumdick, *Joseph Beuys und die Architektur. Perspektiven und Akzente* (Stuttgart: Mayer, 2013).

57 I am repeating this description of the work's materials on the authority of several catalogs and other published sources. In actuality, the exact formula remains obscure. The catalog of a major 2008 retrospective in Berlin, for example, only lists suet and stearin, not paraffin. Eugen Blume and Catherine Nichols, eds., *Beuys. Die Revolution sind wir* (Göttingen: Steidl, 2008), 87. The Joseph Beuys Archive at Museum Schloss Moyland preserves several letters from local industrial supply companies addressed to Beuys, his assistant Heiner Bastian, and the *documenta* administration dating from March and April 1977. These letters provide descriptions of different varieties of wax and plastic, and give quotes for sample quantities. Joseph Beuys-Archiv / Stiftung Museum Schloss Moyland, Inv.-Nr. JBA-B 028482, JBA-B 028833, JBA-B 013266, JBA-B 029437. Beuys had signed a contract for his participation in *documenta 6*, providing for a three thousand deutsche mark honorarium, on December 16, 1976. Joseph Beuys-Archiv / Stiftung Museum Schloss Moyland, Inv.-Nr. JBA-B 004701. Given that the exhibition did not open until July 3, 1977, it is thus demonstrable that Beuys was at least considering alternatives to beeswax several months before the installation of the work.

58 See, for example, *Skulptur. Ausstellung in Münster 1977* (Münster: Landschaftsverband Westfalen-Lippe, 1977), 2:43–45.

59 Tisdall, *Joseph Beuys* (1979), 248.

60 I am grateful to Eugen Blume, former director of the Hamburger Bahnhof—Nationalgalerie der Gegenwart, Berlin, for confirming the details in this paragraph in a personal communication.

61 On Beuys's use of fat, compare Alison Leitch, "Joseph Beuys: Shaman of Fat," in *Fat: Culture and Materiality*, ed. Christopher E. Forth and Alison Leitch (London: Bloomsbury Academic, 2014), 71–89; Eva Huber, "Fett," in *Joseph Beuys. Filz, Fett, Honig, Gold, Blut: Symposium zur Material-Ikonografie*, ed. Uwe Claus et al. (Bedburg-Hau: Stiftung Museum Schloss Moyland, 2008), 52–54; Johannes Am Ende et al., *Joseph Beuys und die Fettecke. Eine Dokumentation zur Zerstörung der Fettecke in der Kunstakademie Düsseldorf* (Heidelberg: Edition Staeck, 1987); Monika Wagner, *Das Material der Kunst. Eine Andere Geschichte der Moderne* (Munich: Beck, 2001), 197–212. Wagner notes that fat and more specifically butter have a particular resonance in Germany due to their associations with both wartime rationing and postwar abundance; these

substances are indexes of the nation's material fortunes.

62 Karl Marx, *Capital: A Critique of Political Economy*, trans. Ben Fowkes (New York: Penguin, 1976), 1:133.

63 Quoted in Franz-Joachim Verspohl, "Plastik = Alles. Zu den 4 Büchern aus: 'Projekt Westmensch' von Joseph Beuys," in *Joseph Beuys. 4 Bücher aus "Projekt Westmensch" 1958*, ed. Franz-Joachim Verspohl (Cologne: Hans van der Grinten, 1993), 9. The quotation is taken from Joseph Beuys and Jost Hebrig, "Die Dinge haben ihre Sprache. Interview mit Joseph Beuys," *Süddeutsche Zeitung*, January 26–27, 1980.

64 Tisdall, *Joseph Beuys* (1979), 44. The schema is included in the catalog entry for an early iron and bronze sculpture, *SàFG—SàUG*, dated 1953–58. On Beuys's cosmology of chaos, movement, and form, compare Stephanie Benedikt-Jansen, *Joseph Beuys. Geordnetes Chaos oder chaotische Ordnung?* (Gelnhausen: Triga, 2001).

65 René Descartes, *The Philosophical Writings of Descartes*, trans. John Cottington, Robert Stoothoff, and Dugald Murdoch (Cambridge: Cambridge University Press, 1984), 2:20–21 (30–31).

66 Robert Morris, "Notes on Sculpture," in *Minimal Art: A Critical Anthology*, ed. Gregory Battcock (New York: E. P. Dutton, 1968), 234.

67 Joseph Beuys-Archiv / Stiftung Museum Schloss Moyland, Inv.-Nr. JBA-B 003976.

68 Blume and Nichols, *Beuys*, 87.

69 Beuys's references to wounding and impairment invite consideration and probably critique from the perspective of disability studies. The fact that the pedestrian ramp on the University of Münster campus would have facilitated wheelchair access makes the association particularly relevant. For some brief indications of a possible approach, see Cary Wolfe, "The Biopolitical Drama of Joseph Beuys," *New Literary History* 51, no. 4 (Autumn 2020): 835–54.

70 Joseph Beuys-Archiv / Stiftung Museum Schloss Moyland, Inv.-Nr. JBA-B HG 75.

71 The commonalities between Beuys and Morris were not lost on contemporaries in the German art world. As Düsseldorf gallerist Hans Strelow noted, "There is in fact an intensive as well as personal connection between the apparently highly subjective artist Beuys and the apparently highly objective Robert Morris, an exponent of 'Minimal Art': Morris's 'Corner Piece' made out of light brown plywood has the same space-determining [*raumbestimmende*] function

as the 'Filzecke' by Beuys. Both sculptures were created in 1964." Strelow is quoted in a pamphlet that was issued by Galerie René Block, Berlin, on the occasion of two concurrent exhibitions in June and July 1968—one devoted to "Minimal Art USA," and the other to "Neue Monumente Deutschland" (New monuments Germany). *Minimal Art, USA Juni 1968: Neue Monumente Deutschland, Juli 1968* (Berlin: Galerie René Block, 1968).

72 Buchloh discusses the Beuys-Morris relationship in "Twilight of the Idol." Art historian James Meyer in turn notes the influence not only of Beuys's *Felt Corner* but also Vladimir Tatlin's *Corner Counter-Relief* and Dan Flavin's *Pink Out of a Corner (to Jasper Johns)* on Morris's *Corner Piece*. James Meyer, *Minimalism: Art and Polemics in the Sixties* (New Haven, CT: Yale University Press, 2001), 113. On relations between Beuys and contemporaneous US artists in the milieu of minimalism and postminimalism, compare Dirk Luckow, *Joseph Beuys und die amerikanische Anti Form-Kunst. Einfluss und Wechselwirkung zwischen Beuys und Morris, Hesse, Nauman, Serra* (Berlin: Gebr. Mann Verlag, 1998).

73 Roland Barthes, *Mythologies*, trans. Annette Lavers (New York: Hill and Wang, 1972), 114.

74 Beuys, interview with Erika Billeter, in Erika Billeter, ed., *Mythos und Ritual in der Kunst der 70er Jahre* (Zurich: Kunsthaus Zürich, 1981), 90.

75 The deployment of the concept of the index in art theory from the 1970s onward depended on a selective reading of philosopher Charles Sanders Peirce's semiotics that privileged these qualities. See Rosalind Krauss, "Notes on the Index: Seventies Art in America," *October* 3 (Spring 1977): 68–81; Rosalind Krauss, "Notes on the Index: Seventies Art in America, Part 2," *October* 4 (Autumn 1977): 58–67.

76 *I Like America and America Likes Me* courts similar overreach, with the added offense of attempting vicariously to heal another nation's "trauma point."

77 Art historian Christopher S. Wood has written subtly about this process. See, for example, Christopher S. Wood, "Countermagical Combinations by Dosso Dossi," *Res: Anthropology and Aesthetics* 49–50 (Spring–Autumn 2006): 151–70.

78 Carrie Lambert-Beatty, "Make-Believe: Parafiction and Plausibility," *October* 129 (Summer 2009): 51–84. An exception in Lambert-Beatty's account is artist Aliza Shvarts's *Untitled (Senior Thesis)* because it remains unclear whether Shvarts

did what she claimed to have done in this piece (namely, repeatedly inseminated herself and then induced miscarriages). Lambert-Beatty argues that this uncertainty is the real intended content of the work, which again seems unlike Beuys since, by all evidence, he very much wanted his audience to believe his propositions.

79 Compare "The Moving Contradiction: The Systematic Dialectic of Capital as a Dialectic of Class Struggle," *Endnotes* 2 (2010), https://endnotes.org.uk/articles/the-moving-contradiction. The phrase is from Marx's *Grundrisse*. On the systematic coherence of Beuys's oeuvre, compare Gronau, *Theaterinstallationen*, 41–58; Wolfgang Zumdick, *PAN XXX ttt. Joseph Beuys als Denker: Sozialphilosophie, Erkenntnistheorie, Anthropologie* (Stuttgart: Mayer, 2002); Wolfram Hogrebe, *Beuysianismus. Expressive Strukturen der Moderne* (Munich: Wilhelm Fink, 2011); Massimo Donà, *Joseph Beuys: La Vera Mimesi* (Milan: Silvana, 2004); Antje Oltmann, *"Der Weltstoff letzendlich ist … neu zu bilden." Joseph Beuys für und wider die Moderne* (Ostfildern: edition tertium, 1994); Theodora Vischer, *Joseph Beuys. Die Einheit des Werkes: Zeichnungen, Aktionen, plastische Arbeiten, soziale Skulptur* (Cologne: Walther König, 1991). Vischer is primarily concerned with the relation between theory (or concept, or simply language) and material form in Beuys's work. I am as well, but I approach the question differently: whereas Vischer works through the theory-practice relation immanently, adopting what she calls a "position of agreement" (*Position des Einverständnisses*) as opposed to a "position of skepticism" (*Position der Skepsis*) with respect to Beuys's spoken and written discourse, I will instead describe the conceptuality of the work as in effect external to itself because the coherence of this conceptual system is keyed to the (in)coherence of capitalism as both a social logic and form of objective irrationality. For a more recent systematic overview of Beuys's life and work organized by keywords, see Bettina Paust and Tim Skrandies, eds., *Joseph Beuys—Handbuch. Leben—Werk—Wirkung* (Stuttgart: J. B. Metzler, 2021).

80 Blumenberg, *Work on Myth*. For an essay on myth that serves to introduce many of the basic propositions in the larger work, see Hans Blumenberg, "Wirklichkeitsbegriff und Wirkungspotential des Mythos," in *Ästhetische und metaphorologische Schriften* (Frankfurt: Suhrkamp, 2001), 327–405.

81 Benjamin H. D. Buchloh, Rosalind Krauss, and Annette Michelson, "Joseph Beuys at the Guggenheim," *October* 12 (Spring 1980): 10. On Beuys and science, compare Magdalena Holzhey, *Im Labor des Zeichners. Joseph Beuys und die Naturwissenschaft* (Berlin: Dietrich Reimer Verlag, 2009).

82 Compare Theodor W. Adorno and Max Horkheimer, *Dialectic of Enlightenment: Philosophical Fragments*, ed. Gunzelin Schmid Noerr, trans. Edmund Jephcott (Stanford, CA: Stanford University Press, 2002).

83 For a Blumenbergian analysis of political myths such as political scientist Samuel P. Huntington's notorious "clash of civilizations," see Chiara Bottici, *A Philosophy of Political Myth* (Cambridge: Cambridge University Press, 2007).

84 Rosalind Krauss, "Grids," in *The Originality of the Avant-Garde and Other Modernist Myths* (Cambridge, MA: MIT Press, 1985), 8–22.

85 Leo Bersani, *The Culture of Redemption* (Cambridge, MA: Harvard University Press, 1990).

86 Quoted in Willoughby Sharp, "An Interview with Joseph Beuys," *Artforum* 8, no. 4 (December 1969): 40–47.

87 For a description of value as an "automatic subject," see Karl Marx, *Capital: A Critique of Political Economy*, trans. Ben Fowkes (New York: Penguin, 1976), 1:255. The concept has been further developed in writings by scholars associated with the so-called critique of value, such as Moishe Postone and Robert Kurz. See, for example, Moishe Postone, *Time, Labor, and Social Domination: A Reinterpretation of Marx's Critical Theory* (Cambridge: Cambridge University Press, 1993), 75; Robert Kurz, "Subjektlose Herrschaft," *Krisis* 17 (1993): 17–94. Compare Beverly Best, *The Automatic Fetish: The Law of Value in Marx's Capital* (London: Verso, 2024).

## CHAPTER 2: CIRCULATORY SYSTEMS

1 The work was produced in an unlimited, unnumbered edition, of which approximately eight hundred copies are signed. Jörg Schellmann, ed., *Joseph Beuys: The Multiples* (Cambridge, MA,

Busch-Reisinger Museum, 1997), cat. no. 105, 133 (ill.).

2 For the catalogs of *documenta 6*, which was touted as the first "media" *documenta*, see Manfred

Schneckenburger et al., *Documenta 6. Kassel 1977, 24. Juni—2. Okt.* (Kassel: P. Dierichs, 1977); Hans D. Baumann et al., eds., *Kunst und Medien. Materialien zur documenta 6* (Kassel: Stadtzeitung und Verlag, 1977).

3 Schellmann, *Joseph Beuys*, cat. no. 292, 243 (ill.).

4 The multiple consists of a cardboard box containing fifteen photographs of the installation together with a single copy of the silk-screen print, a cassette tape, and a booklet. Schellmann, *Joseph Beuys*, cat. no. 544, 499 (ill.).

5 An anonymous review of *documenta 6* in *Der Spiegel* noted the work's "apparently [in the sense of falsely] functional mechanics" (*scheinfunktionellen Mechanik*). "Documenta: Süßer Seim der Medien," *Der Spiegel* 26, June 20, 1977, 156–59.

6 For extensive photographic documentation of *Honigpumpe*, see Klaus Staeck and Gerhard Steidl, *Joseph Beuys: Honey Is Flowing in All Directions* (Göttingen: Steidl, 2022; first edition 1997). Dismantled elements of the installation are now housed in the Louisiana Museum of Modern Art, Humlebæk, Denmark. That a propane generator was somehow involved in the *documenta 6* project is attested in a surviving receipt for two fillings by the Kassel office of the company Drachen-Propangas. Joseph Beuys-Archiv / Stiftung Museum Schloss Moyland, Inv.-Nr. JBA-B 028955, 028961. The presence of propane is not accounted for in the list of materials for the work in various catalog entries, which mention only electric motors.

7 See, for example, Peter Sager, "Im Dschungel der Medien," *Die Zeit*, July 15, 1977.

8 The action was performed at the opening of Beuys's first solo gallery exhibition, … *irgend ein Strang* (… Any strand), at Galerie Schmela, Düsseldorf, on November 26. Part of the action was captured on 16 mm film (black and white, no sound, 6:22). For a DVD transfer, see Eva Beuys and Wenzel Beuys, *Joseph Beuys. Die Eröffnung 1965: Irgend ein Strang, Wie man dem toten Hasen die Bilder erklärt* (Göttingen: Steidl, 2010).

9 On the *Besucherschule*, see Peter Weibel, ed., *Beuys, Brock, Vostell. Aktion. Partizipation. Performance* (Ostfildern: Hatje Cantz, 2014), 242–43. Analyses of Beuys's pedagogy include Christa Weber, *Vom "Erweiterten Kunstbegriff" zum "Erweiterten Pädagogikbegriff. Versuch einer Standortbestimmung von Joseph Beuys* (Frankfurt: Verlag für Interkulturelle Kommunikation, 1991); Cornelia Lauf, "Joseph Beuys: The Pedagogue as Persona" (PhD diss., Columbia University, 1992); Carl-Peter Buschkühle, *Wärmezeit: zur Kunst als Kunstpädagogik bei Joseph Beuys* (Frankfurt: P. Lang, 1997); Carl-Peter Buschkühle, *Beuys and the Artistic Education: Theory and Practice of an Artistic Art Education* (Leiden: Brill, 2020).

10 Joseph Beuys-Archiv / Stiftung Museum Schloss Moyland, Inv.-Nr. JBA-B 028968, 028970, 028972. A set of "Workshop Proposals for Documenta, June–September 1977" on FIU stationery, which evidently date from earlier in the year, is also held in the same archive, but only the description of the workshop Media Monitoring is preserved in full. Joseph Beuys-Archiv / Stiftung Museum Schloss Moyland, Inv.-Nr. JBA-B 028975. Two flyers with schedules are reproduced in Weibel, *Beuys, Brock, Vostell*, 352.

11 For a facsimile, see Stephan von Wiese, ed., *Brennpunkt Düsseldorf, 1962–1987. Joseph Beuys, die Akademie, der allgemeine Aufbruch* (Düsseldorf: Kunstmuseum Düsseldorf, 1987), 99.

12 Getty Research Institute, Special Collections, Alfred Schmela Archive, box 123, folders 11 and 11a.

13 Joseph Beuys-Archiv / Stiftung Museum Schloss Moyland, Inv.-Nr. JBA-B 028976.

14 documenta archiv, Kassel, *documenta 6* files, folder 79. The Getty Research Institute holds two drafts of a letter to Schmela, signed by Beuys's associates Walter Warnach and Siegrid Negelung on FIU stationery, that describes Beuys's plans for *documenta 6* and likewise asks for a financial contribution. Getty Research Institute, Special Collections, Alfred Schmela Archive, box 123, folder 11.

15 Joseph Beuys-Archiv / Stiftung Museum Schloss Moyland, Inv.-Nr. JBA-B 028967.

16 Oskar Negt and Alexander Kluge, *Public Sphere and Experience: Analysis of the Bourgeois and Proletarian Public Sphere*, trans. Peter Labanyi, Jamie Owern Daniel, and Assenka Oksiloff (London: Verso, 2016). First published as *Öffentlichkeit und Erfahrung. Zur Organisationsanalyse von bürgerlicher und proletarischer Öffentlichkeit* (Frankfurt: Suhrkamp, 1972).

17 Some of the latter, though, were transcribed for posterity. Joseph Beuys, *Jeder Mensch ein Künstler. Gespräche auf der documenta 5, 1972*, ed. Clara Bodenmann-Ritter (Berlin: Ullstein, 1975).

18 The artist's use of blackboards was almost certainly motivated by Steiner's precedent. See Lawrence Rinder, ed., *Knowledge of Higher Worlds: Rudolf Steiner's Blackboard Drawings*

(Berkeley: University of California, Berkeley Art Museum and Pacific Film Archive, 1997); Allison Holland, ed., *Joseph Beuys & Rudolf Steiner: Imagination, Inspiration, Intuition* (Melbourne: National Gallery of Victoria, 2007); Barbara Lange, "'Questions? You Have Questions?' Joseph Beuys's Artistic Self-Presentation in *Fat Transformation Piece / Four Blackboards*, 1972," in *Joseph Beuys: The Reader*, ed. Claudia Mesch and Viola Michely (Cambridge, MA: MIT Press, 2007), 177–88.

19 For readings of Beuys's pedagogy that resonate with this interpretation, compare Jan Verwoert, "The Boss: On the Unresolved Question of Authority in Joseph Beuys's Oeuvre and Public Image," *e-flux* 1 (December 2008), http://www.e-flux.com/journal/01/68485/the-boss-on-the-unresolved-question-of-authority-in-joseph-beuys-oeuvre-and-public-image/; Jan Verwoert, "Class Action," *frieze* 101 (September 2006): 150–55; Alex Potts, *Experiments in Modern Realism: World Making, Politics and the Everyday in Postwar European and Experimental Art* (New Haven, CT: Yale University Press, 2013), esp. 366.

20 In addition to Buchloh's "Twilight of the Idol," another attack on Beuys's political naivete can be found in Terry Atkinson, "Beuyspeak," in *Joseph Beuys: Diverging Critiques*, ed. David Thistlewood (Liverpool: Liverpool University Press, 1995), 165–76.

21 Art historian Petra Richter notes this on the basis of an interview with Sassen. Petra Richter, *Mit, neben, gegen. Die Schüler von Joseph Beuys* (Düsseldorf: Richter, 2000), 61. This head would reappear in the artist's final large installation piece, *Palazzo Regale*, 1985. Some accounts of the work claim or imply that Beuys himself sculpted the head. Bastian, for example, says that Beuys created it in 1961. Heiner Bastian, *Straßenbahnhaltestelle* (Berlin: Nationalgalerie Berlin, 1980), unpaginated. Beuys would ultimately produce five casts of this sculpture in iron and bronze, as attested in Simone Scholten, Roland Mönig, and Guido de Werd, eds., *Joseph Beuys, "Straßenbahnhaltestelle": Ein Monument für die Zukunft* (Kleve: Museum Kurhaus, 2000), 196.

22 Beuys had by this time already produced several works that make explicit reference to the concentration camps, such as the small assemblage *KZ = Essen 2, KZ = Essen 1*, 1963 (KZ is the standard abbreviation for *Konzentrationslager*, or concentration camp; *Essen* means food, although it also happens to be the name of a German city near Düsseldorf that was in fact the site of large forced labor camps during World War II) as well as

the vitrine *Auschwitz Demonstration*, a collection of material that bears the date 1956–64. On the latter work, see Mario Kramer, "Art Nourishes Life—Joseph Beuys: Auschwitz Demonstration, 1956–1964," in *German Art from Beckmann to Richter: Images of a Divided Country*, ed. Eckhart Gillen (Cologne: DuMont, 1997), 261–71. Compare the reading in Gerald Schröder, *Schmerzensmänner. Trauma und Therapie in der westdeutschen und österreichischen Kunst der 1960er Jahre: Baselitz, Beuys, Brus, Schwarzkogler, Rainer* (Munich: Wilhem Fink, 2011), 220–31.

23 This phrasing is meant to recall the subtitle of Frederic Jameson, *Archaeologies of the Future: The Desire Called Utopia and Other Science Fictions* (New York: Verso, 2005).

24 Isocrates, "To Demonicus," *Isocrates 1*, trans. George Norlin (Cambridge, MA: Harvard University Press, 1928), 35.

25 Lucretius, *Of the Nature of Things: A Metrical Translation*, trans. William Ellery Leonard (London: J. M. Dent and Sons, 1916), 91.

26 Seneca, "On Gathering Ideas," in *Seneca: Epistles 66–72* (Cambridge, MA: Harvard University Press, 1992), 277, letter 84. I am grateful to Nicola Suthor for providing me with this reference.

27 Virgil, *Eclogues, Georgics, Aeneid: Books 1–6*, trans. H. Rushton Fairclough (Cambridge, MA: Harvard University Press, 1999), 153–54.

28 Plato, *Phaedo*, trans. Harold North Fowler (Cambridge, MA: Harvard University Press, 1914), 284–87 (82). Thomas Hobbes also notes the exceptional sociality of bees and ants in *Leviathan*, part 2, chapter 17, with reference to Aristotle rather than Plato, however. In his *Politics*, Aristotle in fact briefly notes that bees are *less* of a political animal than humans. His longer remarks on bees in the *History of Animals* are limited to their peculiar reproductive arrangements.

29 The poem that is the core of the book—*The Grumbling Hive: or, Knaves Turn'd Honest—*appeared in 1705; Mandeville added his prose exegesis on the occasion of its republication as a book in 1714. A second volume arrived in 1732. A modern edition is available as Bernard Mandeville, *Fable of the Bees: and Other Writings* (Indianapolis: Hackett Publishing, 1997).

30 Mandeville, *Fable of the Bees*, lines 155–56.

31 Caroline Tisdall, *Joseph Beuys* (New York: Solomon R. Guggenheim Museum, 1979), 46, ill. 72.

32 Karl von Frisch, *Aus dem Leben der Bienen* (Berlin: J. Springer, 1927).

33 The multiple is documented in Jörg Schellmann, *Joseph Beuys*, cat. no. 285, 239 (ill.).

34 Hans van der Grinten and Franz Josef van der Grinten, *Joseph Beuys. Zeichnungen, Aquarelle, Oelbilder, plastische Bilder aus der Sammlung van der Grinten: Städtisches Museum Haus Koekkoek, Kleve, 8. Oktober bis 5. November 1961* (Kleve: Museum Haus Koekkoek, 1961), unpaginated.

35 Illustrated in Heiner Bastian and Jeannot Simmen, *Joseph Beuys. Zeichnungen, Tekeningen, Drawings* (Berlin: Nationalgalerie Berlin, 1979), cat. no. 5, 235–36 (ill. unpaginated).

36 Reinhardt Ruttmann and Kurt Zimmermann, "Das Museum der 100 Tage. Erster Bericht von der *documenta 3* in Kassel, 1964" (report on Hessischer Rundfunk, first broadcast June 30, 1964); transcript cited in Helmut Friedel and Lothar Schirmer, eds., *Joseph Beuys im Lenbachhaus und Schenkung Lothar Schirmer* (Munich: Schirmer/Mosel and Lenbachhaus, 2013), 35.

37 Wurmbach was the author of a popular zoology textbook published shortly before Beuys met his daughter. Hermann Wurmbach, *Lehrbuch der Zoologie* (Stuttgart: Gustav Fischer, 1957). He had also been, in the words of biographer H. P. Riegel, a "convinced Nazi and was much more than a fellow traveler" (*Mitläufer*). H. P. Riegel, *Beuys: Die Biographie*, vol. 3, *Dokumente* (Zurich: Riverside, 2021), 80. Wurmbach joined the party in April 1933—shortly after Hitler's rise to power—and delivered an address on the "Biological Foundations for Population Policy" during the war. Hermann Wurmbach, "Biologische Grundlagen für die Bevölkerungspolitik," in *Kriegsvorträge der Rheinischen Friederichs-Wilhelms-Universität Bonn a. Rh.* (Bonn: Verlag Gebr. Scheur, 1940). Whether Wurmbach's views had a strong influence on Beuys is hard to determine. Riegel's supposition that "in fact it may have been that Beuys primarily obtained his scientific and ecological knowledge from the textbook of his father-in-law Hermann Wurmbach" seems dubious, however, since if anything, his work prior to meeting Eva and her father in 1958 is much more strongly marked by natural-scientific preoccupations; the year 1958 is anyway late to posit a formative influence of this sort. Riegel, *Beuys*, 3:88. Beuys's association with Heinz Sielmann, a maker of nature films, while stationed in Posen during World War II as well as his subsequent studies with Ewald Mataré, a sculptor of animals, in Düsseldorf from 1947 onward seem like a more reasonable terminus ad quem for his engagement with the natural world.

38 Rudolf Steiner, *Neun Vorträge über das Wesen der Bienen* (Dornach: Naturwissenschaftliche Sektion am Goetheanum, 1929), available in English as Rudolf Steiner, *Bees*, trans. Thomas Braatz (New York: Anthroposophic Press, 1998). The latter publication features an afterword on Beuys by art historian David Adams, who relays the interesting fact (if it is true) that Beuys would regularly leave his studio doors open while warming beeswax, thus attracting "millions" of bees into the room. Steiner, *Bees*, 194–95. This assertion is quoted from an interview with Beuys contained in a 1971 thesis by Robert Bonybeare that I unfortunately have not been able to consult.

39 Steiner, *Bees*, 159.

40 See, for example, his statement that "all things are connected—plants, animals, the earth … man." This is from a 1982 interview with Max Reithman, cited in Annie Suquet, "Archaic Thought and Ritual in the Work of Joseph Beuys," *Res: Anthropology and Aesthetics* 28 (Fall 1995), 150 (ellipsis in the original).

41 Cited in Tisdall, *Joseph Beuys*, 254. This statement complemented a manifesto-like flyer titled "Das Modell der Free International University," signed by Beuys and his student Johannes Stüttgen, that was distributed at *documenta 6*. A copy is held at Joseph Beuys-Archiv / Stiftung Museum Schloss Moyland, Inv.-Nr. JBA-B 005904. This text was also subsequently published in the Czechoslovak exile magazine *Listy* 17 (December 1977): 18–20. The content of the flyer has to do primarily with economic questions, rather than the artist's work, and presages the doctrines that Beuys would further develop in his 1978 text *Aufruf zur Alternative*, which I discuss below.

42 Joseph Beuys and Volker Harlan, *Was ist Kunst? Werkstattsgespräch mit Beuys* (Stuttgart: Urachhaus, 1986), 55.

43 A term that I am borrowing from Paul de Man's *Aesthetic Ideology*, ed. Andrzej Warminski (Minneapolis: University of Minnesota Press, 1996), in particular the lecture transcript "Kant and Schiller," 129–62.

44 See, for example, Craig Owens, "The Allegorical Impulse: Toward a Theory of Postmodernism," *October* 12 (Spring 1980): 67–86; Benjamin H. D. Buchloh, "Allegorical Procedures: Appropriation and Montage in Contemporary Art," *Artforum* 21, no. 1 (September 1982): 43–56. For reconsiderations of these theories of allegory, see David Joselit, "An Allegory of Criticism,"

October 20 (Winter 2003): 3–13; Gail Day, *Dialectical Passions: Negation in Postwar Art Theory* (New York: Columbia University Press, 2011), 132–81.

45  Joseph Beuys, "Talking about One's Own Country: Germany," in *Joseph Beuys: In Memoriam Joseph Beuys*, trans. Timothy Nevill (Bonn: Inter Nationes, 1986), 48.

46  Joseph Beuys, *Energy Plan for the Western Man: Joseph Beuys in America: Writings by and Interviews with the Artist*, ed. Carin Kuoni (New York: Four Walls Eight Windows, 1990), 56–57.

47  Joseph Beuys, *Kunst = Kapital. Achberger Vorträge* (Wangen: FIU-Verlag, 1992), 30–31.

48  On the circulation metaphor in Beuys, compare Heribert Schulz, *Pulsschlag. Herz- und Kreislaufkonzepte von Joseph Beuys* (Düsseldorf: Richter, 2003). For a discussion of *Honigpumpe* in relation to Beuys's ideas about the circulation system and money, see Schulz, *Pulsschlag*, 115–34. See also Heribert Schulz, "Herz-Kreislaufgestaltungen bei Beuys und Klee. Trennendes und Verbindendes," in *Paul Klee trifft Joseph Beuys. Ein Fetzen Gemeinschaft*, ed. Tilman Osterwold (Ostfildern-Ruit: Hatje Cantz, 2000), 78–87. For another interpretation of the beehive metaphor, see Magdalena Holzhey, *Im Labor des Zeichners: Joseph Beuys und die Naturwissenschaft* (Berlin: Dietrich Reimer Verlag, 2009), 83–87.

49  *Wirtschaftswerte* (Economic values) is the title of an important installation from 1980 in which Beuys paired commodities from the socialist German Democratic Republic (at least some of them smuggled out clandestinely by the artist's friends) with paintings in the host institution's permanent collection dating from Marx's lifetime. For a reading of *Wirtschaftswerte*, see Max Rosenberg, "Through the Wall, Slowly," *Texte zur Kunst* 85 (March 2012): 70–81. For further documentation, see Klaus Staeck and Gerhard Steidl, eds., *Das Wirtschaftswertprinzip* (Heidelberg: Edition Staeck, 1990).

50  Beuys, "Talking about One's Own Country," 51.

51  Joseph Beuys, "Aufruf zur Alternative," *Frankfurter Rundschau*, December 23, 1978, reprinted in Volker Harlan, Rainer Rappmann, and Peter Schata, *Soziale Plastik. Materialien zu Joseph Beuys* (Achberg: Achberger Verlag, 1984), 129–36.

52  Art historian Sven Lütticken has noted that Beuys is inconsistent on this point: "In his 'Aufruf zur Alternative,' Beuys had claimed that money had in fact already come to function in this manner; with the emergence of central banks and modern monetary policy, money 'became a

legal regulatory instrument for all creative and consumptive processes.' What 'Aufruf zur Alternative' presents as an established *fact*—money *is* a tool for regulation—Beuys presents as a *demand* in the 1984 discussion—money *has yet to be* 'legalized.' The real breakthrough in the reconceptualization of money had not yet been made." Sven Lütticken, "Inside Abstraction," *e-flux* 38 (October 2012), http://www.e-flux.com/journal/inside-abstraction/ (emphasis in the original). The "1984 discussion" to which Lütticken refers is a public panel that took place on November 29 of that year, during which Beuys was involved in a heated debate with professional economists. This discussion has been published as Joseph Beuys et al., *Was ist Geld? Eine Podiumsdiskussion* (Wangen: FIU-Verlag, 1991).

53  Beuys, "Aufruf zur Alternative," 131.

54  Note on stationery of the Organisation für direkte Demokratie durch Volksabstimmung, 1972, reproduced in Weibel, *Beuys, Brock, Vostell*, 332.

55  Beuys, *Kunst = Kapital*, 37 (emphasis in the original).

56  This text is obscure enough that it does not appear in art historian Monika Angerbauer-Rau's monumental *Beuys Kompass*, which tabulates no less than 514 interviews, essays, lectures, and so forth dating from 1961 until the artist's death. Monika Angerbauer-Rau, ed., *Beuys Kompass. Ein Lexikon zu den Gesprächen von Joseph Beuys* (Cologne: DuMont, 1998).

57  A second volume was left unfinished at the time of the author's death in 1980. Both are available in English as Jean-Paul Sartre, *Critique of Dialectical Reason*, vol. 1, *Theory of Practical Ensembles*, trans. Alan Sheridan-Smith (London: NLB, 1976); Jean-Paul Sartre, *Critique of Dialectical Reason*, vol. 2, *The Intelligibility of History*, trans. Quintin Hoare (London: Verso, 1991). The first volume appeared in German as Jean-Paul Sartre, *Kritik der dialektischen Vernunft* (Reinbek bei Hamburg: Rowohlt, 1967).

58  Beuys, *Kunst = Kapital*, 46 (emphasis in the original).

59  On Beuys's concept of Gestaltung, compare art historian Pamela Kort's remarks on Beuys's expanded concept of *Plastik* (sculpture) in Pamela Kort, "Beuys: The Profile of a Successor," in *Joseph Beuys: Mapping the Legacy*, ed. Gene Ray (Sarasota, FL: John and Mable Ringling Museum of Art, 2001), 28. Suquet remarks that "Beuys aims at nothing less than a human Gestalt." Suquet, "Archaic Thought and Ritual," 150. The connection

between Beuys's sculpture and social Gestaltung is quite explicit in any number of his statements. For a high-profile example, see his explication of his system in Tisdall's 1979 Guggenheim catalog: "SOCIAL SCULPTURE—how we mould or shape the world in which we live: Sculpture is an evolutionary process; everyone is an artist." Tisdall, *Joseph Beuys*, 7 (emphasis in the original).

60 Beuys often referred to Schmundt in writings and interviews of the 1970s and 1980s. In "Aufruf zur Alternative," for example, he cites Wilhelm Schmundt, *Revolution und Evolution. Auf dem Weg zu einer Elementarlehre des sozialen Organismus* (Achberg: Verlag Edition Dritter Weg, 1973). The FIU-Verlag, the publishing organ of Beuys's FIU, kept the Beuys-Schmundt alliance in print for years after both of their deaths (Schmundt passed away in 1992). See Wilhelm Schmundt et al., *Denkschritte. Auf dem Weg zur Idee des sozialen Organismus* (Wangen: FIU-Verlag, 1999); Rainer Rappmann and Joseph Beuys, *Denker, Künstler, Revolutionäre. Beuys, Dutschke, Schilinski, Schmundt: vier Leben für Freiheit, Demokratie und Sozialismus* (Wangen: FIU-Verlag, 1996); Rainer Rappmann and Joseph Beuys, *Die Kunst des sozialen Bauens. Beiträge zu Wilhelm Schmundt* (Wangen: FIU-Verlag, 1993).

61 Beuys, *Energy Plan for the Western Man*, 56–57.

62 Karl Marx, *Capital: A Critique of Political Economy*, trans. Ben Fowkes (New York: Penguin, 1976), 1:284.

63 Immanuel Kant, *Critique of Judgment*, trans. Werner S. Pluhar (Indianapolis: Hackett Publishing, 1987), 170.

64 Jacques Derrida, "Economimesis," trans. R. Klein, *Diacritics* 11, no. 2 (June 1981): 5 (emphasis and brackets in the original).

65 Joseph Beuys, "Gespräch zwischen J. Beuys, B. Blume und H.G. Prager vom 15.11.1975," *Rheinische Bienenzeitung* 12 (December 1975): 373–76

66 "Money is the root form of representation in bourgeois society. Threats to monetary value are threats to signification in general." T. J. Clark, *Farewell to an Idea: Episodes from a History of Modernism* (New Haven, CT: Yale University Press, 1999), 10.

67 This insight likewise precedes Marx. In a late lecture, Hegel characterized money as both an "existing concept" and "existing universal": "Money is the real existence of the universal. This universal is not only an external, objective universal, but also a subjective universal, a completely different type of universal." Georg Wilhelm Friedrich Hegel, "Philosophie des Rechts nach der Vorlesungsnachschrift K.G. von Griesheim 1824/25," in *Vorlesungen über Rechtsphilosophie 1818–1831*, ed. Karl-Heinz Ilting (Stuttgart-bad Cannstatt: Friedrich Fromman, 1974), 229–30, translation quoted from Helmut Reichelt, "Marx's Critique of Economic Categories: Reflections on the Problem of Validity in the Dialectical Method of Presentation in *Capital*," *Historical Materialism* 15, no. 4 (2007): 12.

68 Admittedly, another situation in which this might happen—which I will not consider further since it is less relevant to the present argument—is that of a collectible coin or banknote that exchanges at higher than its face value thanks to its age and/or rarity. In effect, this likewise shifts money into the sphere of art, or rather into the economic category of the luxury object, to which art also belongs.

69 The multiples to which I am referring here are cat. no. 298, 28 (ill.) in Schellman, *Joseph Beuys*. There exist several related works that feature slightly different inscriptions. The earliest, from 1974, incorporates a one dollar bill signed with the name "John Dillinger." Schellmann, *Joseph Beuys*, cat. no. 139, 156 (ill.). For a later variant of 1978, with two bills, see Schellmann, *Joseph Beuys*, cat. no. 245, 222 (ill.). Dillinger, incidentally, was a figure with whom Beuys identified, to the point of staging an impromptu videotaped "action" miming his violent death during a visit to Chicago in 1974. Schellmann, *Joseph Beuys*, cat. nos. 296 (*Nylon Money*; the inscription reads "fühlt sich an wie Nylon," or "it feels like nylon") and 304 (*Schilling*, with an inscription reading "komme leider nicht," or "sorry can't come") also date from 1979; they feature the artist's signature but not the slogan Kunst = Kapital.

70 Karl Marx, *Grundrisse: Foundations of the Critique of Political Economy (Rough Draft)*, trans. Martin Nicolaus (New York: Penguin Books, 1993), 53–56. For a thorough analysis of the coming to grief of various such schemes, see Jasper Bernes, *The Future of Revolution: Communist Prospects from the Paris Commune to the George Floyd Uprising* (London and New York: Verso, 2025), 81–128.

71 *Marx-Engels Gesamtausgabe* II, 5:37 (emphasis in the original), translation quoted from Michael Heinrich, *An Introduction to the Three Volumes of Karl Marx's Capital*, trans. Alexander Locascio (New York: Monthly Review Press, 2012), 78. This passage appears in volume 1 of the

first German edition of *Capital*, but was removed in Marx's subsequent revisions. Hence it is not found in Ben Fowkes's Penguin translation, which is based primarily on the fourth German edition. Marx here echoes a passage in which Hegel points out "the absurdity of setting a universal *beside* the particulars": "Would anyone, who wished for fruit, reject cherries, pears, and grapes, on the ground that they were cherries, pears, or grapes, and not fruit?" Georg Wilhelm Friedrich Hegel, *Encyclopedia of the Philosophical Sciences in Basic Outline, Part I: Science of Logic*, trans. Klaus Brinkmann and Daniel O. Dahlstrom (Cambridge: Cambridge University Press, 2010), 42. Marx's point is that money in fact incarnates this absurdity.

72 Samo Tomšič, *The Capitalist Unconscious: Marx and Lacan* (London: Verso, 2015), 180.

73 Karl Marx, *Capital: A Critique of Political Economy*, trans. David Fernbach (London: Penguin, 1981), 3:953.

74 In a different way, art historian Thierry de Duve has argued that Duchamp's invention of the readymade marks the threshold to a similarly generic "art as such." With the readymade, the Duchampian judgment "this is art" supposedly replaces the Kantian aesthetic judgment "this is beautiful." See Thierry de Duve, *Kant after Duchamp* (Cambridge, MA: MIT Press, 1996).

75 Beuys, "Talking about One's Own Country," 39. The artist's use of the imperative "must" arguably already hints at an authoritarian dimension.

76 Quoted in Éric Michaud, *The Cult of Art in Nazi Germany*, trans. Janet Lloyd (Stanford, CA: Stanford University Press, 2004), 1, first published in French as *Un Art de l'éternité: L'image et le temps du national-socialisme* (Paris: Editions Gallimard, 1996). The novel is Joseph Goebbels, *Michael. Ein deutsches Schicksal in Tagebuchblättern* (Munich: Franz Eher, 1934).

77 Éric Michaud, "The Ends of Art According to Joseph Beuys," trans. Rosalind Krauss, *October* 45 (Summer 1988): 39, 46. The phrase "to render the concept of politics void" is quoted from Beuys's 1985 lecture "Talking about One's Own Country."

78 Beuys had already campaigned (unsuccessfully) in the 1976 Bundestag election as a candidate for the Aktionsgemeinschaft Unabhängiger Deutscher (Action Group of Independent Germans, or AUD), a predecessor of the Green Party. The AUD's program was straightforwardly democratic, pacifistic, antimonopolistic, and ecological. For a reproduction of an AUD flyer,

see Weibel, *Beuys, Brock, Vostell*, 319. On Beuys's involvement in the early years of the Green Party, see Petra Karin Kelly and Joseph Beuys, *Diese Nacht, in die die Menschen . . .* (Wangen: FIU-Verlag, 1994).

79 Beuys, "Talking about One's Own Country," 37.

80 Joseph Beuys, *Das Geheimnis der Knospe zarter Hülle: Texte 1941–1986*, ed. Eva Beuys (Munich: Schirmer/Mosel, 2000), 376–77.

81 An art historical version of this questionable thesis took shape in the context of the *Orient oder Rom* (Orient or Rome) debate that erupted in response to a book of that title by art historian Josef Strzygowski, who proposed an Eastern origin for Christian artistic culture. Josef Strzygowski, *Orient oder Rom. Beiträge zur Geschichte der Spätantiken und Frühchristlichen Kunst* (Leipzig: J. C. Hinrichs'sche Buchhandlung, 1901).

82 On the Eurasian topos in Beuys, see the catalog of an exhibition that took place in Antwerp in 2017: Anthony Hudek, ed., *Greetings from the Eurasian: Joseph Beuys* (Antwerp: Museum van Hedendaagse Kunst Antwerp, 2017). See also Victoria Walters, "Joseph Beuys and EURASIA," *Tate Papers* 31 (Spring 2019): unpaginated.

83 Philippe Lacoue-Labarthe, *Heidegger, Art and Politics*, trans. Chris Turner (Oxford: Basil Blackwell, 1990) (emphasis in the original). These observations are close to the Derrida of "Economimesis."

84 Partly this is the result of a shift in the meaning of the word "neoliberalism." The German neoliberal economists who came of age during the Weimar Republic and National Socialist period, some of whom assumed active roles in postwar reconstruction, were for the most part critical of the more extreme views associated with the contemporaneous Austrian school (representatives of which included political economists Friedrich Hayek and Ludwig von Mises). In the resurgence of neoliberalism that occurred in the second half of the twentieth century, it was by contrast this more uncompromising position that came to the fore. Many of the doctrines of the German ordoliberals now look highly interventionist from a mainstream economic perspective. For a succinct account of the genesis of the contemporary version of neoliberalism, see David Harvey, *A Brief History of Neoliberalism* (Oxford: Oxford University Press, 2005).

85 See Raphaël Fèvre, *A Political Economy of Power: Ordoliberalism in Context, 1932–1950* (New York: Oxford University Press, 2021).

86 Literature on the social market economy is copious. See, for instance, Ştefan Sorin Mureşan, *Social Market Economy: The Case of Germany* (Cham, Switzerland: Springer, 2014); James C. van Hook, *Rebuilding Germany: The Creation of the Social Market Economy, 1945–1957* (Cambridge: Cambridge University Press, 2004); Mark E. Spicka, *Selling the Economic Miracle: Reconstruction and Politics in West Germany, 1949–1957* (New York: Berghahn Books, 2007); Ralf Ptak, *Vom Ordoliberalismus zur sozialen Marktwirtschaft. Stationen des Neoliberalismus in Deutschland* (Opladen: Leske + Budrich, 2004); Michel Foucault, *The Birth of Biopolitics: Lectures at the Collège de Francy, 1978–79*, trans. Graham Burhell (New York: Picador, 2010). On the economic history of the period in general, see also Hans-Joachim Braun, *The German Economy in the Twentieth Century* (London: Routledge, 2003); Nina Grunenberg, *Die Wundertäter. Netzwerke der deutschen Wirtschaft 1942 bis 1966* (Munich: Siedler Verlag, 2006); Tamás Vonyó, *The Economic Consequences of the War: West Germany's Growth Miracle After 1945* (New York: Cambridge University Press, 2020). Vonyó in particular echoes Fèvre's emphasis on market regulation and state intervention.

87 Labor leaders called for a general strike. The struggle was most intense in Stuttgart, where workers faced off against US tanks. These actions came to be known as the *Stuttgarter Vorfälle* (Stuttgart events).

88 Anthony James Nicholls, *Freedom with Responsibility: The Social Market Economy in Germany, 1918–1963* (Oxford: Clarendon Press, 1994), 294.

89 Quoted in Nicholls, *Freedom with Responsibility*, 147.

90 Quoted in Nicholls, *Freedom with Responsibility*, 61.

91 Quoted in Nicholls, *Freedom with Responsibility*, 280. Rüstow's statement originates from a quotation in an article by Jürgen Eick, published in the *Industrie-Anzeiger* on November 7, 1950.

92 Where Britain's postwar Labour government nationalized vast sectors of industry (such as the nation's railroads), West Germany by contrast collaborated with industrial cartels to maintain both stability and private ownership. Economists Barry Eichengreen and Albrecht Ritschl emphasize that decartelization was not nearly as complete as has sometimes been suggested, although authorities in the US occupation sector especially made concrete efforts toward this end. Barry Eichengreen and Albrecht

Ritschl, "Understanding West German Economic Growth in the 1950s," *Cliometrica* 3, no. 3 (2010): 191–219. For ordoliberals, as underscored in Fèvre, *A Political Economy of Power*, the main danger to a free society was vested interests; the market, as they saw it, was a tool with which to dismantle monopolies.

93 These usually proceeded without a hitch, at least until the wildcat Septemberstreiks (September strikes) of 1969, which made a great impact on the West German Left.

94 Eichengreen and Ritschl, "Understanding West German Economic Growth in the 1950s," 215.

95 On this point, see Robert Brenner, *The Economics of Global Turbulence: The Advanced Capitalist Economies from Long Boom to Long Downturn, 1945–2005* (London: Verso, 2006), 67–69, 129–33.

96 Bureau of Labor Statistics, "International Comparisons of Annual Labor Force Statistics, 1970–2012," tables 2–4 and 2–7, http://www.bls.gov/fls/flscomparelf/lfcompendium.xls.

97 SPD economist Karl Schiller, who was to serve as the BRD's economic minister from 1966 to 1972, spoke of a "third way" in the context of his (ultimately successful) attempt to shift his party to a more market-friendly platform in the early 1950s. See, for example, Karl Schiller, *Thesen zur praktischen Gestaltung unserer Wirtschaftspolitik aus sozialistischer Sicht. Vortrag gehalten auf einer Tagung von Christen und Sozialisten in Königswinter von 3. Bis 5. Januar 1952* (Hamburg: Zentralverband dt. Konsumgenossenschaften, 1952), 7–8. The concept, however, was also widespread in anthroposophy, where it stems from Steiner's writings. Beuys used the term "third way" for one of the many political initiatives with which he was involved in the 1970s: Aktion Dritter Weg. In fact, *Dritter Weg* had been the theme of the first Achberg conference in 1973; I have already quoted from Beuys's contribution to this event. Aktion Dritter Weg seems to have been a direct outgrowth of the artist's association with this anthroposophical circle.

98 An earlier coinage of Erhard's—*Wohlstand für Alle* (prosperity for all), the title of a book that he published in 1957—came to be taken as an epitome of the *Wirtschaftswunder*. Ludwig Erhard and Wolfram Langer, *Wohlstand für Alle* (Düsseldorf: Econ-Verlag, 1957).

99 Rüdiger Altmann, "Die formierte Gesellschaft," in *Abschied vom Staat. Politische Essays* (Frankfurt: Campus, 1998). The essay was written in 1965.

100 Ludwig Erhard, speech to the federal CDU convention, March 31, 1965, quoted in Georg Stötzel and Martin Wengeler, *Kontroverse Begriffe. Geschichte des öffentlichen Sprachgebrauchs in der Bundesrepublik Deutschland* (Berlin: Walter de Gruyter, 1994), 4:66.

101 Hugo Steger, "Sprache im Wandel," *Sprache und Literatur in Wissenschaft und Unterricht* 20, no. 63 (1989): 12.

102 The term "administered world" (*verwaltete Welt*) is pervasive in Adorno's writings after the Second World War and is found in Max Horkheimer's work as well. The transcript of a 1950 radio interview on the topic between Adorno, Horkheimer, and Eugen Kogon has been published as "Die verwaltete Welt oder: Die Krise des Individuums," in Max Horkheimer, *Gesammelte Schriften*, vol. 13, *Nachgelassene Schriften 1949–1972*, ed. Gunzelin Schmid Norr (Frankfurt: Max Fischer Verlag, 1989), 121–42. Kogon was a left-leaning Christian intellectual who had been interned for six years in the Buchenwald concentration camp due to his opposition to the Nazi regime. For Marcuse's concept of the one-dimensionalization of society, see Herbert Marcuse, *One Dimensional Man: Studies in the Ideology of Advanced Industrial Society* (Boston: Beacon Press, 1964).

103 See especially Max Horkheimer, "The Authoritarian State," *Telos* 15, no. 2 (Spring 1973): 3–20.

104 For a later variant of the thesis, see Jürgen Habermas, *Legitimation Crisis*, trans. Thomas McCarthy (Boston: Beacon Press, 1975), originally published as *Legitimationsprobleme im Spätkapitalismus* (Frankfurt: Suhrkamp, 1973). Habermas argues that due to the interdependence of political and economic "steering mechanisms," political and economic crises can no longer be cleanly separated in advanced capitalist societies.

105 Hans-Jürgen Krahl, "The Philosophy of History and the Authoritarian State," trans. Daniel Spaulding and Michael Shane Boyle, *Viewpoint* 4 (September 25, 2014), https://viewpointmag.com/2014/09/25/the-philosophy-of-history-and-the-authoritarian-state-1971/. The ultimate source for these as for nearly all other left-wing accounts of the passing of competitive capitalism is Vladimir Lenin's book *Imperialism, the Highest Stage of Capitalism*, first published in 1917. The SDS was founded in 1946 as the youth wing of the SPD, but split from its parent party in 1961.

106 Krahl, "The Philosophy of History."

107 Dutschke participated in Beuys's discussions on the themes of art and capital at *documenta 6*, where *Honigpumpe* was installed. In 1979, Beuys and Dutschke campaigned together for the newly formed Green Party prior to its official incorporation. Dutschke would die from the aftereffects of a 1968 assassination attempt on December 24 of that year.

108 Habermas, *Legitimation Crisis*, 7.

109 For economic histories of this period, see Gérard Bökenkamp, *Das Ende des Wirtschaftswunders: Geschichte der Sozial-, Wirtschafts- und Finanzpolitik in der Bundesrepublik 1969–1998* (Stuttgart: Lucius & Lucius, 2010); Anseld Doering-Manteuffel and Lutz Raphael, *Nach dem Boom. Perspektiven auf die Zeitgeschichte seit 1970* (Göttingen: Vandehoeck & Ruprecht, 2008); Hartmut Kaelble, *The 1970s in Europe: A Period of Disillusionment or Promise?* (London: German Historical Institute, 2010).

110 Although Nixon's actions did not technically abrogate the Bretton Woods agreements (the basis of international monetary relations between the major industrialized capitalist economies after World War II), they effectively rendered the global monetary system unworkable. Note, however, that in his *The Economics of Global Turbulence*, economic historian Robert Brenner attributes the West German slowdown not to the collapse of Bretton Woods (or the oil shock two years later) but instead to industrial overcapacity and consequent overcompetition between the major advanced economies (the BRD, Japan, and the United States). This dynamic had begun some years earlier, producing its first visible effects in the West German recession of 1966. The prehistory of the 1970s' recession is therefore longer than an emphasis on the punctual end of Bretton Woods would suggest. The abolition of this order was the result of long-standing economic difficulties, not their cause.

111 On Beuys's use of gold, see Wouter Weijers, "Gold," in *Joseph Beuys. Die Materialien und ihre Botschaft*, ed. Peter Bürger et al. (Bedburg-Hau: Museum Schloss Moyland, 2006), 126–30.

112 For an overview of West German monetary policy, see Robert L. Hetzel, "German Monetary History in the Second Half of the Twentieth Century: From the deutsche mark to the Euro," *Economic Quarterly* 88, no. 2 (Spring 2002): 29–64.

113 Joseph Beuys and Friedrich Wolfram Heubach, "Die ideale Akademie," *Interfunktionen* 2 (1969): 58–62. For an interview on a similar topic

that took place in 1976, see Joseph Beuys and Hinrich Gerresheim, *Joseph, was ist eine Freie Akademie?* (Achberg: FIU-Verlag, 2014).

114  Caroline Tisdall, *Report to the European Economic Community on the Feasibility of Founding a "Free International University for Creativity and Interdisciplinary Research" in Dublin* (Dublin: Free University Press, 1976), unpaginated.

115  Art historian Claire Bishop has argued that much participatory art, or more specifically instances of so-called relational aesthetics, involves such a fantasy; Beuys probably falls prey to the same critique, though Bishop has not herself devoted many pages to the artist. Compare Claire Bishop, "Antagonism and Relational Aesthetics," *October* 110 (Fall 2004): 51–79. For a more detailed commentary on Beuys, see Claire Bishop, *Artificial Hells: Participatory Art and the Politics of Spectatorship* (London: Verso, 2012), esp. 243–45.

116  For documentation, see Silvia Gauss, *Joseph Beuys: "Gesamtkunstwerk Freie- und Hansestadt Hamburg" 1983/84* (Wangen: FIU-Verlag, 1995).

117  On Haacke's systems thinking as well as the continuity between his "ecological" and "political" projects, see Luke Skrebowski, "All Systems Go: Recovering Hans Haacke's Systems Art," *Grey Room* 30 (Winter 2008): 54–83. Skrebowski contests Buchloh's thesis of a break between these two phases of the artist's career. Compare Benjamin H. D. Buchloh, "Hans Haacke: Memory and Instrumental Reason," in *Neo-Avantgarde and Culture Industry: Essays on American and European Art from 1955 to 1975* (Cambridge, MA: MIT Press, 2000), 203–42.

118  The exhibitions to which I particularly refer are Asher's at Claire Copley Gallery, Los Angeles, in 1974, and Buren's *Within and beyond the Frame* at the John Weber Gallery, New York, a year earlier. Buchloh is an authoritative interpreter of this period in both artists' production. See especially Benjamin H. D. Buchloh, "Michael Asher and the Conclusion of Modernist Sculpture," in *Neo-Avantgarde and Culture Industry: Essays on American and European Art from 1955 to 1975* (Cambridge, MA: MIT Press, 2000), 1–40; Benjamin H. D. Buchloh, "Conceptual Art 1962–1969: From the Aesthetic of Administration to the Critique of Institutions," *October* 55 (Winter 1990): 105–43.

119  Claus Pias, "Hollerith 'Feathered Crystal'": Art, Science, and Computing in the Era of Cybernetics," trans. Peter Krapp, *Grey Room* 29 (Fall 2007): 110–34. For a transcript of the debate, see Birgit Stöckmann, ed., *Joseph Beuys. Provokation Lebensstoff der Gesellschaft—Kunst und Antikunst* (Berlin: Joseph Beuys Medien-Archiv, 2003), 19–54.

## CHAPTER 3: THE SHAPE OF HISTORY

1  Gallerist Lucio Amelio invited Beuys to Italy in 1971. In November of that year, Beuys's first exhibition in the country opened at Amelio's Modern Art Agency in Naples. It was for this occasion that Beuys produced the poster *La Rivoluzione siamo noi* (The revolution is us), which was subsequently distributed as an independent multiple. This work is based on a photograph of the artist taken by Giancarlo Pancaldi in front of the Villa Orlandi on Capri, the home of gallerist Pasquale Trisorio. Beuys had already used this phrase in a multiple of the same title dating from 1970. The earlier work consists of two postcards of the Swiss village of Sils Baselgia with stamps and the title inscribed in Beuys's own hand; it was published in an edition of thirty-three. Jörg Schellmann, *Joseph Beuys: The Multiples* (Cambridge, MA: Busch-Reisinger Museum, 1997), cat. nos. 24–25, 63 (ill.). For the most thorough documentation of Beuys's sojourns in Italy, see Petra Richter, *Joseph Beuys. Ein Erdbeben in den* *Köpfen des Menschen: Neapel, Rom 1971–1985* (Düsseldorf: Richter, 2017).

2  Joseph Beuys, interview with Martin Kunz, in Marianne Eigenheer and Martin Kunz, eds., *Joseph Beuys. Spuren in Italien* (Lucerne: Kunstmuseum, 1979), unpaginated.

3  Joseph Beuys, *Das Geheimnis der Knospe zarter Hülle: Texte 1941–1986*, ed. Eva Beuys (Munich: Schirmer/Mosel, 2000), 268–69.

4  My account of *Arena*'s genesis and installation is drawn primarily from the catalog of an exhibition at the Dia Art Institute in 1994 (the work is in the Dia collection). Lynne Cooke and Karen Kelly, *Joseph Beuys: Arena—Where Would I Have Got If I Had Been Intelligent!* (New York: Dia Center for the Arts, 1994).

5  This exhibition was a survey of contemporary German art with a focus on the Düsseldorf scene; its title is a palindrome. The catalog, unattributed but likely by the show's organizer, Richard Demarco, is *Strategy: Get*

*Arts* (Edinburgh: Richard Demarco Gallery, 1970).

6 Beuys would restage this action in Basel in 1971; I gave an account of it in chapter 1. *The Pack (das Rudel)* is a sculptural installation in which twenty-four sleds, each bearing a felt blanket, flashlight, and lump of fat, pour out of the rear doors of a Volkswagen van.

7 *Vitex agnus-castus* is a species of tree native to the Mediterranean and traditionally used for medicinal purposes (since ancient times, it has been thought to be an anaphrodisiac). For documentation of the action, see Uwe M. Schneede, *Joseph Beuys. Die Aktionen: kommentiertes Werkverzeichnis mit fotografischen Dokumentationen* (Ostfildern-Ruit bei Stuttgart: G. Hatje, 1994), 318–21.

8 Lynne Cooke, "Installing *Arena*: An Introduction," in *Joseph Beuys: Arena—Where Would I Have Got If I Had Been Intelligent!*, by Lynne Cooke and Karen Kelly (New York: Dia Center for the Arts, 1994), 12.

9 Johann Wolfgang von Goethe, *Italian Journey [1786–1788]*, trans. W. H. Auden and Elizabeth Mayer (London: Penguin Books, 1962), 52. Auden and Mayer's translation is hardly literal. The original text of the final sentence reads as follows: "Wenn es [das Volk] sich so beisammen sah, mußte es über sich selbst erstaunen, denn da es sonst nur gewohnt, sich durch einander laufen zu sehen, sich in einem Gewühle ohne Ordnung und sonderliche Zucht zu finden, so sieht das vielköpfige, vielsinnige, schwankende hin und her irrende Tier, sich zu einem edlen Körper vereint, zu einer Einheit bestimmt, in eine Masse verbunden und befestigt, als eine Gestalt, von Einem Geist belebt." A word-for-word rendering of the last few clauses would look something like this: "[The people] sees itself united into a single noble body, determined as a single unity, bound together and fixed as a mass, as a single shape, animated by a single spirit." Johann Wolfgang von Goethe, *Sämtliche Werke*, ed. Christoph Michel and Hans-Georg Dewitz (Frankfurt: Deutscher Klassiker Verlag, 1993), 15/1:44–45.

10 This recalls the mechanism of "proletarian feedback" that scholar Devin Fore has identified in early Soviet aesthetics. Devin Fore, "Proletarian Feedback: The Mirror of the Soviet Public Sphere," *October* 185 (Summer 2023): 5–29.

11 On this exhibition, see Luigia Lonardelli, "*Contemporanea*: An Exhibition in an Underground Car Park," *Art Journal* 77, no. 1 (Spring 2018): 7–29.

12 Perhaps in quite an absolute sense. As Blume notes, "It is not clear whether Joseph Beuys ever took photographs." Eugen Blume, "Joseph Beuys and Photography," in *Joseph Beuys: Make the Secrets Productive, by Ute Klophaus* (New York: Pace Wildenstein, 2010), 45. In my own research, I have yet to encounter a photograph that was unquestionably snapped by Beuys himself.

13 Barthes writes that the photograph inaugurates "flat death." Roland Barthes, *Camera Lucida: Reflections on Photography* (New York: Hill and Wang, 1981), 92. Theater scholar Barbara Gronau makes the point that Beuys's *Raumskulptur* (spatial sculpture) can also be seen as *Zeitskulptur* (temporal sculpture), in which "the process of storage [*Speichern*] materializes as a temporal process in a spatial object." Barbara Gronau, *Theaterinstallationen. Performative Räume bei Beuys, Boltanski und Kabakov* (Munich: Wilhelm Fink, 2010), 129.

14 For documentation, see Joseph Beuys and Caroline Tisdall, *The Secret Block for a Secret Person in Ireland* (Oxford: Museum of Modern Art Oxford, 1974); Joseph Beuys, Caroline Tisdall, and Dieter Koepplin, *Joseph Beuys: The Secret Block for a Secret Person in Ireland* (Basel: Kunstmuseum, 1977); Heiner Bastian, ed., *Joseph Beuys: The Secret Block for a Secret Person in Ireland* (London: Royal Academy of Arts, 1999). The drawing complex was exhibited at the Hamburger Bahnhof in Berlin on the occasion of the artist's centenary in 2021. See Max Rauschenbach and Nina Schallenberg, eds., *Starting from Language: Joseph Beuys at 100* (Berlin: Hatje Cantz, 2021).

15 In approaching the vitrines, I have consulted Gerhard Theewen, *Joseph Beuys. Die Vitrinen: Ein Verzeichnis* (Cologne: Verlag der Buchhandlung Walther König, 1993). Although this book is called a *Verzeichnis*—an index or catalog—it does not cover Beuys's entire production of vitrines (the *Block Beuys*, the largest single repository of such works, is not represented, for example), nor does it possess the full scholarly apparatus of a catalogue raisonné. Another resource is the catalog of an exhibition that was organized by the Menil Collection and Tate. Mark Rosenthal, Sean Rainbird, and Claudia Schmukli, *Joseph Beuys: Actions, Vitrines, Environments* (Houston: Menil Collection, 2004).

16 For an interview on the topic of Beuys's first vitrines, see Helmut Rywelski, *Da mache ich jetzt eine Kiste drum. Die ersten Vitrinen von Joseph Beuys*, ed. Gerhard Theewen (Cologne: Salon Verlag, 2006). Here it is implied that the

first exhibition of vitrines occurred at Rywelski's Cologne gallery, art intermedia, in 1970. The artist had in fact already installed a vitrine for an exhibition of the Karl Ströher collection at Munich's Haus der Kunst in June 1968. This work is now known as *Vitrine 1* and is dated 1950–67; it is in the *Block Beuys* installation in Darmstadt. A version of the *Auschwitz Demonstration* vitrine was also installed for a show at the Kunstverein in Hamburg in 1968, as documented in Willi Bongard, "Gebissausdruck in Talg: Gebrauchsanleitung zu Joseph Beuys," *Die Zeit*, September 8, 1968. In 1970, the installation of the Ströher collection of Beuys's works at the Hessisches Landesmuseum in Darmstadt—where they became the *Block Beuys*—involved the transfer of many hitherto separate objects into display cases. For a recollection of the event in an interview with art dealer Rudolf Zwirner, see Katrin Sauerländer, ed., *Karl Ströher. Eine Sammlergeschichte* (Frankfurt: Revolver, 2005), 126–28. The cases themselves were often cast-offs from museums. Art historian Mario Kramer, for example, notes that the vitrines used in some (unnamed) works came from the Naturmuseum Senckenberg in Frankfurt as well as the Ny Carlsberg Glyptotek in Copenhagen, whereas the vitrines in room five of the *Block Beuys* installation in Darmstadt formerly belonged to the Bayerisches Nationalmuseum (Bavarian National Museum) in Munich. Mario Kramer, "Joseph Beuys: Auschwitz Demonstration," in *German Art from Beckmann to Richter: Images of a Divided Country*, ed. Eckhart Gillen (Cologne: Dumont, 1997), 263.

17 *Sibirische Symphonie 1. Satz* (Siberian symphony first movement), performed at the *FESTUM FLUXORUM FLUXUS* at the Kunstakademie Düsseldorf on February 2, 1963, is generally considered Beuys's first action, although there exists a plan for an unrealized action titled *Erdklavier* (Earth piano) that dates from 1962. Defining what counts as a "multiple" is not a straightforward matter, given that this term has retrospectively been applied to objects that had not originally been conceived as such. For my dating, I follow Schellmann's catalogue raisonné of the multiples, in which the first entry is the 1965 illustrated book *Von Tod zu Tod und andere kleine Geschichten* (From death to death and other small tales, originally published 1902), a collection of short stories by Richard Schaukal with illustrations by Beuys. Schellmann, *Joseph Beuys*, cat. no. 1, 36 (ill.). This designation is awkward. By most criteria, limited edition illustrated books would not count as "multiples." *Zwei Fräulein mit leuchtendem Brot* (Two

young women with shining bread), from the next year, more clearly fits into the category given that it consists of an object (a typewritten list of words paired with a chocolate bar coated in Braunkreuz) and was distributed as an edition of five hundred enclosed in artist Wolf Vostell's loose-leaf album *dé-coll/age 5*, along with objects by other Fluxus and happenings artists. Schellmann, *Joseph Beuys*, cat. no. 2, 39 (ill.). Even this work, however, is not a "classical" multiple insofar as it was not available as a separate commodity for individual purchase but was rather bundled as part of a larger edition. The first object that unambiguously matches the full description of the category is *… mit Braunkreuz*, 1966, each exemplar of which consists of unique drawings executed between 1948 and 1959 encased in a box with a piece of felt, in an edition of twenty-six. Schellmann, *Joseph Beuys*, cat. no. 3, 41 (ill.). The first exhibition dedicated exclusively to Beuys's multiples appears to have taken place at Schellmann's Munich gallery in 1971. The catalog is Joseph Beuys, *Multiples. Galerie Jörg Schellmann München (Ausstellung Februar-März 1971)* (Munich: Schellmann und Klüser, 1971). For the catalog of an exhibition of an almost complete collection of Beuys multiples, see Andrea Gyorody and Sarah Loyer, eds., *Joseph Beuys: In Defense of Nature* (Los Angeles: The Broad and DelMonico Books, 2024).

18 There is another ambiguous category in Beuys's work: the so-called *plastische Bilder*, or plastic pictures, which are suspended between drawing, painting, collage, and sculpture, although if there is a traditional form that best approximates them it is that of relief. Beuys's use of the term dates from no later than 1961, when it appears as a designation for some of his works in an exhibition of the holdings of the brothers van der Grinten, the artist's first major collectors, at the Museum Haus Koekkoek in Kleve. See Hans van der Grinten and Franz Josef van der Grinten, *Joseph Beuys. Zeichnungen, Aquarelle, Oelbilder, plastische Bilder aus der Sammlung van der Grinten: Städtisches Museum Haus Koekkoek, Kleve, 8. Oktober bis 5. November 1961* (Kleve: Museum Haus Koekkoek, 1961).

19 For documentation of *Hauptstrom Fluxus*, see Schneede, *Joseph Beuys*, 166–85. Note that the proper title of the action makes use of symbols that are not available in standard digital character sets. This work was performed in collaboration with Christiansen at the opening of Beuys's exhibition *Fettraum* (Fat room), Galerie Franz Dahlem, Darmstadt, on March 20, 1967. For documentation

of the *Mundplastik* objects, see Eva Beuys, Jessyka Beuys, and Wenzel Beuys, *Joseph Beuys. Block Beuys* (Munich: Schirmer/Mosel, 1990), 365, 209 (ill.), 214–15 (ill.).

20  Kuspit observes that Beuys's objects were exhibited as "cultic relics, neutralizing the transformative power they acquired through their ritual use in the performance." Donald Kuspit, "Enchanting the Disenchanted: The Artist's Last Stand—Joseph Beuys," in *The Cult of the Avant-Garde Artist* (Cambridge: Cambridge University Press, 1993), 95. For other approaches, compare Irene Small, "Site and Sociality: Joseph Beuys and the Relics of Modern Sculpture," *Yale University Art Gallery Bulletin*, 2009, 86–88; Charity Scribner, "Object, Relic, Fetish, Thing: Joseph Beuys and the Museum," *Critical Inquiry* 28, no. 4 (Summer 2003): 645.

21  Gronau, *Theaterinstallationen*, 120.

22  As becomes clear in Derrida's last paragraph: "The word *vomit* arrests the vicariousness of disgust; it puts the thing in the mouth; it substitutes, but only for example, oral for anal. It is determined by the system of the beautiful, 'the symbol of morality,' as *its* other; it is then for philosophy, still, an elixir, even in the very quintessence of its bad taste." Jacques Derrida, "Economimesis," trans. R. Klein, *Diacritics* 11, no. 2 (Summer 1981): 25. On the nexus of consumption, excretion, and philosophical systematicity, compare Werner Hamacher, *Pleroma: Reading in Hegel*, trans. Nicholas Walker and Simon Jarvis (Stanford, CA: Stanford University Press, 1998). Hamacher's book is closely related to Jacques Derrida, *Glas*, trans. John P. Leavey Jr. and Richard Rand (Lincoln: University of Nebraska Press, 1986).

23  Vitrine seven contains *Filz-TV* (Felt TV), 1970; *Ja Ja Ja Ja Ja, Nee Nee Nee Nee Nee* (Yes yes yes yes yes, no no no no no), 1969; *Evervess II 1*, 1968; *Intuition*, 1968. This list of the vitrine's contents is from Eva Beuys et al., *Joseph Beuys: Block Beuys*, 385. Vitrine seven also contains the object *Arktis Boothia Felix*, 1967, which is not a multiple. On Beuys's multiples, see Maja Wismer, "One of Many: The Multiples of Joseph Beuys" (2015), http://walkerart.org/collections/publications/art-expanded/one-of-many-joseph-beuys; Andrea Gyorody, "'Object into Action and Action into Object': Joseph Beuys and the Political Work of Social Sculpture" (PhD diss., University of California Los Angeles, 2017), esp. chap. 2.

24  There are at least two other works with a similar formal strategy that share the name

*Hasengrab*: one in Lothar Schirmer's donation to the Städtische Galerie im Lenbachhaus, Munich, dated 1962–67, and *Hasengrab 2 01*, 1964, at Museum Schloss Moyland.

25  For a general overview, see John C. Welchman, ed., *Sculpture and the Vitrine* (Farnham, UK: Ashgate, 2013).

26  Christopher S. Wood, *Forgery, Replica, Fiction: Temporalities of German Renaissance Art* (Chicago: University of Chicago Press, 2008), esp. 15.

27  On the irreducibility of tropology in the process of concept formation, in addition to texts by the same author cited elsewhere, see Paul de Man, "The Epistemology of Metaphor," *Critical Inquiry* 5, no. 1 (Fall 1978): 13–30.

28  Hal Foster, "What's Neo about the Neo-Avant-Garde?," *October* 70 (Fall 1994): 5–32.

29  Sigmund Freud, "From the History of an Infantile Neurosis," in *The Standard Edition of the Complete Psychological Works of Sigmund Freud*, ed. James Strachey, trans. James Strachey and Anna Freud (London: Hogarth Press, 2001).

30  Hal Foster, *The Return of the Real: The Avant-Garde at the End of the Century* (Cambridge, MA: MIT Press, 1996), 130–36.

31  In addition to texts that I have cited elsewhere, see Lisa Saltzman, *Anselm Kiefer and Art after Auschwitz* (Cambridge: Cambridge University Press, 1999); Paul Jaskot, *The Nazi Perpetrator: Postwar German Art and the Politics of the Right* (Minneapolis: University of Minnesota Press, 2012).

32  Petra Richter, *Mit, neben, gegen. Die Schüler von Joseph Beuys* (Düsseldorf: Richter, 2000).

33  For a dissertation on this episode, see Colin Lang, "Room 19, 1966–1969" (PhD diss., Yale University, 2010).

34  For an account of the founding of the Deutsche Studentenpartei, see Johannes Stüttgen, "Auszug aus 'DER GANZE RIEMEN': 22. Juni 1967—Die Gründung der Deutschen Studentenpartei," in *Brennpunkt Düsseldorf, 1962–1987. Joseph Beuys, die Akademie, der allgemeine Aufbruch*, ed. Stephan von Wiese (Düsseldorf: Kunstmuseum Düsseldof, 1987), 142–51.

35  Richter, *Mit, neben, gegen*, 76, 162, 190–94. Both LIDL and YIUP are nonsense words rather than proper acronyms, though they were habitually capitalized at the time. YIUP was founded in room nineteen of the Kunstakademie Düsseldorf by artists Peter Angermann, Robert Hartmann, Hans Rogalla, and Hans Henin. The group

disbanded in 1971. Most of the organizations I have listed in this paragraph had overlapping membership to some degree. Immendorff, for example, was a member of the Kommunistischer Studentenverband as well as being a founder of LIDL and participant in the Rote Zelle Kunst group.

36 For useful documentation of Beuys's interactions with the authorities in Düsseldorf, much of it drawn from the city's archives, see Susanne Anna, ed., *Joseph Beuys, Düsseldorf* (Ostfildern: Hatje Cantz, 2008).

37 This generational friction took an almost exaggeratedly Oedipal form in the relationship between Beuys and Immendorff. On this topic, see Norman Rosenthal et al., *Joseph Beuys & Jörg Immendorff: Art Belongs to the People!* (Oxford: Ashmolean Museum, 2014).

38 Getty Research Institute Special Collections, Staatliche Kunstakademie Düsseldorf records, box 890034, folder 5.

39 In a letter he posted on May 13, 1968 (a month after the attempted assassination of student leader Dutschke), Habermas admitted that he would now "avoid using the label of left-wing fascism." Cited in Gerhard Bauß, *Die Studentenbewegung der sechziger Jahre in der Bundesrepublik und Westberlin. Handbuch* (Cologne: Pahl-Rugenstein, 1977), 64.

40 For documentation of these events, see Johannes Stüttgen, *Der ganze Riemen. Der Auftritt von Joseph Beuys als Lehrer: die Chronologie der Ereignisse an der Staatlichen Kunstakademie Düsseldorf* (Cologne: Walter König, 2008), 433–35, 499–500, 543–94; Getty Research Institute Special Collections, Staatliche Kunstakademie Düsseldorf records, 1965–74, box 890034.

41 See Johannes Stüttgen, "Anmerkungen zu Joseph Beuys als Lehrer der Kunstakademie Düsseldorf und die Beuys-Klasse 1961–1972," in *Die Geschichte der Kunstakademie Düsseldorf seit 1945*, ed. Kunstakademie Düsseldorf (Berlin: Deutscher Kunstverlag, 2014), 111–12.

42 For the text of the flyer, see Peter Weibel, ed., *Beuys, Brock, Vostell. Aktion. Partizipation. Performance* (Ostfildern: Hatje Cantz, 2014), 268. For personal accounts of the event, compare Horst Bredekamp, "Beuys als Mitstreiter der Form," in *Joseph Beuys: Parallelprozesse. Archäologie einer künstlerischen Praxis*, ed. Ulrich Müller (Munich: Hirmer, 2012), 31–40; "report" by Ursula Reuter-Christiansen, cited in Stüttgen, *Der ganze Riemen*, 494–95.

43 Gene Ray, "Joseph Beuys and the After-Auschwitz Sublime," in *Joseph Beuys: Mapping the Legacy*, ed. Gene Ray (New York: D.A.P., 2001), 55–74. A version of the essay has been reprinted as a chapter in Gene Ray, *Terror and the Sublime in Art and Critical Theory: From Auschwitz to Hiroshima to September 11* (New York: Palgrave Macmillan, 2005).

44 In his response to Ray's paper (which was originally delivered at a 1998 conference dedicated to new interpretations of Beuys), Buchloh agrees with the proposition that Beuys was perhaps "the first, if not the only, artist of the 1950s and 1960s in Germany, if not in Europe to actually have addressed the conditions of cultural production after the Holocaust." Benjamin H. D. Buchloh, "Reconsidering Joseph Beuys: Once Again," in *Joseph Beuys: Mapping the Legacy*, ed. Gene Ray (New York: D.A.P., 2001), 78.

45 Benjamin H. D. Buchloh, *Gerhard Richter: Painting after the Subject of History* (Cambridge, MA: MIT Press, 2022), 378. In a footnote elsewhere in the same book, Buchloh writes that "if anyone in the German context could be considered a predecessor of Richter it would have to be Beuys, and especially his work of the late 1950s, as for example his preliminary studies and proposals for the International Competition for an Auschwitz Monument and the subsequent collection of these objects in the *Auschwitz Vitrine* (1956–1964)." Buchloh, *Gerhard Richter*, 633.

46 For a discussion of this project, see Peter Chametzky, *Objects as History in Twentieth-Century German Art: Beckmann to Beuys* (Berkeley: University of California Press, 2010), 159–95. It was more extensively documented on the occasion of an exhibition at the Museum Kurhaus in Kleve, for which the work was also conserved. Valentina Vlašić, ed., *Joseph Beuys: Werklinien* (Kleve: Freundeskreis Museum Kurhaus und Koekkoek-Haus Kleve e.V., 2016). For an earlier treatment, compare Holger Brülls, *Kein Kreuz, das Büdericher Mahnmal für die Toten der Weltkriege von Joseph Beuys* (Meerbusch: Geschichtsverein Meerbusch, 1995).

47 Kramer, "Joseph Beuys," 266.

48 Quoted in Chametzky, *Objects as History*, 70. The interview was conducted in German, but has only been published in full in French translation. Max Reithmann, *Par la présente, je n'appartiens plus à l'art* (Paris: L'Arche, 1982).

49 "Joseph Beuys," *Penthouse* 106 (1980): 98, quoted in Ray, "Joseph Beuys and the After-Auschwitz Sublime," 71.

50 Theodor W. Adorno, "Cultural Criticism and Society," in *Prisms*, trans. Samuel Weber

and Sherry Weber (Cambridge, MA: MIT Press, 1981), 34.

51 The action is documented in Schneede, *Joseph Beuys*, 80–84.

52 Quoted in Caroline Tisdall, *Joseph Beuys* (New York: Guggenheim Museum, 1979), 23.

53 For his statement that "wrong life cannot be lived rightly" (*es gibt kein richtiges Leben im Falschen*, or more literally, "There is no right life in the false [one]"), see Theodor W. Adorno, *Minima Moralia: Reflections from Damaged Life*, trans. E.F.N. Jephcott (London: Verso, 2020), 43.

54 Among other texts, see his analysis of *zeige deine Wunde* in Armin Zweite, "'Zeige deine Wunde': Das Münchner Environment von Joseph Beuys," in *Joseph Beuys. Zeige deine Wunde*, by Armin Zweite and Joseph Beuys, vol. 2 (Munich: Schellmann & Klüser, 1980), unpaginated.

55 Joseph Beuys, *Energy Plan for the Western Man: Joseph Beuys in America: Writings by and Interviews with the Artist*, ed. Carin Kuoni (New York: Four Walls Eight Windows, 1990), 179.

56 Current research has found little evidence that this occurred on anything more than a small, experimental scale, if at all. Still, the horrific image of human soap was important for popular understandings of the Holocaust. Several witnesses at the 1945–46 Nuremberg trials testified that soap was produced in the camps. The allegation was repeated in Alain Resnais's documentary *Night and Fog*, which was distributed in Germany in 1956 with a voiceover translated by poet Paul Celan. In "Joseph Beuys and the After-Auschwitz Sublime," Ray highlights the connection between fat and the Nazi period. It is hard to imagine that Beuys was oblivious to it. In his 1964 action at the *Festival der Neuen Kunst* in Aachen, he melted a pat of margarine on a hot plate not long after Brock had played Goebbels's "total war" speech over a loudspeaker. The *Auschwitz Demonstration* vitrine includes two slabs of fat on a decrepit hot plate, perhaps the same one used in the action.

57 The most complex instance being, perhaps, the wide dissemination of a photograph, taken by Thomas Hesterberg in 1967, of the residents of West Berlin's Kommune 1 (the BRD's first political commune and a hub for the city's counterculture). They are shown naked with their backs to the camera and hands up against the wall. The staging of the image suggests a police search at the same time as it participates in the hippie valorization of nudity. It also is reminiscent of the forced stripping of concentration camp inmates.

On the New Left's relationship to the Holocaust, compare Hans Kundnani, *Utopia or Auschwitz? Germany's 1968 Generation and the Holocaust* (New York: Columbia University Press, 2009); Dagmar Herzog, *Sex after Fascism: Memory and Morality in Twentieth-Century Germany* (Princeton, NJ: Princeton University Press, 2005).

58 In more recent years, insistence on the singularity of the Holocaust—associated with the "leftist" position of Habermas and his allies in the *Historikerstreit* of the 1980s—has been challenged in light of new attention accorded to the Herero and Nama genocide of 1904–8 along with other colonial atrocities. The "leftist" position has thus effectively switched to the view that Nazi crimes are better comprehended in relation to wider (and not exclusively German) colonialist, imperialist, and capitalist dynamics, whereas assertions of the singularity of the mass murder of European Jews is now more strongly associated with the German state's support for Israel.

59 An exception is the work of Gerald Schröder, who links the theme of trauma with Beuys's relationship to the New Left, and in particular, its culture of bodily violence, victimhood, and the processing of the Nazi past. Gerald Schröder, *Schmerzensmänner. Trauma und Therapie in der westdeutschen und österreichischen Kunst der 1960er Jahre: Baselitz, Beuys, Brus, Schwarzkogler, Rainer* (Munich: Wilhem Fink, 2011). On a similar topic, but with a focus on German art of the 1980s rather than the 1960s, compare Cornelia Gockel, *Zeige deine Wunde. Faschismusrezeption in der deutschen Gegenwartskunst* (Munich: S. Schreiber, 1998).

60 Another notable early reference occurs in an unsigned article on *documenta 4* that was published in the *Münchner Merkur* on June 8, 1968. The anonymous author compares a bed-like object in the artist's installation to concentration camp barracks. Clipping reproduced in *Interfunktionen* 1 (1968): 43.

61 Dagmar Herzog, "'Pleasure, Sex, and Politics Belong Together': Post-Holocaust Memory and the Sexual Revolution in West Germany," *Critical Inquiry* 24, no. 2 (Winter 1998): 398–99.

62 The columnar element of the work was cast from the remnants of the so-called *Eiserner Mann*, or Iron Man, that once stood at a tram stop on Nassauer Allee in Kleve. For photographs of the 1976 casting process, see Vlašić, *Joseph Beuys*, 251–56. The column originally stood at the entrance to the Baroque "amphitheater" adjacent to

the Kleve Kurhaus, which is now a museum; the latter structure in fact housed Beuys's studio from late 1957 until his permanent move to Düsseldorf in 1964. This amphitheater is another possible point of reference for *Arena*, though it is simply a raised, semicircular viewing terrace at the end of an artificial canal. The house of Beuys's parents, where he lived for much of the 1950s, is only a short walk away. On its original site, the column has now been replaced by a new "Iron Man" created by sculptor Stephan Balkenhol. The *Eiserner Mann* had originally been a monument erected by Johann Moritz, prince of Nassau-Siegen, in the seventeenth century, at which time it bore a statue of Cupid on its pinnacle. The Cupid figure was lost by the end of the century. The nickname *Eiserner Mann* dates from later, when the object's original appearance had already been forgotten. By the time Beuys would have first seen it, presumably in the 1920s or 1930s, it was in a completely ruined condition. Sculptor Dieter von Levetzow restored the column in 1973, adding a new Cupid figure. In other words, the column from which Beuys cast the central element of *Straßenbahnhaltestelle* was exactly *not* the ruined, unrecognizable forms that he would have seen in his youth but rather a new restoration. This displacement of indexical reference as well as the use of a casting technique in the sculpture's production points to a continuity between *Straßenbahnhaltestelle* and *Unschlitt/Tallow*.

63 Tisdall, *Joseph Beuys*, 242. The description of the work in this catalog echoes statements that Beuys had made to art critic Georg Jappe in a 1976 interview. Georg Jappe, "Interview mit Beuys über Schlüsselerlebnisse," *Kunstnachrichten* 3 (1977): 72–81.

64 Incidentally, a different source gives the depth of the hole as twenty-one meters. Klaus Gallwitz, "Stationen der Erinnerung: Joseph Beuys und seine 'Straßenbahnhaltestelle,'" in *Festschrift für Eduard Trier zum 60. Geburtstag*, ed. Justus Müller Hofstede and Werner Spies (Berlin: Mann, 1981), 311–27. I have already noted that the head on the column was originally a work by Sassen, one of Beuys's students. Multiple sources report that Beuys initially wanted to place a gold-plated version of his 1947 *Porträt* (a self-portrait with feminized features) over the entrance to the pavilion as a counterpoint to the head on the column but decided against this at some point during the planning of the installation. *Porträt* is reproduced in Vlašić, *Joseph Beuys*, cat. no. 3, 162 (ill.). For a bronze cast of the same plaster original on a marble base, see Vlašić, *Joseph Beuys*, cat.

no. 23, 182 (ill.). No date is given for the casting of the latter work. Both works are in the collection of the Museum Kurhaus Kleve—Ewald Mataré Sammlung.

65 Heiner Bastian, *Straßenbahnhaltestelle* (Berlin: Nationalgalerie Berlin, 1980), unpaginated.

66 A 2022 exhibition at the National Gallery, Washington, DC, demonstrated the lability of the motif. The catalog is James Meyer et al., *The Double: Identity and Difference in Art since 1900* (Washington, DC: National Gallery of Art, 2022).

67 The trinity formula supplements the more famous "fetishism of commodities" in volume 1 by describing three additional fetishistic effects: land appears to yield rent, labor appears to yield wages, and capital appears to yield interest as if by magic, concealing the fact that "capital is not a thing, it is a definite social relation of production pertaining to a particular historical social formation, which simply takes the form of a thing and gives this thing a specific social character." Karl Marx, *Capital: A Critique of Political Economy*, trans. David Fernbach (London: Penguin, 1991), 3:953.

68 Quoted in Hans-Georg Backhaus, "On the Dialectics of the Value Form," *Thesis Eleven* 1, no. 1 (February 1980): 109. The most widely distributed modern translation of Marx's *Capital* renders the passage as follows: "Exchange, however, produces a differentiation [*Verdopplung*] of the commodity into two elements, commodity and money, an external opposition which expresses the opposition between use-value and value which is inherent in it" (1:199).

69 Backhaus, "Dialectics of the Value-Form," 109 (emphasis in the original). The first part of this passage is a quotation from Marx, *Capital*, vol. 1. The phrase "identity of identity and non-identity" is borrowed from Hegel.

70 Eugen Blume and Catherine Nichols, *Joseph Beuys: Die Revolution sind Wir* (Göttingen: Steidl, 2008), 78. On the motif of doubling, compare Matthias Bleyl, "Doubling as a Principle: Reflections on the Dualisms in the Work of Joseph Beuys / Verdoppelung als Prinzip: Überlegungen zu den Dualismen im Werk von Joseph Beuys," in *Joseph Beuys Symposium*, ed. Förderverein Museum Schloss Moyland e.V. (Kranenburg: Stiftung Museum Schloss Moyland, Sammlung van der Grinten, and Joseph Beuys Archiv des Landes Nordrhein-Westfalen, 1995), 67ff.

71 *Schepser* is a dialect variant of *Schäleisen*, meaning in English "barking iron" or "stripping iron."

72 Helmut Friedel and Lothar Schirmer, eds., *Joseph Beuys im Lenbachhaus und Schenkung Lothar Schirmer* (Munich: Schirmer/Mosel and Lenbachhaus, 2013), 92–94.

73 "The devaluation of the world of things in allegory is surpassed within the world of things itself by the commodity." Walter Benjamin, "Central Park," trans. Edmund Jephcott and Howard Eiland, in *Selected Writings*, ed. Howard Eiland and Michael W. Jennings (Cambridge, MA: Harvard University Press, 2003), 4:164.

74 A term that art historian Erwin Panofsky borrowed from the philosopher Ernst Cassirer in his formulation of iconographic methodology. See, in particular, Erwin Panofsky, "Iconography and Iconology: An Introduction to the Study of Renaissance Art," in *Meaning in the Visual Arts* (Garden City, NY: Anchor Books, 1955), 26–54, esp. 31.

75 For a reading of what this estrangement of things from themselves as they slip into the commodity form might have looked like at an earlier stage of capital's colonization of everyday life, compare T. J. Clark's chapter on Paul Cézanne's painting *Still Life with Apples* (1893–94, Getty Museum). T. J. Clark, *If These Apples Should Fall: Cézanne and the Present* (London: Thames & Hudson, 2022), 63–107.

76 Andreas Malm, *The Progress of This Storm: Nature and Society in a Warming World* (London: Verso, 2018).

77 It is striking that Beuys gravitated toward sculpture as his canon of universal art. In the Western philosophical tradition, the less material and therefore more "spiritual" arts of painting, music, or especially poetry have generally been considered higher and more universal than sculpture, which is by contrast more essentially bound to materiality. This is true in Hegel, who refers to poetry as the "most perfect" and "most unrestricted of the arts." Georg Wilhelm Friedrich Hegel, *Philosophie der Kunst oder Ästhetik. Nach Hegel. Im Sommer 1826. Mitschrift Friedrich Carl Hermann Victor von Kehler*, ed. A. Gethmann-Siefert and B. Collenberg-Plotnikov (Munich: Wilhelm Fink, 2004), 197; G.W.F. Hegel, *Aesthetics: Lectures on Fine Art*, trans. T. M. Cox (Oxford: Clarendon Press, 1975), 2:626. In a reading of Kant's third critique, Derrida comes strikingly close to Marx's theorization of money via his deconstruction of poetry's "economimesis," or the mutual dependency of political economy and aesthetic ideology: "If art is expressive, if speech expresses more than other modes of expression, poetic speech in turn

is the most telling [*la plus parlante*]; interiority is produced there and is better preserved there in its plenitude. And it produces not only the most moral and the truest disinterested pleasure, which is therefore the most present and the highest, but also the most positive pleasure. A priceless pleasure. By breaking with the exchange of values, by giving more than is asked and more than it promises, poetic speech is both out of circulation, at least outside any finite commerce, without any determinate value, and yet of infinite value. It is the origin of value. Everything is measured on a scale on which poetry occupies the absolutely highest level. It is the universal analogical equivalent, and the value of values." Jacques Derrida, "Economimesis," trans. R. Klein, *Diacritics* 11, no. 2 (Summer 1981): 18. Poetic speech is thus like money. That Beuys proffered sculpture as a comparable economimetic universal perhaps indicates that he ranked (socio)plastic Gestaltung above expressive self-presence—though, as we have noted, his socioplastic practice had as its counterpart incessant discursive activity.

78 Derrida, "Economimesis," 9 (emphasis and brackets in the original).

79 Discourses of cognitive or semio-capitalism derive largely from Italian autonomist thought. See, for example, Franco Berardi, *Precarious Rhapsody: Semio-Capitalism and the Pathologies of the Post-Alpha Generation* (London: Autonomedia, 2009).

80 I borrow the phrase "mimetic subsumption" from Marina Vishmidt, "What Do We Mean by 'Autonomy' and 'Reproduction'?," in *Reproducing Autonomy: Work, Money, Crisis and Contemporary Art*, ed. Marina Vishmidt and Kerstin Stakemeier (London: Mute Publishing, 2016), 43.

81 T. J. Clark, "Clement Greenberg's Theory of Art," *Critical Inquiry* 9, no. 1 (September 1982): 155–56.

82 The work on view was the second version of *Straßenbahnhaltestelle*, now in the Erich Marx collection, Berlin (on long-term loan to the Staatliche Museen zu Berlin), not the version exhibited in Venice.

83 Tisdall, *Joseph Beuys*, 224, ill. nos. 388–89. The work's presence at the Guggenheim is attested in Cooke, "Installing *Arena*," 14–15.

84 The *Fond* sculptures on display were *Fond II/3*, 1979, and *Fond IV/4*, 1979, both of which were reworked versions of earlier sculptures. I have discussed these pieces at the beginning of chapter 1. There is another important work from the end of decade that I have so far not considered

at all: *Das Kapital Raum 1970–1977* (The capital room 1970–1977), Beuys's contribution to the 1980 Venice Biennale. (It was therefore not present at the Guggenheim retrospective.) This environment consists of numerous blackboards together with a piano, film projector, and other objects. Given that the title of the work alone is suggestive in the present context, it is legitimate to ask why *Das Kapital Raum* does not occupy a more prominent position in my account. The short answer is that I do not need *Das Kapital Raum* to make my case. The piece is an instructive instance of the themes of creativity, pedagogy, accumulation, and so forth that are objects of my inquiry; in effect, it is a spectacularization of the idea that artistic production is equivalent to capital. But these topics emerge in the analysis of other works and there does not seem much to be gained from integrating constant references to *Das Kapital Raum* in the same way that I have developed a running commentary on my other key artworks. Collector Erich Marx eventually acquired *Das Kapital Raum*; it is on long-term loan to the Staatliche Museen zu Berlin. The work is thoroughly documented. See Mario Kramer, *Joseph Beuys: "Das Kapital Raum 1970–77"* (Heidelberg: Edition Staeck, 1991); Christel Raussmüller-Sauer, ed., *Joseph Beuys und das Kapital. Vier Vorträge zum Verständnis von Joseph Beuys und seiner Rauminstallation "Das Kapital Raum 1970–77" in den Hallen für Neue Kunst, Schaffhausen, ergänzt durch Erläuterungen von Joseph Beuys und seinen "Aufruf zur Alternative"* (Schaffhausen: Die Hallen, 1988)—as the title indicates, this text also contains a reading of Beuys's "Aufruf zur Alternative"; Christel Raussmüller-Sauer, *Eine Entstehungsgeschichte. Das Kapital Raum 1970–1977 & Die Hallen für Neue Kunst Schaffhausen* (Basel: Raussmüller Collection, 2012); Joachim Verspohl, *Joseph Beuys, das Kapital Raum 1970–77. Strategien zur Reaktivierung der Sinne* (Frankfurt: Fischer Taschenbuch, 1984); Mario Kramer, *Joseph Beuys. Das Kapital Raum 1970–1977* (Göttingen: Steidl, 2021). *Das Kapital Raum* was the centerpiece of an exhibition at Berlin's Hamburger Bahnhof in 2016, the catalog of which is Eugen Blume and Catherine Nichols, eds., *Capital: Debt, Territory, Utopia*, trans. Ann Marie Bohan, Tony Crawford, and Fiona Elliott (Dortmund: Verlag Kettler, 2016).

85 As Cooke notes, "Capitalizing on the fact that the Guggenheim consists of a spiral with numerous small lateral bays, Beuys encouraged a very different way of apprehending his works from that which he normally fostered in his actions or environmental installations. Formerly, by giving priority to the process, he had sought to generate a dynamic fluid relationship with the observer. By invoking the stations of the cross in the context of this retrospective, he reinforced the importance of a contemplative response to works now manifest mostly in the guise of batteries, residua, and/or relics." Cooke, "Installing *Arena*," 15.

86 Annie Suquet, "Archaic Thought and Ritual in the Work of Joseph Beuys," *Res: Anthropology and Aesthetics* 28 (Fall 1995): 161.

87 Gronau, *Theaterinstallationen*, 126–29. The second quotation is from Bruno Latour, "On Actor-Network Theory: A Few Clarification Plus More than a Few Complications," *Soziale Welt* 47, no. 4 (1996): 373.

88 De Man argues that there is no language without trope, of which metaphor (that is to say, transference, derived from the Greek μεταφέρω, "to carry over") is the paradigm; furthermore, there is no concept formation without metaphoric totalization—given that even the self or subject is a metaphor too. In addition to texts such as "The Epistemology of Metaphor," which I have already cited, see especially Paul de Man, *Allegories of Reading: Figural Language in Rousseau, Nietzsche, Rilke, and Proust* (New Haven, CT: Yale University Press, 1979).

89 In thinking about Beuys's relation to the Actionists, I have benefited from a chapter in Andrew Weiner, "Times of the Event" (PhD diss., University of California, 2011), 58–77.

90 Despite the earliness of the *Arena* project, there is not much discussion of Beuys in the now sizable literature on the photographic documentation of performance art. He is not mentioned in a foundational article on the topic: Philip Auslander, "The Performativity of Performance Documentation," *PAJ: A Journal of Performance and Art* 28, no. 3 (September 2006): 1–10.

91 The category of the monument occupies a key role as the logical and historical antecedent to modern sculpture in two important essays that are roughly contemporaneous with Beuys's Guggenheim retrospective: Rosalind Krauss, "Sculpture in the Expanded Field," *October* 8 (Spring 1979): 30–44; Benjamin H. D. Buchloh, "Michael Asher and the Conclusion of Modernist Sculpture," in *Neo-Avantgarde and Culture Industry: Essays on European and American Art from 1955 to 1975* (Cambridge, MA: MIT Press, 2000), 1–39, originally published in Chantal Pontbriand, ed., *Penser l'art contemporain: Rapports et documents de la Biennale de Paris* (Montreal: Parachute, 1981), 3:55–64.

Neither Krauss nor Buchloh have room for Beuys in their respective schemata; indeed, given their shared antipathy to the artist, it may not be too much of an exaggeration to say that he is constitutively excluded from their genealogies of legitimate or critical postmodern art.

92 Thierry de Duve, "Joseph Beuys, or the Last of the Proletarians," *October* 45 (Summer 1988): 52 (emphasis in the original).

93 Again, Derrida is useful in making sense of this infinite productivity that traverses the aesthetic and economic: the "pure productivity of the inexchangeable"—art as singular outpouring of genius that asks nothing in return—"liberates a sort of immaculate commerce. Being a reflective exchange, universal communicability between free subjects opens up space for the play of the Fine-Arts. There is in this a sort of pure economy in which the *oikos*, what belongs essentially to the definition [*le propre*] of man, is reflected in his pure freedom and his pure productivity." Derrida, "Economimesis," 9 (emphasis and brackets in the original).

94 Kim Levin, *Beyond Modernism: Essays on Art from the 70s and 80s* (New York: Harper &

Row, 1988), 176–77. The essay was originally published in *Arts Magazine* in April 1980. *Feuerstätte II* (Hearth II), 1978–79, has not previously made an appearance in this book. It is a "sequel" to *THE HEARTH (Feuerstätte)*, originally titled *environment, basel 1974*, 1968–74. But whereas the earlier version of the work is a spare installation of copper rods, felt rolls, and blackboards, among other materials, the second version incorporates a large heap of felt suits.

95 Arguably, the more chilling and therefore more difficult analysis would have been to see in the deadening aspects of the postwar welfare state not a resurgence of fascism, in the sense of an exceptional and aberrant phenomenon, but rather the normal disciplinary operations of capitalist liberal democracy. It was in this spirit that a few dissident communists in the postwar era (notably Amadeo Bordiga, who had been imprisoned by Benito Mussolini's regime from 1926 to 1931) denounced antifascism itself as an alibi for capitalism. See, for instance, Gilles Dauvé, *Fascism/Anti-Fascism* (Birmingham, UK: Kaleidoscope, 1982).

## CODA: TERROR AND ITS DOUBLE

1 This sentence is meant to summarize Buchloh's writings on Broodthaers. See, among other texts, Benjamin H. D. Buchloh, "Marcel Broodthaers: Open Letters, Industrial Poems," in *Neo-Avantgarde and Culture Industry: Essays on European and American Art from 1955 to 1975* (Cambridge, MA: MIT Press, 2000), 65–118.

2 For a facsimile, see Catherine David and Véronique Dabin, *Marcel Broodthaers* (Paris: Editions du Jeu de Paume, 1991), 22. Translation adapted from Claudia Mesch and Viola Michely, eds., *Joseph Beuys: The Reader* (Cambridge, MA: MIT Press, 2007), 67–68; Marcel Broodthaers, *Marcel Broodthaers: Collected Writings*, ed. Gloria Moure (Barcelona: Ediciones Polígrafa, 2012), 196. In both this "letter" and the next that I will quote, ellipses in brackets are my elisions while those not in brackets are in the original. As mentioned in a footnote in the previous chapter, at least one reviewer of this exhibition shared Broodthaers's association of Beuys's work with the Holocaust.

3 The Haacke work in question is *Shapolsky et al. Manhattan Real Estate Holdings, a Real-Time Social System, as of May 1, 1971*, which documents properties owned by New York slumlord Harry J. Shapolsky. For a recounting of this episode, see

Stefan Germer, "Haacke, Broodthaers, Beuys," *October* 45 (Summer 1988): 63–75. The catalog for the Guggenheim exhibition is *Amsterdam, Paris, Düsseldorf* (New York: Solomon R. Guggenheim Museum, 1972).

4 Facsimile in David and Dabin, *Marcel Broodthaers*, 178. Translation modified from Broodthaers, *Marcel Broodthaers*, 387.

5 Compare Trevor Stark, "The Reification of the World: Poetry and Conquest in Marcel Broodthaers's Maps," *Critical Inquiry* 50, no. 2 (Spring 2024): 517–42.

6 A sizable literature has accumulated around this term. Once again, Buchloh's writings are seminal. See especially Benjamin H. D. Buchloh, "Conceptual Art 1962–1969: From the Aesthetic of Administration to the Critique of Institutions," *October* 55 (Winter 1990): 105–43. As interventions of this sort became de rigueur from the 1990s forward, institutional critique in turn accumulated its own metacritique. See Andrea Fraser, "From the Critique of Institutions to an Institution of Critique," *Artforum* 44, no. 1 (September 2005): 100–105. Current artistic strategies rooted in the lineage (such as the work of conceptual artist Cameron Rowland) could be described as

second-order institutional critique, in analogy with second-order cybernetics: they are reflexive both of the institution and of "critical" work's own capture by the institution. Beuys's alternative model of participating in the mainstream art world while simultaneously building counterinstitutions such as the FIU has also had a long afterlife.

7 Buchloh may nonetheless exaggerate when he claims that "everybody who was seriously involved in radical student politics during the 1960s in Germany, for example, and who worked on the development of a new and adequate political theory and practice, laughed at or derided Beuys's public-relations move to found the Grand Student Party [sic], which was supposed to return an air of radicality to the master who was coming of esthetic age." Or rather, much depends on how one defines "seriously." Benjamin H. D. Buchloh, "Beuys: The Twilight of the Idol," Artforum 18, no. 5 ( January 1980); note that in the version reprinted in Neo-Avantgarde and Culture Industry, "Grand Student Party" has been amended to "International Student Party," which is also incorrect since the actual name of the organization was Deutsche Studentenpartei. Presumably Buchloh is confusing it with the FIU. Pace Buchloh, some influential figures in the West German Left were happy to collaborate with Beuys, including Dutschke as well as writer Heinrich Böll, with whom the artist wrote a manifesto for the foundation of the FIU in 1973 (a year after Böll won the Nobel Prize in Literature).

8 The action was filmed by Jürgen Boettcher, a filmmaker and painter. Ausfegen is not documented in Uwe Schneede's catalogue raisonné of the artist's actions and thus occupies something of a gray zone in his production alongside a handful of other works that were performed specifically for film or video recording, such as Filz-TV, 1970. At the time of this writing, a digitized version of the Ausfegen video was available at https://ubu.com /film/beuys_ausfegen.html.

9 The present version of the encasing vitrine dates only from 1985. The artist's widow, Eva, later claimed that the idea to preserve this material in a vitrine was not Beuys's own but rather came from gallerist Block (the vitrine's owner) and hence that the work is not genuine. Since 1999, the Ausfegen vitrine had been on loan to the Neues Museum in Nuremberg. Eva first raised her protest on the occasion of the work's loan to the 2009 exhibition Art of Two Germanys: Cold War Cultures at the Los Angeles County Museum of Art. The catalog of the show is Stephanie Barron and Sabine Eckmann, eds., Art of Two Germanys: Cold War

Cultures (New York: Abrams, 2009). For an abbreviated journalistic account of the affair, compare Andreas Radlmaier, "Neues Museum: Irrer Streit um dieses Beuys-Kunstwerk," Abendzeitung (Munich), July 13, 2009, https://www.abendzeitung-muenchen.de/bayern/neues-museum-irrer-streit-um-dieses-beuys-kunstwerk-art-99916.

10 Peiter's account of the event, from a 1993 letter to curator Pia Witzmann, is quoted in Johannes Stüttgen, Der ganze Riemen. Der Auftritt von Joseph Beuys als Lehrer: die Chronologie der Ereignisse an der Staatlichen Kunstakademie Düsseldorf (Cologne: Walter König, 2008), 980–81.

11 In a discussion of his documenta 5 interventions, Stüttgen goes so far as to say that Beuys's theories represented a "counter-model to RAF terrorism." Stüttgen, Der ganze Riemen, 980.

12 In Schellmann's catalogue raisonné of the multiples, this work is no. 49. As mentioned earlier, the work was produced in an unlimited, unnumbered edition, of which approximately eight hundred copies are signed. Jörg Schellmann, ed., Joseph Beuys: The Multiples (Cambridge, MA, Busch-Reisinger Museum, 1997), cat. no. 105, 133 (ill.). On Beuys's self-presentation in this work, compare Sabeth Buchmann, "Leben als Allegorie. Zu 'La Rivoluzione siamo Noi' von Joseph Beuys," Texte zur Kunst 79 (2010): 88–101. That the pose strongly recalls that of the central figure in Giuseppe Pellizza da Volpedo's painting The Fourth Estate, 1898–1901, has often been remarked given the work's Italian connection. Likely as it is, I can find no conclusive proof that Beuys intended this reference.

13 Ulrike Meinhof, "The Black September Action in Munich: Regarding the Strategy for Anti-Imperialist Struggle," translation modified from J. Smith and André Moncourt, The Red Army Faction: A Documentary History, vol. 1: Projectiles for the People, trans. J. Smith and André Moncourt (Oakland, CA: PM Press, 2009), 223. The original text is in Martin Hoffmann, ed., Rote Armee Fraktion: Texte und Materialien zur Geschichte der RAF (Berlin: ID-Verlag, 1997), 167. German professor Sarah Colvin has analyzed the rhetorical function of Meinhof's distinctive authorial voice in constructing a notion of the revolutionary subject. Sarah Colvin, Ulrike Meinhof and West German Terrorism: Language, Violence, and Identity (Rochester, NY: Camden House, 2009). In the quotation above, note how the logical necessity of revolutionary struggle is repeatedly framed as an if-then deduction followed by a sentence beginning with "this means" (das heißt).

14 Gideon Bachmann, "Pasolini on de Sade: An Interview during the Filming of The 120 Days

of *Sodom,*" *Film Quarterly* 29, no. 2 (Winter 1975–76): 45.

15 For Marx's reproduction schemes, see *Capital*, vol. 2, esp. part 2, chap. 17.

16 On the origins and uses of the term "subsumption" in Marxist discourse, see "The History of Subsumption," *Endnotes* 2 (April 2010), endnotes.org.uk/articles/the-history-of-subsumption.

17 On the "deficiency of concepts," see Hans Blumenberg, "Theory of Nonconceptuality," in *History, Metaphors, Fables: A Hans Blumenberg Reader*, ed. Hannes Bajohr, Florian Fuchs, and Joe Paul Kroll (Ithaca, NY: Cornell University Press, 2020), 262.

18 Beuys and Warhol knew each other slightly. One product of this association was a series of portraits of Beuys that Warhol made in the last few years of his life. Another was the "Warhol-Beuys-Ereignis" (Warhol-Beuys event) that Stüttgen arranged in 1979 at the Galerie Denise René / Hans Mayer, Düsseldorf, which was subsequently commemorated in both a book—namely, Johannes Stüttgen, *Das Warhol-Beuys-Ereignis. 3 Kapitel aus der ganze Riemen* (Wangen: Free International University, 1979)—as well as in a multiple. Kuspit once claimed that Beuys "was everything Warhol was not." Donald Kuspit, "Enchanting the Disenchanted: The Artist's Last Stand—Joseph Beuys," in *The Cult of the Avant-Garde Artist* (Cambridge: Cambridge University Press, 1993), 84. Given that in the same text, Kuspit ("Enchanting the Disenchanted," 92) also writes that "Beuys consciously set himself up as Hitler's opposite in every way," readers may, oddly, have to align Warhol with Hitler.

19 Leo Bersani and Ulysse Dutoit, "Merde Alors," *October* 13 (Summer 1980): 25.

20 Bersani and Dutoit, "Merde Alors," 24 (emphasis in the original).

21 Bersani and Dutoit, "Merde Alors," 22, 24, 25.

22 Bersani and Dutoit, "Merde Alors," 26 (emphasis in the original).

23 Bersani and Dutoit, "Merde Alors," 26.

24 Bersani and Dutoit, "Merde Alors," 25.

25 Bersani and Dutoit, "Merde Alors," 30, 28.

26 On the aesthetics of the withdrawal of affect in the 1960s and 1970s, compare Jacob Stewart-Halevy's work on the "casual" stance in conceptual art. Jacob Stewart-Halevy, "California Conceptualism's About-Face," *October* 163 (Winter 2018): 71–101.

27 Bersani and Dutoit, "Merde Alors," 31.

28 Bersani and Dutoit, "Merde Alors," 31–32 (emphasis in the original).

29 Bersani and Dutoit, "Merde Alors," 35.

30 Jacques Derrida, "Economimesis," trans. R. Klein, *Diacritics* 11, no. 2 (Summer 1981): 25 (emphasis in the original). Kant devotes section 59 of the *Critique of Judgment* to "Beauty as the symbol of morality." Literary critic Werner Hamacher makes closely related points (though of Hegel as opposed to Kant) in his book *Pleroma: Reading in Hegel*, trans. Nicholas Walker and Simon Jarvis (Stanford, CA: Stanford University Press, 1998).

31 Clement Greenberg, "Modernist Painting," in *The Collected Essays and Criticism*, vol. 4, *Modernism with a Vengeance*, ed. John O'Brian (Chicago: University of Chicago Press, 1993), 85.

32 Karl Marx, *Capital: A Critique of Political Economy*, trans. Ben Fowkes (New York: Penguin, 1976), 1:926.

33 Interesting details of which are found in an interview with the Lotta Continua photographer Tano D'Amico, who documented the event. Manuela de Leonardis, "Il Tempo della Vita secondo Tano D'Amico," *Il Manifesto*, August 28, 2011. The Beinecke Library at Yale holds several of D'Amico's photographs of this event. Tano D'Amico, photographs of events in Italy, 1976–81, GEN MSS 655, Beinecke Rare Book & Manuscript Library, Yale University.

34 I accordingly think it is untrue of his relation to Lotta Continua to say that Beuys had "no interest or identification with its cause," as curator Mark Rosenthal has claimed. Mark Rosenthal, "Staging Sculpture," in *Joseph Beuys: Actions, Vitrines, Environments*, by Mark Rosenthal, Sean Rainbird, and Claudia Schmukli (Houston: Menil Collection, 2004), 130. On the relationship with Lotta Continua—another outcome of which was Beuys's multiple *Il thè di Bruno Corà per la lotta continua vera* (Bruno Corà Tea for the real continuous struggle), 1975—see, in addition to her more recent book *Ein Erdbeben in den Köpfen der Menschen*, Petra Richter, "Joseph Beuys: Terremoto, 1981. Ein Erdbeben in den Köpfen der Menschen," *Palinsesti* 2 (2011): 12–23.

35 In a dispute with Bersani, literary theorist Walter Benn Michaels criticized the former's "vision of art as a device for prolonging desire by indefinitely deferring orgasm (like slowly counting backward from ten or silently reciting the entire starting lineup of the 1947 Brooklyn Dodgers)." Walter Benn Michaels, "Fictitious Dealing: A Reply to Leo Bersani," *Critical Inquiry* 8, no. 1 (Fall 1981): 167.

36 T. J. Clark, "In Defense of Abstract Expressionism," *October* 69 (Summer 1994): 22.

# Index

Weber, Helga, 87
Weimar Republic, 26, 126–27, 132
Weiner, Lawrence, 192
welfare state, 23, 127–28, 131, 133–36, 149–50, 155, 235n95
Westfälisches Landesmuseum, 70
Wood, Christopher S., 156
World War II, 5, 31, 39, 49, 137, 145–46, 156–57, 163, 165–67, 193, 220n37

Wright, Frank Lloyd, 68
Wurmbach, Hermann, 97, 220n37

Yi, Anicka, 13
YIUP, 159–60

Zotti, Checco, 204
Zucht, Wolfgang, 87
Zweite, Armin, 164

# Photography and Copyright Credits